Social Structure & Mobility in Economic Development

Social Structure & Mobility in Economic Development

Edited by

Neil J. Smelser & Seymour Martin Lipset

With a new introduction by Neil J. Smelser

Routledge
Taylor & Francis Group

LONDON AND NEW YORK

First published 2005 by Transaction Publishers

Published 2017 by Routledge
2 Park Square, Milton Park, Abingdon, Oxon OX14 4RN
711 Third Avenue, New York, NY 10017, USA

Routledge is an imprint of the Taylor & Francis Group, an informa business

Library of Congress Catalog Number: 2005041892

Library of Congress Cataloging-in-Publication Data

Social structure and mobility in economic development / Neil J. Smelser and
    Seymour Martin Lipset, editors ; with a new introduction by Neil J. Smelser.
        p. cm.
    Originally published: Chicago : Aldine Pub. Co., 1966.
    Papers presented at a conference held in San Francisco, Jan. 30-Feb. 1,
    1964.
    Includes bibliographical references.
    ISBN 0-202-30799-9 (pbk. : alk. paper)
        1. Social mobility—Congresses. 2. Social structure—Congresses. 3.
    Economic development—Congresses.   I. Smelser, Neil J.   II. Lipset,
    Seymour Martin.

HT609.S633   2005
305.5'13—dc22   2005041892

ISBN 13: 978-0-202-30799-2 (pbk)

This volume is the outgrowth of a conference on
Social Structure, Social Mobility and Economic Development
San Francisco, January 30-February 1, 1964
sponsored by
THE COMMITTEE ON ECONOMIC GROWTH
Social Science Research Council

CONTENTS

ALDINETRANSACTION INTRODUCTION

IN THE DISTINGUISHED eighty-year history of the Social Science Research Council, the two decades following World War II stand out as possibly the most productive. This was a period of high optimism for the scientific potential, both empirical and theoretical, of the social sciences as sciences. It was a period in which the prospects for American world hegemony crystallized tangibly, despite the escalating threat from world communism in its Soviet garb. It was a period of anticipation for the newly decolonized world, manifested concretely in theories of development and modernization. And it was a period in which there was ample room for meaningful and path-breaking social-scientific innovation by talented individuals and groups, a period that contrasts with the early twenty-first century, in which every foundation, government funding agency, publisher, and university research center competes aggressively to a fill perceived lacuna with an "invented here" notation.

The Social Science Research Council capitalized effectively on the themes and opportunities of those decades. Its favored mode of operation was to identify what it perceived as a promising area or problem, to form a group—usually interdisciplinary—to collect what was known, and to set a research agenda. This was usually done on the cheap, by today's standards. Committee members were not paid. They would usually design and convene a conference on a topic, secure funding for it, bring the best people they could locate to it, and publish a volume of papers. A list of the most visible committees of that era would include the Committee on Comparative Politics (1954-72), Linguistics and Psychology (1952-61), Mathematical Training of Social Scientists (1952-58), Political Behavior (1945-47, 1949-64), Sociolinguistics (1963-70), and Socialization and Social Structure (1960-67). All made lasting impacts on the knowledge and research agendas in their areas.

The Committee on Economic Growth and Stability (1949-68) was one of those seminal committees. The great quantitative economic historian Simon Kuznets, whose work ultimately gained him a Nobel Prize, chaired it. Its other members wee Bert F. Hoselitz (economics, University of Chicago), Joseph Spengler (economics

vii

and demography, Duke University), Wilbert Moore (sociology, Princeton University), and Melville Herskovitz (anthropology, Northwestern University). In 1961 I was invited to join the Committee. I was clearly a baby (at age thirty-one) in the cast of giants. To have served on the committee was a glorious educational experience for me; it shaped many of my research interests in economic sociology and social change.

As might be expected, with the dominance of Kuznets and the presence of Spengler and Hoselitz, most of the committees work was focused on the economic aspects of growth, and much of that was empirical and quantitative. Moreover, both Moore and I had economic sociology (such as it was in those days) at the core of our interests, and Herskovitz was already a doyen among economic anthropologists. Every one of the members was, however, noted for his interdisciplinary and comparative reach. At one of our meetings in 1961, Kuznets, who evidently had been sizing me up for a while, turned to me and said, "We need another project in sociology; you do it." Needless to say, this was a daunting assignment, but I appreciated his confidence.

In scanning the possibilities, I early came up with the already influential work on comparative social mobility by my Berkeley colleagues, Reinhard Bendix and Seymour Martin Lipset (1960). Yet that research had focused on mobility in the developed countries. It occurred to me that it would be of value to extend our understanding of social structure, stratification, and mobility comparatively and bring the topic to bear on the processes of economic development. I asked Lipset, with whom I had collaborated earlier (Lipset and Smelser, 1961), to join me in this enterprise, and he agreed. Thus was born, and thus were collected the principal ingredients of, the title of the project and volume.

Lipset and I proceeded along established SSRC lines. A planning meeting was held in 1961 in Berkeley, at which we honed topics for papers, identified a list of scholars best fitted and available to contribute, and invited them to a conference. This was held in San Francisco early in 1964. If readers will scan the list of authors who prepared chapters and the names of those additional scholars who attended (listed in the Preface to this volume), it will become evident that we succeeded in securing the best. Almost all were from that set of social scientists whose work turned out to be important and influential in the second half of the twentieth century. The list also testifies to the strength of SSRCs leadership and its power to draw.

After re-reading the contributions to this volume almost forty years after its publication, I can venture a number of observations that were not entirely evident to us at the time. The book is clearly a product of its time, in that it reflects many of the main tenets of modernization theory dominant in the 1960s. The emphasis is positivistic throughout, and included two explicitly methodological chapters (by Duncan and Wilensky). The distinction between industrial and pre-industrial was a meaningful one (see Chapter V by Hoselitz) and many general tendencies involved in the transition from the one to the other were identified, for example, increasing differentiation of the occupational structure and the movement of societies to ascriptive- to achievement-based assignment to social roles (see Chapter VI by Moore and Chapter I by Smelser and Lipset). All the same, the authors revealed a sense of contingency and qualification to this dualistic mode of thinking (see Smith's insistence on the variability of both pre-industrial and industrial societies in Chapter IV); and qualitatively different types of mobility are identified, beyond upward and downward (see Sjoberg's stress on rural-urban mobility in Chapter VIII). For all these reasons the volume tends to avoid the premodern-modern dichotomy found in simpler versions available at the time, for example, Daniel Lerner's *The Passing of Traditional Societies* (1958), and Walt W. Rostow's *The Stages of Economic Growth* (1960).

These qualifications noted, it should also be said that the volume was conspicuously silent on two perspectives, both of which were to become salient in the period of backlash against functionalism and modernization theory in the 1980s. The first was a variety of historicist reactions, represented in the notable studies by Barrington Moore, Jr. (*The Social Origins of Dictatorship and Democracy*, 1966) and Reinhard Bendix (*Nation-Building and Citizenship*, 1966). Different in many respects, these two studies insisted on diverse points of origin, divergent paths, and different outcomes in the historical development of political systems and, as such, constituted an attack on the convergence assumptions of much of developmental theory and less directly an attack on its functionalist underpinnings. The second perspective was internationalist and had two strands—the sociology of dependency and underdevelopment, represented in the works of Cardoso and Faletto (*Dependency and Development in Latin America*) and Frank (*Latin America: Underdevelopment or Revolution?*, 1969), and the world-system analysis advanced mainly by Wallerstein (*The Modern World System*, 1976). This internationalist approach also reflected neo-Marxist and neo-Leninist themes, and gave them and their derivatives a marked but temporary salience in the history of development theory. Both the historicist and internationalist lines of analysis joined with others to dethrone the modernization approach so dominant in the two preceding decades.

Social Structure and Mobility was reviewed by outstanding scholars in two leading national journals, the *American Sociological Review* and the *British Sociological Review*. Both took the volume seriously, and dedicated their reviews to developing their own reflections on the substantive and methodological issues informing the volume. In the first, Nathan Keyfitz welcomed the book, noting that its appearance signals that good minds are once again focusing on modernization, the central problem of sociology in its best days (Keyfitz, 1967, p. 508), thus confirming my retrospective judgment on the quality of the contributors. John Goldthorpe in his turn said the volume maintains a high standard throughout and in fact constitutes quite essential reading for all interested in social stratification or the sociological aspects of development (Goldthorpe, 1976, p. 324). In general the book gained a solid place in the tradition of scholarship associated with the SSRC. I am personally very gratified that it is now being republished.

Another overwhelming but I suppose obvious impression I gained in reading the volume four decades later was how much the world has changed with respect to its subject-matter, and how different such a book it would now have to be. As a mental exercise, I tried to imagine the different kinds of chapters I would want to include in the book if I were asked to do it again today. The following came to mind:

- A chapter on the history of stratification theory in the past half-century, including the perspectives of neo-Marxism, Habermas, Bourdieu, and globalization theory.
- A chapter on the changes of stratification systems in the societies of developed world, focusing mainly on the conquest of these societies by the enormous growth of service occupations and the shrinking of their proletarian classes as manufacturing has moved into the non-Western world and the changing implications for mobility generated by all these changes.
- A chapter on the movement of stratification (and mobility) away from the occupational systems of developed societies, with increasing salience of social welfare, consumption, and lifestyle in the determination of social status—in short, the increase in complexity of the social bases of stratification and mobility.
- A chapter on the changing nature of the units of stratification. Previously assumed to be family units—and most contributors in our volume at least tacitly went along with this assumption—the massive increases of women in the labor force and the evolution of multiple family types (single, single-parent, conjugal, communal, and same-sex) have challenged the assumption, and made more complex the discernment the basic units of stratification and the forms and meanings of mobility.
- A chapter on the changes in stratification systems of the developing world, focusing less on the role of ascription and more on the penetration of multinational corporations in particular and international capitalism in general on their economies, and the implications of those developments for mobility of labor and the development of classes in those societies.
- A chapter on the internationalization of stratification, in two senses, stratification among nations as well as the eclipse of national systems, of stratification by the further internationalization of the economy, and their partial displacement by world-dispersed work forces.
- A chapter on international migration, barely touched in the original volume, that dwells mainly on rural-urban migration within societies. In particular, the migration of great numbers into North America and Europe has significantly altered the picture of stratification and mobility in both the sending and the receiving societies.
- A chapter on the increasing salience of race, ethnicity, and communalism on which the original volume was also largely silent. These facets of social

life have become much more important worldwide, as historical developments have shot down the predictions of liberals, modernization theorists, and Marxists alike. This chapter would also have to develop a new theory of collective mobility that is demanded by the sociological and political realities of such groups. Lipset and I mentioned collective mobility in our introductory essay on theoretical issues, but it played no role in the work of the contributors.

So a new book on the same topic would have to be a very different one. Many of the issues, insights, and findings of the original volume are still alive, but they would have to be adapted, transformed, and sometimes discarded in light of the vast sea of changes that have influenced social inequality in the world through the second half of the twentieth century.

NEIL J. SMELSER
University of California, Berkeley

REFERENCES

Bendix, Reinhard. 1966. *Nation-Building and Citizenship*. Berkeley: University of California Press.
Cardoso, Fernando H. and E. Faletto. 1969. *Dependency and Development in Latin America*. Berkeley: University of California Press.
Frank, Andre Gunder. 1969. *Latin America: Underdevelopment or Revolution? Essays in the Development of Underdevelopment and the Immediate Enemy*. New York: Monthly Review.
Goldthorpe, John H. 1976. Review of *Social Structure and Mobility Economic Development*. *British Sociological Review* 18, pp. 324-25.
Keyfitz, Nathan. 1967. Review of *Social Structure and Mobility in Economic Development*. *American Sociological Review* 32, 3 (June), pp. 507-09.
Lerner, Daniel. 1958. *The Passing of Traditional Societies: Modernizing the Middle East*. Glencoe, IL: The Free Press.
Lipset, Seymour Martin and Reinhard Bendix. 1960. *Social Mobility in Industrial Society*. Berkeley: University of California Press.
Lipset, Seymour Martin and Neil J. Smelser (eds.). 1961. *Sociology: The Progress of a Decade*. Englewood Cliffs, NJ: Prentice-Hall.
Moore, Barrington, Jr. 1966. *The Social Origins of Dictatorship and Democracy*. Boston: Beacon Press.
Rostow, Walt W. 1960. *The Stages of Economic Growth: A Non-Communist Manifesto*. Cambridge: Cambridge University Press.
Wallerstein, Immanuel. 1976. *The Modern World System, Volume 1: Capitalist Agriculture and the Origins of the European World-Economy in the Sixteenth Century*. New York: Academic Press.

PREFACE

THE FOUNDATION of this volume is the notion that the several processes of change constituting economic and social development are systematically interrelated. The essence of development is the appearance of rapid rates of increase in many different indices—output per capita, political participation, literacy, and the like. These quantitative changes are, however, commonly accompanied by vast changes in the social structure—markets emerge, political bureaucracies arise, and new educational systems appear. And finally, development entails a substantial movement of persons in society from rural to urban settings, from one occupation to another, and from one prestige level and another. While a good deal is known about each type of process, very little is known about the relations among them. This volume constitutes, we hope, a modest inroad on this ignorance.

As early as 1961 the Committee on Economic Growth of the Social Science Research Council began to explore the idea of holding a conference on the relations between social structure and social mobility in economic development. Because neither a theoretical framework nor a consolidated tradition of empirical research was available on the subject, the Committee thought this conference should receive especially careful advance planning. The planning committee—whose members were Neil Smelser (chairman), Seymour Martin Lipset, and Wilbert E. Moore—developed subjects for papers and considered potential authors over a period of two years. The bulk of the planning for a conference was done at a special two-day meeting in Berkeley in June, 1962. Besides Smelser, Lipset, and Moore, this planning session was attended by Reinhard Bendix, Clifford Geertz, Bert F. Hoselitz, and Leo F. Schnore.

The conference was held in the Sheraton-Palace Hotel, San Francisco, on January 30 and 31 and February 1, 1964, and was the sixteenth conference sponsored by the Committee on Economic Growth.

The papers delivered at the conference fall under five main headings, which also constitute the basis for organizing the chapters in this volume:

(1) *Theoretical and methodological issues*. The paper by Smelser and Lipset reviews a number of theoretical issues involved in studying the relations between development and social mobility, and comments on recent findings in comparative research on mobility. The papers by Otis Dudley Duncan and Harold L. Wilensky focus on the vast range of methodological problems that arise in the analysis of mobility proper.

(2) *Traditional stratification and modern stratification*. Michael G. Smith explores the different type of pre-industrial stratification systems, while Bert F. Hoselitz, starting from the notion of "dualism," examines the ways in which traditional and modern stratification systems are accommodated to one another during periods of economic change.

(3) *The effects of economic development on social mobility*. Moore's paper summarizes a number of trends in occupational structure—specialization, upgrading, bureaucratization—typically associated with development. Gideon Sjoberg reviews the problems of rural-urban migration, and inquires particularly into some of the ideological influences that impinge on urbanization. Natalie Rogoff Ramsøy, using Norwegian data for illustration, inquires into the differential rates of mobility in various industrial sectors during periods of economic development.

(4) *Non-economic influences on mobility*. Taking late nineteenth-century Japan as an illustrative case, Reinhard Bendix explores the role of cultural values—in this case the samurai ethic—in the genesis of a class of economic innovators. Harry Crockett considers some of the psychological origins of mobility and innovation, reviewing especially the literature on achievement motivation. And in an analysis of the lower reaches of the stratification system, David Matza analyzes some of the social mechanisms involved in producing a more or less permanent stratum of the "disreputable" poor.

(5) *Political aspects of social mobility*. Lester Seligman examines some of the political recruitment and its implications for conflict and stability. Gino Germani turns to the political consequences of rapid social mobility during periods of development, singling out mobility experience as a significant determinant of political and social unrest.

Besides those preparing papers, the following discussants and other participants also attended the conference: John W. Bennett, Dorothy Brady, Richard Hartshorne, Clifford Geertz, Joseph Kahl, Simon Kuznets, Juan Linz, Armando de Miguel, Norman B. Ryder, Leo F. Schnore, Joseph J. Spengler, Charles Tilly, Melvin M. Tumin, and Ralph Turner. Paul Webbink and Elbridge Sibley represented the Social Science Research Council.

After the conference the various authors revised the papers for publication on the basis of discussants' remarks, subsequent conference discussion, and editors' suggestions. The editors wish to express their profound appreciation to Mrs. Karen Renne Many, whose critical review of the conference papers improved their substance, and whose editorial skills sharpened their expression. The staff of the Institute of Industrial Relations at the University of California, Berkeley, typed many of the manuscripts. Finally, we would like to express our appreciation to the Comparative National Development Program of the Institute of International Studies, University of California, Berkeley, for assistance to us at the various stages of preparation of the manuscript.

NEIL J. SMELSER
SEYMOUR MARTIN LIPSET

SOCIAL STRUCTURE

AND MOBILITY IN

ECONOMIC DEVELOPMENT

SOCIAL STRUCTURE, MOBILITY AND DEVELOPMENT

NEIL J. SMELSER AND SEYMOUR MARTIN LIPSET,* *University of California, Berkeley, and Harvard University*

ANALYSIS of economic development often begins by identifying a specific dependent variable—for example, rate of growth of per capita output. The strategy of explanation is to assemble certain independent variables —consumption, investment, labor supply, for instance—and, by assigning values to these variables, to arrive at resultant rates of economic growth.[1] Sometimes a theory of economic development moves beyond the mere assignment of quantitative values to such independent variables, and takes into account changes in the *structure* of the economy, such as shifts in the distribution of industries.[2]

The same strategy of explanation can be followed in analyzing development in non-economic spheres, though frequently it is more difficult to identify variables and specify measures for them. Take educational development, for instance. One salient dependent variable is change in the rate of literacy in a population. The immediate determinants of variations in this rate are the economic and political requirements of the society in question, the availability of teachers and educational facilities,

* Although the authors share equal responsibility for this article, we divided the initial drafting by sections that reflect our varying concerns. Smelser handled the first part, dealing with matters of conceptual clarification, while Lipset dealt primarily with the second, the discussion of research problems and findings beginning on page 17. Some of the remarks in the first part grow from a memorandum entitled "The Allocation of Roles in the Process of Development," prepared jointly by Harvey Leibenstein and Smelser. A portion of the second part was published earlier in S. M. Lipset, "Research Problems in the Comparative Analysis of Mobility and Development," *International Social Science Journal*, 26 (1964), pp. 35-48.

[1] For a summary of the recent literature on such models, cf. Henry J. Burton, "Contemporary Theorizing on Economic Growth," in Bert F. Hoselitz (ed.), *Theories of Economic Growth* (New York: Free Press of Glencoe, 1960), pp. 243-261.

[2] *Ibid.*, pp. 262-267.

and so on. These variables in their turn depend in part on the rates of change in the educational system's social environment.

Development as a whole involves a complex series of changes in rates of growth—of output per capita, of literacy, of political participation, etc.—and major changes in these rates depend on the occurrence of fundamental changes in the social structure of the developing society. To complicate the study of development even more, changes in one institutional sector set up demands for changes in other sectors. Rapid economic development, for instance, establishes pressure for adjustment in the education and training of a new type of labor force. Again, if the educational system produces a large number of literate, skilled, but unemployable persons, this often sets up demands for economic or political adjustments to assimilate these persons into socially meaningful and perhaps economically productive roles.

Viewing development thus, we cannot escape the fact that persons must be shuttled through the social structure during periods of rapid development. Often they have to move to an urban setting. They must fill new occupational roles and positions of leadership. They must learn to respond to new rewards and deprivations and to accept new standards for effective performance. Development often requires more movement of persons than during pre-development periods; certainly it requires different forms of movement. The ease with which this movement is effected, furthermore, depends largely on the character of the social structure of the society in question—in particular, the demands of the developing structure, the characteristics of the traditional social structure, and the emerging tension between the two.

The study of this movement of persons—either as individuals or in groups—through the social structure is the study of *social mobility*. The objective of these notes is to define and explore the relations between social mobility and social structure, especially under conditions of development. We shall first review the concepts of social structure, stratification, and social mobility; then we shall mention several dimensions of social structure that are critical for the study of mobility; finally, we shall explore the impact of rapid development on social structure and on patterns of social mobility.

SOCIAL STRUCTURE AND RELATED CONCEPTS

At the most general level "social structure" as a construct is used to characterize recurrent and regularized interaction among two or more persons. In its contemporary usage in the social sciences, however, this construct can be understood only by referring to two other sets of concepts: the *directional tendencies* of social systems, and the *resources* of social systems. Let us define each briefly, and show how the concept of social structure links them.

1. *Directional tendencies.* One of the most fundamental sets of concepts employed in analyzing social systems concerns the general orientation of social life. Or, some put the question, what exigencies must be met if the social system is to continue functioning? Analysts who attempt to identify these basic directional tendencies use such terms as "functional exigencies," "functional imperatives," "functional prerequisites," and so on.[3] The following exigencies are typically listed: (a) the production, allocation, and consumption of scarce commodities (sometimes called the economic function); (b) the coordination and control of the collective actions of the society as a whole or a collectivity within it (sometimes called the political function); (c) the creation, maintenance, and implementation of norms governing interaction among members in a system (sometimes called the integrative function); (d) the creation, maintenance, and transmission of the cultural values of a system; and so on. Around these exigencies social life revolves; social resources are devoted to meeting each exigency. Some analysts maintain, moreover, that unless these exigencies are met satisfactorily, disequilibrium of the social system will result.

2. *Resources.* A second set of variables that enter propositions about social systems concerns the capacities or resources available to the system. In economics the concept of capacities has been formulated as the "factors of production"; given the general objective of producing goods and services, the capacities of the economy are found in land, labor, capital, and organization. The importance of resources arises in other institutional sectors as well: the level of literacy and training of the population and its physical fitness; the level of information available for action, and so on, are always relevant to structured social action. It is useful to distinguish between two aspects of capacities: (a) obstacles that limit the performance of a system—examples are the limited number of hours in a day, and the limited physical energy that people can expend before becoming exhausted; (b) means that facilitate the performance of a system. Examples are a high level of skill of the actors, a high level of knowledge about the social situation at hand, etc.

[3] Perhaps the best-known discussion of the directional tendencies in society is found in D. F. Aberle, *et al.,* "The Functional Prerequisites of a Society," *Ethics,* 60 (1950), pp. 110-111; elaborated in Marion J. Levy, Jr., *The Structure of Society* (Princeton: Princeton University Press, 1952), Ch. 3. Talcott Parsons offers somewhat different considerations of the same subject. *The Social System* (New York: Free Press of Glencoe, 1951), Ch. 2.

"Social structure" refers to organized bundles of human activities oriented to the directional tendencies of a social system. The business firm, for instance, is a structure devoted primarily to the production of goods and services. The nuclear family is a set of institutionalized roles, one major function of which is to socialize the young in the cultural values of a society. In contributing to such functions, these structures utilize the resources of social systems. Firms utilize the factors of production. Families utilize some of the motivational energy of adults and some of the family income in socializing children. Thus "social structure" is an interstitial concept in that it links the basic directional tendencies of a social system and its resources.

The basic units of social structure are not persons as such, but selected aspects of interaction among persons, such as roles (e.g., husband, churchmember, citizen) and social organization, which refers to clusters of roles (e.g., a clique, a family, a bureaucracy). Social organization refers not only to formal organization (e.g., hospitals, schools, business firms, government agencies) but to informal organizations (such as gangs or neighborhood friendship groups) and diffuse collectivities with only occasional interaction (such as ethnic groupings). The important defining features of social structure are that interaction is selective, regularized, and regulated by various social controls.

In connection with the regulation of social structures, three concepts are particularly important: (a) *Values* refer to beliefs that legitimize the existence and importance of specific social structures and the kinds of behavior that transpire in them. The value of "free enterprise," for instance, endorses the existence of business firms organized around the institution of private property and engaged in the pursuit of private profit. The degree of consensus on any given value in any given system is always an open question. (b) *Norms* refer to standards of conduct that regulate the interaction among individuals in social structures. The norms of contract and property law, for instance, set up obligations and prohibitions on the actors in an economic transaction. As the examples show, norms are more detailed in their control of interaction in social structures than are values. The degree of effectiveness of any given norm in any given social structure is always an open question. (c) *Sanctions,* including both rewards and deprivations, refer to the use of various social resources to control the behavior of personnel in social structures. Aspects of this control include establishing roles, inducing individuals to enter and perform in roles, and controlling deviance from expected performance in roles. Examples of sanctions are coercion, ridicule, appeal to duty, withdrawal of communication, and so on. The degree of effectiveness of any given sanction in any given social structure is always an open question.

Institutionalization is a concept that unifies the elements of social structure—including roles, collectivities, values, norms, sanctions, etc. It refers to distinctive, enduring expectations whereby these elements are combined into a single complex. When we speak of the institutionalization of American business, for instance, we refer to a more or less enduring pattern of roles and collectivities (e.g., businessmen and firms), values (e.g., free enterprise), norms (e.g., laws of contract and property, informal business codes), and sanctions (profits, political controls over business, etc.).

Finally concepts concerning personnel are employed in the analysis of social structure. Here the conceptual level shifts from the interrelations among persons (to which concepts like role, organization, norm, and sanction refer) to the persons themselves. Roles and organizations are always filled by persons. Accordingly, the motivation and behavior of persons in roles is extremely important in analyzing processes within social structures.

The usual basis for classifying social structures is to return to the basic directional tendencies of the social system. Thus we refer to political, economic, familial, religious, educational, aesthetic, etc., structures. This type of classification involves the assignment of *primacies* only. Even though "religious structure" is the concept used to classify a cluster of rites or an organized church, the social significance of this bundle of activities is not exhausted by using this term. From an analytic point of view, this religious structure has a "political aspect," and "economic aspect," and so on. "Social structure," then, refers to concrete clusters of activities devoted primarily but not exclusively to meeting the exigencies of one major directional tendency of a social system.

Classifications of sanctions usually parallel classifications of social structures. We may speak of political sanctions (the use of power or force), economic sanctions (the use of wealth), esthetic sanctions (condemning something as ugly or commending it as beautiful), religious sanctions (giving or withholding blessings), and so on. From one angle sanctions are the distinctive *products* of particular types of social structure. The economic structure, for instance, produces wealth, which can be used as a sanction in a wide variety of social contexts; the political structure produces power, another generalized sanction; and the educational structures produce knowledge or information, still another generalized sanction. From another angle, sanction produced in one set of social structures are resources for other social structures. Wealth acquired by taxation and other means, is one of the basic resources for political effectiveness. Knowledge and training are important economic resources, and so on. The various social structures of a society are thus linked by a series of complex interchanges of resources, or sanctions.

SOCIAL STRUCTURE, STRATIFICATION, AND SOCIAL MOBILITY

Versions of stratification. In its simplest version, stratification means that in any set of social structures, the various roles are characterized by a differential receipt of sanctions.[4] Given this phenomenon, descriptions of the distribution of sanctions in a social system result in statements of the allocation of wealth, the allocation of power, the distribution of educational benefits, the distribution of religious rewards (e.g., grace), and so on. In the first instance, then, "stratification" refers simply to the differential distribution of sanctions.

Stratification can be conceptualized in more complicated ways, which should be kept distinct from the notion just advanced. The following versions are common:

(1) Stratification of *roles* themselves. This involves a summation of the various kinds of sanctions (wealth, power, esteem, etc.) that are received by the various roles in the social structure. Because it is difficult to translate one type of sanction (e.g., wealth) into precise amounts of another (e.g., cultural benefits), the ranking of roles proves to be a difficult empirical operation.

(2) Stratification of *organizations.* This involves summing up the sanctions received (or resources possessed) by collectivities, such as family units, business firms, educational institutions, etc. For any given sanction (such as wealth) this summation is not too difficult, but the summation of the various sanctions leads to methodological difficulties.

(3) Stratification of *individual persons.* This means not only summing a number of different sanctions for a role, but also summing a number of different roles in which an individual is an incumbent. The difficulties in performing such an operation are even greater than in ranking roles or organizations alone.

(4) Stratification of *classes.* This can be formulated in two ways. The first is simply to group certain classes of persons (e.g., peasants, proletarians, etc.) on the basis of some objective measures of the roles they

---

[4] At this point we do not wish to enter the functionalist controversy as to whether in the nature of social life this differential distributon of rewards and deprivations must be so, and if so, why. We wish merely to indicate the widespread empirical fact that we take into account by using the word "stratification."

hold or sanctions they receive. The second is to determine whether those who occupy similar roles conceive of themselves as a group and act collectively. Classes may be either special (based on the distribution of single sanctions, such as wealth) or general (based on an intermeshed system of many different positions and sanctions; an example is the "lower middle class").

Redistribution and social mobility. Given these characterizations of social stratification, the following types of redistributive process can occur in a set of social structures.

(1) Bringing sanctions to fixed personnel in fixed positions. This involves a redistribution of rewards. Examples are largesse, organized charity for the poor, distribution of groceries through a community by the ward politician, progressive redistribution of income through taxation, and so on. This process presupposes neither movement of persons from role to role nor reorganization of roles themselves.

(2) Bringing personnel to sanctions. This is social mobility proper. It may take the following forms: (a) The movement of *individuals* upward through a hierarchy of positions. This type of mobility is conspicuously emphasized in the traditional American ideology. (b) The movement of *collectivities* upward through a hierarchy of positions. The most common form of this type of mobility is the movement of family units, as when the head of the household advances through the occupational hierarchy, and the status of his dependent family members moves along with his. Another form of this mobility is the movement of formal organizations, as when an academic department "breaks into" the ranks of top-ranking institutions. (c) The movement of entire *classes*. This may occur gradually and peacefully, as in the "professionalization" of an occupation such as nursing or suddenly and violently, as in an accession of a class to political power in a revolution.

(3) Reorganizing the roles in a social structure. An example of this is a shifting balance among the primary, secondary, and tertiary industrial sectors in the economy. Such changes in the balance of roles give rise to redistributions of both rewards and personnel.

(4) Introducing new *systems* of stratification. Such changes occur with great rapidity during ideological revolutions (such as the French or the Russian, which partially obliterated entire classes); or they may evolve over long periods (as in the growth of the urban-commercial complex out of the feudal, land-based patterns of stratification of medieval Europe). Since these changes involve a reorganization of the criteria for evaluating social roles, they also occasion redistributions of roles, rewards, and personnel. Most societies undergoing rapid change are characterized not by a single stratification system, but by several systems of co-existing

hierarchies. Social mobility in such societies is often a matter not of simply moving up or down in a single hierarchy, but of moving from one hierarchy to another.

SOCIAL STRUCTURE AND THE ANALYSIS OF MOBILITY

Three features of social structure are critical in determining the *forms* of social mobility in any society: ascription-achievement; level of differentiation of social structures; and locus of control of sanctions. We shall now discuss each of these briefly. Later we shall turn to several social determinants of *rates* of social mobility.

1. *Ascription-achievement.* Societies vary considerably in the degree to which persons are assigned to roles (occupational, religious, political, etc.) on the basis of status ascribed at birth. The basis of ascription may be kinship, age, sex, race or ethnicity, or territorial location. So far as these criteria dominate, the society emphasizes ascription. So far as assignment to roles rests on some sort of behavioral performance, the society emphasizes achievement.

The implication of ascription-achievement for the form of social mobility is this: If ascription is firmly institutionalized, mobility tends to be collective; if achievement, mobility tends to be individual.[5]

To illustrate: Classical India displays a stratification system at the ascriptive extreme. Under ideal-typical conditions, virtually every aspect of an individual's future life was determined by his birth into a particular caste: his marriage choice, his occupation, his associational memberships, his ritual behavior, his type of funeral, and so on. Choices were determined at the instant of birth. In this way the caste system discouraged individual mobility from one caste or caste-associated role to another during his lifetime. What form did mobility take, then? According to Hutton's account, mobility manifested itself as the *collective* splitting off of subcastes, or what he calls the "fissiparous tendencies in Indian castes." Members of a caste were aggregated into a subcaste, which for a time accepted wives from other subcastes but simultaneously refused to give daughters to these subcastes. This established a claim to superiority, which was fortified by some change in occupational duties. The final step was to adopt a new caste name and deny all connection with the caste of origin. Thus, in Hutton's language, "by organization and propaganda a

---

[5] This argument concerns only the movement of persons. Societies that institutionalize ascription also encourage the distribution of rewards to existing "estates" or "classes," whereas societies that institutionalize achievement encourage the movement of persons to rewards.

caste can change its name and in the course of time get a new one accepted, and by altering its canons of behavior in the matter of diet and marriage can increase the estimation in which it is held." [6] This multiplication of castes over the centuries provides the clue to the distinctive form of social mobility in classical India.

American society possesses, ideally, a stratification system at the achievement extreme. An individual is able, in his lifetime, to move away from ascribed positions (based on region, ethnic background, even family of orientation) into new roles. In practice, of course, ascribed characteristics, especially racial ones, prevent the operation of this system in pure form.

One reason for the pronounced hostility toward "welfare" practices in the United States stems from this distinctive American emphasis on achievement. The introduction of welfare measures means bringing facilities and rewards to certain defined classes of persons, rather than having persons move to these facilities and rewards. One of the interesting justifications for introducing welfare measures in the United States—as opposed to continental European states, where state welfare is taken more for granted—is that such measures must presumably *facilitate* equality of opportunity for individuals in the society. If it can be argued that *not* to give welfare somehow impedes the life chances of a potentially mobile individual or class of individuals, then welfare measures are more likely to be accepted as legitimate.

Within the United States some interesting variations on the dominantly individual form of mobility are observable. When a person assumes an adult occupational role and reaches, say, age 30, his mobility as an individual is more or less completed, except perhaps within the same occupational category. Thus adult occupational status is in certain respects an ascribed position, though this ascription is not a matter of position at birth. Under these circumstances mobility tends to become collective. Whole occupational groups try to improve their standing or guard it from erosion. Collective mobility in the American system becomes legitimate, in short, when the battle for individual mobility is in effect closed for an individual, when he becomes lodged in an ascribed group.

Great Britain constitutes a system intermediate between extreme individual mobility and extreme collective mobility. Individual mobility is emphasized but individuals carry with them certan ascribed and semi-ascribed markings—accent, habits, manners, etc.—which reflect family and educational background and operate as important status

[6] J. H. Hutton, *Caste in India* (Cambridge: The University Press, 1946), pp. 41-61, 97-100.

symbols. Full mobility takes place only in the next generation, when mobile individuals can give their own children the appropriate cultivation and education. This case is intermediate because it is the family that moves collectively upward over two or more generations.[7]

2. *Differentiation of social structures.* One point of contrast between simple and complex societies is the degree of differentiation of social structures. In an ideal-typical simple society, little differentiation exists between a position in a kinship group (e.g., elderly men in a certain clan), political authority (since elderly men in this clan hold power as a matter of custom), religious authority (since political and religious authority are undifferentiated), and wealth (since tributes flow to this position). The social structures are undifferentiated, and an individual occupies a high or low position in all roles simultaneously. (M. G. Smith takes a somewhat different view of undifferentiated societies in his contribution to this volume. He argues that within ascribed categories, such as age groups, individual performance or achievement is very important in determining rank.)

In complex societies, by contrast, a position in the age structure does not necessarily entitle a person to membership in specific roles in the occupational structure;[8] a position of importance in the religious hierarchy does not necessarily give an individual access to control of wealth. Thus, though some individuals *may* simultaneously receive great amounts of different rewards—wealth, power, prestige—these rewards are often formally segregated in a highly differentiated social structure.

Many colonial societies of the late 19th and early 20th centuries are intermediate between the simple and the complex. In these societies the social order broke more or less imperfectly into three groupings: first, the Western representatives who controlled economic enterprises and political administration, and who frequently were allied with large landowners; second, natives—when drawn into the colonial economy—were tenant farmers, wage laborers, etc.; and third, a group of foreigners—Chinese, Indians, Syrians, Goans, Lebanese, etc.—who fit "between" the first two as traders, moneylenders, merchants, creditors, etc. This view is oversimplified, of course, but many colonial societies approximated this arrangement. The important structural feature of such systems is that economic, political, and racial-ethnic roles *coincide* with one another.

---

[7] This example is not meant to imply that several-generation mobility is absent in the United States. The contrast between Britain and the United States is a relative one.

[8] Very young and very old persons are generally *excluded* from occupational positions, however. The institutionalization of the seniority principle in industry and elsewhere also constitutes a qualification on the principle of separation of age and occupation.

Two implications of the level of differentiation of social structures for the form of social mobility are: (a) The less differentiated the system, the more difficult it is for individuals to move with regard to a *single* role (e.g., through occupational success). The individual would have to move with regard to all roles—political, economic, ethnic, etc. This means that individual mobility is difficult, and that the distribution of rewards is effected not by movement of the individuals to positions so much as by collective competition among multi-functional groupings. In highly differentiated systems it is possible to move, for example, into a new occupational role thereby achieving economic success without simultaneously having to become a political leader, change one's ethnic identification, etc. Segmental mobility, in short, is conducive to individual mobility. (b) The highly differentiated system leaves room for status disequilibrium (being high in one role and low in another, as in the case of the Negro doctor). This phenomenon is rare in societies with coinciding social hierarchies.

3. *The locus of control of sanctions.* Where does the locus of power to apply sanctions reside in a society? Consider several different types of economic activity: In an ideal-typical paternalistic industrial setting, the industrial manager has at his own disposal both economic and political —and perhaps even moral—sanctions to recruit and control employees. In an ideal-typical free enterprise system, the industrial manager has only economic sanctions to recruit employees, but once they are recruited he also has limited political authority over them. In an ideal-typical totalitarian system, the industrial manager may utilize both economic and political sanctions, but for both he is held accountable to a central political source.

To compare and contrast political situations such as these, and to assess their implications for social mobility, two dimensions are particularly important: (a) Elitist-egalitarian, which refers to the locus of control over rewards and facilities in the stratification system itself. In the elitist case power to allocate sanctions is concentrated in the hands of a few; in the egalitarian case the origin of decisions to allocate is presumably dispersed, even though the implementation of these decisions may rest in the hands of a few. (b) The locus of power in territorial terms: just as the elitist-egalitarian dimension refers to the concentration of power in social space, the dimension of central-local refers to the same concentration in geographical space. (c) The degree to which the several concentrations of sanctions coincide. Are those classes with primary responsibility for decisions concerning economic sanctions the *same* classes that determine educational policy, religious doctrine, and so on? This last dimension, closely related to the concept of differentiation, refers to the relations among the distributions of several types of sanction.

DEVELOPMENT AND THE FORM OF SOCIAL MOBILITY

What are the typical consequences of rapid social and economic development in terms of these dimensions? In a general way the answer is that rapid development sets up tensions between ascription and achievement, between differentiated and undifferentiated structures, between egalitarian and hierarchical principles, and between central and local power. Let us examine each type of tension briefly:

1. As economic and social development proceeds, various criteria of achievement—attainment of wealth, attainment of political power, etc. —begin to intrude on ascribed memberships as bases for assigning persons to roles. Castes, ethnic groups, and traditional religious groupings do not necessarily decline in importance *in every respect* during periods of modernization. As political interest groups or reference groups for diffuse loyalties, they may even increase in salience. As the bases of role assignment and ranking, however, ascriptive standards begin to give way to economic, political, and other standards which gives rise in turn to tension between ascriptive and achievement standards for organizing roles and recruiting personnel to them.

2. Because of the widespread tendency for social structures to become differentiated from one another during periods of rapid development,[9] individual mobility through occupational and other structural hierarchies tends to increase. This signifies the separation of the adult's roles from his point of origin. In addition, individual mobility is frequently substituted for collective mobility.[10] Individuals, not whole castes or tribes, compete for higher standing in society. This phenomenon of increasing individual mobility appears to be one of the universal consequences of industrialization.[11]

3. Most contemporary developing areas, emerging from colonial domination of one sort or another, are committed to egalitarian ideologies.

[9] Neil J. Smelser, "Mechanisms of Change and Adjustment to Change," in Bert F. Hoselitz and Wilbert E. Moore (eds.), *Industrialization and Society* (The Hague: Mouton, 1963).

[10] The degree to which this takes place depends also on the residue of ascription in industrial societies, as well as the locus of power with regard to the control of major social sanctions.

[11] Seymour Martin Lipset and Reinhard Bendix, *Social Mobility in Industrial Society* (Berkeley: University of California Press, 1959), pp. 13ff.

Since most of these societies have traditional hierarchical social arrangements, yet another source of tension—between hierarchical and egalitarian principles—is introduced by rapid development.

4. Most contemporary underdeveloped countries have chosen a highly centralized approach to the management of their economy and social structure. This choice generates many tensions and conflicts, however, since most of the countries in question have strong local traditions of tribalism, community life, etc.

These several tensions frequently make their appearance in the relation between *demands* for mobility imposed by the exigencies of development on the one hand, and the *supply* of potentially mobile individuals and groups with appropriate motivations, attitudes, and skills on the other.

Issues that arise on the demand side of mobility in developing societies. For any society attempting to modernize we must ask which sectors of the social structure provide the developmental vanguard movement, and which lag behind? Under the influence of the classic British model of industrialization and lingering materialist assumptions as well, analysts have tended to assume that economic development leads the way, and that other sectors change in order to adjust. Parliaments are reformed, education is strengthened, etc., as a response to the exigencies imposed by economic change. This is not the only pattern of development, however. Although the *commitment* to economic change is pronounced in many African societies, for instance, these societies have moved much faster into the modern age in the political sphere (with universal suffrage, parliaments, parties, and administrative bureaucracies) than in the economic sphere. In these same societies, moreover, changes in the educational structure seem to be outdistancing actual economic accomplishments. Lester Seligman analyzes certain aspects of these lead-lag relations, especially with respect to the development of various types of political parties and relations in his contribution to this volume.

A related issue concerns the organizing principles employed in fostering development, and the ways in which such principles change the course of development. By "organizing principles" we refer to the kinds of sanctions (rewards and deprivations) used to establish roles and to induce personnel to perform in them. The following organizing principles might be considered:

1. Reliance on monetary sanctions. This refers to the system of wages, salaries, and profits that can be employed to determine the role distribution in a society, the recruitment of individuals into these roles and the degree of effort elicited within them. Such sanctions may

operate positively (e.g., the offer of high wages in industrial operations) or negatively (e.g., the "push" of agricultural wage laborers from the land into urban settings during periods of slack demand).

2. Reliance on political measures. These include physical coercion or the threat of coercion, influence, bargaining, persuasion, the promise of political power, etc. Again, these sanctions may be used to induce individuals into new roles or to force them from old ones, or both.

3. Integrative measures. One focus of integrative pressure is particularism, or membership in some ascriptive group. Membership in a kinship grouping, for instance, not only may set up expectations with respect to roles that a given member may assume, but also may determine the conditions of entry and tenure in a role. Group membership may also be important for controlling a person once he has entered a role. The key feature of particularistic sanctions of this sort is that the sanctioner appeals to the integrative ties (memberships) of the actor in question. Other foci of particularism are caste membership, tribal affiliation, membership in ethnic groups, and so on. Such integrative measures, like the other sanctions, may operate positively (e.g., in the case of particularistic hiring in the Japanese case) or negatively (e.g., in the case of escaping burdens to extended family and tribe, as reported for some African societies).

4. Value-commitments. Commitment to fundamental principles can be used as a lever to induce individuals to enter roles and behave in certain ways, once in them. Specific areas in which fundamental values operate as sanctions are in religious doctrine, nationalism, anti-colonialism, socialism, and communism, or any combination of these. Again, in specific cases entry into a role may be as a result of the pull of a positive commitment to a "modern" value-system, or as a result of the push of alienation from some "traditional" value-system.

The *effectiveness* of these organizing principles refers in the first instance to the ability to stimulate the social mobility requisite for the society's developmental needs. In addition, however, reliance on a particular type of sanction has consequences other than merely stimulating mobility. For example, in some cases political sanctions may be the most effective means for establishing and filling roles necessary for economic production, though these same sanctions may not be the most effective means of allocating roles to foster changes in the educational sector. Furthermore, the wholesale application of political sanctions may set up inflexible political cleavages that paralyze a society, thus making these sanctions ineffective in the long run.

A final issue concerns the locus of power with respect to the organizing principles during periods of rapid development. In any empirical case a society relies on *several* of the organizing principles for development. Broadly speaking, the dominant principles of recruitment into economic roles in American society are: (a) reliance on the belief in fundamental values such as free enterprise, inculcated in potential incumbents of occupational roles during periods of early socialization and education; (b) reliance on monetary compensation, implemented through the market mechanism; (c) reliance on the outcome of political contests among interest groups, especially labor and management; (d) reliance on more centralized political machinery, usually when the second and third principles seem to be functioning inadequately. In general the political controls over these different organizing principles are dispersed in our society; a single political agency is *not* presumed to have direct control over the education of children in the basic values of society, the operation of the labor market, the settlement of industrial disputes, etc. In other societies—e.g., theocratic, totalitarian—the political centralization of control over organizing principles is much greater.

Social mobility may be viewed as a consequence of the organizing principles involved, the capacity of the society to maintain such organizing principles, and their effectiveness in achieving the ends for the society. Mobility in turn is an important variable in determining the rate and form of development, and development in its own turn may feed back to the organizing principles and pattern of mobility by occasioning shifts in the power balance of society, changes in the distribution of wealth, and so on.

Issues that arise on the supply side of mobility in developing areas. On this subject we may be briefer. The effectiveness of the organizing sanctions depends very much on the predisposition of the persons and groups in society to be moved by such sanctions. This depends in turn on their motivation, attitudes, and skills. The social structures that are critical in forming these characteristics are religion, education, community, and kinship, for these structures "specialize" in creating commitment and social outlook. Many of the problems that new nations face revolve around the attempt by those eager for development to undermine traditional familial, community and religious structures and establish new ones—especially in education—so as to modify the supply conditions for mobility.

Any historical case of individual or collective mobility resolves into the interplay of various demand and supply conditions for mobility. One familiar case of mobility involves immigrant groups in the United States during the past 150 years. Roughly speaking, migrants have filled the lowest economic rung—unskilled labor—upon arrival, only to be dis-placed "upward" by a new wave. Although most ethnic groups have remained at the very lowest level for only a short time, they have moved upward economically at different rates, and each wave leaves behind its dregs, who make up an important component of the "disreputable poor" described by David Matza in his contribution to this volume. Four factors appear to determine the relative speed of ascent:

1. Economic conditions of demand. The rise of the Negro during World War II and the postwar prosperity has resulted in large part from increased economic opportunities throughout the occupational structure.

2. The degree to which the ethnic group is "held back" through discrimination by the majority group. Every ethnic minority has experienced some discrimination; but for the Negro this has been extreme. Hence Negroes traditionally have been consigned to manual labor and servant work, and are underrepresented in professional, business, and clerical occupations. Discrimination may be direct, when employers resist employment of Negroes because they are Negroes; or indirect, when employers refuse to hire Negroes because they are less technically qualified for employment (which usually means that they have experienced discrimination elsewhere in the system, especially in education).

3. The internal resources of the ethnic group itself, both financial and socio-cultural. Thus the Jews, Greeks, and Armenians, with a much more highly developed commercial tradition than the Polish, Irish or Italian peasants, possessed an initial advantage in terms of capital and commercial skills. Also the Irish pattern of kinship and community loyalties fit Irishmen particularly for American political-party life, in which the Irish have been notably successful.

4. The continuing strength of particularistic ties. Once an ethnic group makes an inroad on a new higher-level occupation, the successful few will allocate their new talent and resources to bringing in people of their own kind to reap the advantages. This particularistic pressure applies in varying degree to every ethnic group.

A final issue arising on the supply side of mobility concerns not the *conditions* under which persons become mobile, but rather the psychological and social *consequences* of mobility once it has occurred. Two potentially disruptive consequences of mobility are: (a) The creation of individuals and groups who have moved upward rapidly according to one set of rewards, but whose advance is constricted in other spheres. The "unemployed intellectuals" so frequently found in the developing areas are an example. Sometimes groups of such persons do constitute a vocal portion of public opinion calling for changes in the pattern of development. In such a case the "supply" side of mobility begins to affect the nature of development itself and hence the "demand" side for mobility. In his article in this volume, Gino Germani attributes the absence of a revolutionary proletariat in Latin American cities partly to the relative speed with which rural migrants were able to achieve economic security. (b) The creation of individuals and groups that are forced to move downward by virtue of the changes in the social structure. Examples are handicraft workers displaced by factory production, traditional chiefs displaced by the growth of centralized political structures, peasants displaced by programs of land reform, and so on. Both the irregularly upwardly mobile and the downwardly mobile groups in the developing societies provide many candidates for protest movements. The political stability of these societies depends in large part on the extent of this protest and on the ways in which the constituted authorities respond to such protest.

RESEARCH PROBLEMS IN THE COMPARATIVE ANALYSIS OF MOBILITY AND DEVELOPMENT

Our discussion thus far has dealt with the general relations between different elements of social structure and various patterns emerging around the creation of new roles in a developing economy. Empirical analysis of these relationships, however, requires a detailed look at the processes through which new structures such as governments, business organizations, trade unions, the military, political parties, and so on locate individuals to fill roles at all levels, particularly at the important summit or elite positions. An investigation of the problem of mobility must also involve an analysis of the relations between individual and collective social mobility. The first, of course, refers to the changes in position, within or between generations; the second, to changes in the relative income, power or status of entire strata which may be occasioned by major economic or political changes.

Drastic social change on the scope of significant economic growth or social revolution must, in and of itself, result in a sizable increase in the amount of social mobility in a society. A shift from an agrarian system toward an urban and industrial one means that many who began life in peasant or artisan families must become workers, clerks or entrepreneurs; politically a change in fundamental patterns of rule will open many positions in government and the military to those of low origin. Conversely, of course some in stable positions, e.g., peasants and artisans, may find it difficult to retain their positions and may lack the flexibility to adjust to the requirements of the new occupational structure, while those from a more insecure background may be more willing to take the risks necessary to improve their circumstances. In major social revolutions certain classes are often downgraded as a matter of policy.

The phenomenon of "collective mobility" has been little analyzed by social scientists. A given stratum, such as skilled workers, or those possessing a certain level of education, may find its social bargaining power sharply increased when a society commits itself to rapid industrialization. This pattern has occurred in the Soviet Union and other Communist countries, and probably in a number of the developing countries in other parts of the world. Social revolution may increase the status and opportunities of given classes as a consequence of the downgrading of others. In some Communist countries, workers and peasants and their children were given greater opportunities to secure education and to achieve good positions as a matter of deliberate policy. The organized strength of certain classes may equalize rewards to some extent. Changes in the relative income position of the manual and white collar strata reflect differential political and trade union strength.

In the long run, however, such discrepancies between status and opportunity tend to disappear. In the Soviet case, for example, it seems clear from the available materials that being a member of a higher status stratum is a major asset in enhancing the status of one's kin. The children of the higher classes and the better-educated do better in the educational system and have a better chance to secure high status positions than do those of lowly background. The ideological commitments to discriminate in favor of the lowly are gradually downgraded or ignored under the pressures from those who control the new system and seek to maintain privilege for themselves.

The analysis of social mobility patterns in rapidly changing societies is also bedeviled by the problem of relating data concerning shifts from one role to another to assumptions concerning movements up or down the class structure. A move from the status of peasant or artisan to that of factory worker is clearly mobility but it is not clear whether it should be regarded as upward, downward, or parallel movement. A man who has given up "control" over his pace of work, his economic independence, etc., to accept factory employment has made a drastic change in the social relationships linked to the job. From one perspective the changes may involve an increase in income or in status. Yet, from another perspective, self-employed peasants and artisans are more conservative politically, acting as part of the "have" classes, as contrasted with manual workers who develop antagonisms to their employers. And in Western society, petty businessmen and lower white-collar workers demonstrate a closer affinity to upper-middle-class values and general styles of life than do manual workers whose incomes are higher than theirs.

Many discussions of the rates, causes, and consequences of social mobility by sociologists have ignored this extremely difficult question of distinguishing between mobility that involves a change of "social setting" and mobility that clearly involves upward or downward movement. The literature assumes, on the whole, that most movement can be classified roughly as upward or downward, with the manual-non-manual line as the main dividing point. Farm or peasant owners have been left out because it is too difficult to fit them into this dichotomous division. This approach may be plausible in advanced industrial societies where rural-urban movement is of relatively small importance but it creates obvious difficulties for analysis of mobility in rapidly developing nations. Some scholars (e.g., David Glass) have attempted to surmount this problem by locating all occupations on a social status scale (social rankings given to them by a sample of the population), or by some sort of socio-economic classification established by the researcher (differential weights to income, skill, presumed status, etc.). This latter method presents the difficulty that certain kinds of movement are not counted as social mobility, since they are classified as movements within the same stratum. Thus, English students of mobility classify most shifts from skilled to lower white-collar worker or the reverse, as job changes occurring within the same class, and most rural-urban moves are also by definition not social mobility. A common change in newly developing countries—from farm laborer to manual laborer—would not be counted as mobility under some of these methods.

These difficulties, as well as those analyzed in detail by Otis Dudley Duncan in his contribution to this volume, must be kept in mind in evaluating the research findings and interpretation presented here. Much of what seems puzzling and contradictory, either to common or to theoretical sense may be, in fact, a consequence of the lack of reliability of the indicators, and often the generalization under discussion cannot be tested given the way in which the data were collected and classified. A further limitation is that the existing literature on the subject is by and large confined to analysis of patterns of total labor force movement, omitting considerations of important problems such as recruitment into elite positions.

There is a puzzling lack of association between indicators of economic development and measures of social mobility. Data assembled by Lipset, Zetterberg, and Bendix suggest considerable "upward mobility," as measured by shifts across the manual-nonmanual line even in traditionalist and preindustrial society.[12] Miller and Bryce have attempted to relate variations in nations' mobility patterns (e.g., combinations) of high upward and low downward movement, or high upward and high downward, low upward and high downward, etc.) to various indicators of economic growth drawn from Kuznets, as well as to current variations in productivity. The one significant relationship they uncovered is between current national income and such patterns. There is little association between mobility patterns, percentage growth in national product, percentage growth in per capita income or percentage growth in population.[13] As Miller and Bryce suggest, "this finding is surprising since we would expect a rather strong relationship between economic forces and the patterns of mobility."

These findings so contradict the logical expectation that economic growth should result in a pattern of high upward and low downward mobility (one which has been suggested by the data from the Harvard Russian refugee sample as characteristic of Soviet life before World War II) that we wonder whether these negative results are a function of the methodological weaknesses suggested above. Do we really have a reliable way to estimate upward or downward mobility in developing countries? As of now, we do not: a systematic effort must be made to relate the data of changes, classified in different ways, to the estimates of growth.

STATUS VALUES AND THE POTENTIAL FOR ECONOMIC GROWTH

If we can question the hypothesis that high rates of economic growth give rise to high rates of social mobility, we can also question the frequent assumption that a strong concern for social mobility in a society will invariably contribute to economic growth presumably because those most anxious to succeed will seek ways to maximize resources. (Reliance on this assumption is characteristic of the literature on achievement motivation cited by Harry Crockett in his article in this volume.) Under some conditions the desire for social mobility, inherent in the logic of any

[12] Lipset and Bendix, op. cit., pp. 11-75; see also S. M. Miller, "Comparative Social Mobility: A Trend Report," Current Sociology 9, no. 1 (1960).

[13] S. M. Miller and Harrington Bryce, "Social Mobility and Economic Growth and Structure," Kölner Zeitschrift für Soziologie, 13 (1961), pp. 303-315.

system of socal stratification, may actually serve to reduce the supply of talent available for economic development. Thus, in cultures that emphasize the worth of occupations associated with traditional aristocratic status, the desire for higher status may lead men out of more economically productive tasks into occupations less significant from the point of view of the economy. Sons of the successful businessmen go to a university and enter the learned professions, the civil service, politics, the arts, or other similar occupations. Such behavior presumably diminishes capital investment.

The conditions under which new, socially important roles acquire the status necessary to recruit and maintain a high level of talent must therefore be considered. Some have suggested that variations in rates of development among certain countries are partly due to differences in values attached to entrepreneurial occupations. Thus, the emphasis on mobility through entrepreneurship in the United States has been causally linked to the absence of aristocratic status patterns and to the "purity" of the tie between economic achievement and social status. Foreign travelers early in American history described American materialism as a reflection of the values of a new society without a traditional upper class.[14]

Conversely, the ability of the English entrepreneurial strata to recruit from the established upper class has been explained in part by pressure for downward mobility among the "younger sons" of the privileged in a society emphasizing primogeniture. To avoid downward mobility, younger sons had to find occupational roles that would give them the income appropriate to their background.[15]

Similarly, primogeniture has been credited with facilitating industrial development in Japan. "[Y]ounger sons were both economically and emotionally drawn to the new urban occupations. These younger sons . . . appear to have been especially responsive and adaptive to the introduction of new styles of life." [16]

Analyses of Latin societies have stressed the presumed desire of Latin Americans and Europeans to secure property, either in land or business, as a source of family solidarity and status, but they also have indicated

[14] Seymour Martin Lipset, *The First New Nation. The United States in Historical and Comparative Perspective* (New York: Basic Books, 1963), pp. 57-59, and *passim*.

[15] Robert Ulrich, *The Education of Nations* (Cambridge: Harvard University Press, 1961), p. 95; Nancy Mitford, "The English Aristocracy," in Mitford (ed.), *Noblesse oblige* (Harmondsworth: Penguin Books, 1959), pp. 36-37.

[16] James C. Abegglen, "The Relationship Between Economic and Social Programming in Latin America," in Egbert DeVries and José Medina Echaverria, eds., *Social Aspects of Economic Development in Latin America*, Vol. I (Paris: UNESCO, 1963), p. 268.

that the traditional Latin values emphasize preservation of property once attained, and dictate an extreme unwillingness to risk capital to make enterprise more efficient.[17]

Many middle developed countries retain important elements of the status and political power structure of a pre-industrial society. Their situation has been well described by Harbison and Myers:

> Landlords, lawyers, government officials, owners of large family enterprises, and often military leaders enjoy both high status and political power. They are the elites. And access to their ranks is likely to depend largely upon political and family connections rather than demonstrated competence or high intellectual ability. The status of professional engineers and scientists is usually inferior, since in most cases they are employed and perhaps managed by these elites. And in some countries, a so-called "humanitarian tradition" may strengthen the tendency to downgrade agronomists, physicists, chemists, and engineers . . . Professional managers in private enterprises, as distinguished from owners or family managers, are not very high either on the status ladder . . .
>
> A social structure of this kind obviously is an obstacle to growth along modern lines; and it must be drastically changed if the newly articulated goals of the partially developed countries are to be achieved. In China, of course, the required changes have been made in a completely ruthless and arbitrary fashion. There, the scientist, the engineer, the technician, and the factory worker are glorified, and other "intellectuals" who are not members of Communist ruling elites are roundly castigated.[18]

There is considerable empirical evidence drawn from studies of the behavior and attitudes of aspiring (university students) and actual elites

---

[17] On France, see various articles by David Landes, "French Entrepreneurship and Industrial Growth in the XIXth Century," *Journal of Economic History*, 9 (1949), pp. 49-61; "French Business and the Business Man: A Social and Cultural Analysis," in Edward H. Earle, (ed.), *Modern France* (Princeton: Princeton University Press, 1951), pp. 334-353; and "Observations on France: Economy, Society and Polity," *World Politics*, 9 (1957), pp. 329-350; See also, John E. Sawyer, "Strains in the Social Structure of Modern France," in Earle, ed., *op. cit.*, pp. 293-312; and Roy Lewis and Rose Mary Stewart, *The Managers: A New Examination of the English, German and American Executive* (New York: Mentor Books, 1961) pp. 182-187. For a discussion of similar attitudes and behavior in Italy, see Maurice F. Neufield, *Italy: School for Awakening Countries* (Ithaca: New York State School of Industrial and Labor Relations, 1961), p. 35 and *passim*. For Quebec, see Norman W. Taylor, "The French-Canadian Industrial Entrepreneur and His Social Environment," in Marcel Rioux and Yves Martin (eds.), *French-Canadian Society* (Toronto: McClelland and Stewart, 1964), pp. 271-295. For discussions of values and economic behavior in Latin America see T. C. Cochran, "Cultural Factors in Economic Growth," *Journal of Economic History*, 20 (1960), pp. 515-530; John Gillin, "Ethos Components in Modern Latin American Culture," *American Anthropologist*, 57 (1955), pp. 488-500.

[18] Frederick Harbison and Charles A. Myers, *Education, Manpower and Economic Growth* (New York: McGraw-Hill, 1964), p. 92; see also William F. Whyte and Allan R. Holmberg, *Human Problems of U. S. Enterprise in Latin America* (Ithaca: New York State School of Industrial and Labor Relations, 1955), p. 9.

of many underdeveloped nations which sustain the conclusions reached by Harbison and Myers.[19] There are important national variations in the propensity to sustain business careers; successful businessmen often turn to other more traditional high status pursuits on a part or full time basis. More important, perhaps, is the propensity of the economic elite of such nations to follow the values of pre-industrial society in the operation of their businesses, e.g., strong emphases on family particularism. Such behavior by the elite, however, is not reflected in major differences in occupational prestige ranking reported in various sociological studies in many nations, both developed and underdeveloped.[20]

Although much more research, both between and within nations, is needed before any definitive conclusions can be drawn concerning the factors that determine occupational prestige, the data in hand suggest that certain common underlying forces affect these rankings in all societies. And if emphasis is placed not on the descriptive content of specific occupations as such, but rather on their functions, financial rewards, and requirements, it seems evident that varying types of societies accord high status to positions that convey considerable power in key institutions, i.e., government, economy, education, religion, to those that alleviate tension, e.g., physicians, and to those requiring prolonged education, training, and intelligence.[21] Both modern and traditional roles seem to be judged according to such underlying assumptions, although the old elites strongly, and often successfully, resist according equal status to the *nouveaux riches* "materialistic" positions of the encroaching industrial society.

MOBILITY AND THE INTEGRATION BETWEEN
TRADITION AND MODERNITY

One of the greatest difficulties in generalizing about mobility in the developing societies involves the relations between tradition and modernity in periods of transition. The principal socio-economic change with

---

[19] For a discussion of this literature in the context of an analysis of Latin American development problems see Seymour Martin Lipset, "Elites, Education and Entrepreneurship in Latin America," in Seymour Martin Lipset and Aldo A. Solari (eds.), *Elites and Development in Latin America* (New York: Oxford University Press, forthcoming).

[20] Robert W. Hodge, Donald J. Treiman, and Peter H. Rossi, "A Comparative Study of Occupational Prestige," in Reinhard Bendix and Seymour Martin Lipset (eds.), *Class, Status, and Power: Social Stratification in Comparative Perspective* (New York: Free Press of Glencoe, 1966), pp. 309-321.

[21] For a more detailed effort to suggest such general factors, see R. Murray Thomas, "Reinspecting a Structural Position on Occupational Prestige," *American Journal of Sociology*, 57 (1962), p. 565; see also Hodge, Treiman, and Rossi, *op. cit.*

which development is associated is the change from technically simple production to complicated modern production methods, a change that creates a demand for individuals who are motivated to train for or create new positions in the secondary and tertiary sectors of the economy. This change, however, is comparatively rapid in some countries and slow in others, and it does not progress at a uniform rate among various regional sectors in a single country. As a result, certain parts of a developing country, especially the industrialized urban sectors, have acquired a new stratification structure, while other sections still possess a more traditional, less differentiated structure of social relations. Though often neglected in the past, analyses of these contrasts in economic life should be related to any effort to specify the causes and consequences of social mobility in emerging societies.

Some of the first analysts of such differences emphasized the way in which the imposition of a Western modern economy, stressing a nationally centralized production-oriented system, in countries where the great majority of the population were engaged in an agricultural, consumer-oriented economy, destroyed the organic political and social unity of essentially *Gemeinschaft* societies. A "dual" society and economy results, in which the larger but weaker traditional one ultimately loses its ability satisfactorily to fulfill many functions it had handled before changes were originated from outside. Colonial domination or indigenous efforts to industrialize, by bringing in Western values, undermined the social utility of many traditional institutions for the population. Many customs were abandoned. Anti-social forces were released, hastening the disintegration of organic solidarity. According to this view, the efforts of the rulers of such nations to control these anti-social forces through chiefs and tribal or other local authorities, or by establishing modern governmental rule, failed to provide a socially accepted integrative or organizing principle. Both parts of the "dual" society operated inefficiently.[22]

This thesis stresses the social dysfunctions inherent in cultural diffusion and efforts to modernize. Others have criticized its failure to recognize the positive effects an emerging cultural pluralism may have on a society, or the varying consequences of "dualism" under different conditions.[23] In his paper in this volume Bert Hoselitz points out that the imposition of a modern economy on a traditional and less advanced so-

[22] J. H. Boeke, *Dualistische Economie* (Leiden, 1930); Boeke's inaugural lecture at Leiden, "Dualistic Economics," reprinted in *Indonesian Economics: The Concept of Dualism in Theory and Policy* (The Hague, 1961); J. H. Boeke, *Oriental Economics* (New York: Institute of Pacific Relations, 1947); J. S. Furnivall, *Colonial Policy and Practice* (Cambridge: The University Press), p. 5.

[23] Manning Nash, "Introducing Industry in Peasant Societies," *Science*, 130 (Nov. 27, 1959), pp. 1456-1462.

ciety can have varying results: (1) the economically simpler societies may be completely destroyed or absorbed or become a welfare-maintained portion of the advanced population; (2) the non-Western population may adopt quickly the basically different and new pattern of economic, social, and political organization; (3) the indigenous tribal population may persist for a long time in self-centered and separate groups; and (4) the more westernized and less westernized economies of a developing nation may integrate successfully. The contrasts between different sectors of the society and between different spheres of peoples' lives are a major factor in the alteration of the original social stratification system, helping to motivate some individuals to enter new and previously non-existent social groups. Accordingly, intrusions may be viewed as a means of encouraging new structures of social relations which permit an increase in the standard of living rather than as sources of the disintegration of structures that embody traditional customs and ideals, such as the family and religion.

Though it is impossible to present a detailed discussion of the changing stratification patterns in developing countries in Asia and Africa in terms of these alternatives, since relatively little research has been done, it is possible to point to examples of the varying alternatives. Hoselitz himself cites Japan as an example of the second pattern, successful adaptation to an industrial society, and points to Indonesia, India, Pakistan, and other areas of Asia as examples of nations attempting the fourth possibility, the integration of tradition and modernity in one society and economy—e.g., village handicraft and large factories. In his research on stratification and social mobility in Malaya, Gayl Ness asserts that British rule had for the most part strengthened the traditional Malayan social organization. In the pre-independence period, "Malaya appeared as a plural society with a dual economy." And while the heads of strong traditional local communities kept the peace and supported efforts to develop national centers of authority, the new sector, though involving only a minority of Malays, laid the basis for a more integrated modernized national society.

The modern sector of the economy found participants from all communities . . . [if] compared with other sub-systems, the economy appears to have been a significant nationalizing force, in the sense of bridging communal barriers.[24]

The existence of separate social stratification systems within the disparate cultural, caste, religious, regional, and linguistic communities of many underdeveloped communities makes it virtually impossible to assess

[24] Gayl D. Ness, "Occupational Prestige Rankings in Malaya" (unpublished mimeographed paper presented to the Conference on Stratification and Mobility in East Asia, Tokyo, April 1964), p. 2.

directly the relations between economic change and social mobility, especially since gross rates may conceal significant variations in the rates and patterns of various groups with different cultures. Studies do exist, however, of mobility in the urban areas of some developing societies. These indicate that in the cities, at least, mobility rates resemble those of Western societies. Thus, some observers point to the fact that a relatively unchanged agricultural and rural stratification system may exist in one country simultaneously with a high (*i.e.*, Western) rate of mobility in the urban sectors. In his paper in this volume on the problem of maintaining a balance between urban and rural sectors in industrializing economies, Gideon Sjoberg points out that education rather than rural poverty encourages the needed rural out-migration. The more highly educated leave the rural scene for urban centers in relatively greater numbers than do the poorly educated. These findings suggest that increased expenditures for rural education may increase the numbers who seek to better themselves by modernizing their country. In this regard Sjoberg implicitly criticizes those who favor efforts to attain economic development by repeating the alleged Western model, first creating a rural economic surplus by enhancing agricultural productivity. This gives disproportionate importance to the rural sector, and neither threatens the traditional power structure nor supports the modern values that are a necessary condition for economic development and increased social mobility.

A related problem discussed in this volume by Lester Seligman concerns the effects that the intrusion of foreign political concepts into a rather undifferentiated socio-political system may have on mobility orientations. In many underdeveloped countries the adoption of Western (including Marxist) legalistic political ideas has produced many occupational positions, such as political party worker, toward which new vocational aspirations are directed. Knowing that the distribution of power directly influences decisions about the allocation of economic resources, we can expect that the structure of political stratification will seriously affect patterns of mobility in developing nations. Ambitious educated men are more likely to seek to advance themselves within the powerful political-public sector than within the private and production sectors than was true in Western nations while they were developing.

In general, of course, political elites are legitimated by their incorporation or evocation of sacred, traditional values. In the developing countries where new states are coming into existence, programs of modernization are usually interwoven with the goals of nationalism. Consequently, both nationalism and modernization are major conditions of legitimating the governing elites. As Seligman suggests, nationalism supported by all may encourage political pluralism by identifying traditional groups and institutions with the new state. In this sense the new nationalism may itself sustain interest in old loyalties and avenues of status mobility.[25]

Ironically, certain recent Western innovations may become "traditional" barriers to modernization because they are identified with the struggle for national independence and pride. For example, the impact of Western education on contemporary Africa has in many cases been a source of controversy because African administrators and new nationalist leaders who as products of "academic" or general education resist proposals for introducing widespread technical and agricultural education. Because an elitist "academic" system of education contributed to increased aspirations for political independence, and is characteristic of developed European countries, many leaders therefore contend that a "traditional" British or French type educational system is a prerequisite for economic growth. In Ghana the government finds itself in a painful dilemma, betwen the need to deal with advocates of African and Western "traditionalisms," and the need to open modern roads to economic development. On one hand, students and faculty at the elitist university modeled on Oxbridge have strongly resisted efforts to give the university a more vocational or utilitarian emphasis on the grounds that this will denigrate the culture of the Ghanaian elite and shame the nation before the world. On the other hand, though committed to modernization, it is forced to celebrate the virtues of traditional society while its aggressive nationalist ideology assumes that Western education in the colonial period robbed Africans of their traditional heritage. Thus, the most acculturated individuals in Ghana demand the "Africanization" of the schools.[26] The persistence of neo-colonial and traditional values and practices among a political elite that openly rejects both, makes it difficult to establish and legitimate universalistic values, including perhaps an ideological program that formally sanctions processes and structures of social mobility.

The gap between economic aspirations and the facts of underdevelopment, brought about by the spread of modern media of communication, especially the motion picture and the transistor radio, may result in political instability, even in very backward areas with little direct exposure to modern education or to industrial urban society. The isolated, almost totally non-urban kingdom of Cambodia has been cited as a society in

[25] See Rupert Emerson, *From Empire to Nation* (Cambridge: Harvard University Press, 1960), p. 329.

[26] The discussion of Ghana is based on Philip J. Foster, *Education and Social Change in Ghana* (Chicago: University of Chicago Press, 1965), Chapter IX.

which the lure of industrial civilization, reaching now even into the most remote section forces the peasants to change many attitudes and encourages them to want more manufactured goods.[27] The processes of change may contain the seeds of social unrest and foster support for revolutionary movements which have appeared in nations seemingly unaffected by economic or other structural changes. Peasants become receptive to varied forms of propaganda and appeals to violence as a result of upheaval of traditional patterns, the inept establishment of modern values, and perhaps premature aspirations for mobility.

The assumption in much of literature in this field is that the sociological problem of development can largely be expressed in terms of a conflict between the forces supporting tradition and modernity. This assumption is challenged by Reinhard Bendix in his paper in this volume. He suggests that the key "question is how cultural ideals that support tradition can give rise to cultural ideals that support modernity," or in other words, that the shift from tradition to modernity need not involve a rejection of a nation's basic values. Bendix notes that Weber's study of the resolution of the contradiction betwen the traditional and the modern in a developing society begins with the observation that the Protestant reformers continued to be concerned with their salvation and accepted the traditional, Christian devaluation of worldly pursuits. The emergence of the "spirit of capitalism" represents a direct outgrowth of this early anti-materialistic tradition of Christianity wherein the individual did not cease to be concerned with his salvation. Applying Weber's approach to the preconditions for Japanese development, Bendix points out that the samurai under the Tokugawa regime became a demilitarized aristocracy which remained loyal to the traditional samurai ethic of militancy, although the Tokugawa regime pursued a public policy of disciplined pacification and discouraged conflict or competitive struggles to change status or power relations among the feudal lords. After the Meiji Restoration of 1868, the virtues of competition were socially accepted. The traditional samurai ethic applied to a competitive world meant now that any self-expecting samurai was obliged to show his ability and desire to win. Thus in 19th century Japan, as in Reformation Europe, the emergence of "modern" economic orientations involved the application of traditional values and sources of individual motivation to new structural conditions, rather than the supplanting of one set of values by another. This conclusion concerning two cultural areas that have successfully developed has obvious implications for those now seeking to industrialize.

EDUCATION AND ECONOMIC GROWTH

When it comes to suggesting a relationship between possible deliberate action and changes in values and behavior that might affect the emergence of a modern elite, more thought has been given to the effects of increases in educational facilities than to any other variable.[28] In spite of this, however, the various *ad hoc* generalizations that have been made in this area remain largely in the category of "unproven," and, not surprisingly, some of them contradict each other. Most writers generally accept the thesis that heavy investment in education will pay off in economic growth because it increases the amount of skill in a society and the motivation of the educated to create new development-fostering positions.[29] This positive thesis has been countered by several arguments: that a transfer of educational and research techniques from developed to underdeveloped societies sometimes results in efforts at innovation that are dysfunctional to the country; that an "overexpansion" of educational resources may create a frustrated and hence politically dangerous stratum whose political activities undermine the conditions for growth; that the "educated" often develop diffuse elitist status and cultural sustenance demands which lead them to refuse to work in the rural or otherwise "backward" parts of their country; that the educated often resist doing anything which resembles manual employment; and that rapid educational expansion results in many being poorly educated, while reducing the opportunities available to the small minority of really bright students.[30]

Apparent evidence for the thesis that increased education makes for growth is found in the history of the United States, Japan, and the Soviet Union. In these three countries, high levels of national expenditure on education preceded industrialization.[31] North America has led the world in educational attainments almost from its establishment as a nation.

[28] Adam Curle, *The Role of Education in Developing Societies* (Accra: Ghana University Press, 1961).

[29] See T. W. Schultz, *The Economic Value of Education* (New York: Columbia University Press, 1963).

[30] H. Myint, "Education and Economic Development," *Social and Economic Studies*, 14 (1965), pp. 8-20.

[31] John Vaizey, *The Economics of Education* (London: Faber and Faber, 1962), pp. 55-56.

There is general agreement that this investment has played a major role in its economic success. The United States Census of 1840, the first to deal with literacy, reported that only 9 per cent of the white population 20 years old and above were illiterate.[32] It is often forgotten that both Japan and Russia were strongly oriented toward popular education before they entered their modern rapid development stages, that is in the pre-Meiji and pre-Communist eras. Close to half the Japanese male population were literate at the end of the Tokugawa era,[33] and the rulers of Meiji Japan initiated a campaign of educational investment on all levels, resulting in close to 95 per cent elementary school attendance by the beginning of the present century. Similarly in Czarist Russia, the Census of 1897 indicated that 44 per cent of males aged 30-39 were able to read; in urban areas, 69 per cent were literate, including 60 per cent of the workers. while almost 40 per cent of the rural population were reported as literate.[34] A much higher percentage of school-age youth were enrolled in elementary school. Thus the Bolsheviks, like the Meiji elite of Japan, took over a country which had already gone a long way toward providing a seeming prerequisite for economic development, a literate population. And both, of course, on taking over, enlarged the national commitment toward educational growth as a means of fostering economic development. It is obviously difficult to separate out the extent to which any given aspect of national policy has contributed to high rates of economic development. But there is no question that both Japan and the Soviet Union entered on a policy of heavy investment in education at all levels, long before any one could argue that the demand for the educated equaled the increased supply. Today, the Soviet Union spends more per capita on education than any nation except Kuwait. Similarly, Communist China has increased its educational expenditures enormously. Although in 1949 China and India were approximately at the same level of development, the Chinese have invested far more than India in expanding educational facilities, with particular emphasis on higher education.[35]

[32] U.S. Bureau of the Census, A Statistical Abstract Supplement, Historical Statistics of the U.S. Colonial Times to 1957 (Washington: 1957), p. 214.

[33] Herbert Passin, "Japan," in Coleman (ed.), op cit., p. 276; Ronald Dore, Education in Tokugawa Japan (Berkeley: University of California Press, 1965), pp. 317-322.

[34] C. A. Anderson, "Footnote to the Social History of Modern Russia: the Literacy and Educational Census of 1897," Genus, 12 (1956), pp. 1-18; see also Arcadius Kahan, "Russian Scholars and Statesmen on Education as an Investment" in C. Arnold Anderson and Mary Jean Bowman (eds.), Education and Economic Development (Chicago: Aldine, 1965), pp. 3-10.

[35] Adam Curle, "Education, Politics and Development," Comparative Education Review, 7 (1963), pp. 236-238.

It is interesting that a report of the discussions at a conference of the International Economic Association on factors in raising productivity states "that economists from around the world believed that the educational system of the United States was the reason for its achieving by a fair margin the highest productivity of labor of any country . . . [T]he economists at the conference pointed out that what was different was that the United States was the first country to have the land grant institutions based on the idea that the university would contribute to all of society. The Communists and others at the conference shared this view: the secret of the United States was not the fact that it was a democracy or a capitalist society, or that it had the greatest physical resources, but rather that it got started very early using education largely, or at least philosophically, for political reasons, and then this turned out to be a great economic asset." [36]

A number of studies have provided evidence for the close links between the distribution of literacy and education to economic development. An analysis of the relation between levels of educational achievement and industrialization indicates that literacy and levels of industrialization correlate quite highly on an international level (.87 for 70 countries in 1950), and that these two factors have been associated historically in the development of industrialized nations. The author concludes:

The differential rates of economic advance for the educationally retarded and the educationally advanced countries point to the importance of the dissemination of literacy and education in the transformation of peasant-agricultural nations into urban-industrial nations . . . [T]he countries that today are ahead educationally will find it easier to achieve this goal [increased industrialization] than those that are behind. The latter countries . . . will need to spend a great share of their goal of mass education before they can aspire to become modern industrial states.[37]

There seems to be a close association between a high degree of literacy and high per capita income, and between very low literacy rates and quite low incomes. Thus of 24 nations in the early 1950's whose adult populations were over 90 per cent literate, 21 had a per capita income of $500 or more; conversely, of the 25 countries with less than 30 per cent literate, only one had an income of over $200, oil-rich North

[36] Clark Kerr, "Presentation," in Council on Higher Education in the American Republics, *National Development and the University* (New York: Institute of International Education, 1965), p. 10.

[37] Hilda H. Golden, "Literacy and Social Change in Underdeveloped Countries," in Lyle Shannon (ed.), *Underdeveloped Areas* (New York: Harper and Row, 1957), pp. 108-113.

Borneo.[38] The relationship is less striking but still present for nations falling in the intermediate categories.

The relationship between levels of literacy and education and subsequent economic development is obviously much more complex than any two variable relationship statements such as those made here would indicate. Identical rates of literacy or proportions enrolled in universities will have different consequences for societies with varying values, levels of economic development, types and quality of schooling, opportunities for educational mobility, and the like. Such factors do not appear in the national parameter statistics employed in most studies of the issues. A look at gross national data, for example, indicates that for "Western and Far Eastern countries 1930, primary attendance seems to be the best of . . . three educational predictors [primary, post-primary, and adult literacy] of 1955 incomes; for Latin America, the Middle East, and Africa adult literacy best predicts subsequent income." [39] There has been no adequate effort, as yet, to account for such regional differences. The correlations between educational levels and economic development also seem to be affected by the seeming "occurrence of important, distinct stages in educational lead and lag; an early stage of education-economic breakthrough; a plateau on which diffusing education is still not sufficient to support a high-level economy; and a third stage in which another economic breakthrough is possible, based on a well-educated population." [40]

A number of recent studies do suggest high positive relationships between levels of secondary and higher education and statistical indicators of economic development.[41] Harbison and Myers, in fact, conclude that in moving from one stage of economic development to a higher one the investment in secondary and higher education increases about three times as fast as productivity.[42] Such relationships, of course, do not indicate which is cause and which effect. However, a study comparing rates of technological growth between 1952 and 1958 (as indicated by changes in use of electric power), and higher educational enrollments, found that those countries that had relatively high levels of university

---

[38] Mary Jean Bowman and C. Arnold Anderson, "Concerning the Role of Education in Economic Development," in Clifford Geertz (ed.), *Old Societies and New States* (New York: Free Press of Glencoe, 1963), pp. 251-252.

[39] C. Arnold Anderson, "Economic Development and Post-Primary Education," in Don C. Piper and Taylor Cole (eds.), *Post-Primary Education and Political and Economic Development* (Durham: Duke University Press, 1964), p. 5.

[40] Bowman and Anderson, "Concerning the Role . . . ," *op. cit.*, pp. 266, 277.

[41] J. Tinbergen and H. Correa, "Quantitative Adaption of Education to Accelerated Growth," *Kyklos*, 15 (1962), pp. 776-786; Curle, *op. cit.*, pp. 227-229; for a somewhat different result see Anderson, *op. cit.*

[42] Harbison and Myers, *op. cit.*, pp. 23-49, 182-187.

enrollment in 1950 had much higher rates of technological growth during the 1950's than did the nations with relatively low levels of enrollment.[43] It is significant that "higher education enrollments bear an even closer relation to rates of economic growth in the 1950's than secondary education does."[44]

These findings are clearly relevant for specifying the ways in which education, particularly higher education, is related to the role of the elite in contributing to political modernization and economic growth. First, as Arthur Lewis has suggested, there is some reason to suspect that the status concomitants that are linked to education should vary with the proportion and absolute size of the population that is educated. A relatively small higher education establishment will encourage the retention or even development of traditional diffuse elitist values among university graduates, while where a large proportion of the university age population attend school, the pressures should be in the opposite direction.[45] In much of Latin America, university students almost automatically "become part of the elite. It matters little whether a student is the son of a minister or the son of a workman. His mere enrollment at the university makes him one of the two per thousand most privileged in the land."[46] Conversely in the United States, with its mass educational system, few university graduates may expect to attain high status; many of them will hold relatively low non-manual positions, and a certain number will even be employed in manual occupations. Where comparatively few attend university, as in Britain, graduates who fail to achieve a status comparable to that of most of their fellow graduates will feel discontented, for their reference group will be a more highly successful group. The same analysis may be applied to the different implications of education for status concerns in the Philippines as contrasted, say, with Senegal. A Filipino who attends the massive University of the Far East must know that few of his fellow students can expect an elite position; Senegalese students, however, know that among their classmates at the University of Dakar are the future and economic and political leaders of the nation.

Some further evidence that the reality of the opportunity structure

[43] David McClelland, "Does Education Accelerate Economic Growth?" (unpublished dittoed paper), p. 23.

[44] *Ibid.*, p. 22.

[45] For a discussion of the consequences of moving from a small elite system to mass higher education in Japan, see Herbert Passin, "Modernization and the Japanese Intellectual: Some Comparative Observations," in Marius B. Jansen (ed.), *Changing Japanese Attitudes toward Modernization* (Princeton: Princeton University Press, 1965), pp. 478-481.

[46] Rudolph P. Atcon, "The Latin American University," *Die Deutsche Universitätszeitung*, 17 (February, 1962), p. 16.

also affects the aspiration level of students in developing countries on a lower level may be found in a study of Ghanaian secondary school students. Contrary to many assumptions about the unrealistic elitist aspirations of African students, those in Ghana, though aspiring to high-status positions, have adjusted their career expectations to the actual structure of opportunities, which favors white-collar employment for the large majority of graduates. Over two-thirds of the 963 questioned were found to prefer a career in the natural sciences and their related technology in physics, chemistry, meteorology and engineering, while the remainder indicated a preference for biology and agricultural science. But the number who expect to enter scientific and technical fields if they should not be able to proceed with full-time study beyond the fifth form drops to 7 per cent, and virtually no students believe that it will be possible for them to enter professional or semi-professional employment. In fact, 84 per cent of all students *expect* to enter low-level clerical employment or primary and middle school teaching, and the bulk of secondary school graduates are employed in clerical positions. Graduates, then, tend to obtain precisely the jobs which they expect. While the Ghanaian students would like to have various professional positions, their perception of the occupational value of a secondary school education is realistic. And most of them realize that a secondary education has become increasingly terminal, given the small numbers admitted to higher education.[47]

There is good reason to believe, however, that growth in the numbers who attain higher levels of education should result in an increase in the amount of high achievement orientation in a population. Studies of the occupational goals of college students in nations with tiny systems of higher education suggest that the large majority of them expect positions in government work.[48] Since some form of white-collar employment must be the goal of college and secondary students, a sharp increase in their numbers should make talent available for a variety of technical and entrepreneurial roles. As Tumin and Feldman have indicated: "From the point of view of a theory of stratification, education is the main dissolver of barriers to social mobility. Education opens up the class structure and keeps it fluid, permitting considerably more circulation through class positions than would otherwise be possible. Education, further, yields attitudes and skills relevant to economic development and such development, in turn, allows further opportunity for persons at

[47] Foster, *op. cit.*
[48] See K. A. Busia, "Education and Social Mobility in Economically Underdeveloped Countries," *Transactions of the Third World Congress of Sociology,* Vol. V (London: International Sociological Association, 1956), pp. 81-89.

lower ranks." [49] These assumptions are borne out in a comparative analysis of the relationship between national rates of social mobility and various characteristics of nine western European nations, plus Communist Hungary, Japan, and the United States; this analysis reports that the education variable emerges as the individually most important and ostensibly reliable determinant of manual outflow mobility. "Higher levels of upward mobility are associated with higher levels of education . . . ." [50] School enrollment correlated more highly with upward mobility than did other parameter items such as gross national product per capita, or population in localities over 20,000. However, investment in education affects only the amount of *upward* mobility; the relationship between rates of down mobility and education was insignificant, lower than with any of the other variables examined. Although there are some contradictory reports, the weight of the available evidence supports the thesis that increased expenditure for education increases the number of individuals available and motivated to seek new and more prestigious roles.[51]

Educational expansion, however, has been criticized for impeding economic growth by fostering dysfunctional values in some countries, by reinforcing "status values and/or special privileges that are incompatible with economic advance." [52] "[I]t has been suggested that the labour-shortage for sugar-cane cutting in some of the West Indian islands may be due to the spread of primary education among the younger people." [53] There is no doubt, of course, that a rapid expansion of an educational system may result in an over-supply of persons with relatively high expectations of employment, salary, and status. The increase in the numbers of educated people in a developing economy necessarily means that as education becomes less scarce it should command less status and income. The process of adjusting expanded levels of education to reduced rewards is obviously a difficult one, and often results in political unrest.

[49] Melvin Tumin with Arnold S. Feldman, *Social Class and Social Change in Puerto Rico* (Princeton: Princeton University Press, 1961), p. 7.

[50] Thomas Fox and S. M. Miller, "Economic, Political, and Social Determinants of Mobility: An International Cross-Sectional Analysis," *Acta Sociologica*, 9 (1966), pp. 76-93.

[51] See C. Arnold Anderson, "A Skeptical Note on the Relation of Vertical Mobility to Education," *American Journal of Sociology*, 66 (1961), pp. 560-570. Anderson indicated that in countries in which many received prolonged education, the level of an education does not affect mobility. But an opposite finding is reported in a detailed analysis of the relationship between education and mobility in the United States. Otis Dudley Duncan and Robert W. Hodge, "Education and Occupational Mobility: A Regression Analysis," *American Journal of Sociology*, 68 (1963), pp. 629-644.

[52] Bowman and Anderson, *op. cit.*, p. 227.

[53] Myint, *op. cit.*, pp. 18-19.

And as W. Arthur Lewis has pointed out, "upper classes based on land or capital have always favored restricting the supply of education to absorptive capacity, because they know the political dangers of having a surplus of educated persons." [54] One must, however, separate the problem of the possible political consequences of educational expansion from the economic ones. As Lewis indicates, "as the premium for education falls, the market for the educated may widen enormously. . . . The educated lower their sights, and employers raise their requirements. . . . As a result of this process an economy can ultimately absorb any number of educated persons. . . . One ought to produce more educated people than can be absorbed at current prices, because the alteration in current prices which this forces is a necessary part of the process of economic development." [55] The argument against expansion is largely a political, rather than an economic one, and calls for a detailed examination of the sociological consequences. The history of a rapidly growing post-revolutionary country, Mexico, affords an example of the way in which economic growth and emphases on new values may reduce the tensions inherent in rapid educational expansion. William Glade contends that though the educated were often frustrated in prerevolutionary Mexico, "the more or less steady expansion of the private sector activity since the mid-1920's" has meant a continuing demand for trained persons. "Secondly, . . . with the over-all expansion of the social, economic, and political structure there came a widening range of socially approved channels for the realization of achievement." [56]

The main criticisms of educational growth, however, have usually not involved so much opposition to expansion, *per se*, but rather have raised questions as to the *type* of education provided. There is considerable controversy as to the relative value of varying amounts of concentration on the elementary, secondary, and higher levels, an issue which we do not want to treat here in any detail; or the suggestion is made that underdeveloped nations are more in need of semi-professional trained talent, e.g., nurses, technicians, and the like, than university graduates, but that institutions designed to fulfill these needs are rarer than universities. And a considerable amount of the sociological and

[54] W. Arthur Lewis, "Priorities for Educational Expansion," O.E.C.D. *Policy Conference on Economic Growth and Investment in Education, III. The Challenge of Aid to Newly Developing Countries* (Paris: O.E.C.D., 1962), p. 37.

[55] *Ibid.*, pp. 37-38.

[56] William P. Glade, Jr., "Revolution and Economic Development; Mexican Reprise," in Glade and Charles W. Anderson, *The Political Economy of Mexico. Two Studies* (Madison: University of Wisconsin Press, 1963), pp. 44-46; for a general discussion of the conditions which affect student participation in various forms of politics see S. M. Lipset, "University Students and Politics in Underdeveloped Countries," *Minerva*, 3 (1964), pp. 15-56, and the special issue on "Student Politics," *Comparative Education Review*, 10 (June 1966).

political analysis has concentrated on the supposed dysfunctions inherent in the "elitist" educational systems common in these societies. Such critics argue that the humanistic emphases which were introduced by the English and French into their African and Asian colonies, or developed on European models in Latin America, are to a large extent dysfunctional for a society seeking to modernize its economy. The American, Japanese, and Communist university systems with technical and vocational courses within the university would seem more appropriate for developing nations. As one of the foremost students of comparative higher education concludes, once universities have been separated from "their upper class associations," once they have been viewed as agencies of training for a wide variety of occupations, rapid expansion need not lead to unrest.[57]

Although western European universities, from which the emphasis on a humanistic orientation derived, are changing rapidly in this respect, many in the "third world" resist. Statistics provide a clear picture of this. As of 1958-59, 34 per cent of all West European university students were studying science or engineering, in contrast to 23 per cent in Asia (excluding Communist China and India), 19 per cent in Africa, and 16 per cent in Latin America.[58] The comparable figure for the major communist countries including the Soviet Union and China is 46 per cent.[59] China now trains more engineers per year than any country except the two leading ones, the Soviet Union and the United States. And 90 per cent of all China's scientists and engineers have been trained since 1949.[60] In 1958, by contrast, 58 per cent of Indian students were enrolled in faculties of humanities, fine arts, and law.

The rulers of Meiji Japan have provided an excellent example of the way in which a development oriented elite consciously used the educational system both to provide the needed cadre of trained and highly motivated people and to enhance the status of those occupations that were needed for modernization. Shortly after the restoration, technical "education was introduced at the university and middle-school levels, and it covered a broad range of theoretical science and practical instruction in agriculture, trade, banking, and, above all, industrial technology."[61] In addition to the various government schools in these fields,

[57] Joseph Ben-David, "Professions in the Class Systems of Present-Day Societies," *Current Sociology*, 12 (1963-1964), pp. 276-277.

[58] J. Tinbergen and H. C. Bos, "The Global Demand for Higher and Secondary Education in Underdeveloped Countries in the Next Decade," O.E.C.S. *Policy Conference on Economic Growth and Investment in Education, III, The Challenge of Aid to Newly Developing Countries* (Paris: O.E.C.D., 1962), p. 73.

[59] Harbison and Myers, *op. cit.*, p. 179.

[60] *Ibid.*, p. 88.

[61] Johannes Hirschmeier, *The Origins of Entrepreneurship in Meiji Japan* (Cambridge: Harvard University Press, 1964), pp. 127, 128-131.

Japanese businessmen helped start private universities such as Keio and Hitotsubashi designed to train for executive business positions students who could absorb the norms of modern business rationality as part of their education.[62]

The problem, therefore, is not so much the number of graduates as such, but the content of education and the status orientations and curricula that encourage vast numbers to work for degrees in subjects that are not needed in large quantity. Educational policy often encourages such maladjustments by making it much easier to secure a degree in subjects like the law or the humanities than in the sciences or engineering. Clearly the policy to pass students in the former fields for less and easier work than in the latter is an implicit policy decision, a decision which says, in effect, "We will over-train and over-encourage a section of our youth." An analysis of these problems in Egypt points out that while the numerous graduates in the humanities and in law contribute to revolutionary forces, those in fields in which employment may be found "have by contrast a vested interest in what the regime is already accomplishing and are hence its conservative supporters."[63] The Egyptian system is like many in other less developed societies, in that it rations admission to engineering, medicine, and the sciences, which are costly, but permits unrestricted enrollment in the others. Malcolm Kerr's comment about these policies applies to many countries:

> The passively accepted assumption is that in these fields, where tuition fees are very low and nothing tangible is sacrificed by increasing the attendance at lectures, freedom of opportunity should be the rule. In reality, of course, a great deal is sacrificed, for not only does the quality of education drop, but a serious social problem is made worse, and thousands of students beginning their secondary schooling continue to be encouraged to aim for the universities rather than for the secondary technical education which would be more useful to themselves and to the economic progress of the country.[64]

As we have previously noted, the many studies of occupational prestige in both developed and underdeveloped countries suggest that occupations that are perceived as "academic" or intellectual in character are quite universally highly valued. To a considerable extent, the difference in the relative attractiveness of technical or managerial positions in various countries may be a function of the extent to which these occupations have been incorporated into the university system, and have taken over some of the aura of that system. Even in the United States, a study based on interviews with business executives in the largest

    [62] *Ibid.*, pp. 164-171.
    [63] Malcolm H. Kerr, "Egypt," in James S. Coleman (ed.), *Education and Political Development* (Princeton: Princeton University Press, 1965), p. 190.
    [64] *Ibid.*, pp. 190-191.

corporations and with leading intellectuals, designed to learn how they perceived each other, reported that the executives were disturbed concerning their low status with intellectuals. Many of them argued that their jobs required a high order of creativity, a quality which intellectuals presumably valued but did not realize was as much an aspect of managerial as of intellectual work.[65] The various efforts to professionalize business occupations through the establishment of graduate business schools in leading universities, and other devices, testify to the continuing tribute which American businessmen pay to the attainment of "academic status."

Seemingly a general problem of many underdeveloped societies is the desire of students to use university training as a means toward attaining diffuse high status, most often affirmed through the free professions or governmental position, rather than through achievement in business.[66] Even in the second most developed Latin American country, Argentina, a report on national values points out that the traditional landed aristocratic disdain for manual work, industry, and trading continues to affect the educational orientations of many students. When an Argentine seeks to move up, "he will usually try to do so, not by developing his manual skills or by accomplishing business or industrial feats, but by developing his *intellectual* skills. He will follow an academic career typically in a field that is not 'directly productive' from an economic point of view— medicine, law, social sciences, etc." [67]

North American, Japanese and Russian experiences indicate that the introduction directly into the university curriculum of such vocational subjects as animal husbandry, accounting, elementary school teaching, engineering, and so forth, as well as the wide dispersion of colleges and universities in provincial and small communities, can have the effect of creating a trained stratum of talent that is motivated to work outside of metropolitan centers, willing to accept employment that has little appeal to college graduates in more elitist systems. To create a mass system of higher education that includes highly vocational subjects may lower the status of university graduates as compared to their status in a society with a small, elitist university system, but it may also raise the status of positions that do not require university training in elitist systems. The

[65] See "The Intellectual's Challenge to the Corporate Executive," *Public Opinion Index for Industry* (September, 1961).

[66] Joseph Fisher, *Universities in Southeast Asia* (Columbus: Ohio State University Press, 1964), pp. 6, 81-82, 96.

[67] Tomas Roberto Fillol, *Social Factors in Economic Development. The Argentine Case* (Cambridge: The M.I.T. Press, 1961). For a detailed discussion of many of these problems in a Latin American context see Lipset, "Elites, Education and Entrepreneurship in Latin America," *op. cit.*

contrast between Puerto Rico and Jamaica may be relevant here. Many occupations that involve university education in Puerto Rico are held in Jamaica by men who did not go to university. It may be suggested that both the level of competence and, perhaps more significant, the achievement motivation of the former will be higher.[68] Similarly in the Philippines, which has absorbed the American emphasis on the worth of a massive higher educational system, and has the second highest percentage of the relevant age cohort in universities in the world, there is some evidence that the investment is worth while. "While the quality of education is low by Western standards, the system produces an impressive flow of graduates with minimum technical and professional skills . . . enrollment in technical and agricultural courses is increasing rapidly." [69]

Concern with fostering egalitarianism and achievement through manipulation of the educational system is often perceived as necessarily involving a reduction in the class recruitment bias, which denies many of the potentially most able the opportunity to enter the elite. In all societies, the higher one goes in the educational system, the larger the proportion of students from privileged backgrounds. Many talented youth from less well-to-do families lack the opportunity or motivation to attend university. To some extent, the discrimination against the lowly is associated with size of the educational establishment. The larger the system in relation to the relevant age cohort, the greater the relative proportion from lower-class backgrounds who can go on. But this varies by country, in part reflecting the extent of conscious concern and efforts to create opportunities for the brighter lower-class students, and in part reflecting aspects of the pre-university system, for example, whether it is costly or not. The proportions in education at various levels will, of course, also be related to the size of the national income, and to its distribution. Where most families have no possible economic reserve to sustain a student through school, he will not go. And the evidence indicates that less developed countries give financial aid to a much smaller proportion of secondary and university students than do developed ones.[70] In Latin

---

[68] "[I]n almost all underdeveloped countries, there is still too great an emphasis on literary-historical and narrowly legal training." Bert Hoselitz, "The Recruitment of White-Collar Workers in Underdeveloped Countries," in Shannon (ed.), *op. cit.*, p. 188.

[69] Frank H. Golay, *The Philippines: Public Policy and National Economic Development* (Ithaca: Cornell University Press, 1961), pp. 201-203; Curle, *op. cit.*, p. 54; "[A] high emphasis in the Philippines is placed on mass education, and education accounts for nearly one-quarter of the nation's total governmental expenditures." Edward A. Tiryakian, "Occupational Satisfaction and Aspiration in an Underdeveloped Country: The Philippines," *Economic Development and Cultural Change*, 7 (1959), p. 442.

[70] Frank Bowles, *Access to Higher Education*, Vol. I (Paris: UNESCO, 1963), pp. 188-189.

America, about two-thirds of all secondary school students attend fee-charging private schools, a factor that undoubtedly operates to increase class discrimination. Latin America has done little to "identify and encourage able students . . . to provide programmes for part-time students, although it is known that a sizable proportion of the students in higher education support themselves through employment, and there is no programme for external or correspondence students. Perhaps most important of all, the number of students who receive financial assistance must be discounted as negligible." [71] This situation, of course, means that the overwhelming majority of students at Latin American universities are from quite privileged backgrounds.[72] The distribution of class backgrounds may become more rather than less discriminatory in the future, if higher education does not expand rapidly. For greater selectivity, brought about by a more rapid increase in demand than in places, will increase the relative advantage of those from well-to-do, culturally privileged homes, who can prepare for admission examinations with the advantage of having attended good private schools, or having private examination tutors.[73]

It is important to note that a universalistic and achievement oriented educational system does not necessarily produce an egalitarian society. In fact, given the cultural, economic, and other advantages that go with higher status, the more emphasis a society places on locating people in the occupational hierarchy through educational attainments, the less equal will be the origins of those above the working class unless the educational system expands greatly. In Japan, very few elite university students are from lowly background. The latter simply cannot compete in the rigorous entrance examinations. Similar findings and conclusions are reported in a recent survey of the backgrounds of university students in the Soviet Union which, like Japan, has a universalistic competitive admissions system:

> According to the survey, the children of white-collar workers have a far better chance for higher education than have the children of industrial workers and farmers. A sample survey showed that 90 per cent of the youngsters living on farms went to work after graduation from high school and only 10 per cent went on to higher schools.
>
> Of the children of white-collar workers, 15 per cent go to work after high school and 83 per cent continue their studies. The remaining 3 per cent combine work and study.

[71] *Ibid.,* p. 148.

[72] Robert W. Burns, "Social Class and Education in Latin America," *Comparative Education Review,* 6 (1963), pp. 230-238.

[73] Robert J. Havighurst and J. Roberto Moreira, *Society and Education in Brazil* (Pittsburgh: University of Pittsburgh Press, 1965), pp. 104-105.

The investigators point out that the larger graduating classes of the post-war generation will increase the competition for admission to college and further handicap the children of workers and peasants who usually are less prepared for college than the children of the so-called urban intelligentsia.[74]

"OTHER-DIRECTEDNESS," VALUE ORIENTATIONS, AND ECONOMIC GROWTH

Much of the analyses of the social requisites for economic development has suggested that a highly industrialized society requires the breakdown of traditional ties, a considerable degree of flexibility in role relationships, the willingness to treat market forces and individuals impersonally, and a system of recruitment to important positions that is based largely on universalistic and achievement criteria. A brief look at the fulfillment of these requisites in different societies suggests some additional complexities in the ways in which education contributes to development.

It has been suggested that "other-directedness," sensitivity to the opinions of others, contributes to economic growth. This thesis rests in part on the assumption that concern with general opinion facilitates a breakdown of traditional loyalties. "The transition to the new order is certainly likely to be helped if people can learn to listen to what 'other people' say is the right thing to do." [75] An analysis of the correlation between estimates of the relative emphasis on "other-directedness," as reflected in the content of children's readers, for several nations, and their economic growth in two different time periods, revealed that the two variables are related to each other, that an emphasis on other-directedness "predicts" growth. It may be noted further that the association with rates of growth is increased greatly when nations are

---

[74] Theodore Shabad, "Job Lack Face Young in Soviet," *New York Times,* June 30, 1965. This article summarizes a report by a group of sociologists of the Economic-Mathematical Research Laboratory of Novosibirsk University, published in the journal *Voprosy Philosofii* (Problems of Philosophy). Similar results have been reported for Poland. See Jerzy Janicki, "Choice of Vocation by Warsaw School Pupils," *Polish Sociological Bulletin,* 1 (June-December, 1961), pp. 88-89; and Slowzimierz Michajlow, "Higher Education," *Twenty Years of the Polish People's Republic* (Warsaw: Warszawa Panstwowe Wydawnictwo Ekonomiczne, 1964), p. 199.

[75] David C. McClelland, *The Achieving Society* (Princeton: D. Van Nostrand, 1961), p. 194. See pp. 192-203 for a comprehensive discussion of other directedness and economic development. Albert Hirschman argues that the ability to "engineer agreement," to deal with others, officials, subordinates, and the like is a key component of entrepreneurship. Albert Hirschman, *The Strategy of Economic Development* (New Haven: Yale University Press, 1958), pp. 17-18.

ranked on measures of achievement orientation as well as other-directedness.[76]

It may seem curious to argue that "other-directedness" serves to reinforce strong achievement drives in stimulating individual initiative, since many have linked "inner-direction" to a strong emphasis on technological development and capital accumulation.[77] Before coining the term "inner-direction," David Riesman referred to those so oriented as having a "Protestant Ethic" personality type, thus reflecting a common interpretation of Max Weber's analysis of the role that Protestantism played in fostering economic growth in northern Europe. This interpretation rests on the assumption that Calvinism produced a thoroughly inner-directed individual. In fact, however, Max Weber did not make this case. Rather, he urged that one of the significant components distinguishing ascetic Protestantism, and particularly Calvinism, from other religious groups was precisely its pressure to conform to the judgment of others:

> The member of the [Protestant] sect (or conventicle) had to have qualities of a certain kind in order to enter the community circle. . . . In order to hold his own in this circle, the members had to *prove* repeatedly that he was endowed with these qualities. . . . According to all experience there is no stronger means of breeding traits than through the necessity of holding one's own in the circle of one's associations. . . . The Puritan sects put the most powerful individual interest of social self-esteem in the service of this breeding of traits . . . to repeat, it is not the ethical *doctrine* of a religion, but that form of ethical conduct upon which premiums are placed that matters. . . . The premiums were placed upon "proving" oneself before God in the sense of attaining salvation—which is found in *all* Puritan denominations—and "proving" oneself before men in the sense of socially holding one's own within the Puritan sects.[78]

A key difference between the Puritans who fostered economic initiative and the Lutherans and Catholics who did not, in Weber's judgment, lay in the extensive use of an appeal to "social self-esteem" or the power of group opinion by the former, and imposing religious discipline "through authoritarian means" and punishing or placing premiums on "concrete individual acts," by the latter two.

It is interesting to note in this connection that the educational system of Communist China, in addition to strongly stressing individual achievement, has also initiated changes from aspects of pre-Communist China which correspond to the differences between the mechanisms of control of the Protestant sects and Catholicism. It emphasizes the role of "public

---

[76] McClelland, *op. cit.*, pp. 201-202.

[77] David Riesman, *The Lonely Crowd* (New Haven: Yale University Press, 1950), p. 115.

[78] H. H. Gerth and C. Wright Mills (eds.), *From Max Weber: Essays in Sociology* (New York: Oxford University Press, 1946), pp. 320-321 (emphases in the original).

opinion or 'other directedness' rather than institutional norms." [79] And the Chinese Communists have established a system of social control that resembles the Protestant sects, as described by Max Weber, in which there is a strong emphasis placed on securing "the personalized approval of one's group." [80]

An effort to account for the seeming presence of "other-directedness" early in American history (as indicated by the comments of many "foreign travelers") indicates that this quality has been a consequence of the fluidity of the American status system.[81] That is, where there is a general emphasis on achieved status, and a reduction in ascribed status, participants in a social system are much more likely to be concerned with the opinion of others. Status in an open and egalitarian society depends largely on others' judgments. If this be true, then the massive introduction of institutions that upset normal status definitions should increase the amount of other-directedness in the culture. The *arrivistes* are the other-directed *par excellence*. The quickest way to create a large group of other-directed is to enlarge the higher educational system.

If egalitarianism and consequent "other-directedness" contribute to economic growth, then egalitarianism and investment in education should be positively correlated. A comparison of the nations of Latin America, Africa, the Middle East, and Europe, which divided countries within each area into "egalitarian" and "non-egalitarian" groups according to the extent to which they emphasized ascribed qualities in determining opportunity for high position, reports that within each region the more egalitarian nations spend much more on education per capita and have a higher average income.[82] Separating out the factors indicated the "egalitarianism, rather than national wealth, is the important corollary of high per capita expenditure on education." [83] Of course these findings do not demonstrate that a presumed increase in other-directedness is the principal intervening variable between egalitarianism, education, and economic development. A greater commitment to egalitarian values is usually also associated with greater emphasis on universalism rather than particularism, and on specificity, particularly in role definition, rather than diffuseness.[84] And these values, together with egalitarianism and achievement constitute a large part of what we mean by modern as distinct from traditional values.

[79] John Wilson Lewis, "Party Cadres in Communist China," in Coleman (ed.), *op. cit.*, p. 424.

[80] *Ibid.*, p. 429.

[81] Lipset, *The First New Nation, op. cit.*, pp. 101-139.

[82] Curle, *op. cit.*, pp. 232-244.

[83] *Ibid.*, p. 244.

[84] See Lipset, *op. cit.*, pp. 209-213.

Relating the strength of national emphases on achievement to educational investment and economic development shows the independent strength of this variable also. When comparing technological growth rates for 1929-1950 and 1952-1958, McClelland finds that "achievement motivation [as measured by content analyses of children's readers] facilitates economic growth; knowledge (as represented by more education) facilitates economic growth, but motivation plus knowledge has a significantly greater effect than motivation or knowledge alone." [85]

The assumptions that economic development is fostered by emphases on "other-directedness," egalitarianism, universalism, and achievement appear to be congruent with the success of the major protagonists in today's world, the United States and the Soviet Union. The ideologies and practice of both Americanism and Communism, as well as their stress on education, subsume these orientations and values. Many have pointed to the relatively low emphases on these factors in much of Latin America and the other less developed regions as among the principal inhibitions on economic development.

DOWNWARD MOBILITY

Analyses of the problem of mobility and motivation in developing nations have usually assumed that these societies emphasize the maintenance of high-status non-manual positions more than in the developed nations because the demand for such positions is higher, and consequently the gap in the rewards betwen manual and non-manual status is much larger. Presumably, therefore, it is much more difficult to get people who have a claim to a higher-status position to accept a lower one. As Bert Hoselitz has put it:

Very low prestige . . . is attributed to manual work which "dirties one's hands." . . . Some employees endure their economically unenviable position, because being a white-collar worker gives the illusion . . . that one is above the ordinary crowd of common labourers. . . .

In many underdeveloped countries the relative social prestige which attaches to white-collar jobs is even greater, and that is in close correlation with the relatively greater scarcity of literate persons. . . .[86]

Attitudes toward manual work in underdeveloped as compared with developed nations, particularly the United States, probably are very different. But the evidence does not justify the conclusion that those with

[85] McClelland, "Does Education Accelerate Economic Growth," *op. cit.*, p. 22.
[86] Hoselitz, *op. cit.*, p. 183.

a claim to white-collar status in underdeveloped societies view manual work with such abhorrence that they will refuse to accept such positions if they are more readily available or if they pay more than nonmanual jobs. The rates of movement from non-manual to manual positions in a number of these countries are similar to those reported for various industrialized nations. Thus, in a recent survey of labor mobility in Taiwan, based on data from the files of those who registered for a job or a change in position at the Taiwan Employment Office, 22.6 per cent of those whose job experience had been limited to one "high white-collar" position stated as their preference a manual position. Among those who had been salesmen, 27 per cent asked for a manual job. If we look at the actual shifts in job status among those who had had at least two jobs, we find that 7 per cent of those who began in white-collar work and 18 per cent who started in sales took a manual job as their second position. Conversely, among those who began in low manual jobs, 27 per cent secured a white-collar position as their second job, and 22 per cent shifted to sales work.[87] A survey of mobility in Poona, India, which compared inter-generational mobility, reports that one-quarter of those whose fathers were in non-manual positions had become manual workers, while 27 per cent of those of manual origin had risen into the middle classes.[88] In São Paulo, Brazil, similar data indicate that 19 per cent of those of non-manual origins were in manual positions when interviewed, while 30 per cent of those with manual family backgrounds had secured a white-collar position.[89]

The most comprehensive analysis of social mobility in a developing nation, Tumin's study of stratification in Puerto Rico, indicates that the Commonwealth has the highest rate of downward mobility ever reported. Over half the sons (58 per cent) of middle-class fathers, urban and rural, were in manual jobs when interviewed; among the sons of the urban middle-class, the proportion who had fallen in occupational status is 44 per cent.[90] This downward mobility is not primarily a result of movement from low-status non-manual to manual occupations: Tumin reports a high rate of movement into the working class from "elite" middle-class status.[91] Thus, 42 per cent of the sons of "elite" fathers were

[87] Wolfram Eberhard, "Labor Mobility in Taiwan," *Asian Survey*, 2 (May 1962), pp. 38-56.

[88] V. Sovani and Kusum Pradhan, "Occupational Mobility in Poona City Between Three Generations," *The Indian Economic Review*, 2 (1955), pp. 23-36.

[89] Robert J. Havighurst, "Educação, mobilidade sociale e Mundança social em quatro sociedadas—estudo comparativo," *Educação e Ciencias Socias*, 2 (1957), pp. 103-131.

[90] Tumin with Feldman, *op. cit.*, p. 441.

[91] The elite groups are professionals, semi-professionals, and owners of businesses other than "one-man enterprises at very low levels of capitalization." *Ibid.*, p. 428.

in manual occupations when interviewed. And, significantly, a comparison with rates in 11 other European nations and Japan indicates that the two countries with the highest rate of downward mobility from the "elite" strata are the two among them that are currently in the process of emerging industrially—Italy, with 36 per cent moving downward into manual positions from the elite strata, and Japan, with a downward rate of 27 per cent.[92]

The phenomenon of extensive "downward" mobility occurring within emerging industrializing societies is a feature of European history as well. Sorokin amassed considerable evidence from a variety of studies in late nineteenth and early twentieth century Europe indicating that sizeable proportions of the manual work force had been recruited from the offspring of middle-class and even elite fathers.[93]

One structural cause of downward mobility has been suggested in an interesting paper by the Argentinian sociologist Di Tella. His data indicate that in the early stages of industrialization economic growth may decrease the percentage of the labor force in middle-class occupations rather than increase it. Within Chile, he finds that the more developed a province the smaller the proportion of its middle class. He suggests that in underdeveloped areas, urban areas are largely centers of trade with a middle-class composed of merchants and government workers, including teachers. With the growth of industry, the artisans and petty traders find it difficult to compete for workers or to compete in the market. Consequently there is an absolute or relative decline in the numbers of such establishments.[94]

In his chapter in this volume dealing with changes in the occupational structure and their effects on mobility, Wilbert Moore refers to this process as one resulting from bureaucratization, which inhibits mobility from manual to non-manual occupations via an independent business, or movement between employers. Bureaucratization increases demand for more highly educated workers, but it also reduces the category of the self-employed, many of whom are uneducated and unskilled.

[92] *Ibid.*, p. 443.

[93] Pitirim Sorokin, *Social and Cultural Mobility* (New York: Free Press of Glencoe, 1959), pp. 435-440, 447-449. This work first published in 1927, which is rarely cited today, is not only a rich source of comparative data, but contains highly sophisticated analyses of both the causes and consequences of social mobility. Much of the recent work in this field touches precisely on the issues Sorokin dealt with, and often "rediscovers" processes he specified. Unlike some of the more recent writers, Sorokin recognized the difficulties involved in trying to be overprecise in comparative research, and did not try to draw precise conclusions from what was and is only roughly comparable data.

[94] Torcuato S. Di Tella, "Economía y estructura ocupacional en un pais subdesarrollado," *Desarrollo Económico*, 1 (1961), pp. 123-153.

The presence of high rates of upward mobility in emerging societies has never struck observers as surprising since it has always been assumed that industrial expansion results in a rapid increase in the proportion of higher status as contrasted with lower status positions. (Di Tella, of course, has thrown this assumption into doubt.) The assumption that particularistic and ascriptive values are emphasized in traditionalist and underdeveloped societies more than in industrialized nations implied that low rates of downward mobility should occur in such nations as they began to develop economically. Those with a privileged background, and a strong motivation to retain high status, should in an expanding economy find it relatively easy to retain or improve their status. The fact that many actually fall in status suggests that the skills and orientations necessary to adapt successfully to the new roles of an industrializing society may be at variance with those linked to "middle-class" status in pre-industrial society. The offspring of such strata who seek to preserve or advance status using traditional methods may be at a disadvantage with the ambitious sons of low status families who more readily reject or do not even know of the customary behavior patterns associated with privileged status.

These findings also suggest consequences for the behavior of the industrial work force in emerging societies if we assume that it includes a significant proportion of workers who have been downwardly mobile in status terms. The downwardly mobile may provide a reservoir of potential leadership for class organization (union or leftist party), or conversely, they may contribute heavily to the ranks of those who serve as work force leaders, e.g., foremen and supervisors. As yet, we know little about the consequences of downward mobility in such situations. Studies of this phenomenon in developed nations suggest that the downwardly mobile remain oriented towards middle-class values and behavior with respect to politics (they are much more conservative and less likely to join unions than workers of lower-status background) and work habits (they are more likely to possess a commitment to steady work).[95]

Wilensky and Edwards report, in the most comprehensive study of

---

[95] See Lipset and Bendix, *Social Mobility in Industrial Society, op. cit.,* pp. 64-71; Seymour Martin Lipset and Joan Gordon, "Mobility and Trade Union Membership," in Reinhard Bendix and Seymour Martin Lipset (eds.), *Class, Status and Power. A Reader in Social Stratification* (New York: Free Press of Glencoe, 1953), pp. 491-500; Arnold Tannenbaum and Robert Kahn, *Participation in Union Locals* (Evanston: Row, Peterson, 1958), pp. 142-148; Harold Wilensky and Hugh Edwards, "The Skidder: Ideological Adjustments of Downward Mobile Workers," *American Sociological Review,* 24 (1959), pp. 215-231; and Alain Touraine and Bernard Mottez "Classe ouvrière et société globale," in Georges Friedmann and Pierre Naville (eds.), *Traité de sociologie du travail,* Vol. II (Paris: Librarie Armond Colin, 1962), pp. 238-241.

downwardly mobile American workers, that as compared with non-mobile workers they are more likely to "reject identification with the working-class . . . ; believe in an open class system and in ability as a proper basis for promotion . . . ; aspire to middle class position for themselves, attach importance to promotion opportunities, and say they would accept the job of foreman if offered . . . ; anticipate leaving the factory soon . . . ; and expect their children to achieve middle class position." [96] And in suggesting consequences for the larger social structure of the presence of a large group of downwardly mobile among the workers, they suggest that these men "with their adherence to the free mobility ideology, constrain tendencies toward political extremism among two-generation workers, who, sharing the same grievances and perspectives, if unexposed to the deviant views of skidders would be more susceptible to totalitarian solutions." [97]

Wilensky and Edwards thus cast doubts on the argument that an excess of middle-class ambitions caused by changes in various structural factors, e.g., education, urbanization, are a major source of political tension.

Recent research has also raised questions about the general validity of the proposition that the sharp discontinuities in social relationships and values occasioned by the rapid recruitment of an industrial labor force from rural areas predisposes, the "new workers" to accept radical ideologies or theologies.[98] A comparative study of Indian, American, and English textile mills during the period of rapid industrial growth concludes these causal analyses are wrong:

Scholars have spent a good deal of effort describing the profound adjustments that were required by the shift of workers into factory employment and the violence of the reactions to that new discipline. The striking feature of the Bombay pattern is that there was no violent reaction to factory work . . . Similarly, in New England, no violent antagonisms manifested themselves among those who worked in the mills during the early phase.[99]

[96] Wilensky and Edwards, op. cit., p. 226.

[97] Ibid., p. 230.

[98] See Walter Galenson, "Scandinavia," in Walter Galenson (ed.), Comparative Labor Movements (New York: Prentice-Hall, 1952), esp. pp. 105-120; Val Lorwin, "Working-Class Politics and Economic Development in Western Europe," American Historical Review, 63 (1958), pp. 338-51; Reinhold Niebuhr, The Irony of American History (New York: Charles Scribner's Sons, 1952), pp. 112-18; Seymour Martin Lipset, Political Man (Garden City, N.Y.: Doubleday & Company, 1960), pp. 68-71; William Kornhauser, The Politics of Mass Society (New York: Free Press of Glencoe, 1959), pp. 150-158.

[99] Morris David Morris, "The Recruitment of an Industrial Labor Force in India, with British and American Comparisons," Comparative Studies in Society and History, 2 (1960), p. 327.

A similar argument based on Brazilian experience has been presented by Herbert Blumer.[100] He suggests that the growth of an industrial work force in the expanding petroleum industry had increased social integration rather than reduced it among the workers recruited from rural environments. And Japan is, of course, the classic case of a nation that has endured the strains inherent in rapid industrialization without the emergence of significant working-class protest. Explanations for some of these variations have been offered, referring to the extent to which a new working class retains strong links to the rural communities from which it was recruited, or the relative difference in economic standard and living conditions between pre-industrial and industrial positions. The fact remains, however, that a systematic analysis of the variations in reactions to the dislocations inherent in rapid industrialization has not been accomplished.

CONCLUSION

In these introductory comments we have explored the problems of social structure and social mobility—with reference to economic development—at two levels, theoretical and empirical. In the first section we advanced definitions of social structure and social mobility, and suggested some of the broad consequences of social structure for the overall pattern of social mobility in any society. In the second portion, we selected certain research areas about which scholars and policy makers have definite opinions and judgments, but on which the empirical evidence is far from clear. In particular we examined the general relations between rates of growth and rates of mobility, the relations between education and patterns of mobility; and the relations between economic development and downward mobility. The chapters that follow elaborate on these themes in more specific contexts.

[100] Herbert Blumer, "Early Industrialization and the Laboring Class," *The Sociological Quarterly*, 1 (1960), pp. 5-14.

2

METHODOLOGICAL ISSUES IN
THE ANALYSIS OF SOCIAL MOBILITY *

OTIS DUDLEY DUNCAN, *University of Michigan*

THE JUXTAPOSITION of themes—social mobility and economic development—in the title of the conference may invite acceptance of an unwarranted assumption. In point of fact there is and can be no fixed and
determinate general relationship between measures of economic growth
and indexes of social mobility, either over time in one country or between
countries at a point in time. A whole set of auxiliary postulates, each
empirically contingent, must be adopted before a relation between
mobility and growth can be deduced.

The work of Kuznets, Clark and others has indeed supported the
proposition that economic growth, in the sense of sustained increase in
output per capita, is accompanied by a redistribution of the working
force by functional categories—industries or occupations. Yet, such a
proposition, even if accepted as an axiom, implies very little about the
kinds, amounts, and patterns of social mobility that will be observed
during a sequence of economic growth.

To see why this must be so, consider observations on an economy
taken at two times, t_0 and t_1. Let the functional distribution of the working force be described as the frequency of employment in each of k
classes (including, possibly, null frequencies for some classes). If we

* This paper was prepared in the course of a project, "Differential Fertility and
Social Mobility," supported by research grant GM-10386 from the National Institutes
of Health. This is a companion project to one on "Intergenerational Occupational
Mobility in the United States," supported by a grant from the National Science Foun-
dation, of which the principal investigator is Peter M. Blau, University of Chicago.
I should like to mention the contribution to the paper made not only by the oppor-
tunity to work with Blau but also by communication and collaboration with Robert
W. Hodge, Albert J. Reiss, Jr., and Norman B. Ryder. Indispensable assistance in the
statistical work summarized in the paper was provided by J. Michael Coble, Bruce L.
Warren, and Ruthe C. Sweet.

designate the distribution at t_0 as a vector u_0 and that at t_1 as a vector u_1, the issue of social mobility arises in trying to account for the transformation of u_0 into u_1. Evidently, such a transformation includes the following component processes of "social metabolism:" exits from u_0 produced by death, migration out of the country, and retirement from economic activity; entries into u_1 produced by initiation of gainful employment or migration into the country; and, for personnel included in both distributions, change of functional class, i.e., mobility. Note that mobility is but one of the components of the transformation. Observe, moreover, that mobility from, say, class i at t_0 to class j at t_1 may be balanced by mobility from class j at t_0 to class i at t_1. Thus, even if mobility were the only component, our axiom only tells us that a *net* redistribution of the working force must occur, while a given net redistribution can be accomplished by an indefinitely large number of patterns of *gross* mobility. As soon as the other components are allowed, it is evident that any redistribution whatsoever can be accomplished by them alone, in the absence of any mobility whatsoever; or, on the other hand, the redistribution produced by mobility as such can be compensated or amplified, in any manner or degree you care to specify, by the other components.

In the foregoing account the only type of mobility considered is the change of occupational position on the part of a constant set of individuals, i.e., intracohort or so-called intragenerational mobility. If we introduce the possibility that an individual's position at either t_0 or t_1 depends in some fashion on his "origin" (say, his father's occupation) the analysis is complicated and the possibility of a determinate relation between economic growth and mobility pattern is, if anything, reduced. Foremost among the complications is the fact that a distribution of the fathers of those in the working force at a given time is not, and in the nature of the case cannot be, a distribution of the working force at some definite prior instant of time. This follows from the facts (a) that fathers vary in the number of sons they may have, from zero to some not well-defined upper limit; and (b) that age at paternity is a variable, i.e., a father may be no more than 20 years (or even less) older than his son, or as much as 50 years (or even more) older. Ordinarily, in the conventional study of intergenerational mobility, the origin distribution represents fathers in proportion to the number of their sons of a given age, and aggregates into a single distribution the positions they occupied over a considerable period of time.

Another way to express the predicament is this. Presumably, there is an actual, though unknown, transformation T which takes into account all the sources of change in an occupation structure, so that $u_0 T = u_1$. We could then write $u_0 = u_1 T^{-1}$. But suppose a transformation S exists such that $u_0 = u_1 S$. Can we then infer that $S = T^{-1}$ and accordingly $T = S^{-1}$, yielding a solution for T? Unfortunately, no. That is, to discover a transformation that *could* have sent u_0 into u_1 is not necessarily to learn what transformation actually did that job.

The upshot of these considerations is that the connection, if any, between economic growth and social mobility falls into the domain of *contingent* rather than *necessary* relationships. To be sure, some of the contingency may be removed by introducing assumptions that restrict, or even eliminate, certain of the components of occupational redistribution. Thus, for purposes of constructing a model of social mobility the analyst may choose to consider a population closed to migration. But this is to abstract from the real process of economic growth as well as the real process of occupational mobility. While partial deductive models, therefore, have their analytic uses, the generalizations reached concerning interrelations of mobility and economic development must be in large part empirical generalizations, supported or rationalized as well as they may be by some not very specific deductions from apparently applicable postulates.

This situation has already been encountered in the paper by Smelser and Lipset, wherein they refer to the logic that economic growth should result in a pattern of high upward and low downward mobility, whilst noting that the "logic" is not always borne out by the data. Apparently, the "logic" rests on one or more assumptions that are contrary to fact. They themselves, at this juncture, call for a resort to inductive procedure: "What is necessary is a systematic effort to relate the data of changes, classified in different ways, to the estimates of growth."

These remarks suggest, among other things, that a sharp separation of issues in "theory" from problems of "method" is no more justified in the study of social mobility than in any other domain of inquiry. The methodologist is concerned with the grounds for accepting bodies of data as evidence for or against propositions. If he can show how verbal formulations place logically irreconcilable demands on bodies of data— those in existence, or those that might conceivably come into existence— then revision of the formulations is in order. Rather than "answering" the questions posed by theory, fundamental study of analytical methods is likely to make two questions grow where only one flourished before.

This paper makes two kinds of contribution. In the next section, the issue of how occupational mobility may be related to changes in occupational structure is considered in greater detail. Some positive results are obtained, but the topic is left at the point where the "theorist" must vouchsafe a revised formulation as a basis for further methodological and empirical explorations. The remaining sections of the paper deal with a selection of technical and methodological issues raised in the literature on intergenerational occupational mobility. The issues are ones I consider important and on which I profess to have something to say. They hardly exhaust the agenda of pressing problems. The vexing topic of what effect errors in mobility data have on conclusions, treated cursorily in the first draft of this paper, is omitted for lack of space. Other matters meriting discussion but ignored here are covered in a recent methodological paper by Yasuda,[1] with most of whose points I am in general agreement, despite some reservations about specific procedures.

OCCUPATIONAL MOBILITY AND THE TRANSFORMATION
OF OCCUPATIONAL STRUCTURES

If the reader, like the writer, finds it helpful to have the problem posed concretely rather than in purely abstract terms, he may refer to Table 1, where occupational distributions for two years are exhibited in columns (a) and (b). The years, 1960 and 1930, were selected so as to be about a "generation" apart. (The median age of all men who have sons born in a given year usually is around 30 or 31.) The net changes in the male occupational distribution in the U.S. during this period are matters of common knowledge—the rapid increases in proportions of white-collar, particularly professional and technical jobs; the likewise appreciable increases of occupations involving skilled or semi-skilled manual work; the marked decline in proportion of laborers; and the even more pronounced decrease in percentage of farm workers, both farm operators and farm laborers. Over the period in question, moreover, the absolute size of the male labor force increased by about one-fourth.

The character of the transformation that produced these changes is not so well understood. Indeed, the information needed for a complete analysis of it is not now and may never become available. We can, nevertheless, profitably study the problem of whether certain components of the transformation could, in theory, be related to the idea of occupational mobility.

A convenient point of departure is the well-known discussion by Kahl,[2] which is noteworthy as an explicit formulation of the problem, superseding a mass of prior literature. Although the conclusion of the present discussion is that Kahl's effort was a failure—and for fundamental

---

[1] Saburo Yasuda, "A Methodological Inquiry into Social Mobility," *American Sociological Review*, 29 (February, 1964), pp. 16-23.

[2] Joseph A. Kahl, *The American Class Structure* (New York: Holt, Rinehart and Winston, 1957), Ch. 9.

TABLE 1

CHANGE IN OCCUPATIONAL DISTRIBUTION (PERCENTAGE) OF THE TOTAL
MALE WORKING FORCE IN THE UNITED STATES, 1930-1960, AND
PERCENTAGE DISTRIBUTION OF MEN 25 TO 64 YEARS OLD IN THE 1962
WORKING FORCE BY OWN OCCUPATION AND FATHER'S OCCUPATION

Major occupation group	Total male working force 1960 (a)	1930 (b)	Male working force 25-64 years old, 1962 Own Occupation (c)	Father's Occupation (d)	Inter-annual Change (a) - (b)	Inter-generational Difference (c) - (d)
All occupations	100.0	100.0	100.0	100.0	......	......
Professional, technical, and kindred workers	10.4	4.8	12.9	4.8	5.6	8.1
Managers, officials, and proprietors, except farm	10.8	8.8	16.2	11.8	2.0	4.4
Sales workers	7.0	6.1	5.2	4.0	0.9	1.2
Clerical and kindred workers	7.2	5.5	6.6	3.4	1.7	3.2
Craftsmen, foremen, and kindred workers	20.7	16.2	20.8	18.5	4.5	2.3
Operatives and kindred workers	21.2	15.3	18.6	15.4	5.9	3.2
Service workers including private household	6.5	4.8	5.5	4.8	1.7	0.7
Laborers, except farm and mine	7.8	13.6	6.5	6.5	—5.8	0.0
Farmers and farm managers	5.5	15.2	5.9	28.0	—9.7	—22.1
Farm laborers and foremen	2.9	9.6	1.8	2.8	—6.7	—1.0

Source: U.S. Bureau of the Census, *1960 Census of Population*, Supplementary Reports,
PC (S1)—40 (Washington: December 31, 1962); *Occupational Trends in the United States,
1900 to 1950*, Bureau of the Census Working Paper, No. 5 (Washington: 1958); March 1962
Current Population Survey of the Bureau of the Census and supplementary questionnaire,
"Occupational Changes in a Generation," unpublished tables.

reasons, not merely because of flaws in the data available to him—it falls
into the class of honorable failures which needed to be made in order
to force a re-examination of the problem.

Kahl looked at U.S. data on occupational distributions in 1920 and
1950 (which showed much the same sort of changes as those for 1930

and 1960 reproduced here). He also had available a conventional father-son mobility table derived from a 1947 survey. He then reasoned somewhat as follows. The "sons" in the mobility table represent a current occupational distribution, the "fathers" the occupations being pursued a "generation" ago. Equating interperiod change, 1920-1950, with intergenerational net change as depicted in the marginals of the mobility table, Kahl supposed that the gross mobility revealed in the table might be decomposed into components due to "four causes of movement:" technological, reproductive, and immigration mobility, and mobility due to the fact that "some people slip down and make room for others to move up," later referred to as "individual mobility." Certain additional data were used to make estimates of mobility induced by differential reproduction and immigration. Technological mobility was estimated from the dissimilarity of the two census occupational distributions for 1920 and 1950. With total mobility given in the intergenerational table and with the other three components estimated from other sources, Kahl obtains as a residual the amount of "individual mobility."

There would be no point in criticizing Kahl's statistical procedures in detail. They are, as a matter of fact, ingenious uses of defective materials. Leaving aside the problem of data quality, the argument to be presented here is that the estimates fail because the conceptual framework for the estimates harbors fatal internal inconsistencies. The heart of the problem is Kahl's forthrightly stated assumption "that all the men in the labor force in 1920 have been replaced by their sons by 1950." This assumption, as will be shown, represents a confounding of the notions of occupational redistribution as it may be observed in comparing structures separated approximately by a "generation" of time (i.e., a span of years approximately equal to the average father-son age difference), and intergenerational mobility as it is commonly measured by comparing occupations of a "generation" of fathers with those of the "generation" of their sons.

Let us recollect how intergenerational mobility tables ordinarily are compiled. In the survey method, a sample of respondents is contacted and they are interrogated concerning their own occupations and those of their fathers. The investigator designing the survey confronts some difficult decisions. Usually he will want to know the current occupations of the respondents as well as those they may have pursued at certain times in the past. It is by no means obvious, however, how he should construe the concept of father's occupation. The latter could itself refer to a current (as of the survey date) occupational pursuit; but then a large number of fathers, deceased or retired, would have to remain unclassified. More often, the question used to elicit father's occupation is a variant of one of the following phrasings: father's last main occupation; father's longest job; father's occupation at age x (say, 30 or 50); father's occupation when you (the respondent) were growing up. In studies using records or registers the situation is somewhat different. Information on the father's occupation typically refers to the date of the record, e.g., that of the son's birth or marriage.

Consider the predicament of a research worker in 1960 designing a survey of intergenerational occupation mobility with the aim of repeating Kahl's analysis. He might well entertain the notion of asking respondents to designate the occupations in which their fathers were engaged in the year 1930. (Actually, this form of the question on father's occupation has seldom if ever been used.) On first thought, this might seem to offer a neat solution, for the investigator could have estimated in advance that there would be about 34.9 million men in the 1960 labor force whose fathers were in the 1930 labor force (see Table 2), while the entire 1930 labor force (ages 15-74) included some 37.3 million males. The second thought would be less sanguine. Surely, some of the fathers in the 1930 labor force had more than one son who was economically active in 1960. What about the men at work in 1930 who never had a son, or did not have one whose working life continued to 1960? This is not so easy to estimate, but an "informed" guess is that perhaps half of the men in the 1930 labor force did *not* have a son at work in 1960; the other half had, perhaps, an average approaching two sons apiece.

Now we are in a position to see how important it is to evaluate Kahl's assumption that "all the men in the labor force in [1930] have been replaced by their sons by [1960]." In point of fact, a goodly proportion of the fathers are not fully "replaced" within a generation. That is, of all currently (1960) working men with fathers in the 1930 labor force, nearly one-third have fathers who are still in the labor force in 1960. About half the men in the 1930 labor force were not fathers of men destined to be working in 1960 and were not, therefore, "replaced by their sons." There are, on the other hand, 12.0 out of the 46.9 million members of the 1960 male labor force (ages 15-74) who cannot answer a question on "father's occupation in 1930," because their fathers were still too young to be working then or had already died or ceased to work. Finally, the "fathers" in the intergenerational mobility table are about twice as numerous as the actual men who sired the sons, since each son reports for his father even though all his brothers do likewise.

The last problem could be handled by asking respondents to state how many brothers they have who are in the labor force. Size of fraternity then could be used as a deflation factor so as to secure an unbiased estimate of the occupation distribution of fathers in 1930. Such a proce-

TABLE 2

MALE LABOR FORCE 15 TO 74 YEARS OLD, 1960, BY EXPOSURE TO
INTRA- AND INTERGENERATIONAL OCCUPATIONAL MOBILITY,
1930-60: ILLUSTRATIVE ESTIMATES FOR THE U. S.
(In Millions)

Father's Labor Force Status	Members of 1960 labor force by 1930 status		
	Not in 1930 labor force	In 1930 labor force	Total
In 1930 labor force	26.1	8.8	34.9
In 1960 labor force	10.7	0.1	10.8
Not in 1960 labor force	15.4 *	8.7	24.1
Not in 1930 labor force	5.5	6.5	12.0
In 1960 labor force	2.2	0.0	2.2
Not in 1960 labor force	3.3	6.5	9.8
Total	31.6	15.3	46.9

* This is the only subgroup it is strictly correct to describe as "men in the labor force in 1930 who have been replaced by their sons by 1960;" note that the unit of enumeration, however, is the son, not the father.

dure, however, would require some innovations in the analysis of inter-generational mobility tables.

Some of the estimates just cited, together with other figures of interest, appear in Table 2. It is a temptation to discuss at length the procedures by which these estimates were derived, since we do not automatically secure data of this kind from official sources. Suffice it to say, however, that the estimates, although they involve tedious and circuitous demographic calculations, are highly approximate and are intended only to give some notion of orders of magnitude.

Looking at the matter from the point of view of men pursuing occupations in 1960, Table 2 indicates the size of the base populations exposed to various kinds of mobility over the 3-decade period. As already noted, about 34.9 million, or three-fourths of the men, were exposed to the risk of intergenerational mobility. Of these, however, some 8.8 million were in the 1930 labor force along with their fathers and, therefore, were subject to intragenerational as well as intergenerational mobility, 1930-1960. This leaves 26.1 million, only some 56 per cent of the 1960 labor force, who could have experienced "pure" intergenerational mobility. About 14 per cent (6.5/46.9 million) of the 1960 labor force was subject to "pure" intragenerational mobility, 1930-1960; that is, the men themselves were in the 1930 labor force but their fathers were not. Finally, for nearly one-eighth of the 1960 labor force (5.5/46.9 million) neither intra- nor inter-generational mobility can be defined with reference to the dates 1930 and 1960. Cross-cutting these distinctions is the classification of men according to whether their fathers were in the 1960 labor force. Actually, there were some 13.0 million men, with fathers currently economically active, for whom "cross-sectional" intergenerational mobility could be defined by comparing current pursuits of sons and fathers. For only one-third of the labor force (15.4/46.9) does it make sense to regard the sons as having "replaced" fathers who were at work in 1930.

One way of summarizing the import of the quantities in Table 2, therefore, is to suggest that they render untenable any simple concept of "replacement." When and by whom is a member of the labor force replaced? Is a father replaced when his (first) son enters the labor force? when the father leaves the labor force? when the son attains the age of his father at the son's birth? Who "replaces" the man who has no son? Put it this way: The transformations that occur via a *succession of cohorts* cannot, for basic demographic reasons, be equated to the product of a *procession of "generations."* The writer is prepared to argue, though this is hardly the place to do so, that this brute fact is a profound key to the understanding of social continuity and social change. Indeed, a characteristically human type of society might well be impossible were the demography of the species structured differently.

At the risk of tedium, let us take another approach to demonstrating that occupational change over a period of time equivalent to a "generation" in length cannot be equated to a set of "intergenerational" changes observed in a father-son mobility table. The point can be illustrated with somewhat more adequate data than were at Kahl's disposal—a 1962 survey, "Occupational Changes in a Generation" (OCG), conducted by the Bureau of the Census as an adjunct to its Current Population Survey on behalf of projects directed by Peter M. Blau and the present writer.[3]

In Table 1, columns (c) and (d) show the distributions of OCG respondents by their own occupations and by the occupations pursued by their fathers at the time the respondents were 16 years of age. The last two columns reveal a general resemblance between the net interannual changes in the overall occupation distribution, 1930-1960, and the net intergenerational shifts shown in the OCG table. Yet these are clearly not the same set of changes, and the explanation of the discrepancies

[3] Bureau of the Census, *Current Population Reports,* Series-P-23, No. 11, "Lifetime Occupational Mobility of Adult Males: March 1962" (Washington: Bureau of the Census, 1964).

between them does not lie wholly in data error or defects in comparability between census and OCG, although such defects exist. Even supposing, for example, that many sons of farm laborers erroneously reported in OCG that their fathers were farmers, the intergenerational difference in proportion of total farm workers (-23.1 per cent) is not the same as the interannual change (-14.4 per cent).

This particular example is pursued further in Table 3, since a declining proportion of farm workers has been such an outstanding feature of U.S. occupational transformation, while intergenerational mobility out of farming is conceded to be a highly significant form of mobility. If the intergenerational and interperiod comparisons here are of different orders of magnitude, then it is clear that the two are not interchangeable.

The point of Table 3 is to call attention to a set of conceptual distinctions, rather than to interpret a collection of facts. Line (1) depicts the familiar *trend* of decline in farm pursuits, known to us from *aggregate* data on the entire working force at successive points in time. In lines (2) to (8) observations are shown for selected cohorts (those making up the central age group, 25 to 64, at each census year); the data on each line depict *intracohort* (net) *changes* in proportion in farming. Although not all age groups are shown, it is evident at once that the aggregate figure is an average (weighted) of rather widely varying proportions in the component age groups. The aggregate decrease in farming, moreover, is seen to involve two processes: the intracohort changes revealed by reading lines (3) through (7) horizontally (all but one of which changes are actually decreases); and the *intercohort changes* ascertain by reading the data in lines (2) through (8) along upper left to lower right diagonals (all of these changes being decreases).

In the lower half of the table are data derived from the survey of inter- and intragenerational mobility. Respondents are classified into four groups of cohorts, approximately matching four of the cohort groups independently observed in census data. (Ideally, of course, the cohort matching could be made exact.) The survey data, however, do not concern the respondents' occupations at successive decennial dates. Instead, each respondent was asked to report his father's occupation as of the time the respondent was 16 years old; and the respondent's own first full-time job, at whatever age entry into regular full-time work occurred. Both father's occupation and first job refer to experiences spread out over an interval of years.

For each of the four groups of cohorts, therefore, we have three observations—father's occupation, first job, and current (1962) occupation—variation among which represents, again, intracohort change. Here, however, intracohort change is viewed in terms of the relationship between generations. Father's occupation is here regarded as the respond-

TABLE 3

PER CENT OF MALE WORKING FORCE ENGAGED IN FARM WORK, 1900 TO 1960, AND PER CENT OF 1962 MALE WORKING FORCE WITH FARM ORIGINS AND FIRST JOBS AND CURRENTLY IN FARM WORK, FOR THE U. S.

Cohort	Line No.	Year 1900	1910	1920	1930	1940	1950	1960
Decennial Census Data								
Total male working force	(1)	41.7	34.7	30.4	24.8	21.7	14.9	8.4
Male working force, selected cohorts, by date of birth								
1865-74	(2)	......	......	... ..	30.3	......	......	......
1875-84	(3)	......	......	......	25.0	26.0	......	......
1885-94	(4)	......	......	......	20.2	20.0	17.2	.....
1895-1904	(5)	......	......	......	18.8	17.0	14.0	10.9
1905-14	(6)	......	......	......	......	16.9	12.6	8.7
1915-24	(7)	......	......	......	......	......	11.4	6.5
1925-34	(8)	......	......	......	......	......	......	5.5

1962 Survey, Occupational Changes in a Generation

Fathers occupation by respondent's date of birth	Line No.	Respondents age 16 in: 1913-22	1923-32	1933-42	1943-52	
1897-1906	(9)	......	41.3	......	......	......
1907-16	(10)	......	......	34.6	......	......
1917-26	(11)	......	......	......	29.5	......
1927-36	(12)	......	......	......	......	22.3	......

Respondent's first job and 1962 occupation by date of birth	Line No.	Respondents 15-24 years old in: 1911-30	1921-40	1931-50	1941-60	(1962)
1897-1906	(13)	......	......	25.5	......	......	11.3
1907-16	(14)	......	......	.....	21.8	......	7.8
1917-26	(15)	......	......	......	......	16.5	6.3
1927-36	(16)	......	......	......	......	11.1	5.6

Sources: Line (1): U.S. Bureau of the Census, Working Paper No. 5, "Occupational Trends in the United States: 1900 to 1950" (Washington: 1958), Table 2; *1960 Census of Population,* Subject Report PC(2)-5B, "Educational Attainment" (Washington: Government Printing Office, 1963), Table 8. Lines (2)-(8): A. J. Jaffe and R. O. Carleton, *Occupational Mobility in the United States: 1930-1960* (New York: King's Crown Press, 1954), Appendix Table 1; *1960 Census,* PC(2)-5B, Table 8. Lines (9)-(16): March 1962 Current Population Survey of the Bureau of the Census and supplementary questionnaire, "Occupational Changes in a Generation," unpublished tables.

ent's "origin status," first job as the initial status in his own career. A common pattern of changes occurred in all four groups of cohorts: mobility from father's occupation to first job—compare line (9) with the first entry in line (13), etc.—resulted in a net reduction in farming; and mobility from first job to 1962 occupation—compare the two entries in line (13), etc.—again resulted in a net reduction in farming.

The capital observation in the present context is this. Neither father's occupation nor first job represents the aggregate proportion in farming at any specifiable period. This is not mere happenstance but would occur whenever an ocupational structure was being transformed by a combination of inter- and intracohort changes. It is, therefore, a basic fallacy to suppose (as was suggested at one point in the conference discussions) that the father-son mobility table provides in effect two "samples in time." If the sons in the mobility table are, in fact, representative of the occupational structure at some recent point in time, then the distribution of sons by their fathers' occupations cannot represent the occupational structure at some definite prior moment in time. This has nothing to do with the fallibility of retrospective reports on father's occupation. Nor can the problem be avoided by asking for a time-specific or age-specific report on father's occupation.

The crux of the matter is that in human demography (unlike that of, say, certain insects), birth cohorts and "generations" are not coincident. There is, moreover, no ready translation formula for converting "generational" changes into intercohort or aggregate interannual changes.

Students of occupational mobility may not relish this complication of their problem. They will have to learn to live with it nonetheless. However inconvenient it may be, the fact is that the intergenerational mobility table can tell us less about how occupational structures are transformed in the course of economic development than we had hoped.

Does this mean that the conventional type of mobility study is without value? The remainder of this paper rests on the contrary assumption. Even though "intergenerational" mobility plays no simple and straightforward role as a mechanism in the transformation of occupational structures, we can give a straightforward rationale for analyses of the data in an intergenerational mobility table.

Instead of thinking of the classification of father's occupation as conveying information about a "generation" of "fathers," think of it as describing the origin statuses of the sons. Particularly if the data on father's occupation apply to a time point proximate to the opening of the son's career,[4] this origin status provides a natural base line against which one can measure the son's subsequent occupational achievement.

[4] Cf. Yasuda, *op. cit.*, pp. 20-21.

The father-son mobility table, then, becomes a table showing a cross-classification of origin by destination statuses of the cohorts included in the study. All changes—whether net shifts or gross mobility—are then subject to straightforward interpretation as intracohort changes.

I do not claim that this type of analysis will answer all or even the most pressing questions that might be asked about occupational change by a student of economic development. But surely it is worth knowing how and to what extent the subsequent achieved statuses in a cohort depend on the statuses in which they started. Indeed, the recent popularity of "the inheritance of poverty" as a diagnostic concept in public policy discussions suggests that we need to know a good deal more about this relationship.

Regarding mobility research as a species of cohort analysis clarifies at least one point on which there has been confusion. Although data in the typical mobility study are collected retrospectively (by questioning the respondent about the past), this is only a convenience in data collection. While it introduces problems of data reliability and validity, it does not commit the analyst to a backward-looking conceptual framework. The difference between retrospective and prospective designs in mobility research is probably no greater than in cohort fertility research, where we have the alternatives of collecting (retrospective) census data on children ever born and fertility history, or cumulating annually reported vital statistics.

COMPARISONS OVER TIME: REGRESSION APPROACH

Rogoff's well-known study [5] affords the only suitable published example of an intertemporal comparison of two intergenerational mobility tables derived from independent information on two otherwise comparable cohorts of sons separated by an appreciable span of time. Any other such comparison that might now be attempted would be confronted with almost insuperable problems of establishing comparability, or with a time lapse between the two terms of the comparison so short as to be of little interest.

After working up much of the material for this section, I came across the following remark:

. . . in the full report of the important study by Natalie Rogoff, the publisher has included, in a special attachment to the book, a large basic data sheet

[5] Natalie Rogoff, *Recent Trends in Occupational Mobility* (New York: Free Press of Glencoe, 1953).

which permits recombining the data in a variety of ways . . . it obviously offers many opportunities for research, yet no one to my knowledge has published anything employing these data in new ways.[6]

The data in question consist of two father-son mobility tables for white males, with the respective occupation classifications comprising rather more than 100 occupation titles. One table is for the period around 1910, the other for the period around 1940. Rogoff's information, it will be recalled, was drawn from marriage license applications, and therefore concerns predominantly young adult males. The occupations reported are presumably the current occupations (as of the date of application) of the young men themselves and of their fathers; there is no retrospective element in the reports. Since uniform procedures were followed in processing the two sets of data, comparability is doubtlessly as good as it could be, although there is no evidence that biases, if any, resulting from loss of information due to nonreporting of either or both occupations were the same in the two periods.

A report of some further analysis of Rogoff's data will furnish occasion for presenting several methodological matters that could be relevant in contexts other than intertemporal comparison. (I shall assume that the reader is familiar with the published Rogoff material.)

The data compiled by Rogoff included the titles of occupations copied from documents. In her analysis she resolved the problem of occupational classification by employing the then current major occupation group categories of the U.S. Bureau of the Census, and all her analysis is carried out in terms of these categories, or combinations thereof. Evidently the publication of the two large tables with detailed categories was an afterthought, and the text contains no analysis of them.

In the light of recent work on the status of occupations[7] and the proposal to use a new index of occupational socio-economic status in mobility research,[8] the outcome of an alternative to Rogoff's method of analyzing mobility is interesting.

The new index of occupational socio-economic status is available for each occupation in the Census Bureau's detailed list, which appeared with only minor changes in the censuses of 1940, 1950 and 1960. The census detailed classification includes quite a few more titles than even Rogoff's detailed classification. The first problem, therefore, was to derive

        [6] S. M. Miller, "Comparative Social Mobility," *Current Sociology*, 9 (1960), pp. 5-6.

        [7] Albert J. Reiss, Jr., with collaborators, *Occupations and Social Status* (New York: Free Press of Glencoe, 1961), Chs. 6-7.

        [8] Otis Dudley Duncan and Robert W. Hodge, "Education and Occupational Mobility: A Regression Analysis," *American Journal of Sociology*, 68 (May, 1963), pp. 629-44.

occupational SES scores for her categories. In most cases, this simply involved combining two or more census categories. In doing this, weighted averages were computed, with frequencies found in the 1940 census occupation tables for Indianapolis men as the weights. On the whole, the census categories to be combined were reasonably similar and the process of deriving the scores for Rogoff's categories was straight-forward though involving some arbitrary decisions on minor interpreta-tions. It does not seem worthwhile to go into details on this problem.

Once each of Rogoff's 114 occupation categories was assigned a 2-digit occupational SES score, her mobility table could be handled as an ordinary correlation table. Following the pattern of the previously-cited paper of Duncan and Hodge, the regression of son's occupational status (Y) on father's occupational status (X) was computed from the data for each year. A summary of relevant statistics appears in Table 4.

The striking result is that it would take the sociological equivalent of a micrometer to detect a difference between the 1940 and the 1910 regression equations. The occupational status of a lad marrying in Indianapolis depended just as strongly, but no more strongly, on the occupational status of his father in 1940 as in 1910.

Unfortunately, Rogoff's detailed data were published without sub-division by other respondent characteristics, so that is is impossible to pursue the lead of the Chicago research into a multivariate analysis. Her data, however, do offer possibilities for exploring a couple of interesting points about the regression model.

The question one might raise is how much the result depends on the particular method of scoring occupations—which, though reasonable, is arbitrary. In the presentation of the status index [9] a transformation of the score was provided, the so-called population decile scale, which has a range of 1 to 10, as compared with the range of 0 to 96 for the status score. The decile scale is a rather drastic transformation, com-pressing the values at the upper end and stretching the scale at the lower end of the range, but the transformation has a relatively small effect on the correlation and regression slope (means, standard deviations, and intercepts, of course, are different). (See Table 4.) Both the slope and the correlation are slightly lower when the decile scale is used. Again, however, the difference betwen years is negligible.

A matter of some confusion to persons acquainted with hitherto con-ventional analyses of mobility tables is the relation between the extent of "occupational inheritance," often used as an indication of the depend-ence of the son's upon the father's occupation, and the coefficients ob-tained in the regression analyses. If all sons followed directly in their

[9] Reiss, *op. cit.*, Appendix Table B-1.

TABLE 4

REGRESSION ANALYSIS OF ROGOFF'S DATA ON OCCUPATIONS OF SONS (Y) AND FATHERS (X), WHITE MALES MARRYING IN MARION COUNTY, INDIANA, c. 1940 AND c. 1910

| Description and year | Number of cases | Occupational SES | | | | Regression (Y on X) | | |
| | | Means | | Standard deviations | | Inter-cept (a) | Slope (b) | Corre-lation (r) |
		Y	X	Y	X			
Occupations scored on SES index [a]								
Total cases								
1940	9,892	34.7	31.7	21.4	21.1	22.8	.376	.370
1910	10,253	32.5	27.3	20.4	20.3	22.6	.362	.361
Omitting farmers' sons								
1940	8,257	35.7	35.1	21.7	21.5	22.0	.389	.385
1910	7,568	33.7	32.0	20.4	21.8	21.5	.381	.407
Omitting cases of occupational inheritance								
1940	8,602	35.2	31.8	21.3	21.0	26.6	.272	.268
1910	8,618	33.9	27.8	20.3	20.5	27.1	.246	.249
Occupations scored on decile scale [a]								
1940	9,892	6.28	5.82	2.39	2.57	4.48	.309	.332
1910	10,253	6.00	5.13	2.52	2.60	4.29	.334	.345

[a] Reiss, *op. cit.*, Appendix Table B-1.

fathers' footsteps the association between occupational statuses in the two generations would, of course, be perfect. The mean of Y would equal the mean of X, the two standard deviations would be the same, the regression slope would be unity, and the correlation likewise unity. A perfect association between fathers' and sons' occupations is possible without perfect occupational inheritance; if the association were linear, the regression slope would differ from unity while the correlation would still be 1.0. This could only happen, however, if there were an inter-generational difference in the standard deviations, representing an increase or decrease in the dispersion of the distribution between generations. When the association is not perfect, even though linear to a good approximation, and when the dispersion of occupation scores is roughly the same in the two generations, the regression slope is necessarily less than unity. In other words, there is a "regression toward the mean," in the sense of Francis Galton, who coined the term "regression" precisely because he observed that fathers at the lower end of the distribution (of biometric traits) had sons averaging higher than themselves, while fathers at the upper end had sons averaging lower than themselves. The phenomenon of regression toward the mean is observed in all ordinary occupational mobility tables, and is as important a feature of such tables as any tendency toward occupational inheritance. Evidently, the two tendencies work in opposite directions. At the extreme of perfect occupational inheritance there would be no regression toward the mean. At the extreme of regression toward the mean—where sons have the same average irrespective of their fathers' scores, i.e., the son-father correlation is zero—there could be no occupational inheritance except for sons of fathers located precisely at the mean.

For theoretical reasons one should expect occupational inheritance, in the sense of the transmission of a specific occupational pursuit from father to son, as when a son follows his father into a professional practice, a business, a craft, a trade, or a farm enterprise. For many occupations, however, identity of father's and son's occupation may not signify any specific mechanism of transmission, as when a professor's son becomes a professor. However that may be, there is popular interest in the question of how many sons follow their fathers' occupations. In Rogoff's data this interest is recognized by printing the frequencies in the diagonal cells of the mobility table in boldface type. The total number of such cases, of course, is a function of the breadth and heterogeneity of occupation categories, and despite the detail of her classification, some of Rogoff's categories are rather heterogeneous. As it turns out, about 16 per cent of the sons in the 1910 table and 13 per cent in the 1940 table are on the diagonal. (Even lower figures turn up in Chicago and U.S. data, using a more detailed occupation classification.)

How does occupational inheritance of this order of magnitude affect the regression? Evidently, if we remove the cases of occupational inheritance from the analysis, the tendency of "regression toward the mean" will be enhanced. What happens to the coefficients depends somewhat on where the cases of inheritance are located. Interestingly enough, in Rogoff's data occupational inheritance is widely scattered over the SES scale, so that the means and the standard deviations of both fathers and sons remain virtually unaffected by this statistical surgery. In this event, the regression coefficient and the correlation are reduced; omitting cases of occupational inheritance, the correlations and regression slopes shown in Table 4 are about ⅔ or ¾ as large as those for all cases. The comparison between years is hardly affected.

If we discount the estimate of occupational inheritance from Rogoff's data for two reasons—some spurious resemblance due to broad categories, and some father-son identity due only to happenstance or to nonspecific mechanisms of transmission—we reach the conclusion that analysis in terms of occupational inheritance is not a very fundamental way to look at a mobility table for a general population. This does not, of course, gainsay its occurrence, nor its importance in the case of some specific occupations. Most farmers in a developed country are farmers' sons, and may be thought to have inherited their occupations; but many farmers' sons leave farming. Farming, moreover, is probably an extreme example of an occupation recruited from sons of men pursuing the occupation.

Mention of farming brings up the point that Rogoff's data pertain to an essentially urban population, and farming is represented primarily as an occupation of fathers whose sons have taken up nonfarm pursuits. In the Chicago study using the regression model it was found that farmers' sons had poorer chances in the urban structure than did respondents of nonfarm origin.[10] This does not seem to be the case in the Indianapolis data. Since farming scores relatively low (14) on the status scale, omission of farmers' sons from the regression analysis raises the mean scores for fathers appreciably and for sons slightly. It also produces a small upward shift in the correlation and regression coefficients, but does not particularly affect the between-years comparison. On the basis of the regression equation for the total group, the expected average score for sons of farmers was 28.1 in the 1940 data, 27.7 in the 1910 data; these figures compare with the respective observed averages for sons of farmers, 29.6 in 1940 and 29.1 in 1910. In both years, therefore, farmers' sons did just slightly better than expected on the basis of the regression for the whole population.

One further comment on the regression model at this point concerns its use in relation to the notion of "mobility." As the reader has observed, the linear regression model as such makes no statement about the kind or amount of intergenerational mobility revealed in the data. It is concerned rather with the extent to which the son's status is dependent on the father's, so far as that dependence is represented by the slope of a straight line. A direct implication of "regression toward the mean" (a slope less than unity), however, is that upward mobility is the average,

[10] Duncan and Hodge, op. cit., pp. 641-42.

or expected, pattern for sons with low origins, while downward mobility is the average pattern for sons with high origins. In geometric terms, one can represent the (X, Y) plane with father's occupational status as the horizontal and son's occupational status the vertical axis, and plot thereon the line, $Y = X$. Any point lying to the right and below this line represents a son who undergoes downward mobility, while a point above and to the left represents upward mobility. Now, if the observed regression line, $\hat{Y} = a + bX$, is plotted on the same graph, it will intersect the former line. In the case of the 1910 regression line, the intersection occurs between $X = 35$ and $X = 36$, that is, $a/(1 - b)$ lies between these two scores. Thus, the regression equation *implicitly* predicts upward mobility for sons originating at fathers' occupational status levels of 35 or less and downward mobility for sons originating at 36 or more. For the 1940 regression line, the analogous point is between 36 and 37. Again, one is most impressed by the similarity between the two years.

The analyst using the regression model will also pay attention to the means of Y and X. A positive value for $\bar{Y} - \bar{X}$ implies a net balance of upward over downward mobility, in the sense of average "distance" moved, though not necesarily in terms of the respective numbers moving up and down. The Rogoff data reveal an average intergenerational movement that is positive in both years, though slightly greater in 1910 (5.2 score points) than in 1940 (3.0 points). The same two pairs of means also show that the intercohort shift, 1910-1940, was 2.2 points for sons (34.7 minus 32.5) and 4.4 points for fathers. Some, but not all of these effects are attributable to the smaller proportions of farmers' sons in the 1940 population, as the reader may verify by making the corresponding calculations from the means in the second panel of Table 4.

If it were necessary or worthwhile to do so, significance tests associated with the analysis of covariance could be carried out to check the null hypotheses that the regressions are the same for the two years and that the inter-year shift in $\bar{Y}$ is attributable to that in $\bar{X}$, with the common within-year regression taken into account. Such tests were not made for purposes of this discussion, since the data do not constitute a probability sample from a well-defined actual universe.

In concluding the discussion of the regression model as applied to Rogoff's data, it is appropriate to take note of one of Rogoff's own conclusions: ". . . the processes by which men selected and were selected for occupations were more closely related to social origins in 1940 than they had been in 1910." [11] The foregoing results suggest the following revision of this conclusion: the socio-economic status of occupations held

[11] Rogoff, *op. cit.*, p. 106.

by white Indianapolis men marrying in 1940 was no more closely related
to the socio-economic status of their occupational origins than had been
the case for white men marrying in 1910.

COMPARISONS OVER TIME: MATRIX APPROACH

In both the foregoing analysis and in Rogoff's original work with
social distance mobility ratios (somewhat misleadingly termed "rates"),
the analysis involves a considerable abstraction from the observed facts
about the occupation structure. In the regression model, of course, the
parameters are scale values (e.g., means) and dimensionless numbers
(coefficients) that only purport to quantify a particular aspect of the
structure and the mobility process. In the ratio approach, the calculations are justified on the basis that structure, as represented by the relative frequencies in the several occupational classes in the two generations,
must be "partialled out" before the amount of mobility can be taken to
measure the degree of "openness" of a society. Legitimate and necessary
as such abstractions are, there is also reason to be interested in methods
of analysis that stick closer to the way a cohort actually is redistributed
over a set of structural categories. The matrix approach [12] has an appeal
from this point of view.

The transition matrix, or what Miller [13] proposes to call the "standard
outflow table," is an array of rows, each row consisting of a set of proportions that sum to unity. The number in the jth column of the ith row
is the proportion of all sons originating in the occupation class i whose
destination is class j. It is also useful to think of the distribution of all
sons according to their origin classes as a single row (vector) of proportions and similarly of their destination distribution as a probability vector.[14] Under these conventions, together with those of matrix algebra, the
following notation is convenient for the discussion at hand. Let a_0 be the
origin vector, A the transition matrix, and a_1 the destination vector. We
then have the identity, $a_0 A = a_1$, and we may speak of the transition
matrix, A, as sending the origin vector into the destination vector.

Now, if we think of the mobility experience recorded in Rogoff's data
as being summarized by the two transition matrices, A (1910) and B
(1940), then we may consider a comparison between A and B in terms

[12] Gösta Carlsson, *Social Mobility and Class Structure* (Lund, Sweden: CWK
Gleerup, 1958), Ch. 5.
[13] "Comparative Social Mobility," *op. cit.*, p. 7.
[14] Judah Matras, "Comparison of Intergenerational Occupational Mobility Patterns: An Application of the Formal Theory of Social Mobility," *Population Studies*,
14 (November, 1960), pp. 163-69.

of the structures they would produce under various assumptions. Table 5 sets forth a number of origin and destination vectors (written for convenience as columns rather than rows and in percentages rather than proportions) which are useful in making the comparison.

Note, first, that the origin vectors are in fact somewhat dissimilar. The

TABLE 5

COMPARISON OF ACTUAL AND HYPOTHETICAL OCCUPATION DISTRIBUTIONS (PER CENT) FOR WHITE MEN MARRYING IN MARION COUNTY, INDIANA C. 1940 AND C. 1910 (ROGOFF DATA)

Major occupation group	Origin distributions		Destination distributions		Hypothetical destination distributions		Fixed point distributions	
	1910	1940	1910	1940			1910	1940
	a_0	b_0	a_0A	b_0B	a_0B	b_0A	a_∞	b_∞
Professional	3.68	4.79	3.79	5.54	5.06	4.11	3.79	6.60
Semi-professional	0.72	1.15	1.85	3.10	2.76	2.12	2.64	4.12
Proprietors, managers and officials	12.22	12.16	7.13	6.63	6.52	7.29	6.19	6.09
Clerical and sales	6.43	11.04	18.23	22.12	20.38	19.91	22.31	25.32
Skilled	26.53	27.59	31.99	21.87	22.19	32.16	32.89	20.07
Semi-skilled	9.17	15.36	17.10	27.07	27.08	17.60	17.74	26.79
Unskilled	12.25	7.28	11.95	6.91	8.56	9.95	9.29	5.48
Protective service	1.56	2.44	0.96	2.32	2.46	0.91	0.79	1.94
Personal service	1.26	1.66	3.65	3.38	3.58	3.53	3.45	3.18
Farming	26.19	16.53	3.36	1.06	1.42	2.42	0.91	0.41
Total	100.01	100.00	100.01	100.00	100.01	100.00	100.00	100.00

	Differences between distributions				
	$b_0 - a_0$	$b_0B - a_0A$	$a_0B - a_0A$	$b_0B - b_0A$	$b_\infty - a_\infty$
Professional	1.11	1.75	1.27	1.43	2.81
Semi-professional	.43	1.25	.91	.98	1.48
Proprietors, managers and officials	—.06	—.50	—.61	—.66	—.10
Clerical and sales	4.61	3.89	2.15	2.21	3.01
Skilled	1.06	—10.12	—9.80	—10.29	—12.82
Semi-skilled	6.19	9.97	9.98	9.47	9.05
Unskilled	—4.97	—5.04	—3.39	—3.04	—3.81
Protective service	.88	1.36	1.50	1.41	1.15
Personal service	.40	—.27	—.07	—.15	—.27
Farming	—9.66	—2.30	—1.94	—1.36	—.50
Index of dissimilarity	14.7	18.2	15.8	15.5	17.5

Note: See text for notation used to identify columns.

column of differences in the bottom panel, $b_0 - a_0$, shows where the most important changes occurred over the 30-year period. Likewise, the two destination distributions exhibit some lack of resemblance. In 1940 as compared with 1910, there was an excess of professional, semi-professional, clerical and sales, semi-skilled, and protective service workers, and a deficiency of proprietor-managerial, skilled, unskilled, personal service, and farm workers. The "index of dissimilarity" is the sum of the positive differences in the column above it. (An index of dissimilarity computed between an origin distribution and a destination distribution is identical with the percentage of net mobility. The same index also serves to compare two origin or two destination distributions, but in this case it is not interpretable as an amount of mobility.)

The third and fourth columns of differences are perhaps the most interesting. Granted that the 1910 and 1940 destination distributions differed considerably, may this not be due primarily to the fact that the respective origin distributions, as we have just seen, were not alike? The answer appears to be that the difference between the two destination distributions is *not* due so much to the origin difference, but rather to the difference between the two transition matrices, A and B. In one calculation, the 1910 origin distribution is applied to the 1940 matrix, to produce a hypothetical destination distribution, a_0B, which may be compared with the actual 1910 destination distribution, a_0A. In the other calculation, the same difference between matrices is seen under the condition of b_0 (1940 origin distribution) as the origin distribution. Casual inspection will reveal that either of the two comparisons of a hypothetical with an actual distribution comes out at much the same place as the comparison of the two actual destination distributions. The difference between the latter, then, inheres primarily in the matrices that produced them, not in the origins whence they came.

How big is the difference? Is an index of dissimilarity of 15-18 points a "large" or a "small" value? As in all such cases, assessment of magnitudes as important or unimportant depends on a background of typical variation in the index. In the present instance, 15 points is not a trivial magnitude, although we would expect larger index values if we compared occupation distributions separated by a longer time period, or the distribution for whites with that for nonwhites, or the distribution for men with that for women.

One final comparison is suggested by the treatment of mobility transition matrices from the viewpoint of Markov processes. I have reservations about the utility of Markov analysis for the subject of "intergenerational" mobility, which arise from consideration of the issues discussed in the first section of this paper. Leaving this point aside, however, one can still regard one of the statistics derived from the Markov approach as a summary of the transition matrix. This is the so-called "fixed point" of the matrix. If there is an origin distribution, a_∞, such that $a_\infty A = a_\infty$, then a_∞ is the fixed point vector of the transition matrix A. It is the origin distribution which is unaffected by the transition. The fixed points of the matrices A and B are shown in the last two columns of the top panel of Table 5. The last column of the lower panel reveals that the pattern and degree of differences between the two fixed points are much like those observed in the other comparisons between actual and hypothetical destination distributions.

We evidently cannot escape the conclusion that a real difference of some appreciable magnitude exists between the mobility processes represented by the 1910 and 1940 transition matrices for Indianapolis. The 1940 matrix produces more white-collar and semi-skilled workers in the destination distribution, and fewer skilled and unskilled, than the 1910 matrix. If one wants to argue, as Rogoff does in her Chapter 2, that the difference between the 1910 and 1940 occupation structures was due to shifts in "demand" for workers of the several types of qualification, then one must regard the mobility process, as described by the transition matrix, as the *dependent variable*.

This suggestion leads to still another approach to the comparison of two mobility tables. Is it possible that differences in the 1910 and 1940 mobility patterns are due solely to shifts in the distribution of job opportunities open to young men? (The term "opportunities" is used in place of "demand," to acknowledge that factors on the "supply" side, such as the educational qualifications of these men, may influence the kinds of jobs they get.) Can we, in other words, contrive a comparison between the two mobility tables putting the change in occupation structure in the role of an exogenously determined factor, which then induces a change in mobility patterns?

The starting point of the comparison is to test the null hypothesis that all changes in the mobility table are due to proportional adjustments occasioned by changes, 1910 to 1940, in the two marginal distributions—the distribution of sons by their fathers' occupations, and the distribution of sons by their own occupations. When this hypothesis is rejected, attention will be turned to the pattern of nonproportional shifts, which cannot be attributed to changing marginal distributions.

One initial simplification will entail no loss of useful information. The frequencies in the 1910 table are reduced by a factor of 9,892/10,253, so that the two tables have the same total N: 9,892.

Let n_{ij} be the number of sons in occupation j whose fathers were in occupation i, according to the 1910 table (as reduced), and N_{ij}, the frequency in the corresponding cell of the 1940 table. Define $R_{ij} = N_{ij}/n_{ij}$ and $R.. = N../n.. = 1.0$. The rationale for the analysis [15] is given by the model identity, $R_{ij} = R + a_i + b_j + e_{ij}$, where $R = 1$, and $i = 1, 2, \ldots, r;\ j = 1, 2, \ldots, r$. The quantities on the right side of the identity are to be computed from the data (including R_{ij}) on the following assumptions: $\Sigma_i n_{ij} e_{ij} = \Sigma_j n_{ij} e_{ij} = \Sigma_i n_{i.} a_i = \Sigma_j n_{.j} b_j = 0$. These conditions imply the following set of normal equations:

$$n_i.a_i + \Sigma_j n_{ij} b_j = N_i. - n_i. \qquad (r - 1 \text{ equations, } i = 1, 2, \ldots, r - 1)$$
$$\Sigma_i n_i.a_i \qquad\quad = 0 \qquad (1 \text{ equation, } i = 1, 2, \ldots, r)$$
$$\Sigma_i n_{ij} a_i + n_{.j} b_j = N_{.j} - n_{.j} \qquad (r - 1 \text{ equations, } i = 1, 2, \ldots, r - 1)$$
$$\Sigma_j n_{.j} b_j = 0 \qquad (1 \text{ equation, } j = 1, 2, \ldots, r)$$

Given the solution of these equations, further manipulations of the data and computed quantities are carried out to exhibit the pattern and magnitude of departures from proportionality of change. Under the null hypothesis these departures are, of course, nil; that is, $e_{ij} = 0$ for all i,j.

Let us first observe that the total sum of squares (SS) of the cell ratios, R_{ij}, which is defined as $\Sigma_i \Sigma_j n_{ij} (R_{ij} - R)^2$, can be broken down as in the following tabulation, where verbal descriptions are given for the components of this total:

$\Sigma_i n_i.a^2_i$ — SS due to (net) proportional change in distribution by father's occupation (1)

$\Sigma_j n_{.j} b^2_j$ — SS due to (net) proportional change in distribution by son's occupation (2)

$2\Sigma_i \Sigma_j n_{ij} a_i b_j$ — SS due to proportional change in both distributions, reflecting the initial correlation between son's and father's occupation (3)

$\Sigma_i \Sigma_j n_{ij} e^2_{ij}$ — SS due to nonproportional change, or interaction (4)

Sum — Total SS, $\Sigma_i \Sigma_j n_{ij} (R_{ij} - R)^2$

From the data at hand, we secure the following results:

component	SS	per cent
total	3,326	100
(1)	1,133	34
(2)	1,384	42
(3)	252	7
(4)	557	17

[15] W. Edwards Deming, *Statistical Adjustment of Data* (New York: John Wiley, 1943), Ch. 7.

Since Rogoff's data do not represent a random sample, but rather consist of the entire universe of observations for Marion County for the specified periods (less certain omissions), we do not consider the question of the "statistical significance" of the SS due to nonproportional change. There actually was some appreciable departure of the 1940 table from the table that would have been produced by proportional changes in the 1910 table, since the interaction component amounts to about one-sixth of the total sum of squares.

If one regards this amount of nonproportionality as "small," he may conclude that the bulk of the difference between the 1910 and 1940 mobility tables is, indeed, due to changes in occupational distribution, as reflected in the shifts in the marginals. Had only the 1910 table been available, plus the 1940 marginals, the assumption of proportional changes would have been a reasonable basis for estimating the 1940 table.

If, on the other hand, the amount of nonproportionality seems "large," the investigator is sensitized to the need for searching out determinants of the change in mobility pattern other than mere shift in the occupational structure. For example, the mobility of white men may have been affected by the entry into the Marion County labor force of larger numbers of white women and Negroes. There is also the question of how the elevated unemployment level of 1940 may have influenced mobility patterns.

Although the issue as between the two interpretations will not be resolved here—since this paper is not concerned to reach substantive conclusions—some alternative indications of the amount, as well as the pattern, of nonproportional change may be given.

In Table 6, the actual frequencies in the 1940 table are shown as positive or negative deviations from the frequencies that would have been observed in the event of strictly proportional changes. For example, 59 fewer men moved from unskilled origins to semi-skilled occupations than would have appeared in the 1940 table had it shown only proportional differences from the 1910 table. The total of these deviations must, of course, add to zero. If we sum the positive deviations alone, however, we find that at least $723/9,892 = 7$ per cent of the men were in classes other than those in which they would have been, in the event of proportional change, 1910-1940.

In Table 7, the comparison of the hypothesis of proportional change with the 1940 actuality is given in terms of percentages of occupational inheritance for each origin class. Interestingly enough, the hypothesis produces just the right amount of inheritance over the table as a whole; but deviations, some of them sizable, occur for specific origin classes. In

TABLE 6

DEVIATION OF FREQUENCIES IN ROGOFF'S 1940 MOBILITY TABLE FROM
THOSE EXPECTED ON THE BASIS OF PROPORTIONAL ADJUSTMENT OF THE
1910 TABLE TO 1940 MARGINALS (WHITE MEN)

Father's occupation class	Son's occupation class									
	(1)	(2)	(3)	(4)	(5)	(6)	(7)	(8)	(9)	(10)
(1) Professional	12	6	—14	16	5	—24	1	—1	—2	
(2) Semi-professional	13	—15	—5	—3	17	—4	—1	—3	2	
(3) Proprietors, etc.	—27	—10	—10	9	24	49	—10	—9	—16	
(4) Clerical	11	16	8	—35	—19	30	—6	5	—4	—4 *
(5) Skilled	15	9	8	32	—81	7	5	4	—4	
(6) Semi-skilled	—6	3	13	46	—85	41	—43	13	19	
(7) Unskilled	7	0	1	—9	10	—59	53	—5	2	
(8) Protective service	2	0	—8	1	—19	14	4	8	—4	
(9) Personal service	6	0	3	—3	6	1	—8	0	—5	
(10) Farming	—33	—10	3	—54	141	—56	4	—12	14	4

* This combination of cells was made in computing total and interaction SS, but not in computing other SS components or in securing the a_i and b_j coefficients.

Note: Columns may not sum to zero exactly, owing to errors of rounding.

the case of three origin classes the proportionally adjusted percentage of inheritance is farther from the 1940 observation than was the unadjusted 1910 percentage. (The reader may, of course, form other kinds of comparisons to summarize the pattern of nonproportionality, making use of Table 6 and Rogoff's published tables.)

If we now compare the results of the regression analysis in the preceding section with the outcome of comparisons between matrices in this section, we are threatened by a paradox. The regression approach (and the same is actually true, on the whole, of Rogoff's results based on social distance mobility ratios) discloses very little difference between 1940 and 1910 in regard to the degree to which the young man's occupational achievement, up to the time of his marriage, depends on his origin status. Yet the 30-year period had witnessed some genuine alteration of occupational structures and, as an apparent consequence thereof, some appreciable modification of mobility patterns. The paradox is resolved, of course, by the observation that the two kinds of analysis address different questions. It is well to bear in mind the fact that invariance with respect to some aspects of the mobility process is com-

TABLE 7

OCCUPATIONAL INHERITANCE (PER CENT OF SONS IN SAME
OCCUPATIONAL CLASS AS FATHER) IN ROGOFF'S 1910 AND 1940
MOBILITY TABLES, AND IN HYPOTHETICAL TABLE OBTAINED BY
ADJUSTING 1910 TABLE TO 1940 MARGINAL DISTRIBUTIONS
(WHITE MEN)

Father's Occupation Class	Observed Mobility Tables		1910 Table Adjusted to 1940 Marginals
	1910	*1940*	
All classes	29.4	27.1	27.3
Professional	21.0	28.3	25.7
Semi-professional	27.0	19.3	32.5
Proprietors, managers, officials	21.1	17.6	18.4
Clerical and sales	43.7	42.2	45.4
Skilled	48.6	32.2	35.2
Semi-skilled	31.6	43.2	40.5
Unskilled	34.2	28.6	21.2
Protective service	2.5	8.3	4.8
Personal service	14.7	10.4	13.7
Farmers	10.6	4.2	3.9

patible with variation in other aspects. The evidence from intertemporal comparisons suggests that the invariance is not to be uncovered by direct inspection of the transition matrix, even though this is precisely where Lipset and Bendix [16] sought to discover it. This little irony of research strategy is worth some elaboration with additional empirical materials.

COMPARISONS BETWEEN PLACES

At an early point in their ambitious comparative study, Lipset and Bendix forthrightly state a far-reaching conclusion: "*the overall pattern of social mobility appears to be much the same in the industrial societies of various Western countries. This is startling. . . .*" [17] The authors are led by their assessment of the evidence favoring this proportion to question whether rates of social mobility and of "economic expansion" (development?) are correlated.

One might observe that Lipset and Bendix are in the position of

[16] Seymour M. Lipset and Reinhard Bendix, *Social Mobility in Industrial Society* (Berkeley: University of California Press, 1959).

[17] *Ibid.*, p. 13 (italics in original).

affirming the null hypothesis—no international differences—and an investigator who accepts the burden of proof for such an affirmation is in a difficult position. The present discussion deals with only one of the many pieces of evidence Lipset and Bendix adduce. It is treated in some detail to illustrate certain points of method, and not with the idea of assessing the general proposition.

In their Table 2.2 Lipset and Bendix show the father-son transition matrix, with occupations grouped into four broad classes, for Aarhus (Denmark) based on Geiger's [18] 1949 data and for Indianapolis based on Rogoff's 1940 data. Similarities and differences between the two studies are not discussed, except for the remark that the "two excellent studies" pertain to "two somewhat comparable provincial cities." The reader is not advised how to compare the two matrices. He is simply given the conclusion summarily: "It is clear that there is no substantial difference in the patterns of social mobility in Aarhus and Indianapolis." [19]

If this conclusion is correct, it belongs in the category of statements that are true for the wrong reasons. Rogoff's data are for young men getting married; three-quarters of the men in her 1940 table were under 31 years of age. Geiger's data were secured in a complete census covering men of all ages; only three-tenths were in this age group. Obviously, the bulk of Geiger's data concern men whose exposure to intragenerational mobility was much greater than that of the men in the Indianapolis table. While the proportion of men with deceased fathers must have been considerably smaller in Rogoff's study, she was forced to omit them from consideration. Yet the older respondents in Geiger's study, in substantial proportions, must have reported occupations that their presently deceased fathers held at some indefinite time in the past. Thus intragenerational mobility of fathers, as well as of respondents, introduces uncontrolled variation into the comparison. In addition, Lipset and Bendix elect to report on data pertaining to only nine-tenths of the Indianapolis occupation structure. They show a condensation of Rogoff's table for white men but ignore her data on Negroes. While aggregation of the occupation categories used in the two studies is necessary to approximate comparability of the classifications, Lipset and Bendix show data so highly aggregated as to obscure structural differences that are significant for mobility patterns. In sum, if there really is "no substantial difference" between the "patterns of social mobility" revealed by the two tables the authors present, there is a good possibility that a more meticulous comparison would disclose differences worth noting.

[18] Theodor Geiger, *Soziale Umschichtungen in einer Dänischen Mittelstadt,* "Acta Jutlandica," Vol. 23, No. 1 (Copenhagen, 1951).

[19] Lipset and Bendix, *op. cit.,* p. 31.

The first step in re-examining this evidence is to settle on an occupational classification into which one can fit the categories originally used in the two studies. This is a difficult problem, for general occupational designations are usually both vague and ambiguous. In Rogoff's material we have definite indications as to what actually goes into such a category as "semi-professional;" Geiger, unfortunately, does not give equally explicit definitions. Clearly recognizing the doubtful character of certain of the equations, I propose to use the following groupings to compare the two studies:

Group	Rogoff categories	Geiger categories
I.	Professional Semi-professional	Freie Berufe (4) Geistliche und Lehrer (6) Höhere Privatangestellte (7) Sonstige Gehaltempfänger 12)
II.	Proprietors, managers, and officials	Unternehmer (2) Gewerbetreibende (3) Höhere öffentliche Beamte (5)
III.	Sales workers	Verkaufsangestellte (10)
IV.	Clerical workers	Öffentliche und privat Büro-Angestellte (11)
V.	Skilled workers City fireman Policeman, detective, sheriff, patrolman	Technische angestellte (9) Gelernte Arbeiter (13)
VI.	Semi-skilled Unskilled Guard, watchman Soldier, sailor Personal service	Öffentliches Verkehrs-Personal (8) Ungelernte Arbeiter (14) Lehrlinge (15)
VII.	Farmer	Landwirtschaft (1)
(Omit)	Unknown, poorly reported, etc.	Studierende (16) Personen im Ruhestand (17) Unidentifizierte (18)

The proposed groups are, in all cases, direct combinations of the Geiger categories (his code numbers are shown in parentheses). In reclassifying the Rogoff material, Clerical and Sales, as well as Protective Service Workers, were subdivided. This required reference to the detailed mobility table in the case of white respondents and some arbitrary, but quite minor, estimates in the case of Negroes. The temptation to provide translations for Geiger's categories was resisted, since it would be all too easy to manipulate nominal synonyms in such a way as to enhance the apparent comparability. It is doubtful, moreover, that researchers realize sufficiently well that translatability of occupational titles does not guarantee compatibility of occupational classifications. The present illustration will proceed on the assumption that the indicated combinations yield roughly comparable occupational classifications. If the reader's knowledge of German occupational titles and Danish occupational structure requires him to reject this assumption, then the correct conclusion is that the Indianapolis and Aarhus mobility data are not comparable—*not* that "there is no substantial difference in the patterns of social mobility."

The next step is to extract from Geiger's tables a set of statistics approaching comparability with Rogoff's in respect to age distribution. Since the problem admits of no exact solution, a simple arbitrary device was used. A "synthetic" mobility table for Aarhus was prepared by combining the tables for the respondents born in 1924-1928 with those born in 1919-1923 and one-third of those born in 1909-1918. This yielded a table based on 8,003 cases.

TABLE 8

TRANSITION MATRICES FOR INDIANAPOLIS, 1940, AND AARHUS, 1949 (IN PERCENTAGES)

Father's Occupation Group °	Son's Occupation Group °						
	I	II	III	IV	V	VI	VII
	Indianapolis (Marion County, Indiana) Whites plus Negroes						
I	32.86	6.92	11.48	12.74	16.19	19.65	0.16
II	10.94	17.70	13.84	16.09	14.48	26.47	0.48
III	10.41	8.45	28.20	17.65	14.18	20.96	0.15
IV	16.40	6.29	12.13	23.38	17.54	24.04	0.22
V	6.13	4.28	7.47	11.07	32.16	38.34	0.55
VI	3.97	3.45	5.91	7.88	15.52	62.84	0.43
VII	5.14	5.41	6.49	7.14	21.63	50.51	3.68
	Aarhus, "Synthetic" Table for Young Men						
I	28.70	8.44	10.55	18.14	20.04	13.71	0.42
II	11.06	14.93	12.32	8.70	32.43	20.06	0.50
III	9.58	8.68	20.96	14.36	26.96	19.16	0.30
IV	11.69	5.19	15.58	20.78	24.68	22.08	0.00
V	5.90	4.56	7.09	6.23	45.63	30.38	0.21
VI	4.28	4.52	6.55	6.00	31.49	46.16	1.00
VII	12.30	13.22	7.72	5.63	24.21	32.59	4.32

° See text for definition of groups.

Table 8 shows the transition matrices computed from the mobility tables. It is no longer "clear" that "no substantial difference" exists between the mobility patterns of the two cities. Careful inspection discloses a number of interesting differences. There was more occupational inheritance in Indianapolis than in Aarhus for sons originating in each white-collar group as well as for those from group VI. In Indianapolis a son originating in V was more likely to move to VI than to stay in V, while the reverse was true in Aarhus. A considerably higher proportion of farmers' sons had found upper white-collar positions in Aarhus. On the other hand, the overall proportion of occupational inheritance was 34 per cent for the Aarhus table, as compared with 32 per cent for Indianapolis, a difference that may not seem to warrant emphasis.

As in the case of the 1910 vs. 1940 Indianapolis comparisons, we may compare the Indianapolis and Aarhus transition matrices by looking at the distributions they produce under alternative assumptions. Table 9 assembles the relevant distributions and shows selected indexes of dissimilarity. These data help considerably in discerning the contrast in "patterns" of mobility between the two cities. Note that Indianapolis and Aarhus differed as much in respect to their origin distributions as in regard to their destination distributions. Yet the former difference explains little of the latter. The contrast is nearly as great when the distribution of origins is held constant; compare either columns (3) and (5) or (4) and (6). The (nearly) equal amounts of net mobility in the two cities were required to accomplish rather different types of transition. In Aarhus a much more drastic intergenerational reduction occurred in group II occupations. In Indianapolis the proportion of group V occupations was reduced considerably, while in Aarhus it increased markedly. Correlatively, a pronounced intergenerational increase occurred in group VI occupations in Indianapolis, but none in Aarhus. In short, the contrast in structure of the two cities produced differences in mobility patterns.

Additional insight into the structural contrast is gained from comparisons that go beyond the data used in the mobility analysis proper. For Indianapolis it was possible to assemble data from the 1940 census on occupations of all men in the experienced labor force (except on public emergency work) and of men 20 to 34 years of age, and to group the figures into the categories suggested here. Since the Aarhus data derive from a local census, we have the distribution for men of all ages as well as for those in the "synthetic" mobility table for younger men. Without presenting the respective census figures, one may summarize the situation by stating that the Aarhus and Indianapolis structures bear a closer resemblance when the comparison refers to the entire working

TABLE 9

COMPARISON OF ACTUAL AND HYPOTHETICAL OCCUPATIONAL
DISTRIBUTIONS (PERCENTAGE), FOR WHITE PLUS NEGRO MEN MARRYING
IN INDIANAPOLIS (MARION COUNTY), C. 1940, AND FOR AARHUS
"SYNTHETIC" DISTRIBUTION FOR YOUNG MEN, 1949

Occu-pation Group	Observed Origin Distributions		Observed Destination Distributions		Hypothetical Destination Distributions *	
	Indianapolis (1)	Aarhus (2)	Indianapolis (3)	Aarhus (4)	Indianapolis (5)	Aarhus (6)
I	5.78	5.92	8.09	8.85	8.85	8.41
II	11.30	24.85	6.23	8.36	7.67	7.81
III	6.03	4.17	9.23	9.15	9.01	9.62
IV	4.04	0.96	11.02	7.90	8.11	11.44
V	26.53	23.29	20.89	33.38	32.91	19.73
VI	29.52	31.26	43.57	31.42	32.27	42.24
VII	16.80	9.55	0.97	0.94	1.18	0.75
Total	100.00	100.00	100.00	100.00	100.00	100.00

Indexes of dissimilarity: Net mobility:

Col. (1) vs. Col. (2)   15.4   Indianapolis, (1) vs. (3)   26.5
(3) vs. (4)   15.4   Aarhus, (2) vs. (4)   25.1
(3) vs. (5)   14.4
(4) vs. (6)   14.8
(3) vs. (6)   2.7
(4) vs. (5)   1.3

* Origin distribution for given city times transition matrix for the other city.

force instead of to younger men only. The between-city index of dissimilarity is 13.4 for men of all ages, 19.3 for men 20 to 34 in Indianapolis vs. the Aarhus "synthetic" distribution. Most noteworthy, perhaps,
is the comparison of proportions in group V ("skilled" workers). For men
of all ages, this proportion was 21.4 per cent in Indianapolis and 27.6
per cent in Aarhus. At the youthful ages the respective proportions are
17.0 and 33.4 per cent. This, together with other information that may
be gleaned from the census data, permits one to suggest at least one
major difference in mobility "patterns." In Aarhus large numbers of youth
enter apprenticeship (no less than 45 per cent of those born in 1929-
1933, according to Geiger's figures), and by the time they are in their
20's or early 30's, they already are engaged in skilled occupations. By
contrast, for whatever reasons, intragenerational mobility into skilled
work occurs later for Indianapolis men. The conclusion that the two

cities have similar mobility patterns might have appeared stronger, had a more mature group of sons been available for the comparison. The above discussion should have made evident the uncertainties surrounding interspatial comparisons of mobility patterns where the two (or more) terms of the comparison derive from studies defining their universe and key variables in noncomparable ways. It seems not at all unlikely that the differences we should like to detect in a comparison between places will be small relative to discrepancies that can be produced by varying research procedures. If this conjecture is sound, then the answer to the problem of comparative research is plain, if discouraging—the research must employ rigidly standardized procedures from the initial collection to the final tabulation of data. In the field of social mobility I know of only one example of this kind of standardization: the Six-City Survey.[20] Until a similar device of *literal replication* can be applied to international studies, juxtaposition of data from various countries will require of the analyst as much skill in effecting comparability as in making comparisons.

OCCUPATIONAL CLASSIFICATION

The issue of occupational classification has already become apparent, despite postponement of the topic to a late point in the paper. This issue is important not only when we inquire whether one of two places or periods has the greater or lesser mobility, or a different pattern of mobility. It is equally pressing when we consider determinants of mobility or factors affecting occupational achievement. Yet at this juncture we may be in a more favorable position than when we try to compare mobility patterns as such. In fact, the argument put forward now—albeit somewhat tentatively—is that *for some purposes* a kind of comparability can be effected, even though specific occupational categories differ.

Suppose the analyst is concerned with so-called "vertical mobility," or more precisely, with the correlates of high and low occupational achievement. It could happen that studies conducted in different countries use different occupational classifications, but that in each country it is possible to grade or scale the occupations on such a dimension as occupational prestige or occupational socio-economic status. The dependent variable is no longer occupation as such, nor occupational mobility strictly speaking, but the standing of the individual's occupation in the occupational system of his own country.

[20] Gladys L. Palmer, *Labor Mobility in Six Cities* (New York: Social Science Research Council, 1954).

The problem of scaling occupations has been approached in various ways. Major studies of occupational mobility in Britain and Denmark included extensive preliminary investigations of occupational prestige.[21] In this country some use was made of the North-Hatt occupational prestige scores [22] in mobility research during the 1950's. A systematic approach to the construction of occupational scales specifically for use in mobility research was taken by Bogue in research conducted in 1958 [23] and by Duncan a little later.[24] Both projects contributed methods of scaling census detailed occupations in terms of "socio-economic status," conceived as an average of the occupation's standing with respect to its income and educational levels. They were anticipated in this respect by Blishen's work in Canada.[25] Still a fourth set of status scores for detailed occupations has now been provided by the U.S. Bureau of the Census.[26]

Blishen observed that occupational status is a very good predictor of occupational prestige in the sense of the North-Hatt ratings. This relationship was built into the Duncan status scores, the weights for which were derived from a multiple regression equation, with occupational prestige rating as the dependent variable, occupational education and income levels, the independent variables.

What is one to make of this proliferation of closely similar occupation scaling systems? The fact is that they are all highly intercorrelated, and it is difficult to believe that substituting one for the other would have much effect on the conclusions of most research studies. For specific purposes, however, there may be reasons to prefer one system of scoring to another. Bogue's scores, for example, provide a good deal of differentiation at the lower end of the status scale. This was appropriate for his purpose, which was to study a predominantly downwardly mobile, Skid Row population. For studies of mobility in the general population, where upward mobility prevails, it may be more important to emphasize differentiation among higher-status occupations. In Bogue's scoring system, which does not take full advantage of the census detailed occupational classification, bankers and filling-station proprietors receive the same

---

[21] D. V. Glass (ed.), *Social Mobility in Britain* (New York: Free Press of Glencoe, 1954); Kaare Svalastoga, *Prestige, Class and Mobility* (Copenhagen: Gyldendal, 1959).

[22] Reiss, *op. cit.*, pp. 111-12.

[23] Donald J. Bogue, *Skid Row in American Cities* (Chicago: Community and Family Study Center, University of Chicago, 1963), Ch. 14 and Appendix B.

[24] Reiss, *op. cit.*, Chs. 6, 7; Duncan and Hodge, *op. cit.*

[25] Bernard R. Blishen, "The Construction and Use of an Occupational Class Scale," *Canadian Journal of Economics and Political Science*, 24 (November, 1958), pp. 519-31.

[26] U.S. Bureau of the Census, *Methodology and Scores of Socio-economic Status*, Working Paper No. 15 (Washington, 1963).

score, while in Duncan's system the two occupations are separated by more than 50 points, or over two standard deviations.

To illustrate the possibility of cross-national comparisons in analyzing the determinants of occupational achievement, reference is made to a French study wherein an interesting procedure for scaling occupational status was proposed some years before the Canadian and American work reviewed above. The substantive question has to do with the role of marriage in determining the occupational status achieved by the subject in France and the United States; that is, how does the status of the father-in-law relate to that of the subject, independently of their respective relations to father's status? The methodological proposition to be illustrated is that comparative analysis is aided, first, by treating occupational status as a variable to be scaled by some plausible device and analyzed quantitatively, and second, by using correlation and regression methods of data reduction. Data for France are taken from the well-known investigation of Bresard, which covered some 3,000 men 18 to 50 years of age in 1948.[27] U.S. data from the Blau-Duncan-Census research on Occupational Changes in a Generation (OCG) pertain to a sample of over 20,000 men 20 to 64 years of age in 1962.[28] (The analysis of the OCG data is provisional, since qualifications may be required when controls for age and other factors are introduced during further analysis.)

Bresard's study is noteworthy for two points relevant to the present discussion. He gave explicit attention to the problem of placing occupations on a "social scale" without, however, investigating occupational "prestige." He then treated his "scale" values, expressed as ranks, as a quantitative variable for summary purposes where it was natural to compute average ranks. This computation was somewhat incidental to the bulk of his analysis, however, and it did not lead into a straightforward development in terms of correlation and regression.

Bresard's data on occupational status are assembled and reproduced in Table 10. He states that there are three criteria of the rank of an occupation: the level of education, external signs of the level of living, and the average age of persons engaged in the occupation. The latter criterion assumes that cross-sectional age-grading patterns can substitute for information on careers of individuals or cohorts. Thus Bresard states that occupations with high average ages are those into which entry is made only upon gaining experience, maturity, and responsibility. Average

---

[27] Marcel Bresard, "Mobilité sociale et dimension de la famille," *Population*, 5 (July, 1950), pp. 533-66.
[28] Peter M. Blau and Otis Dudley Duncan, "Eine Untersuchung beruflicher Mobilität in den Vereinigten Staaten," *Kölner Zeitschrift für Soziologie und Sozialpsychologie*, special issue, *Soziale Schichtung und soziale Mobilität* (1961), pp. 171-88.

TABLE 10

DATA ON SOCIAL STATUS OF OCCUPATIONS, FRANCE, 1948 (AFTER BRESARD)

Occupation	Age (1)	Education (2)	Property (3)	Auto (4)	Servant (5)	Phone (6)	Rank (7)	Score (8)*	
				Level of Living					
Industriels	41.8	12.0	84	82	67	87	11	100	95
Professions libérales	37.4	14.7	57	56	46	75	10	90	
Fonctionnaires I	38.8	14.4	33	25	25	34	9	80	
Cadres industriels et commerciaux	38.0	12.9	47	26	21	30	8	70	75
Commerçants et artisans	37.1	8.6	59	52	25	45	7	60	
Cultivateurs exploitants	37.3	7.5	75	31	39	14	6	50	
Fonctionnaires II	35.4	11.7	32	16	12	9	5	40	
Employés	34.9	9.2	31	5	2	6	4	30	35
Ouvriers qualifiés	32.9	7.7	18	2	1	1	3	20	
Manoeuvres	31.3	6.7	13	2	0	0	1	0	18
Ouvriers agricoles	32.2	6.5	10	2	1	1	2	10	
All occupations	35	8.6	44	22	18	16	....	....	

Definitions and sources:

(1) Mean age in years, shown in Bresard, *op. cit.*, p. 564.
(2) Mean number of years of schooling (age left school, minus 6), Tables XXI and XXII.
(3) Per cent owning property, p. 563.
(4) Per cent having an automobile, p. 563.
(5) Per cent "disposent d'une aide domestique," p. 563.
(6) Per cent having a telephone, p. 563.
(7) Mean rank of subjects "dans l'échelle social," Table XI.
(8) Score = 10 (Rank − 1). Braces show combinations that had to be made in computing correlations shown in the text.

age would be a misleading indicator in the United States. Professional occupations, for example, show a reverse age-grading, due to the rapid recent expansion of the category, even though each birth cohort increases its proportion of professionals over time, in accordance with Bresard's assumption about career patterns. Ignoring this difficulty, Bresard proceeds to average the four indicators of level of living, and then to average level of living with age and education to secure the "rank" shown as column (7) in Table 10. The "score" in column (8) was used as a matter of convenience for the present re-analysis. Why Bresard ranks farm laborers above laborers is not wholly clear.

One reason for presenting Bresard's data on occupational status in detail is that they throw light on the controversial question of "the empirical adequacy of . . . the distinction betwen manual and non-manual as a basis for comparative research" (to quote the terms of reference for this paper as stated in the initial conference outline). One thing is made clear by the data in Table 10. The only variable that consistently ranks all the white-collar occupation groups above each of the manual and farm occupations is educational attainment. It also happens to be the variable that shows the lowest average intercorrelation with the other variables. For education, the five Spearman rank correlations range from .49 with property to .79 with age. All the remaining ten rank correlations involving variables other than education are .82 or higher. Insistence on the white-collar vs. manual distinction, therefore, is tantamount to an insistence on level of educational attainment as the dominant, if not the sole, criterion of the status of occupations. Even so, it ignores the considerable variation of this criterion within both categories of the dichotomy.

Work with American data points to the same conclusion when a slightly different approach to the problem is taken. In the course of preparing the index of occupational SES, occasion was taken to formulate the problem as one of statistical discrimination between *persons* classified on the basis of their occupations as white-collar or manual (looking only at men, and disregarding farm occupations). Taking as the optimum cutting point on the discriminator variable the one that results in misclassifying the smallest number of individuals, it was found that the income indicator misclassified 21 per cent, the education indicator only 8 per cent. The status index, a composite of the two, misclassified 12 per cent.[29] Thus, if occupations are classified solely by an educational indicator and this indicator is dichotomized at the right point, the two categories are virtually identical to the conventional white-collar vs. manual split. There is rather less redundancy between a dichotomy based

[29] Some of these results are given in Reiss, *op. cit.*, p. 159.

on an income classification of occupations and the white-collar vs. manual split. The evidence indicated that the American public, in supplying occupational prestige ratings, attends not only to the educational level of an occupation but also to its income level, since each of the two variables has an appreciable net correlation with prestige ratings. The status index, which incorporates these relationships into its formula, is guided more by the popular view of the subject than by the theoretical or pragmatic preference of some investigators for the apparent neatness of the white-collar vs. blue-collar distinction.

The issue of the overlap of white-collar and manual occupations with respect to occupational prestige had been somewhat confused by the original presentation of the NORC results on occupational prestige,[30] where it appeared that the mean North-Hatt score for "clerical, sales, and kindred workers" was only 0.2 points higher than that for "craftsmen, foremen and kindred workers." An analysis of the occupational status index by major occupation groups showed that this was misleading: the mean status scores for both "clerical and kindred workers" and "sales workers" were clearly higher than that for "craftsmen, foremen, and kindred workers." The original NORC results for major occupation groups were slightly faulty, owing to failure to sample adequately the specific occupational titles in the major occupation groups and to weight for relative size of the occupations in terms of employment.

The question remains as to whether there is "something more" to the white-collar classification than the occupational status index picks up. One way to look at this is from the occupational prestige standpoint. Is there any *systematic* tendency for respondents to evaluate white-collar above blue-collar jobs, *beyond* the rating implicit in the education and income correlates of those jobs? The answer is *no*. This is easily seen in Table VI-1 of *Occupations and Social Status*, where one can find the "error of estimate," the status index minus the prestige rating, for each of the 45 occupations on which the status scores are based. The mean error is 0.8 points for the 24 white-collar occupations, and —0.7 for the 21 blue-collar occupations. Besides being small, these errors are in the wrong direction for us to suppose that there is a "white-collar bonus" for prestige that goes beyond the income and education components of occupational status.

Actually, the distinction between white-collar and manual is not so neat as it may seem. In the first place, a number of white-collar jobs clearly involve "manual" elements to a high degree and precious little

[30] National Opinion Research Center, "Jobs and Occupations: A Popular Evaluation," reprinted in Reinhard Bendix and Seymour M. Lipset (eds.), *Class, Status and Power* (New York: Free Press of Glencoe, 1953), pp. 411-26.

"head work." Secondly, the classification of all occupational titles as belonging to one or the other category is by no means perfectly reliable. In the example at hand, Bresard's categories include one combining shop-keepers and artisans, which would, in the American system, fall on opposite sides of the white-collar vs. manual distinction. In the American system, however, although the nominal definitions are clear enough, study of statistical discrepancies between census and Current Population Survey data reveals difficulty in identifying some kinds of proprietors and distinguishing them from self-employed workers in other occupations.

This is, therefore, a convenient point to enter my opinion that the distinction between white collar and manual is of no vast theoretical merit in and of itself. The purposes it can serve are those of very crude comparison and reconnaissance. If research workers are seriously inter-ested in socio-economic classification of occupations, they can follow the lead of Bresard in France, Blishen in Canada, and Bogue in the U.S., and subject the matter to careful investigation.

Assuming, then, that the French and the American occupational status scales are valid in their respective situations, the inter-country comparison of correlates of occupational achievement is quite straight-forward. For the problem at hand, let Y be the occupational status score of the son (respondent), X his father's score, and Z that of his father-in-law. The following zero-order correlations are obtained:

	France	*U. S.*
YX	.45	.42
YZ	.38	.41
XZ	.36	.33

From these, along with the means and standard deviations, we secure the following multiple regression equations:

$$\text{France:} \quad \hat{Y} = 15 + 0.37\,X + 0.26\,Z \quad (R = .50)$$
$$\text{U. S.:} \quad \hat{Y} = 17 + 0.36\,X + 0.35\,Z \quad (R = .51)$$

Despite the large sample sizes, none of the three differences between corresponding zero-order correlations in the two countries is significant. In France, however, r_{YX} is significantly greater than r_{YZ} although the two hardly differ in the U.S. This shows up in the differential weights for *père* and *beau-père* in the multiple regression equation.

On the face of the matter, the French have a slightly different pat-tern in which, as compared with the U.S., the status of one's marriage

partner has a little less influence in determining occupational achievement than one's father's status. The purpose of this exercise, however,
is not to reach a substantive conclusion. There are obstacles to the
comparison of the French and American data other than the use of
different occupational classifications.

In view of the necessary qualifications, the regression results probably
will not serve to resolve the controversy about the relative rigidity of
the French and American stratification systems.[31] The critic who would
take issue with the results reported here, however, has some explicitly
stated assumptions and procedures to criticize. In any event, the correlation analysis treating occupational status as a variable seems rather
more natural than an attempt to compress all the variation in occupational status into a simple white collar vs. manual dichotomy. This
exercise demonstrates that we need not resort to such drastic simplifica-
tions to secure a certain useful kind of analytical comparability.

INFERRING CONSEQUENCES OF MOBILITY

Suppose a sociologist conducted a survey of a representative sample
of married couples, ascertaining the number of children ever born to
each couple, the occupation of the husband, and that of his father. After
classifying the occupations into broad categories, he characterized the
husbands whose occupations fell in a higher category than those of their
fathers as having undergone "upward" mobility, those in a lower category as "downward" mobility, and those in the same category as "static"
or "stable." Aggregating the couples in each of these three groups and
similarly the numbers of births to the couples, he calculated the average
number of children ever born per couple and obtained the following
results:

upward	2.57
static	2.73
downward	3.01

Assuming he was confident that sampling variation could not account for
these differences, the investigator would be perfectly correct in concluding that "those who moved down are characterized by having larger
families than those who moved up."[32] Other students of social mobility

---

[31] As reviewed by Lipset and Bendix, *Social Mobility in Industrial Society,
op. cit.*, pp. 28-29, fn. 25.

[32] Jerzy Berent, "Fertility and Social Mobility," *Population Studies*, 5 (March,
1952), p. 250.

might then examine these results and present them in a summary in which they "stress the restriction of the size of the 'family of procreation' by upwardly mobile parents: . . . family size restriction is both a condition and consequence of upward mobility." [33]

The purpose of this discussion is to suggest that the inference from the observed pattern of fertility differentials by mobility group to a conclusion about "conditions" and "consequences" is not so straightforward as it might appear. The argument hinges on the issue of how a set of data like these should be analyzed. There is, however, no intention of criticizing Berent's work or, indeed, of calling into question any of his results, which he summarized quite circumspectly. On the contrary, Berent's study remains, a decade after its publication, the only worthwhile investigation of its subject. The point of view developed here is only slightly different from that of Berent, and the conclusions suggested differ from his, if at all, in respect to emphasis rather than substance. The main excuse for additional discussion of Berent's problem is that it may serve as a prototype for cases in which some quantitative characteristic or measure of behavior is the dependent variable and "mobility" is the independent variable. Indeed, the same example illustrates the problem of interpretation encountered whenever the independent variable is some kind of discrepancy measure—not only mobility between statuses held at two points in time, but also heterogamy, "cross-pressure," status disequilibrium, or like indicators encountered in stratification research and so-called relational analysis of sociometric choices.

The gist of the argument is that one is not entitled to discuss "effects" of mobility (or other status discrepancy measures) until he has established that the apparent effect cannot be due merely to a simple combination of effects of the variables used to define mobility.

Berent's data are set forth in Tables 11 and 12. The first thing one might notice in Table 12 is this. Not only do mobile couples differ in their fertility from nonmobile couples of similar origin (or destination), but also nonmobile couples differ considerably among themselves according to their class position. Thus in citing at the outset a single average for "static" couples, we suppress a good deal of variation in occupational status within this group. Aside from looking at the averages on the diagonal, it is perhaps not obvious just how to extract a conclusion from Table 12. Berent himself presents no less than four rearrangements of the data in this table in an effort to convey to the reader his interpretation of their import.

[33] Lipset and Bendix, *Social Mobility in Industrial Society, op. cit.*, p. 244, fn. 39.

TABLE 11

NUMBER OF COUPLES BY PRESENT SOCIAL CLASS AND CLASS OF
ORIGIN OF HUSBAND (BERENT DATA)

Class of Origin	Present Class				
	I	II	III	IV	All
I	65	43	23	11	142
II	38	197	150	68	453
III	37	154	431	244	866
IV	5	45	162	220	432
All	145	439	766	543	1,893

The suggestion put forward here is that the analyst should investigate
the plausibility, for the data in question, of a simple model of additive
effects. In Table 12 there are 16 combinations of an origin class with a
destination class. Now suppose that the "effect" of each combination, as
represented by mean fertility in the corresponding cell of the table, is
regarded as a simple sum of three quantities: (1) a mean effect that
applies to all couples in the sample; (2) an increment thereto for class
of origin, which applies irrespective of class of destination; and (3) an
increment for class of destination, which applies irrespective of class of
origin.

TABLE 12

MEAN NUMBER OF LIVE BIRTHS PER COUPLE, BY PRESENT SOCIAL
CLASS AND CLASS OF ORIGIN OF HUSBAND (BERENT DATA)

Class of Origin	Present Class				
	I	II	III	IV	All
I	1.74	1.79	1.96	2.00	1.81
II	2.05	2.14	2.51	2.97	2.38
III	1.87	2.01	2.67	3.69	2.81
IV	2.40	3.20	3.22	3.68	3.44
All	1.88	2.17	2.73	3.56	2.77

A calculation of effects based on this additive model appears in
Table 13. By comparing Tables 12 and 13, the reader may perhaps perceive that the model reproduces the data to a reasonably good approxi-

mation; that where sizable departures from the model calculations occur, they typically pertain to a few cases only; and that there is not much "pattern" to the deviations. If this perception is valid, there is no need to postulate any "effect" for "mobility" qua mobility. The couples in the study behaved *as if* they determined their fertility by combining the fertility pattern of their class of origin with the fertility pattern of their class of destination in a simple additive or averaging process.

TABLE 13

AVERAGE NUMBER OF LIVE BIRTHS PER COUPLE, BY PRESENT
SOCIAL CLASS AND CLASS OF ORIGIN OF HUSBAND, CALCULATED
FROM BERENT DATA USING MODEL BASED ON ASSUMPTION OF
ADDITIVE EFFECTS

Class of Origin	Present Class				
	I	II	III	IV	All
I	1.60	1.70	2.13	2.85	1.81
II	1.97	2.07	2.50	3.23	2.38
III	2.17	2.27	2.70	3.42	2.81
IV	2.59	2.70	3.12	3.85	3.44
All	1.88	2.17	2.73	3.56	2.77

Consider what happens when we aggregate the calculated means in Table 13, using the frequencies in Table 11 as weights and grouping the couples according to type of mobility, as in the initial results quoted from Berent:

	observed	calculated
upward	2.57	2.60
static	2.73	2.76
downward	3.01	2.94

If one may ignore a discrepancy no larger than 0.07, it is obvious that *"mobility" produces no differences in fertility that cannot be fully accounted for by the additive mechanism* implied by the model. From this point of view, mobility has no "consequence" to be discussed, except the consequence that the mobile couple combines the fertility patterns of two classes. The "restriction" of fertility observed in upwardly mobile couples reflects the fact that they necessarily move to a class with a prevailing level of fertility lower than that of the class whence they originated and, in some measure, take on the pattern of their class of destination. The critic could, of course, insist that it is a matter of preference (or "theory") whether the genuine differences between mobile and non-mobile couples are to be "explained" by mobility or "explained away" by a statistical model that posits separate effects for origin and destination classes. The critic, however, will then have to explain the variation in mean fertility on the diagonal of Table 12. The additive model accounts for this variation as well as for the difference between upwardly mobile, static, and downwardly mobile couples. An interpretation using the additive model thus enjoys an advantage due to the rule of parsimony over the interpretation in terms of a "mobility effect."

I have skipped over the statistical aspects of the problem, since these are treated in accessible expositions.[34] Just a few notes are set down for the interested reader. The model is as follows:

$$\bar{Y}_{ij} = \bar{Y} + a_i + b_j + e_{ij},$$

where $\bar{Y}_{ij}$ is the observed mean fertility in the combination of origin class i and destination class j; $\bar{Y}$ is the grand mean (here, 2.77) for the whole sample; a_i is the "effect," expressed as a deviation from the grand mean, of belonging to the ith origin class; b_j is the effect for the jth destination class; and e_{ij} is the "error" or "interaction" that appears as a deviation of the observed mean from the mean expected on the basis of the sum of the three effects. The normal equations whose solution yields the numerical values are the same in form as those introduced above in adjusting one set of frequencies in a mobility table to the marginal frequencies in another table.

According to the calculations made for this example, the respective (net) effects of the two bases of classification are as follows:

class	origin	destination
I	—0.58	—0.60
II	— .21	— .50
III	— .01	— .07
IV	.42	.66

Thus, for couples moving from class IV to class III, the estimate appearing in Table 13 is computed as 2.77 (grand mean) + 0.42 (origin effect) —0.07 (destination effect) = 3.12.

[34] T. P. Hill, "An Analysis of the Distribution of Wages and Salaries in Great Britain," *Econometrica*, 27 (July, 1959), pp. 355-81; K. A. Brownlee, *Statistical Theory and Methodology in Science and Engineering* (New York: John Wiley & Sons, 1960), pp. 515-21.

If the data are a probability sample from a well-defined universe, it is reasonable to carry out significance tests for the several effects that may be represented in the data. In the present example, standard formulas for analysis of variance for multiple classification with disproportionate subclass numbers were used. At a conventional .01 level of significance, the tests showed: (1) there is non-chance variation among the sub-group means in Table 12; (2) there is non-chance variation among the means calculated from the additive model in Table 13; (3) the first source of variation, though greater than or equal to the second by algebraic necessity, is not *significantly* greater; that is, *interaction* of origin with destination is not significant (whence the willingness to discount completely any specific "mobility effect"); (4) the net effects for both origin class and destination class, each independently of the other, are significant.

Substantively, this last finding suggests a way to summarize the consequence of mobility for marital fertility. As far as Berent's data are concerned, one's class of origin and one's class of destination both make a difference. The "consequence" of mobility is membership in two classes, and one's behavior is best accounted for on the assumption that one combines the patterns of both.

Only one further comment is needed to link this discussion to the theme of comparative analysis. If studies of "mobility effects" are carried out in two or more countries (say), we can compare the several sets of results by inquiring whether they agree or disagree as to the relative magnitudes of the origin and destination effects, the independent significance of each, the significance or nonsignificance of interactions, and hence the need or lack of need for an interpretation invoking "mobility effects." In making such comparisons, of course, we shall require some comparability as to definition of universe and study design. But detailed consistency between studies in procedures for delimiting "classes" is not essential, provided that we are willing to accept the procedures followed in each country as suitable for its particular situation. Thus, there is some merit to the suggestion (communicated orally by Morris Janowitz) that, in principle, it is easier to advance our knowledge of the "consequences of mobility" than to establish similarities or differences in respect to "patterns of mobility" in a comparative framework.

IN SUMMARY

One who takes up the topic of this paper should always remember the observation of Frank Knight, to this effect: A man writing on methodology is in the same position as one who plays the slide trombone; unless he is very good at it, the results are more likely to interest him than his audience. No doubt the tedious exposition has served to obscure the handful of basic propositions the paper seeks to sustain:

Section 1 ("Occupational Mobility and the Transformation of Occupation Structures"): The transformation of occupational structures in the course of economic development is accomplished by a combination of elementary demographic processes, no one or combination of which is identical with or directly translatable into the pattern, volume, or rate of occupational mobility as this may be observed in a conventional intergenerational occupational mobility table. This is not a mere methodological detail but a fundamental structural principle of social metabolism. Assumptions contrary to fact about the translatability of occupational change into occupational mobility and vice versa are most likely to produce derivations which are meaningless or, if not meaningless, simply false.

Sections 2 and 3 ("Comparisons over Time"): Intergenerational mobility, even if it is not easily related by a translation formula to the processes of occupational transformation, is worthy of study in its own right. Its effective study requires improvements in measurement techniques, classification procedures, and analytical models. Regression analysis, with occupational status appropriately scaled, is a straightforward and effective method of measuring the dependence of the son's achieved status upon his level of social origin. In the only published set of fully comparable data comprising two series separated by a sizable time span (Rogoff's data for Indianapolis, 1910 and 1940), it is remarkable that the regression relationships hardly changed during a three-decade period. There were, however, some considerable modifications of the mobility *pattern.* Using either matrix analysis or an approach involving fitting constants, one gains the strong impression that these modifications occurred in consequence of the change in "structure" represented by alterations of the frequency distributions of origin and destination classes. The analysis of occupational inheritance is much less useful, informative, and central, from the point of view of father-son correlation or mobility patterns, than has hitherto been assumed. This statement is made in awareness of recent proposals for models of social mobility that emphasize occupational inheritance, although there is no space to review these proposals here.[35]

Section 4 ("Comparisons between Places"): Interspatial comparisons

[35] Harrison C. White, "Cause and Effect in Social Mobility Tables," *Behavioral Science,* 8 (January, 1963), pp. 14-27; Leo A. Goodman, "On the Statistical Analysis of Mobility Tables," *American Journal of Sociology,* 70 (March, 1965), pp. 564-85.

of mobility patterns or "rates" are seriously compromised by noncomparability of study procedures. Nevertheless, to show that two mobility tables are not fully comparable is *not* to show that the two patterns of mobility are the same. Because interspatial comparisons almost always concern situations with different "structures," differences in mobility patterns are to be expected. The transition matrix will reflect such differences in patterns when analyzed in several alternative ways.

Section 5 ("Occupational Classification"): Interspatial comparisons of factors determining (and, for that matter, consequences of) occupational mobility will be facilitated by the adoption of comparable methodology for the measurement of occupational status. It may be possible, by this strategem, to mitigate somewhat, the fact that intrinsic structural differences render any equating of occupational categories dubious. Occupations can, for example, be scaled as to socio-economic status by procedures suggested more or less independently by three or four investigators. The regression analysis of such scale values then allows comparisons of results between communities or nations that are rather more precise than can be produced by conventional methods. In carrying out the steps implied by such an approach, there is no special value in classifying occupations as "white-collar" vs. "manual." Indeed, reliance on this kind of crude distinction can conceal more than it reveals and lead to erroneous conclusions concerning the nature of relationships.

Section 6 ("Inferring Consequences of Mobility"). Students who have sought to infer consequences of mobility for individual behavior have approached the problem in an inverted order. Instead of classifying cases by type of mobility and showing an association between mobility type and the behavior indicator (the conventional procedure), the investigator should test the sufficiency of a model that postulates simple additive effects of the two statuses whose difference serves to define mobility. When, as happens to be the case in the illustrative material presented here, such a model is sufficient to reduce the data, there is no need nor warrant to postulate a "mobility effect" as such. It is enough to observe that one or both of the two statuses (origin and destination) are associated with the dependent variable.

3

MEASURES AND EFFECTS

OF SOCIAL MOBILITY

HAROLD L. WILENSKY, *University of California, Berkeley*

SOCIAL SCIENTISTS undertaking comparative, macro-sociological analysis of "whole societies," of an institutional sphere (the economy), or even of selected aspects of stratification take on a heavy burden. Weaknesses of data and problems of method loom so large that the web of theory they spin is seldom entangled in any intimate way with systematic, reliable evidence. Nowhere is this more true than in the comparative analysis of the incidence, sources, and effects of social mobility, as the contributions to this book make abundantly clear. This chapter adds emphasis to the several notes of caution running through the book, especially in the chapters by Duncan, Ramsøy, Moore, and Sjoberg; suggests some directions for research implied by the methodological troubles; and reports the results of factor analyses of 20 measures of "Objective Mobility and Economic Deprivation" and 26 measures of "Mobility Orientation" carried out to assure the coherence, economy, and independence of mobility measures in a larger study of "Work, Careers, and Leisure Style." [1] I shall give special attention to problems of concept and method in tackling the social and psychological effects of mobility. I shall concentrate on two issues that concern students of modernization —how to specify the content of various social discontinuities presumably involved, and how economic, political, and organizational contexts shape responses to these discontinuities. Although a detailed treatment of sev-

[1] A program of research on sources of social integration made possible by the generous support of the National Institute of Mental Health (M-2209, 1958-63), the University of Michigan, the University of California, and the Center for Advanced Study in the Behavioral Sciences. The aim of the larger study is to discover those aspects of work and leisure that bind individuals and groups to community and society and those that foster alienation and estrangement. This paper is based on a forthcoming book. I am grateful to John C. Scott and Michael T. Aiken for research assistance.

eral ideas about occupations and mobility will be necessary, I hope to strike a balance between completeness and specificity, on the one hand, and economy and theoretical relevance, on the other.

SOURCES OF ERROR AND THEIR IMPLICATIONS

Duncan's paper and others in this volume point to sources of grievous error in the current comparisons of rates of intergenerational occupational mobility from which some students of stratification have inferred international similarities or differences. These cannot be overemphasized. It will be useful to repeat them, elaborate them, and examine the moral to be drawn. Such methodological difficulties apply not only to studies from diverse countries and time periods but also to studies within one country in one period and to countries at various levels of development.

1. *The categories compared are both heterogeneous and non-comparable.* Received labels for occupational information are, like racial stereotypes, convenient and misleading. It is no news that census-type categories encompass vast variations in rights and duties on and off the job. For example, the U.S. Census "Professional, Technical, and Kindred" covers authors and draftsmen, strip tease artists and mechanical engineers; "Managers, Officials, and Proprietors" embraces the credit man and the political appointee at the board of elections, the entrepreneur of the hot-dog stand and the big business executive; "Clerical and Kindred" includes bank teller and mail carrier; "Sales Workers," newsboy and ad man, big-ticket salesman and the lady at the notions counter.[2] I suppose it is a tribute to sociological zeal that some students have

[2] Standard sources of occupational information—the Census Occupational and Industrial Classification, the *Dictionary of Occupational Titles*, and vocational guidance literature—typically give a better account of "skill," training, and physical task than of any of the following sociological variables: relations with clients, customers, or colleagues; off-work career-determined obligations and hence hours of labor; administrative and financial duties of non-administrative personnel; personnel work of those not defined as personnel workers; the manager's relations with his bosses; the internal and external intelligence functions served by a variety of specialists; quasi-legal activities; degree of discipline or freedom. Even homogeneous occupational groups in one type of organization display vastly varied work routines. See, e.g., the excellent account of the controller's position in large multi-plant companies (e.g., "keeping score," "attention-directing," "problem-solving" and the varied work relations implied in Herbert A. Simon, *et al.*, *Centralization and Decentralization in Organizing the Controller's Department* (New York: Controllers Institute, 1954). Cf. the varied jobs and functions of labor's staff experts, described in Harold L. Wilensky, *Intellectuals in Labor Unions: Organizational Pressures on Professional Roles* (New York: Free Press of Glencoe, 1956), Parts II and IV.

begun to classify occupations in other terms—Miller and Swanson used bureaucratic vs. entrepreneurial to show variations in child-training practices and philosophies; [3] Reiss used Carr-Saunders's classification of professions to show that limited mobility into and within the Census "professions" characterizes established professions (which constitute a minority) much more than new, semi, would-be, or marginal professions; [4] Kerr and Siegel explained the propensity to strike in terms of degree of physical and social isolation of industries and occupations; [5] Hatt used the concept situs.[6] Perhaps it is time to go beyond these forays and launch a major assault against received labels, even in mass surveys, and work out a set of categories that are more relevant to an understanding of both social class and occupational groups.[7]

In short, in modern societies, to say "white collar" or "working class" is to obscure most of what is central to the experience of the person and the structure of society. To say "professional, technical, and kindred" captures more of social life but not much more. "Lawyer" and "engineer" move us closer to social reality, for these men develop quite different styles of life, rooted in diverse professional schools, tasks, work schedules, and organizational contexts. To say "independent practitioner" is to say even more, and finally, to particularize the matter with "solo lawyer" vs. "firm lawyer" is to take account of the sharp contrasts in recruitment base (social origins, religion, quality of professional training), career pattern and rewards which divide the two.

That these comments apply to international comparisons is evident in Ramsøy's demonstration that "percentage of the labor force in agricultural occupations" is a poor indicator of "modern" influences. Farm boys in one rural area may be oriented to urban occupations and culture;

[3] Daniel R. Miller and Guy E. Swanson, *The Changing American Parent* (New York: John Wiley & Sons, 1958). Cf. Lewis Corey, *The Crisis of the Middle Class* (New York: Covici, Friede, 1935), an early discussion of "new" vs. "old" middle classes.

[4] "The range in the percentage with stable attachments among professional status groups in fact is greater than that observed when the percentage for all professionals is compared with that for any of the eleven major occupation groups. . . ." Albert J. Reiss, Jr., "Occupation Mobility of Professional Workers," *American Sociological Review*, 20 (December, 1955), p. 699.

[5] Clark Kerr and A. Siegel, "The Interindustry Propensity to Strike—An International Comparison," in Arthur Kornhauser, Robert Dubin and Arthur M. Ross (eds.), *Industrial Conflict* (New York: McGraw-Hill, 1954), pp. 189-212.

[6] Paul K. Hatt, "Occupation and Social Stratification," *American Journal of Sociology*, 55 (May, 1950), p. 539.

[7] See Harold L. Wilensky, "Labor and Leisure: Intellectual Traditions," *Industrial Relations*, 1 (February, 1962), pp. 1-12. Cf. discussions of styles of life within the "working class" by S. M. Miller, Lee Rainwater, and Gerald Handel in Arthur B. Shostak and William Gomberg (eds.), *Blue-Collar World* (Englewood Cliffs, N.J.: Prentice-Hall, 1964).

those in another may not.[8] If census categories are heterogeneous in rich countries of the social-science-conscious West, the same categories applied to stratification in the new nations must constitute a veritable mine field of error. An increase in the size of the "middle class" is often said to be essential to economic growth and political stability in less developed countries. But surely a large number of small-scale traders, under-employed lawyers, professors, doctors, and civil servants have an effect sharply different from that of an equal number of secondary school teachers, engineers, technicians, and agronomists.[9] Some minimum level of occupational specificity seems necessary in an analysis of stratification systems and modernization.

2. *The samples are non-comparable,* especially when we compare intergenerational mobility among populations drastically differing in age distribution, and *sampling error is large,* especially when we compare rates of movement from one stratum to another. Here, Duncan has said everything that must be said. It should be noted that when we increase specificity to overcome the problem of heterogeneous categories, we generally intensify the problem of sampling error; without very large samples, too few respondents are available to fill meaningful social categories.

3. *Measures in diverse studies are non-comparable.* It is not trivial that the parental base from which men move is tapped by questions variously phrased: father's occupation or line of work, father's main job, father's best job, etc., "most of his working life," or when you "were about 16," "in your 'teens'," "growing up" or during some indefinite time span. And the whole discussion of intergenerational mobility founders fatally on the fact that both the respondent and his father are on the move (the frequency of job change doubtless varying by level and rate of economic growth and, again, by the age of the population sampled). Which of the dozen or so jobs each man holds in four or five decades of his worklife are to be compared? Perhaps the chief contribution of labor market studies is to emphasize the astonishing amount of shifting across industrial and occupational lines within one worklife. Since the total mobility pattern of father and of son alike often involves many ups and downs, it seems arbitrary to single out one job, especially the one the respondent happens to recall or chooses to report. Even more precision in questioning cannot overcome the essentially arbitrary

[8] Natalie Rogoff Ramsøy, Chapter VII in this volume. Cf. Wilbert E. Moore on "agriculture," and Gideon Sjoberg on "rural-urban" migration, Chapters VI and VIII.
[9] Cf. Edward Shils, "Political Development in the New States, I and II," *Comparative Studies in Society and History,* II (1960), pp. 267-292 and 379-411, and Lester Seligman, Chapter XII in this volume.

classification involved. (For an effort to increase precision see Appendix, pp. 133-140 below.)

4. *Data-gathering efficiency varies greatly.* Anyone who has trained interviewers to obtain occupational information knows that interviewer performance, combined with ambiguities and variation in concepts and measures, can produce large differences in reported mobility. Some evidence suggests that the more precise the questions and the more efficient the interviewers, the more self-employment, moonlighting, and hours of work show up. I would attribute the Current Population Report's "excess" of entrepreneurs, noted by Duncan, to superior field operations. Similarly, the "upswing in moonlighting" reported in both academic and popular articles plainly reflects improved enumeration procedures. The national rate of 5 per cent (number of persons who hold two or more jobs in the survey week divided by the number of employed), reported in surveys from 1950 to 1959, is compared with earlier estimates of 3 per cent from surveys of January 1943 and July 1946. As they assert that Americans are responding to the new leisure by filling the gap with feverish economic activity, interpreters of the American scene remain oblivious to the Bureau of the Census's own warnings about the non-comparability of these figures. All these estimates may be low, and whether the rate is going up or down is unknown. Hours of work may also be understated and the trend distorted.[10]

The combination of obstacles is so formidable that I wonder if anything can be said with confidence about rates of intergenerational occupational mobility and their trend. I agree with the judgment that our picture of mobility rates by stratum, country, region, or period may be less a reflection of reality than a spurious product of heterogeneous and non-comparable occupational categories, non-comparable samples and measures, and variations in field work efficiency. Although Duncan's call for "rigidly standardized procedures from the initial collection to the final tabulation of data" may be utopian, we must at least inject more caution than usual into discussions of those rates.

If our interest is theoretical, however, and we do not try to measure population parameters or gauge trends in rates of intergenerational occupational mobility, but instead aim to delineate the most important types of mobility, individual and social, and discover their sources and effects, then much can be done. The problems of heterogeneity of the bases from which men move can be overcome, the sampling problem

[10] For an assessment of evidence on trends and rates and an explanation of multiple job-holding, see Harold L. Wilensky, "The Moonlighter: A Product of Relative Deprivation," *Industrial Relations,* 3 (October, 1963), pp. 105-124. For similar analysis of hours of work, see Wilensky, "The Uneven Distribution of Leisure: The Impact of Economic Growth on 'Free Time,'" *Social Problems,* 9 (Summer, 1961), pp. 32-56.

can be minimized, measurement and interview performance greatly improved.

1. *The platform: family of origin vs. one's own past.* Let us make two assumptions about modern and modernizing societies: First, position in the economic order is sufficiently distinct to exert an independent influence on behavior, so that the effects of occupational mobility may be substantially independent of or at least different from those of other forms of social mobility. Second, while the demands of modern technology impose no rigid mold on a culture, all modern societies face similar problems and their solutions to these problems are similar. For instance, every industrial system requires some competition for occupational position on the basis of criteria relevant to the performance of the role, as well as some system of special reward for scarce talents and skills.[11] It is plausible to assume that these universal structural features of modern economies foster similar mobility ideologies, that in the most diverse political and cultural contexts, doctrines of economic individualism take root: increasing portions of the population in modernizing sectors believe that everyone has an equal opportunity to achieve a better job, everyone has the moral duty to try to get ahead, if a man fails it is at least partly his own fault, and so on. Such notions are widespread in the U.S., again in its most modern sectors, but they appear in countries where the welfare state is more popular, too.[12]

If these assumptions are correct, then students of the effects of social mobility might divert some of the effort now devoted to measuring intergenerational occupational mobility to the study of worklife mobility. For both theoretical and empirical reasons, we can assume that job patterns in one lifetime are more fateful than patterns of intergenerational mobility. Where mobility rates are high and a success ideology prevails, the coercive comparisons men make in evaluating their class situation vary by age, and the comparison with the father may be relevant only for young men; it may be irrelevant for most of the labor force, for most social behavior. Young men have scanty labor market experience; they have not been in the labor force long enough to feel a sense of failure or success, or to be greatly affected by its status implications. Further, they are fresh from the controls of the family of origin; "mobile" young men fear coming out second best in a comparison

[11] Wilbert E. Moore, *Industrial Relations and the Social Order*, rev. ed. (New York: Macmillan, 1951), pp. 426-427, and *Industrialization and Labor: Social Aspects of Economic Development* (Ithaca, N. Y.: Cornell University Press, 1951); Harold L. Wilensky and Charles N. Lebeaux, *Industrial Society and Social Welfare* (New York: Free Press paperback, 1965), pp. 44 ff.

[12] The data in Alex Inkeles, "Industrial Man: The Relation of Status to Experience, Perception, and Value," *American Journal of Sociology*, 65 (January, 1960), pp. 1-31, are consistent but the argument should still be considered speculative.

with their fathers. As they grow older, however—even by the time they are 30 years old—the intergenerationally mobile men adapt to the culture of their class of destination (or occupation, community, or country of destination): the success ideology holds that what they are has little to do with their fathers' status; less and less do they remind themselves or are asked by their peers, "What did your father do?" The important comparisons are made with their own pasts; and consequent interpretations of success or failure are made in the context of contemporary reference groups.[13]

This argument can best be asssessed by studies that bring together data on worklife mobility, intergenerational mobility, and their social and psychological correlates in societies whose cultures support economic individualism in varying degrees. The relative effects of the two types of mobility might be compared in allegedly collectivist contexts and in America, where doctrines of private property, the free market, and minimum government presumably have their strongest grip and reinforce the success ideology. If in societies at high levels of economic development, worklife mobility does not have more effect than intergenerational mobility among men who have been in the labor market for a decade or so, then my assumptions are doubtful.

2. *The platform: occupational origin vs. other clues to social position and group life.* If we want to consider the base of departure as a determinant of later behavior—that is, analyze outcomes firmly anchored in early socialization—then comparing a man's current occupational stratum with the stratum of his father at some arbitrary point in the latter's career may be the least effective alternative in terms of theoretical rele-

---

[13] Pursuing these hypotheses, a study of class ideologies among 495 factory workers found that slipping from a better job in their own past shaped attitudes of these men much more than moving down from their father's status. Harold L. Wilensky and Hugh Edwards, "The Skidder: Ideological Adjustments of Downwardly Mobile Workers," *American Sociological Review*, 24 (April, 1959), pp. 215-231. Cf. W. Read, "Some Factors Affecting Upward Communication at Middle-Management Levels in Industrial Organizations" (unpublished Ph.D. thesis, University of Michigan, 1959), which reports a correlation of + .41 (p < .01) between upward worklife mobility and holding back "problem" information from the boss among 52 middle-level executives (mean age 37), but no correlation for intergenerational mobility. Few studies of the impact of mobility have brought worklife and intergenerational data together. Even the mere description of worklife mobility is rare. In view of the uncommon agreement that the study of types and rates of mobility is crucial to an understanding of modern society, it is remarkable that detailed work histories that cover a decade or more have been reported in only about a dozen American studies. Of these, the Six City Survey of Occupational Mobility contains the most adequate data and most extensive and representative sample. For the list see Harold L. Wilensky, "Work, Careers, and Social Integration," *International Social Science Journal*, 42 (Fall, 1960), pp. 553-554. More recently, see Gladys L. Palmer, *et al.*, *The Reluctant Job Changer* (Philadelphia: University of Pennsylvania Press, 1962).

vance and accuracy. Other patterns of experience involving social discontinuity and contact should receive more attention. For some purposes—for instance explaining ideology or cultural values and beliefs—the educational level attained by the father or mother, their ethnic or racial origins, or the mother's religious preference (assuming the mother is the chief socializing agent here) may be far more important. And, following the argument above concerning the increasing importance of adult experiences, the respondent's level and quality of formal education, and the job training and indoctrination of a workplace or occupational group, count for more than "intergenerational mobility."

Bringing into view these other platforms for social mobility—ethnicity and religion (aspects of "descent" that can be changed through affiliation and assimilation), level and type of formal education, past jobs and job patterns—has two great advantages: it taps group experience more directly and it greatly simplifies measurement problems. As take-off points for mobility, all these variables are clearer in time order than intergenerational occupational mobility, and they can be tapped in survey interviews with greater reliability and adequacy. The mother's religious preference, about how many years of school the father completed, the respondent's national or racial origin, his religious preference and whether it has changed, his education, current job, even his job history and the record of residential shifts—all these are subject to less error in measurement and far less conceptual confusion than intergenerational occupational mobility.

In short, the problems of method plaguing this area—heterogeneous and non-comparable occupational categories, non-comparable samples and measures, and variations in fieldwork efficiency—can be partly overcome by giving attention to worklife mobility, and by broadening the analysis to include status shifts in institutional areas other than the economy.[14]

3. *Minimizing the problem of sample and subclass size.* If our prob-

[14] In a regression analysis of 17 predictors of exposure to books, magazines, newspapers and television, a sensitive measure of intergenerational mobility (see Chart 1) was less important than these variables: (1) an index of level and quality of the respondent's formal education—by far the single most important predictor of "brow level"; (2) an index of "generation American, religion, and status of religious preference" (which permits comparison of established Protestant elites, established or rising Catholic populations, and Catholics of more recent vintage); (3) work context (size of workplace and self-employment status). Intergenerational mobility ranked far behind these simple attributes of origin, status, and group affiliation—ninth as a predictor of exposure to highbrow print and television, twelfth as a predictor of exposure to the shoddiest programming on television. See Harold L. Wilensky, "Mass Society and Mass Culture: Interdependence or Independence," *American Sociological Review*, 29 (April, 1964), pp. 184-185, in which the case for the theoretical importance of these bases of social differentiation relative to occupational stratum and stratum of origin is also discussed.

lem is not to estimate rates of mobility but instead to gauge the effect of various types of cultural and social discontinuity, the problem of sampling error can be minimized. Suppose our hypothesis is that where the technical and social organization of work provides an orderly career in which one job normally leads to another, related in function and higher in status, then work attachments are strong, work is integrated with the rest of life, and ties to community and society are solid. Conversely, if the work history is punctuated by unexpected periods of unemployment, and disorderly shifts among jobs, occupations, and industries, then work attachments are weak, work sharply split from leisure, and ties to community and society uncertain.[15]

Sampling error is not so devastating if we view each sample as a separate test of the hypothesis and merely assure a reasonable approximation to a measure of orderliness of career in diverse studies. If social discontinuity rooted in economic change is linked to a withdrawal from community life, this will be evident among unemployed workers in Marienthal, Austria, or Greenwich, England, employed workers with chaotic work histories in Detroit, lawyers without clients in Nazi Germany, displaced or prematurely retired workers in Chicago, unemployed rural migrants in urban slums anywhere.

NINETEEN IDEAS BEHIND THE LABEL "SOCIAL MOBILITY"

What are the possible measures of social mobility to consider when we deal with its effects, individual and social, which can be elicited in interviews? In the labor-leisure study, I had the opportunity to delineate several types of mobility and tap all of them in one very detailed interview.[16] The interview covered intergenerational and intragenera-

---

[15] Data in Harold L. Wilensky, "Orderly Careers and Social Participation: The Impact of Work History on Social Integration in the Middle Mass," *American Sociological Review*, 26 (August, 1961), pp. 521-539, support this hypothesis.

[16] Mobility hypotheses requiring specification of the types appear in Harold L. Wilensky, "Life Cycle, Work Situation, and Participation in Formal Associations," in R. W. Kleemeier (ed.), *Aging and Leisure* (New York: Oxford University Press, 1961) and "Work, Careers, and Social Integration," *op cit.* The samples include 1,354 men ranging from highly-educated professors, lawyers, and engineers and executives matched for age and income, through a cross-section of the lower middle class and upper working class (the "middle mass") of the Detroit area, and down through 186 men unemployed and on relief. The analysis, in process, is based on interviews with probability samples or universes of six professional groups (100 solo lawyers; 107 firm lawyers in the 19 Detroit firms with 10 or more partners and associates; 31 professors at "Church University"; 68 professors at "Urban University"; 91 engineers at "Unico," 93 at "Diversico"—generally research and development specialists, supervisors, or executives); a probability sample of the middle mass

tional movement as well as aspirations and expectations for movement in all systems of ranking—occupation in workplace and society, education, income, descent (ethnic-religious origin), marriage, and to a lesser extent, resident. The relevant questions are reproduced in the Appendix below.

I felt when I began this study that direction and distance of occupational mobility were not the same as the orderliness of the job pattern, and the latter was not the sheer number of job changes; that marrying up was not the same as increasing one's income; that projecting aspirations on to one's children was not the same as retaining them for oneself; that we could not lump together the worker whose ambitions are limited to the next step in the workplace hierarchy and the worker whose gaze is directed toward higher goals in other settings—independent proprietorship or further training for a semi-professional career. But I was not at all sure that my respondents experienced it that way. And no study can report data on all these dimensions; time and space run out. Thus, for the limited purpose of establishing coherence, independence, and economy of my measures, I combined all samples and carried out two factor analyses—one of objective mobility and economic deprivation, the other of mobility orientation. The results are summarized in Charts 1 and 2.[17]

Since the factors are orthogonal, the factor loadings indicate the correlation of the particular item with the cluster of items defining the factor. Thus "much intergenerational occupational mobility," with a loading of .927, is the best clue to "intergenerational climbing of the couple (occupation and education)," Factor 1 in Chart 1. "Defining items" are items whose factor loadings rank high and have low loadings

---

(N=678); and, as a sharp contrast, two samples of underdogs, 81 Negro and 105 white, who were severely deprived. The interviews took place in the first half of 1960. Only males who were in the labor force, 55 years old or younger, and currently or previously married were interviewed. All the professionals had college degrees. The special selection criteria are described in Wilensky, "The Uneven Distribution of Leisure," *op. cit.*, p. 38; "Orderly Careers," *op. cit.*, pp. 529-530; and "The Moonlighter," *op. cit.*, pp. 106-108.

[17] The two matrices of intercorrelations among 20 objective mobility variables and 26 mobility orientation variables were factor analyzed separately by the method of principal axes. Factors were rotated according to Henry F. Kaiser's varimax criterion. *Psychometrica*, 23 (September, 1958), pp. 187-200. Because missing data ranged from none on "orderliness of work history" to 1170 on "highest occupational level achieved by children," the computer program was designed to take account only of the data available; no arbitrary assignment of responses "not ascertained" to the mean was necessary. In interpretation, loadings below 25 per cent of the average communality of the factors were ignored. I am grateful to James S. Lingoes and William L. Hays of the University of Michigan for statistical consultation.

CHART 1

A FACTOR ANALYSIS OF 20 ASPECTS OF OBJECTIVE MOBILITY AND
ECONOMIC DEPRIVATION AMONG 1,354 MEN *

Per cent of variance explained	Factor	Factor Loadings

26   1. *Intergenerational climbing of couple (occupation † and education)*

         Defining items: 1. Much upward intergenerational occupational mobility (respondent's father's stratum → respondent's stratum using a 5-point scale from much up to much down.†   .927

                             2. Much upward intergenerational occupational mobility for wife (her father's stratum → respondent's stratum; 5-point scale)—i.e., R married down.   .571

                             3. Much upward educational mobility (father's educational level → respondent's, 7-point scale from less than father to five steps more than father). See Factor 8.   .518

         Related items: 4. Most orderly work history.   .398

                             5. High educational level of R compared with wife's—i.e., R married down.   .364

27   2. *Many jobs and employers*

         Defining items: 1. High number of jobs in work history.   .903

                             2. High number of different employers.   .843

         Related items: 3. Highly fluctuating job pattern. (Many ups and downs; some; stable. 416 cases of "only upward" and "only downward" were treated as missing data.)   .388

                             4. Least orderly work history.   .262

12   3. *Little fluctuation in worklife*

         Defining item: 1. Job pattern shows few or no ups and downs.   .773

         Related item: 2. No on-the-job training experience.   .282

6   4. *Non-entrepreneurial worklife*

         Defining item: 1. Self-employed for a low percentage of worklife.   .585

CHART 1 (*Cont.*)

Per cent of variance explained	Factor	Factor Loadings
12	5. *Disorderly worklife with a high rate of recent income loss*	
	Defining items: 1. Least orderly worklife.	.635
	2. Least gain or most loss in family income 1955-59 (8-point scale from decrease of over 50 per cent to increase of more than 150 per cent).	.443
6	6. *Job-relevant self-improvement leisure*	
	Defining items: 1. No on-the-job training experience.	.441
	2. Has had job-relevant self-improvement training or activity off work.	.428
4	7. *Upward mobility involving social and cultural discontinuity (ethnic-religious, neighborhood)*	
	Defining items: 1. Much upward religious mobility (mother to R, 5-point scale from down two steps in status of religious preference to up two).	.303
	2. High residential mobility. (Low mean years per house in the metropolitan area now lived in. Data on inter-city moves not obtained.)	.278
	3. Married up ethnically.	.269
9	8. *Educational mix-up* (complex factor dropped)	
	Defining items: 1. Low education level of R compared with wife's—R married up educationally (loads .364 on Factor 1 and slightly on Factors 2-5).	.564
	2. Low educational level of R compared with father—R is educational skidder (loads .518 on Factor 1 and slightly on others).	.434

° For explanation see text and footnote 17.

† Where occupational prestige was at issue for measures in Charts 1 and 2, all jobs were coded in four strata—high non-manual, low non-manual, high manual, low manual. See Wilensky, "Orderly Careers . . . ," *op. cit.*, p. 524. In comparing fathers and sons, I used the respondent's modal job class (the job held for the longest period since 1945) and the respondent's father's "occupation" (job held for two or more years while the respondent was a teen-ager, a crucial period for his life chances).

elsewhere; they may be taken as phenomena that go together in the mobility experience of these 1,354 men and are independent of other factors. "Related items" rank high and make sense, but the loadings are either too weak or appear on two or more factors; these phenomena are sufficiently associated with the defining items to be taken as subsidiary meanings of the factor, but they may measure other phenomena as well.

The results affirm the need for diversified analysis of social mobility fitting the diversity of modern life. They underscore the wondrous variety of phenomena encompassed by "mobility," placing intergenerational occupational change in perspective as one among a dozen types of movement. Momentous changes in status and aspiration occur in adult life, whatever the parental base of departure. The results suggest that in approaching adult "careers," whether we use simple concepts and measures (frequency of job change, entrepreneurship in the work history) or more sophisticated concepts and measures (number of ups and downs, orderliness of the job pattern, degree of cultural and social discontinuity)—our tasks of measurement will not be so horrendous as those we confront in handling intergenerational mobility.

Finally, the two factor analyses provide leads for both measurement and theory in stratification research. Some indicators of mobility that are typically lumped together are in reality discrete and some that are usually separated belong together. The factors also suggest substantive conclusions concerning the workings of a modern stratification system. In the rest of this paper, I shall interpret the main results of the charts, mention patterns of mobility unrelated to these results, including types so difficult to measure that they might well be abandoned in empirical research, and explore the implications for our picture of stratification in modern societies. I assume that these data, from American men in a modern metropolis, are relevant to our understanding of modernizing societies, for the technological, economic, and demographic changes that underlie mobility patterns in the rich countries take place in the rising poor countries. Although cultural context shapes the effects of mobility patterns on social life, and their incidence varies, the major patterns themselves are probably similar at similar levels of growth.

Interpreting the objective mobility results

Chart 1 and other data not here reported suggest a consolation prize theory of social mobility. The ladders up which a man can climb in modern society are so numerous that falling behind on one or falling off another may neither cause an irrevocable loss of social position nor

yield much sense of deprivation; some other basis of social differentiation will provide a new start. The following signs of the consolation
prize in action appear in these data:

1. *Occupational mobility between generations and educational mobility between generations go together, but intergenerational skidders
marry up.* Factors 1 and 8 indicate that men who achieve less education
than their fathers or who stay on the same level (which in America
means losing out) tend to marry women with superior education from
families with occupational status higher than their own.

2. *During the worklife, diverse economic opportunities appear; many,
perhaps most men who miss one receive another.* In Chart 1 the following patterns of opportunity tend to be independent of one another: holding onto a job for a long time; experiencing few ups and downs in
occupational status; having entrepreneurial opportunities; moving
through an orderly, predictable career (a large portion of the worklife
in jobs that are functionally related and hierarchically arranged); and
leisure mobility (self-improvement that pays off).

Chart 1 contains some guides for students of the psychological and
social correlates of mobility. Large differences between the mobile and
the non-mobile in attitudes and behavior presumably rooted in cultural
and social discontinuity are seldom reported in the literature. One
reason is that much of mobility is in no sense discontinuous—that is,
the breaks in social relations or the changes in social position we
ordinarily measure are neither unpredictable nor sudden; and often
they involve no disruption of ties to kin and friends. To analyze the
impact of the mobility that does involve discontinuity, we should look
to the orderliness of the work history (Factor 5), the number of times
a man has crossed broad occupational strata in his worklife (Factor 3),
blocked mobility strivings,[18] and finally the cluster of discontinuities represented by intermarriage, changes in the status of religious preference,
and shifts in residence (Factor 7).[19] Note that the degree to which a

[18] Suffering blocked mobility vs. never having been thwarted in one's mobility
strivings is a dichotomous variable unrelated to anything in Chart 1, i.e., it loaded
on no factor. Men in the blocked mobility category tried unsuccessfully to enter a
different line of work with higher status or to go into business for themselves; or
they voluntarily undertook self-improvement activity relevant to a white-collar job
but never made it out of the working class. This is another significant worklife pattern seldom considered in studies of mobility.

[19] In a separate analysis of objective participation data, change in religious
preference (disregarding the direction of change) was included as a measure of
fluid social relations. It turned out to be related (.243) to "kin-church avoidance"—
a factor defined by infrequent contact with relatives and little or no attendance at
church. Also, an analysis of assimilation among professionals revealed that as minor-
ity-group men head toward good jobs in Protestant work contexts, they shuck off
both religious identity and minority friends and relatives. (Harold L. Wilensky and

work history fits the model of "career"—orderly rather than chaotic job sequences—is quite independent of the sheer number of jobs. and employers represented. A highly fluctuating job pattern, however, is slightly related (.388) to a pattern with many jobs and employers.

If we seek to locate orderly patterns of mobility and explore their meaning, we can use the obverse of these measures—orderly careers, the absence of ethnic-religious mobility, and so on. Beyond this, the data contain some interesting sidelights. In so far as upward occupational and educational mobility is gratifying, the gratification is doubled, for the intergenerational climbers carry their upwardly mobile women with them (see Factor 1). That mobile men tend to marry mobile women moving in the same direction should at least ease the strain of their journey.[20]

The appearance of entrepreneurial work history as a single item defining Factor 4 in Chart 1 is consistent with a pattern of findings in my study: the persistence, importance, and discrete social character of self-employment. No analysis of American society that writes off the free enterprise ideology—the unique emphasis on private property, the free market, and minimum government—can do justice to the work experience of the American population. Despite a decline in self-employment as a proportion of the labor force, the chance to go into business for oneself, however risky, is still widespread. The supporting doctrines of economic individualism cannot be dismissed as anachronistic, slated

---

Jack Ladinsky, 'From Religious Community to Occupational Group: Structural Assimilation Among Professors, Lawyers, and Engineers," paper presented at the annual meeting of the American Sociological Association, Montreal, September, 1964.)

Together these results suggest that unstable religious preference is at once an expression of status striving, an escape from lowly family origin, and part of a pattern of weak but wide-ranging attachments. Further confirmation is in a study of the religious vitality of undergraduates at the University of Michigan, done under the direction of Guy E. Swanson. Students whose mothers had changed denominations (mother's preference vis à vis maternal grandfather's) scored lower on religious vitality (including church attendance) than students with stable religious preferences, especially if they grew up in entrepreneurial families. The changers among these mothers had overwhelmingly shifted from Lutheran and other low-status Protestant denominations to Episcopalian and other high-status denominations. See Harry C. Dillingham, "Occupational Bureaucratization, Denominational Structure, and Religious Vitality," unpublished Ph.D. dissertation, University of Michigan, 1961, Chapter 3 and Table 75.

[20] If mobility from an unequal base imposes a strain (e.g., uneasy relations outside the nuclear family), then migration may ease it (the couple can move away from in-laws and friends of disparate status and seek a more comfortable identity, often favoring the partner with highest origin). A measure of "similarity of social origin of husband and wife," devised to explore this idea, is independent of the entire mobility matrix. Further analysis was not pursued.

quickly to give way to a "social ethic;" they reflect a basic reality in
the economy. In the labor-leisure samples taken together (this includes
men only a few years in the labor force—middle mass, aged 21-29—and
excludes anyone over 55), 30 per cent have at one time or another, now
or in the past, been in business for themselves. Of those men in the
middle mass who are not now self-employed, 16 per cent have in the
past worked on their own. Other studies have reported similar results.[21]
It is safe to say that the more detailed and reliable our work history
interview, the more self-employment we uncover. There is no doubt that
at least a quarter of the urban labor force has had a taste of the free
enterprising life.

The decline of self-employment has been exaggerated and its meaning
missed. First, the push is mainly out of farming; one in three non-farm
residents in the U.S. was farm-reared. Thus, even if urban self-employment *were* disappearing, many millions who have learned entrepreneurial values and interests in early life would remain with us for
decades to come. Second, the decline of *urban* entrepreneurial opportunities is a myth. The proportion of self-employed in the non-agricultural labor force has remained steady at about 10 per cent for almost
a quarter century; it was 10.6 per cent in 1940, 10.5 per cent in 1960,
and 9.7 per cent in 1963. This actually meant an increase in the number of self-employed—from 4.59 million in 1940 to 6.20 million in 1963.[22]
Put another way, our economy has cast up a large minority who were
brought up in entrepreneurial families, or themselves have had (or will
have) a taste of entrepreneurship before their worklives are over, or
both.

To attempt entrepreneurship is to move in a very special labor
market. The self-employment histories of men in the labor-leisure samples show that most salaried and wage employees remain employees,
while the self-employed alternate between bosses and business: of all

---

[21] Of the manual workers in a cross-section of household heads in Oakland,
California, whose work histories were gathered in 1949-50, 67 per cent reported that
they had thought of going into business for themselves, over 40 per cent had made
some effort to start a business of their own, and 22 per cent had in fact been self-
employed. Seymour M. Lipset and Reinhard Bendix, *Social Mobility in Industrial
Society* (Berkeley: University of California Press, 1959), pp. 102 ff. This study
analyzes lifetime work histories of 935 heads of families in Oakland, a probability
sample of segments of blocks (17 highest—and lowest—SES tracts were omitted;
non-completion rate for the remaining 55 was about 18 per cent). Previous self-
employment includes both farm and non-farm jobs.

[22] *Sixteenth Census of the United States, 1940, Population, Volume III, The
Labor Force, Part 1, United States Summary*, Table IV, p. 7, and *Statistical Ab-
stracts of the United States, 1964*, Table 309. Cf. Simon Kuznets, "Income Distribution and Changes in Consumption," in Hoke S. Simpson (ed.), *The Changing
American Population* (New York: Institute of Life Insurance, 1962), Table 2, p. 26.

those self-employed now, a whopping 94 per cent once worked for someone else, but of those not now self-employed only 19 per cent were ever self-employed.

The "free" professions provide a variation on this theme; they nevertheless illustrate the occupational concentration of self-employment. Take lawyers. Solo practitioners are by definition entrepreneurs—and their biographies show that four in five have been self-employed for more than two-fifths of their careers. But three in four of the firm lawyers have also been self-employed at one time or another—42 per cent, at least two-fifths of the worklife. Thus, in a profession two-thirds of whose members are solo practitioners, even "bureaucratic" men are likely to have worked on their own sometime in the past, or they will before they retire. In contrast, only four of our 99 academic men, two of our 184 engineers, and 19 of the 186 men on relief have ever worked on their own. *Brief attempts at self-employment are apparently confined largely to the middle mass, especially its white-collar segment* (one in six of the salaried white-collar men still in their twenties have already tried it), *or to professionals in occupations with a substantial solo segment.* Many millions move in and out of entrepreneurial jobs, but together they comprise a world apart from the majority, who are lifetime salaried employees.[23]

Finally, this analysis of dimensions of objective mobility suggests several concepts whose measures should be dropped. In my opinion, the *number of "occupations"* in the worklife (as distinct from jobs and employers) cannot be coded with sufficient reliability to consider seriously. Based on a 15 per cent check (102 cases) of the middle-mass sample, the code for number of occupations has only 79 per cent reliability; the errors were concentrated in the upper working class. The highest occupation achieved by the respondent's sons and sons-in-law, included on a first factor analysis of mobility data, was a single-item factor; low residential mobility was somewhat related to sons' high achievement, suggesting a pattern of established local success, but the missing cases, 1170, are too many to permit further analysis. *Data on proportion of worklife in large organizations,* sought in the interviews, were too weak to code; with skillful and repeated questioning respondents can remember jobs and employers in the distant past, even periods of unemployment and whether job changes represented ups or downs,

[23] It is no wonder, then, that in a separate factor analysis of objective work situation, "Small entrepreneur" accounts for more than twice the variance of any other factor; no other attribute of work situation—hierarchy, freedom, pressure, use of skills, chance for sociability on the job, etc.—is so important.

but the number of employees is apparently difficult to relate to particular jobs and employers, perhaps not merely because of ignorance but also because the number fluctuates so much.

I have said little about the dimension of worklife mobility most discussed in the literature: *direction and distance moved.* In the first factor analysis I eliminated fluctuating job pattern and substituted *"upward mobility"* (much up, some up, and stable, treating fluctuating and "down only" as missing data). It was a weak singlet (.405; the next loading, married down, was .263); like fluctuating mobility in Chart 1, it was more or less independent of the matrix. Working with these measures leads me to believe that movement across occupational strata is at least as important as intergenerational occupational mobility as a predictor of individual attitudes and behavior, but that it is less important than the other patterns of mobility described in Chart 1; in any case, it is distinct from them.

Interpreting the mobility orientation results

In delineating the individual's mobility stance, I tried to maintain distinctions between aspirations and expectations, high and low, fantasy and reality-tested aspirations (the latter are similar but not identical to "expectations"), retrospective and prospective, workplace-oriented and society-oriented, self-oriented and child-oriented. I aimed also to explore the changing meanings of "success," and as before, to tap aspirations in diverse ranking systems—occupation, income, education, leisure style. The results in general confirm the empirical reality of these distinctions and again provide leads for measurement and description in stratification research. Several patterns that emerged from the factor analysis deserve special note.

First, the need to separate modest workplace aspirations from aspirations pointed toward a society-wide stratification order is abundantly confirmed. For instance, compare "occupational aspirations—past, present, and for the next generation" (Chart 2, Factor 1) with "workplace aspirations and promotion plans" (Factor 5) and "stable, bureaucratic expectations" (Factor 8). If the researcher aims to locate men with serious, driving ambition, Factor 1 is the measure to use.

Second, aspirations for money are properly distinguished from occupational aspirations, but the clearest independence shows up in how *fast* a man expects his income to rise (Factor 2) and how *strongly* he cherishes monetary ambition (Factor 3). What income *level* he expects to reach and the steadiness of the climb are more ambiguous: they are

CHART 2

A FACTOR ANALYSIS OF 26 ASPECTS OF MOBILITY ORIENTATION AMONG
1,354 MEN

Per cent of variance explained	Factor	Factor Loadings
25	1. *High occupational aspirations—past, present, and for the next generation.*	
	Defining items: 1. Aspired to high position in the past. Highest job mentioned in responses concerning what R would do if he could start over, and whether he ever tried a different line.	.935
	2. Aspires to high position now.	.777
	4. Has reality-tested college aspirations for children. (Scale: 1. R's children now in college or completed college or R plans to send one or more and has savings of $2,000 or more. 2. Aspires, but fantasy. 3. No college aspirations.)	.327
	Related items: 3. Peak income expected in lifetime is high (6-point scale). Complex: loads also on Factors 2, 4, and 7.	.623
	5. Expects steady rise in income—i.e., does not expect ups and downs. Leads loadings on Factor 8.	.310
19	2. *High expected rate of income climb.*	
	Defining items: 1. Expected average yearly increase in income as per cent of 1959 personal income is high.	.936
	2. Expected average increase in income, dollars per year, is high.	.904
	Related item: 3. Peak income expected in lifetime is high.	.268
11	3. *Persistent income drive* (sacrifices R would make to get a job paying 50 per cent more than he's making now).	
	Defining items: 1. Would live in an undesirable neighborhood for awhile.	.642
	2. Would take some risk to his health.	.620
	3. Would do less interesting or enjoyable work.	.448
	Related item: 4. Would go without vacations for several years (loads higher on Factor 9).	.305
13	4. *Reality-tested (vs. retreatist) aspirations, retrospective.*	
	Defining item: 1. Highest retrospective job aspiration was reality-tested (e.g., actually tried to get into or now holds highest job ever wanted).	.848
	Related items: 2. Aspires to high occupation now (defines Factor 1).	.537
	3. Peak income expected in lifetime is high.	.323

116

CHART 2 (*Cont.*)

Per cent of variance explained	Factor	Factor Loadings

[A low score on the single defining item is likely to mean that highest past aspiration was fantasy and R has now given up hope—a retreatist pattern]

7   5. *Workplace aspirations are low, promotion plan absent.*

Defining items: 1. Does not aspire to promotion where he now works.   .557
2. Has never planned ahead for a better job (from checklist of things "ever planned as much as five or six years ahead of time").   .327

Related items: 3. Does not expect workplace promotion (loads higher on Factor 8).   .246
4. Would not take added responsibility for a higher paying job (see Factor 9).   .223

8   6. *Realistic aspirations for the future.*

Defining items: 1. No fantasy aspirations for future self-employment.   .564
2. Highest aspiration for future job is reality tested   .553

Related item: 3. Never aspired to self-employment in the past (see Factor 8).   .298

4   7. *In deep on a house* (Veblenian orientation).

Defining item: 1. Market value of a house as a percentage of family income is high.   .500

5   8. *Stable, bureaucratic orientations.*

Defining items: 1. Expects steady rise in income.   .380
2. Never aspired to self-employment in the past.   .358
3. Expects promotion in workplace.   .350

5   9. *Responsibility avoidance* (leisure orientation).

Defining items: 1. Would not take added responsibility for a higher paying job.   .511
2. Would not go without vacations for several years.   .322

3   10. *Adherence to classic American dream* (in responses to the question "What do you have in mind when you speak about 'getting ahead'—just what does that mean to you?").

Defining items: 1. Security theme absent.   .423
2. American dream theme present—unlimited success in a competitive struggle is possible.   .242
3. Leisure style theme—possessions, consumption, development of free time—is absent (but loading of .148 is below rule).

117

related to occupational aspirations in various ways (see Factors 1, 4, and 8).[24]

The persistence of traditional meanings of success and the emergence of new meanings are weakly confirmed by Factor 10, "adherence to the classic American dream." An accent on leisure style may be new, but it goes together with a faith in economic success in a competitive struggle so often that its correlation with the cluster (security theme present, leisure theme present, American dream theme absent) is very low.

The frequent use in stratification research of questions in the form "What would you give up to get ahead?" led me to a more detailed analysis of what I have labeled "persistent income drive" (Factor 3). In one study using a similar measure [25] the professionals turned out to be less aspiring than lower middle-class workers. I thought that this might reflect the verbal habits of the educated—high-status respondents might be reluctant to admit to crude striving—and that the proper procedure would be to rank the aspirations of each man relative to the typical response of his occupational stratum. With an eye to variations by occupation, I therefore examined the nine-item battery of sacrifices men would make to take a better-paying job. Two is the median number of items checked by lawyers and professors; three by engineers, the middle mass, and the white underdogs—close enough to justify an analysis cross-cutting classes.

The most important problem here is not class rhetoric activated in a survey interview; it is the various meanings of each component of the index. In an earlier factor analysis of mobility orientation, all of the "sacrifice" items were included. Table 1 reproduces the relevant portion of the rotated matrix.

Expressing a willingness to hide one's religious and political views for a better-paying job indicates something different from the ambitions

---

[24] Men scoring very high on "occupational aspirations" (Factor 1) display a pattern of interdependent aspirations embracing both occupation and income, workplace and the world, which in some cases persists through blocked entrepreneurship. These men are more likely to expect a steady rise to a high income peak, feel they have good, visible jobs, want a promotion where they work, feel they are better off than their parents were, have once wanted to go into business for themselves, have received job offers since holding their present jobs (weakly related); they also do not put much of their income into housing and they do not mention any aspect of leisure style as the meaning of getting ahead.

[25] Charles F. Westoff, Robert G. Potter, Jr., Philip C. Sagi, and Elliot G. Mishler, *Family Growth in Metropolitan America* (Princeton: Princeton University Press, 1961).

TABLE 1

LOADINGS AND RANKS OF LOADINGS IN TWO FACTOR ANALYSES OF
SACRIFICES MEN WOULD MAKE TO TAKE A BETTER-PAYING JOB, AN
AMBIGUOUS MEASURE OF AMBITION

Item in order asked °	Factors, loadings, ranks of loadings when all items were included †				Factors, loadings, ranks of loadings when indicated items were dropped	
	2	5	6	11	3	9
1. Would be away from family 4-5 months a year	.355 / 8	.216 / 4	.119 / 5		dropped	
2. Would hide political views	.431 / 7		.596 / 2		dropped	
3. Would hide religious views	.309 / 9		.619 / 1		dropped	
4. Would go without vacation for several years	.494 / 3			—.122 / 5	.305 / 4	—.322 / 2
5. Would leave friends and move to a new part of the country with family	.564 / 2				dropped	
6. Would live in undesirable neighborhood for a while	.586 / 1			.285 / 3	.642 / 1	
7. Would take some risk to health	.448 / 6			.425 / 1	.620 / 2	
8. Would do less interesting or enjoyable work	.468 / 5			.162 / 4	.448 / 3	
9. Would take a lot of added responsibility	.475 / 4		.119 / 5	—.310 / 2	.187 / 5	—.511 / 1
10. High total number of sacrifices he'd make for the higher paying job				—.135 / 3	dropped	
11. Aspires to high level occupation (prospective)		.549 / 2				
12. Highest retrospective aspiration is reality tested		.850 / 1				

° The questions appear in the Appendix.

† From a larger matrix of 34 mobility orientation variables. Varimax rotation. Signs are changed to conform to meaning. The ranks of defining items are underlined. Negligible loadings are not reported except where they rank high. Numbers heading the first four columns are factor numbers for the first try; factor numbers for the second try (columns headed 3 and 9) are those in Chart 2, which reports the full results.

tapped by the rest of this battery.[26] Viewing the theme as "expedient conformity," I shifted these items, together with a measure of the ready willingness to drop friends, to a factor analysis of the quality of social participation, where they again formed an orthogonal factor. I eliminated them and several ambiguous measures from the analysis of mobility orientation reported in Chart 2, with the result reported in Table 1. Items on living in an undesirable neighborhood, risking health, and doing less interesting work now form a stronger, more discrete factor, "Persistent income drive," Factor 3. The items on giving up vacations and taking added responsibility form "Responsibility avoidance" (Factor 9 in Chart 2). The same items load weakly but negatively on Factor 11 in Table 1—men who would give up some other things tend to refuse to take more responsibility or give up vacations. The pattern indicates a population whose mobility stance is leisure-oriented, but it is too weak to be more than suggestive. In short, this "sacrifice battery" mainly taps three separate phenomena: (1) expedient conformity, a measure of the quality of social participation; (2) the zest for money, the strength of one type of ambition; and (3) responsibility avoidance, the weakness of another kind of ambition.

Finally, Chart 2 contains leads for handling "aspirations" in mobility research. It confirms the need to distinguish fantasy aspirations from more serious ambitions (see Factors 4 and 6 for the patterns); and the need to give attention to the chronology of aspirations. Note that the respondent's recollections of what he once wanted and what he did about it and his reports on his present hopes and what he is doing about it almost always load together (see Factors 1, 5, 6, and 8 and their correlates). These men, like all men, live in their memories of the past and their expectations of the future—and we cannot separate the two.

---

[26] Forty-three per cent of the engineers in Diversico would hide their political views compared to about one in three of the white-collar workers in the middle mass and engineers in Unico, one in four of the lawyers, one in five of the blue-collar workers in the middle mass, one in ten of the professors. Hiding one's religion to get ahead is less popular but yields the same pattern—one in five of the engineers in Diversico, one in 20 of the professors, about one in ten of the other samples. Diversico was chosen for the structural attributes I thought might foster the mentality of the organization man: a unit with a tall hierarchy, diversified operations and a history of stable growth, which is a recruiting ground for central headquarters of a multi-plant nationwide corporation. These and other data confirm the hypothesis.

THE INTERACTION OF STATUS, MOBILITY, AND ASPIRATIONS: AN ILLUSTRATIVE APPLICATION

The analysis above suggests that in approaching the effects of mobility in modern stratification systems we should specify types of discontinuity, combine past social mobility with present mobility orientation, and then discover how men variously located in the structure respond to their experience and prospects.

Discussion of discontinuous mobility generally assumes that it fosters alienation from society or self or both. Table 2, holding *status* (SES) constant, combines *a type of past discontinuity* (blocked mobility) *with a pattern of aspirations* (occupational aspirations in the past and present and for the next generation), and relates the resulting mobility types to alienation from society. If we agree that a man is alienated when in politics he adheres to a conspiracy theory, in economics he feels that another Great Depression is imminent and that distributive justice does not prevail, and for the nation as a whole he expects a nuclear holocaust, then alienation is to an impressive degree rooted in these stratification variables, but perhaps in ways that do not fit received theory.

What fosters alienation (row 3)? In general, low aspirations (columns 9 and 12) together with low social and economic status are related to alienation, whatever the mobility experience. Wherever he has been, the most alienated man is nowhere now and is going nowhere. In this case, blocked mobility strivings alone count for nothing. But if we look at all the percentages, including those for attachment (row 1) and alienation (row 3), the contribution of each of the three variables is visible. In general, social-economic status conditions the relation between mobility pattern and alienation in the following ways.

1. In high strata, fulfilled ambition (strivings never blocked) fosters attachment whether current aspirations are high or low (columns 1 and 7); the straight-line movers and the contented among the higher strata are highly attached. That is to say, if you give men quite a lot and never thwart their strivings, they will love the system.

2. High SES overcomes the alienating effect of low aspirations (compare columns 7 and 8, 9, and 10) but status has little effect among ambitious men (compare columns 1 and 2, 4, and 5).

3. Blocked mobility, while not as important as status and aspirations, does have some independent effect but only among the ambitious. Among men with high aspirations, blocked mobility lessens attachment whatever the SES. High-status men who have never been blocked

TABLE 2

LOW ASPIRATIONS FOSTER ALIENATION FROM SOCIETY AMONG MEN OF LOW STATUS WHATEVER THEIR MOBILITY EXPERIENCE, BUT THE MOST STRONGLY ALIENATED AND LEAST ATTACHED ARE LOW-STATUS MEN WHO ARE THWARTED AND RETREAT *

Index of Alienation from Society	Mobility Not Blocked, High Aspirations (Straight-Line Ambition)			Mobility Blocked, High Aspirations (Ambitions Redirected)			Mobility Not Blocked, Low Aspirations (Contented)			Mobility Blocked, Low Aspirations (Thwarted and Retreats)		
	(50-69) High SES	(30-49) Low SES	Total	(50-69) High SES	(30-49) Low SES	Total	(50-69) High SES	(30-49) Low SES	Total	(50-69) High SES	(30-49) Low SES	Total
	(1)	(2)	(3)	(4)	(5)	(6)	(7)	(8)	(9)	(10)	(11)	(12)
Low alienation, high attachment (0-1)	39%	40%	39%	28%	24%	26%	47%	21%	25%	60%	18%	20%
Medium alienation, medium attachment (2-3)	54	44	52	63	68	65	44	41	41	40	45	45
High alienation, low attachment (4-8)	7	16	8	9	8	9	9	38	34	0	38	36
Total	100	100	99	100	100	100	100	100	100	100	101	101
Total N	(543)	(109)	(652)	(32)	(25)	(57)	(68)	(484)	(552)	(5)	(88)	(93)

* The index of alienation is based on four measures, each scored from 0 to 2 points and weighted equally. The highest scores go to men who think that getting to the top is more a matter of luck than ability, that there is at least a 50-50 chance of World War III, the same chance of a big depression, and who evidence racial or ethnic scapegoating at least once in the interview (they blame minority groups for unemployment or name them as behind-the-scenes conspirators or as "groups of people trying to get ahead at the expense of people like you"). The cutting points are 0-1, 2-3, 4-8. Blocked mobility is described in footnote 18. High aspirations (past, present, and for the next generation) is Factor 1 in Chart 2; the scores were dichotomized. SES combines occupational stratum, education, and family income in a factor score (low is 30-49, high is 50-69).

(column 1) have an 11 per cent edge in attachment over high-status men who have been blocked (column 4); low-status men who have never been thwarted (column 2) have a 16 per cent edge over low-status men who have (column 5).

Table 2 illustrates an approach to stratification as a source of social order and disorder, individual attachment and alienation. It also supports Duncan's plea for a simple model of additive effects, but suggests an alternative in which we do not give up our pursuit of mobility variables. Duncan says that "one is not entitled to discuss 'effects of mobility' until he has established that the apparent effect cannot be due merely to a simple combination of the effects used to define mobility." "The 'consequence' of mobility," he says, "is that you have held membership in two classes and your behavior is accounted for on the assumption that you combine the patterns of both."

The argument has merit, but we need not abandon the search for the discrete effects of mobility experience and orientation. We can simply control for status, in the manner of Table 2, and then examine the influence of various types of social and cultural discontinuity or economic deprivation. The result will usually show that where a man is, where he has been, and where he thinks he and his children are going, all contribute to an understanding of his behavior and attitudes.

Finally, it should be noted that while SES is an important variable, a dissection of its components reveals heterogeneity relevant to our understanding of the sources of alienation. The distribution of mean alienation scores by education is slightly curvilinear. This is because the rank order (from high to low) of societal alienation in these samples is (1) Negro underdogs, (2) white underdogs, (3) blue-collar men in the middle mass, (4) Urban University professors, (5) solo lawyers, then, the least alienated, (6) Diversico engineers, (7) Unico engineers, (8) white-collar men in the middle mass, (9) firm lawyers, (10) Church University professors.[27] The most alienated groups in these samples range from "lower lower class" to "upper middle;" the least alienated from lower middle to upper middle. This again calls attention to fateful variations in tasks, work schedules, organizational contexts, work groups, and job patterns obscured by the occupational categories we ordinarily use.

[27] This is the order of the adjusted means in a regression analysis, in which occupational group was by far the leading independent predictor of alienation, followed by occupational aspirations—consistent with Table 2.

ECONOMIC, POLITICAL, AND ORGANIZATIONAL CONTEXTS SHAPE
THE EFFECTS OF MOBILITY

The most impressive theoretical and empirical discussions of the effects of social mobility concentrate on various social or cultural discontinuities presumably involved. Thus, in this volume Smelser and Lipset are concerned with what they call the "irregularly upwardly mobile" or the "downwardly mobile." And in discussions of urbanism, industrialism, and mass society students of modern life find such words as "discontinuity" almost as indispensable as "rootlessness." [28] I have suggested that sociologists generally imply three ideas by the term discontinuity: major, not minor, movement between positions; sudden and unpredictable movement; and disruption of ties to kin and friends —whatever the direction of movement. I have presented three types and measures of mobility that approximate this idea: (1) a disorderly or partially disorderly job pattern, (2) a fluctuating job pattern in which the ups and downs involve shifts across major occupational strata, (3) a pattern of discontinuity including upward mobility involving changes in religion, ethnic intermarriage, and frequent shifts in residence.

Once we have given content to the idea of discontinuous mobility and begin to compare groups with varying rates, we still have the problem that the effects of discontinuity depend heavily on the economic, political, and organizational contexts in which they are experienced. I shall close with some speculation about how context determines the psychological and social correlates of discontinuous mobility.

Economic context

In less developed countries characterized by low per capita income, low levels of education, few ladders for mobility, and an explosion of both population and expectations, a high rate of discontinuous mobility is likely to produce social disorganization and political disruption. The loosening of traditional ties without the immediate substitution of new ones provokes disaffection; nationalist and other extremist movements provide the context for the fervent expression of this disaffection. This view, widely accepted, is elaborated throughout the present volume.

In rich countries the effect of similarly high rates of discontinuous mobility is more variable, although again there is general consensus on

[28] Cf. Louis Wirth, "Urbanism as a Way of Life," *American Journal of Sociology*, 44 (July, 1938), pp. 1-24; Robert A. Nisbet, *The Quest for Community* (New York: Oxford University Press, 1953); William A. Kornhauser, *The Politics of Mass Society* (New York: Free Press of Glencoe, 1959).

one line of argument. These countries are characterized by high per capita income, a high proportion of men educated beyond elementary school, and much social differentiation—therefore a large number of discrete ladders for mobility. They can sustain a large population, contain the political effects of a rise in expectations, and cushion or contain the effects even of high rates of downward mobility. The more education and income, the more urgent and widespread are great expectations; but the more differentiation, the more opportunity for their fulfillment and the more consolation prizes for those who lose out.

Reinforcing these structural constraints in rich countries are the cultural correlates of economic growth, particularly a success ideology which accents personal responsibility for work performance and job fate. Poor countries usually lack this ideology, so that the response to intergenerational or worklife "skidding" is eternalized; it is readily channeled into collective political protest. In rich countries the same skidding leads to self-blame, a sense of shame, and withdrawal from social contact.[29] At the extreme, skidding and other forms of discontinuity produce suicide—self destruction, not societal destruction.[30] In the typical case, however, skidding is rationalized, often realistically, as a temporary setback; in American data we usually find that skidders and fluctuators are more like upwardly mobile than non-mobile men.[31]

Although it may be true, as Germani argues (see his paper in this

---

[29] Part of the labor-leisure study was an intensive analysis of the effects of economic deprivation in the worklives of 147 older, high-seniority blue-collar and low-income white-collar workers. It shows that economic deprivation reduces the vitality of social participation. One in four had experienced at least 20 months of unemployment or layoff; one in three, none. Men who had been most deprived in the past had fewest and weakest ties to formal associations and to relatives in the present. The cumulative impact of this form of discontinuity was greatest among better-educated, higher-income younger workers. See Hallowell Pope, "Economic Deprivation and Social Participation in a Group of 'Middle-Class' Factory Workers," *Social Problems*, 11 (Winter, 1964), pp. 290-300.

[30] Comparing 103 white male suicides, age 20 to 60, and 206 men matched for race and age, Breed found that three in four of the suicides had suffered at least one form of downward mobility (intergenerational skidding, 53 per cent, recent income loss, 51 per cent, recent worklife skidding, 35 to 43 per cent depending on the base and scale used)—far more than the controls. Also, only half the suicides were working full-time just before they did away with themselves. Warren Breed, "Occupational Mobility and Suicide Among White Males," *American Sociological Review*, 28 (April, 1963), pp. 179-188. Cf. similar findings in Andrew F. Henry and James F. Short, Jr., *Suicide and Homicide* (New York: Free Press of Glencoe, 1954); Austin L. Porterfield and Jack P. Gibbs, "Occupational Prestige and Social Mobility of Suicides in New Zealand," *American Journal of Sociology*, 66 (September, 1960), pp. 147-152, confirming the original formulation in 1897 of Emile Durkheim, *Suicide* (New York: Free Press of Glencoe, 1951).

[31] Skidders retain the values and practices of the class from which they slipped and to which they expect to return. Wilensky and Edwards, *op. cit.*, and Peter M. Blau, "Social Mobility and Interpersonal Relations," *American Sociological Review*, 21 (June, 1956), pp. 290-295.

volume), that high rates of social mobility become institutionalized in an affluent society, it is unlikely that the discontinuities at issue become an accepted way of life. The demand for secure and orderly careers is sharp and, though the number of such careers is increasing, the majority of the population experiences substantial chaos in the labor market,[32] and we can guess that they do not learn to think of it as normal. Responses vary from apathy to increased striving, from social isolation to personal disorganization (suicide, alcoholism, mental illness).

Finally, in the rich countries of the sixties, we cannot rule out political responses to social discontinuity until we study vanguard populations such as engineers and technicians. We have no reason to suppose that when these college men are displaced or thwarted they will be as apathetic or personally disorganized as displaced manual workers in the same affluent context. Even small reverses (or threats of reverses) due to industry cutbacks or area recessions can provoke a collective political response. An obvious research implication is to discover types of discontinuities in the lives of Goldwater activists in the mid-sixties and their counterparts in other rich countries.

Political context

At the extreme, skidders in stable democratic societies do away with themselves; in totalitarian police states they may find themselves in a position to do away with others. The data are more scanty here, but modern totalitarian countries may contain the political effects of discontinuity by channeling the discontented into the state apparatus—the party, the military, the police or simply into jails and concentration camps. In Nazi Germany, one-fourth of the SS elite had previously received the doctorate.[33] According to Kogon's account of the Nazi concentration camps, a large fraction of the recruits of the SD and SS corps who supervised the execution of Jews from central and Southeastern Europe were men whose ambitions had been thwarted in civilian life. Persons with a history of failure, skidders poorly adapted to their class of origin, were apparently prominent in the SS corps. On the other hand, Hilberg reports that a majority of the officers of the *Einsatzgruppen*, Himmler's "mobile killing units" assigned to the Russian front, were at least moderately successful professional men—among them a physician, a professional opera singer, and a large number of lawyers. "These men were in no sense hoodlums, delinquents, common criminals or sex maniacs;" they were instead intellectuals in their thirties who wanted

---

[32] Wilensky, "Orderly Careers . . . ," *op. cit.*
[33] Kornhauser, *op. cit.*, p. 188.

more power, fame, and success than they could derive from their ordinary occupations.[34] While skidders and men whose strivings were blocked in Nazi Germany were joining the SS, their counterparts in the U.S. were becoming integrated into the establishment through the labor movement or New Deal agencies, or they were entering hospitals or jumping out of windows on Wall Street. In the first case we see socially-sanctioned aggression against others; in the second, socially-sanctioned careers in reform movements or socially-disapproved aggression against the self. Political culture, including customary ways of expressing discontent, and political organization, including institutional constraints on extremism, exert an independent influence on the consequences of discontinuous mobility.

Organizational context

That the effects of social discontinuity are conditioned by economic and political context is even more readily grasped if we examine work establishments and occupational groups. If an entire stratum, craft, or profession is declining, there is more chance of unity in misery and a collective protest—scapegoating or lashing out against symbols of oppression. The tendency is evident in the populism of family farmers facing corporate competitors or of grain growers dependent on banks and railroads, in the anti-Semitism of obsolescent craftsmen, of frustrated young war veterans, and of the early followers of Hitler recruited from the sinking lower middle class; and, finally, in the political extremism of small businessmen—the franchised dealer dependent on the big-business supplier, the small manufacturer dependent on one corporate customer, the retail proprietor threatened by chain stores and discount houses.[35] Such responses are less likely, and do not spread

[34] Raul Hilberg, *The Destruction of the European Jews* (Chicago: Quadrangle Books, 1961), pp. 182, 189-190. Cf. Eugene Kogon, *The Theory and Practice of Hell: The German Concentration Camps and the System Behind Them* (New York: Farrar, Straus & Giroux, 1950), pp. 16-17, 23, 262-264 (Pages cited from Kogon are from paperback reprint by Berkeley Publishing Corp., New York, no date). That these men would fit the categories, "blocked mobility" and "skidder" is my own inference.

[35] In my samples, as in many other studies, the "little man" who feels squeezed by both big enterprise and big labor is more prone to both extremism and scapegoating than others in the same social class. For instance, of the 29 self-employed men of the middle mass who felt squeezed, 38 per cent recalled Senator Joseph McCarthy with enthusiasm—this in 1960, several years after his demise. Of the 37 comparable entrepreneurs who did *not* feel squeezed, only 14 per cent were retrospective McCarthyites. Felt power squeeze is generally a better predictor of McCarthyism than blocked mobility strivings, especially among small entrepreneurs. Cf. Martin Trow, "Small Businessmen, Political Tolerance, and Support for McCarthy," *American Journal of Sociology*, 64 (November, 1958), pp. 270-281; and David

if they occur, when the position of the group or stratum is stable while the individual is threatened.

Similarly, organizational contexts shape both the rate and severity of social discontinuity and the reactions to it. Consider the mobility of managers, engineers, and scientists in research and development in the IBM Corporation, epitome of the large, complex, growing enterprise based on sophisticated technology.[36] Intense competition between individuals, small teams, projects, and departments is the mode; job reassignments are frequent and universal; much of the mobility is unpredictable and at first blush even chaotic. A man's project can be cancelled, shelved, or cut back; his unit abolished, taken off the project, reduced in force; he can be transferred to another unit or his unit head can be replaced by someone hostile to him or his specialty; his unit can be transferred to a different department or division where there is no place for his particular skills and experience. Despite keen competition, despite an extraordinary amount of moving about, IBM and similar corporations are able to foster rugged individualism and yet minimize the usual chaos in the lives of the competitors. When everyone is rootless, the sting of sudden loss of status is lessened and timetables of progress are rendered comfortably ambiguous. More important is a favorable structure of opportunity; a multi-unit, science-based corporation characterized by growth at once diversified, swift, and stable, requires a labor force heavily recruited from upper and lower middle-class and upper working-class occupations. For men with high ambition such a context provides plenty of room at the top; for those who do not arrive it assures many horizontal transfers or, at worst, many ups and downs within a narrow but rewarding range. A further force for steady growth emerges in the case of IBM: construction, maintenance, and service work is contracted out

---

Rogers, "The Automobile Dealer: A Study of the Status and Ideology of the Small Businessman," unpublished Ph.D. dissertation, Harvard University, 1960. On rural radicals see Seymour M. Lipset, *Agrarian Socialism* (Berkeley: University of California Press, 1950). A French sociologist, studying 206 randomly-selected furniture-makers of the Seine Department, finds that they tend to lead solitary lives; two in five of the artisans in this declining occupation evidenced anti-Semitic sentiments. In contrast to American findings, however, the most deprived individuals within this generally obsolescent, anti-Semitic group were no more prejudiced than the least deprived. Simone Francès, *Où va L'Artisanat français?* (Paris: Centre National De La Recherche Scientifique, 1961), pp. 100-105, 121. Cf. Bruno Bettelheim and Morris Janowitz, *Social Change and Prejudice* (New York: Free Press of Glencoe, 1964), Chapter 2 and p. 164.

[36] The rest of this paragraph is based on my informal interviews with several middle-managers of IBM in 1962 and on Fred H. Goldner, "Demotion in Management," an unpublished paper summarized in part in *Trans-action,* 1 (November, 1963), pp. 2-4.

wherever possible; the brunt of recessional and seasonal fluctuations is thus taken by subcontractors. All this makes a "no layoff" policy practical; hardly anyone is ever fired, few are clearly "demoted."

If we view many such structures from the perspective of the whole economy, we see that the "negative" personal and political effects of discontinuous mobility are concentrated in the less-trained strata on the fringe of modern developments (e.g., the lower working class) and among the subcontractors and their employees. For the rest of the population, especially those in the giant establishments dominating growing industries (e.g., education, electronic data processing equipment), the institutional cushions are numerous and effective.

Such devices as contracting out work that is unstable and alienating, banishing a man to the "sticks" or "kicking" him "upstairs," even such trivial tactics as the ceremonial dinner or exit interview to ease the passage up or out [37]—these obviously vary in availability and institutionalization. In comparative studies of mobility effects we must not only specify and elaborate the content of "irregular" or "discontinuous" mobility and attend to the larger economic and political context; we must also examine the ways in which various types of organizations handle the discontinuities they create.

SUMMARY AND IMPLICATIONS

The rule of parsimony has not been closely observed in this paper, but by bringing the great range of data discussed under the label "mobility" into one analysis, we may avoid hopelessly over-simplified and erroneous generalizations about the social and psychological consequences of mobility. To recapitulate:

1. *The channels for mobility are multiplying as modernizing societies develop and as rich countries become richer.* If we wish to deal with the individual's mobility experience as a source of personal and social organization and change, we must *bring into view all the orderly ladders that integrate and all the discontinuities that disrupt.* They have been listed repeatedly in introductory texts: stratification by descent (religious, ethnic, and racial origin); occupation; education; income; authority; residence, possessions, and leisure style. But systematic empirical studies of mobility give almost exclusive attention to "occupational mobility"

---

[37] Cf. Anselm L. Strauss and Norman H. Martin, "Patterns of Mobility within Industrial Organization," *Journal of Business,* 29 (April, 1956), pp. 101-110; and Erving Goffman, "On Cooling the Mark Out: Some Aspects of Adaptation and Failure," *Psychiatry,* 15 (November, 1952), pp. 451-463.

including the shift from rural to urban economies, especially between the generations.

2. *For reasons of both theory and method, intergenerational occupational mobility may be the least promising variable in stratification research.* On the theoretical side, as sources of social differentiation multiply, as doctrines of economic individualism accenting individual responsibility for work performance and occupational fate take root even in collectivist contexts, the comparison with the father may decline in importance. On the methodological side, we find heterogeneous and non-comparable categories (e.g., which job goes in which stratum), non-comparable samples (e.g., how do the populations compare in age composition), non-comparable measures (which jobs in the variable job cycles, orbits, or trajectories of father and son are to be compared), and, of course, variations in fieldwork efficiency—methodological troubles that are virtually insurmountable. To cope with them I have suggested the following strategy:

a. Give more attention to worklife mobility; for all but very young men in modern societies it may be more important than intergenerational mobility.

b. Broaden the analysis to include status shifts in institutional areas other than the economy.

c. Recognize the limits of attempts to estimate rates of intergenerational occupational mobility by country or community and give more attention to other equally important theoretical problems such as the effects of various types of cultural and social discontinuity, thereby minimizing sampling problems. The measures described in this paper that are most useful in tackling the problem of discontinuous mobility are blocked mobility, the degree of orderliness in the work history (Chart 1, Factor 5), the number of times a man has crossed broad occupational strata in his worklife (Factor 3), and the cluster of discontinuities represented by ethnic intermarriage, intergenerational changes in the status of religious preference, and shifts in residence (Factor 7). Crucial for an understanding of modern America, but hardly confined to this country, are entrepreneurial discontinuities; perhaps they are best indicated by the percentage of years in the worklife a man has been self-employed (Factor 4). Each measure may be seen as an independent dimension of social mobility.

To achieve conceptual clarity and accurate measurement in this area will never be easy, but we need not *ask* for trouble with quite the zest students of intergenerational occupational mobility have displayed. Other types of mobility, powerful in their effects, are subject to less error in measurement and far less conceptual confusion.

3. *Equal attention should be given to objective mobility and mobility orientation; combinations of the two are promising for research on the social and psychological correlates of mobility. There is no reason to believe that an individual's subjective mobility orientation is a weaker source of social integration than his objective mobility experience.* Indeed, in my study occupational aspirations are often more important predictors of behavior than measures of either worklife or intergenerational mobility. The most powerful mobility analysis is one that simultaneously takes account of where a man has been, where he is now, and where he expects to go. By combining measures of past mobility, present social status, and mobility orientation, we can construct simple types of mobility stance, in the manner of Table 2, and discover the distinct effects of mobility experience and prospects.

a. In measuring mobility orientation, my analysis suggests the empirical reality of the following distinctions: between modest workplace aspirations and aspirations pointed toward a society-wide stratification order; among aspirations for high occupational prestige, expectations for a quick increase in income, and a persistent drive for income; and between fantasy aspirations and serious ambitions. The analysis also shows that recall of past aspirations, and reports of present aspirations for self and children tap the same underlying dimension.

b. Similarly, in measuring objective mobility some indicators of mobility that are typically lumped together are in reality discrete. For instance, direction and distance of movement in the worklife is not a good indicator of social discontinuity; some upward moves, like some horizontal moves, are orderly—involving gradual, predictable changes and anticipatory socialization, others are chaotic. "Instability" of job holding (generally based on number of jobs or employers) is also independent of orderliness in the job pattern. Conversely, many indicators of mobility usually separated might be handled together or used as substitutes for one another. For instance, occupational mobility between generations and educational mobility between generations are sufficiently related that the simpler measure based on educational level achieved by son and father might be advantageous, although for analysis of the impact of status incongruity or "skidding," we must still focus on strategic minorities—e.g., college men in the working class.

c. The general need for specificity in occupational analysis applies even more to the analysis of rural-urban mobility. It seems plain that if we are to understand the impact of such migration on social structure and person, we will have to devise better classifications of the occupations and communities of origin and destination. Whether rural-urban migration is personally or socially disorganizing, whether aspirations rise faster than the economy can stand, might depend on whether the shift is out of commercialized manorial systems (involving an apathetic, backward, and disenfranchised peasantry) or family-sized tenancy (an enfranchised, formally free, skilled, politically alert peasantry), a family small-holding (free, but low political competence), plantation agriculture (a proletarian peasantry), or a ranch system (dispersed and unorganized radicalism); and whether the shift is into urban manufacturing; large or small workplaces; paternalistic, company towns; urban entrepreneurial trades and services; unemployment, squatting, begging, or scavenging, and so on.[38]

4. *A discriminating analysis of mobility that fits the diversity of modern life and brings into view the multiple moves of each person leads to a consolation prize "theory" of mobility.* Aspirations may exceed rewards and yield disaffection if we look only at job chances. But if we bring into view other ranking systems and consider changes through marriage (endogamy surely does not increase with modernization) then the place of mobility in the social integration of modern society becomes clearer. For instance, my data show that intergenerational skidders marry up; Factors 1 and 8 of Chart 1 indicate that men who achieve less education than their fathers or stay on the same level tend to marry women with superior education from families with occupational status higher than their own.[39] Data not reported here show that many skidders marry up ethnically. Other studies have reported a low correlation between income and occupational prestige; many note the high economic and occupational status of some minority groups.

These phenomena are usually described, not in terms of mobility experience, but in terms of the strains generated by status inconsistency, incongruity, or low status crystallization.[40] Smelser and Lipset formulate the general principle that highly differentiated systems foster individual mobility and status "disequilibrium," and Germani offers many propositions about the politically disruptive effects of such a condition.

To view the matter in terms of status incongruity has the advantage

[38] Ramsøy, Moore, and Sjoberg (in this volume) have given us important leads here. Cf. Arthur L. Stinchcombe, "Agricultural Enterprise and Rural Class Relations," *American Journal of Sociology*, 67 (September, 1961), pp. 165-176.

[39] The massive emigration of men from the British Isles in the 19th century must have been in one way a source of political stability. It left a large pool of excess women of every rank, many of whom became intergenerational skidders or, put another way, it provided opportunities for many men to marry up. British novels of the period are full of downwardly mobile men or workers who wooed women of station.

[40] Gerhard Lenski, "Status Crystallization: A Non-Vertical Dimension of Social Status," *American Sociological Review*, 19 (August, 1954), pp. 405-413, and George C. Homans, "Status Among Clerical Workers," *Human Organization*, 12 (Spring, 1953), pp. 5-10.

of simplifying measurement, but it may not capture much of the experience of mobility implied by the observed incongruity. Most men may experience the shifts that produced the high-status portion of that "disequilibrium" as a compensatory reward—something instead of nothing in an imperfect world.

An important qualification to my consolation-prize hypothesis concerns education. The most alienated men in my study are Negro high-school graduates on relief; in table after table these men, whose educational opportunities exceed the place allotted to them, are the most disaffected. If educational opportunity whets the appetite for a better life but does not lead to job opportunity and income, it serves less as a compensatory reward than as a source of resentment. Thus, as their educational opportunities exceed their economic rewards and living standards, American Negroes will become more militant. Educated whites already receive roughly congruent rewards and their political discontents are kept within manageable proportions; uneducated whites, if they are unlucky in the labor market, at least have a chance to escape lower ethnic or religious origins or marry up. In countries both rich and poor, cases similar to that of the educated American Negro on relief appear: displaced engineers in the most modern sectors of West coast defense industries; rootless "intellectual" proletarians in the modernizing countries of Asia, Africa, and Latin America that are long on education but short on job opportunity.

The formula for treating the effects of mobility, then, is: specify the types and devise measures to match; be alert to the restiveness of the "over"-educated, whose consolation prize is a burden; keep in view the economic, political, and organizational contexts within which men act out their strivings.

APPENDIX

I. *Objective Mobility*
  A. Occupational Mobility in the Worklife
    *78. Next we would like to find out about the jobs you've had and also about the times you were out of work. What is your job *now*? (RECORD ANSWER WITHOUT PROBE)
    78a. Specifically, what do you do on your job? (GET TYPE OF MACHINE OPERATED; NUMBER TENDED; PROFESSIONAL SPECIALTY; ETC.)

* Numbers refer to original question numbers on schedule used for "Work, Careers, and Leisure Styles," the study of which this is a part.

80. How long have you been working there at the same job?
81. Now let's move back to your last position. What did you do then?

(IF NOT CLEAR) 82. Were you working for yourself or not? (1. Yes; 2. No)

(IF NOT SELF-EMPLOYED) 83. Whom were you working for then? (IF NOT CLEAR: What did this company do?)

84. When did you first get this job and when did you leave it? [Questionnaire contained chart with title headings as to Type of Work, Self-Employment, Type of Company and/ or Product, Duration of Job, Size of Workplace, No. Supervised, Reason for Leaving, and Pay Change. Qs. 81-84 WERE REPEATED FOR EACH JOB R HAD SINCE LEAVING HIGH SCHOOL, proceeding job by job from the latest job to the earliest until each job listed had been accounted for. Interviewer skipped every other line on chart to leave space for other jobs which respondent might recall on second round of questions. PART-TIME AND SUMMER JOBS WHILE IN COLLEGE WERE NOT INCLUDED. PERIODS OF UN-EMPLOYMENT LASTING SIX WEEKS OR MORE WERE RECORDED. AFTER ALL JOBS AND UNEMPLOYMENT PERIODS WERE LISTED, Qs. 85-88 WERE ASKED ABOUT EACH JOB as follows:]

(Now I have a few more questions about each of these jobs you've told me about. Let's start with the earliest.) 85. About how many people were working at (NAME) when you were there?

86. Did anyone work under you at (NAME), that is, were you in charge of the work of others? (1. Yes; 2. No.)

87. How did you happen to leave this job?

(IF NOT CLEAR) 88. Did your next job pay better, the same, or worse than this job? (1. Better; 2. Same; 3. Worse.)

Let's see now—the next thing was (NEXT LISTING). Was there anything in between—another job or some unemployment? (IF YES, RECORD ON CHART AND ASK PROPER Qs)

Repeat Qs. 87-88 UNTIL ALL PREVIOUS JOBS ARE COVERED.

[NOTE: Separate batteries on multiple job holdings, schedules, and hours of work were also included.]

B. Intergenerational Mobility: Occupational, Education, Ethnic, Religious

(IF R RAISED IN ORPHANAGE OR OTHER INSTITUTION, SKIP TO Q. 216)

203. What was the best job your father (step-father, etc.) ever held while you were growing up? (BE SPECIFIC)

204. About how old were you when he got that job?
205. How many years did your father hold this job? ....
   (Years)
(IF ABOVE JOB NOT HELD FOR TWO OR MORE YEARS WHILE R WAS
TEEN-AGER)
206. What was the best job your father had most of the time
   while you were a teen-ager?
(IF "FARMER" BEST JOB HELD FOR 2 YEARS OR MORE WHILE R IN
TEENS)
207. Did your father own his farm or what?
   (1. Owner; 2. Manager; 3. Farm laborer; 4. Tenant farmer;
   5. Share-cropper; 9. DK)
(IF OWNER OR MANAGER) 207a. How many acres did he farm?
   (1. Under 30; 2. 30-49; 3. 50-99; 4. 100-199; 5. 200
   or more; 9. DK)
   207b. Did he have anybody working for (under) him on
   a more-or-less steady basis? (1. Yes; 2. No; 9. DK)
   (IF YES) 207c. How many men worked for (under) him?
(IF "FARMER" IS *not* BEST JOB HELD FOR 2 YEARS OR MORE WHILE R
IN TEENS)
208. On this job, did your father work for himself or someone
   else? (1. Self; 2. Someone else; 9. DK)
   (IF SELF) 208a. How many people did he have working
   for him? (0. None; 1. 1-3; 2. 4-9; 3. 10-99; 4. 100-
   499; 5. 500+; 9. DK)
   (IF SOMEONE ELSE) 208b. About how many people were
   employed by the company he worked for? (1. 1-3;
   2. 4-9; 3. 10-99; 4. 100-499; 5. 500+; 9. DK)
   208c. Did anyone work under your father—was he in
   charge of the work of others? (1. Yes; 2. No; 9. DK)
   (IF YES) 208d. Did anyone work under these people? (1.
   Yes; 2. No; 9. DK)
209. How many years of school did your father complete? (4
   or less; 5-8; <u>9; 10; 11; 12</u>; <u>13; 14; 15; 16</u>; Graduate training)

          High School   College

210. What kind of work did your father's father do most of his
   life? (BE SPECIFIC)
211. What is the original nationality of your family on your
   father's side? (IF "American": What country did his family
   come from originally?)
212. Was your father born in the United States? (1. Yes; 2. No)

213. Was your mother born in the United States? (1. Yes; 2. No)
214. And how many of your grandparents were born in the United States? (0. None; 1. One; 2. Two; 3. Three; 4. Four; 9. DK)
215. How many years of school did your mother complete? (4 or less; 5-8; 9; 10; 11; 12; 13; 14; 15; 16; Graduate training)

         High School   College

ALL RESPONDENTS

216. What was the highest grade of school or college you completed? (4 or less; 5-8; 9; 10; 11; 12; 13; 14; 15; 16; Graduate training)   High School   College

(IF 4 YEARS OF COLLEGE OR MORE) 216Xa. What college degrees do you have—from which institutions?

217. Did you ever take any other special courses or formal training—things like trade school, business school, correspondence course, or job training program? (1. Yes; 2. No)
(IF YES) 217a. What were they? (Anything else?) [Questionnaire contained chart with title headings as to Type of Training, When Started, and When Ended.] (Qs. 217b-217c were asked of each)
217b. What year did you begin (NAME)?
217c. And when did this training end?

218. Do you have a religious preference? That is, are you Protestant, Catholic, Jewish, or something else? (Prot; Cath; Jewish; Other; No pref)
(IF PROT) 218a. What specific denomination is that, if any?
(IF JEWISH) 218b. Do you consider yourself Orthodox, Conservative, Reform, or none of these? (Orth; Con; Ref; None)

219Xf. Would you say your religion and nationality ties have, in general, helped, hindered, or made no difference in your career? (1. Helped; 2. Hindered; 3. No difference)
(IF HELPED OR HINDERED) 219Xg. In what ways? (Could you tell me a bit more about that?)

220. Have you always been a (SPECIFIC PREFERENCE)? (1. Yes; 2. No)

(IF NO) 220a. What other preferences have you had?

221. What is, or was, your father's usual religious denominational preference? (BE SPECIFIC, E.G., BAPTIST, ORTHODOX JEW, ETC.)

222. What is, or was, your mother's usual religious denominational preference? (BE SPECIFIC)

C. Mobility through Inter-marriage: Religious, Education, Occupational, Ethnic

(IF R NOT NOW MARRIED, SKIP Qs. 222X-229)

222X. And what is your wife's religious preference?

224. How many years of school did your wife complete? (4 or less; 5-8; 9; 10; 11; 12; 13; 14; 15; 16; Graduate training)

<u>High School</u>   <u>College</u>

225. What was your wife's father's usual occupation while she was growing up?

226. What is the original nationality of your wife's family on her father's side?

227. Was her father born in the United States? (1. Yes; 2. No; 9. DK)

228. Was her mother born in the United States? (1. Yes; 2. No; 9. DK)

229. And how many of your wife's grandparents were born in the United States? (0. None; 1. One; 2. Two; 3. Three; 4. Four; 9. DK)

D. Residential Mobility

236E. How long have you lived in the (.................... metropolitan) area?

(IF NOT ALL LIFE) 236a. Where were you born? (Town) (State or Country)

236b. Where did you live when you were in your teens? (Town) (State or Country)

236c. Have you ever lived on a farm? (1. Yes; 2. No)

(IF YES) 236d. Between what ages? .... to ....

236e. About how many times have you changed addresses in the last ten years?

237E. About how many other houses or apartments have you lived in here in the (———— metropolitan) area?

(IF ANY) 237a. How long have you lived at your present address?

II. *Mobility Orientation*

A. Occupational Aspirations and Expectations

93. What type of work would you try to get into if you could start all over again?

(IF DIFFERENT FROM PRESENT TYPE OF WORK) 93a. Why would you prefer this to the work you are doing now?

93b. Have you ever thought of going into business for yourself? (1. Yes; 2. No)

(IF YES) 93c. About how long ago was that?

94. Have you ever *actually tried* to get into a line of work that was different from any you've been in? (1. Yes; 2. No)

(IF YES) 94a. What did you do? (IF NOT CLEAR: What sort of work did you try to get into?

94b. When was that?

95. About how long do you expect to be working at the very same job you have now? .... (years)

96. What do you expect to be doing after you leave this job? (IF EXPECTS TO WORK FOR SOMEONE ELSE AND NOT NOW SELF-EMPLOYED) 96a. Would this next job be at the same place you now work? (1. Yes; 2. No; 9. DK)

97. Considering all the jobs you've had or will have, what would be the best job you expect to have in your lifetime? (IF NOT PAST OR PRESENT JOB) 97a. Just as a guess about how many years do you think it will be before you'll get this job? .... (years)

105. Do you have a good chance for promotion where you work? (1. Yes; 2. No; 9. DK)

(IF YES) 105a. Would it make much difference to you if you didn't have a good chance for promotion? (1. Yes; 2. No; 9. DK)

(IF NO GOOD CHANCE FOR PROMOTION) 105b. Does it bother you very much that you don't have a good chance for promotion? (1. Yes; 2. No; 9. DK)

106. Since you have been working at (PRESENT JOB), have you had any job offers or chances for jobs elsewhere which you could seriously consider? (1. Yes; 2. No)

B. Income Expectations and Drive

98. What would be the highest income you expect to earn in any one year during your lifetime (figured in today's dollars)? $................. per ....

99. About when would you expect to have earned that much

—that is, was it sometime in the past, right now, or will it be sometime in the future? (1. Past; 2. Right now; 3. Future)

(IF FUTURE) 99a. Just as a guess, how many years before you'll be making that much? .... (years)

99b. As you look to the years ahead, do you expect a *steady rise* in your income until retirement; *some rise but a decline* before retirement; or do you expect many *ups and downs* in your income? (1. Steady rise; 2. Some rise, then decline; 3. Ups and downs; Other)

115. Suppose you were offered a job that paid 50 per cent more than you're making now. (That is, if you're making $5,000 now, the new job would pay $7,500.) Would you take the better paying job even if you had to be away from your family four or five months a year? (1. Yes; 2. No; 9. DK)

116. Would you take the job if you had to hide your political views? (1. Yes; 2. No; 9. DK)

117. Would you take the job if you had to hide your religious views? (1. Yes; 2. No; 9. DK)

118. Here are some other sacrifices you might have to make to get the job paying 50 per cent more. (SHOW CARD) Which of the things on this card would you be willing to do to get the job? (CHECK IF PICKED) (0. None)
    ....a. Go without vacations for several years
    ....b. Leave your friends and move to a new part of the country with your family
    ....c. Live in an undesirable neighborhood for a while
    ....d. Take some risk to your health
    ....e. Do less interesting or less enjoyable work
    ....f. Take a lot of added responsibility

230. What was your total family income before taxes in 1959—considering all sources such as rents, profits, wages, interest and so on? [Card shown with 15 categories of income ranging from under $2,000 in the first category to $35,000 or more in the 15th category, using income steps of $1,000 for categories 2-9, and income steps of $5,000 for categories 10-14.]

231. And in which of the groups on this card did your family income fall five years ago? [Card shown with income categories as above.]

C. Educational Aspirations and Expectations for Next Generation
126. Did you ever think about how much education you would like your children to get? (1. Yes; 2. No)
    (IF YES) (IF HAS SON) 126a. How much education do (did) you want for your son(s)? (IF VAGUE: Well, what is the minimum you think they should get?)
    (IF DOES NOT HAVE SON) 126b. How much education do (did) you want for your daughter(s)? (IF VAGUE: Well, what is the minimum you think they should get?)
(IF ANY CHILDREN OUT OF SCHOOL)
127. (So far) What was the most education any of your children got?

D. In Deep on a House (Veblenian orientation)
(IF OWNS OR BUYING HOUSE) 132a. Could you tell me what the present value of your house is? I mean about what would it bring if you were to sell it today. (I don't mean what you paid for it—but what would it bring today.) $............................

E. Self-Image and Ambition
77. Now, on another topic . . . almost everyone has a pretty good idea of the way he is seen by the people he likes and feels comfortable with. How about you—for example, are you known as a person who tries hard to get ahead? (1. Yes; 2. No; 9. DK)
    (IF YES) 77a. Would it make much difference to you if you were not known as a person who tries hard to get ahead? (1. Yes; 2. No; 9. DK)
77b. What do you have in mind when you speak about "getting ahead"—just what does that mean *for you?*
    (IF NAMES SPECIFIC JOB: Why would that mean success to you?)

4

PRE-INDUSTRIAL
STRATIFICATION SYSTEMS

M. G. SMITH, *University of California, Los Angeles*

SOCIETIES that rely primarily on human or animal sources of productive power are usually regarded as "pre-industrial." This label involves no expectations about their future. Although pre-industrial societies vary greatly in their structure and developmental level, at this stage we need only distinguish traditional pre-industrial societies from the "national" units in which they are currently incorporated. Even when both these units are equally pre-industrial, they differ sharply in structure, boundaries and orientation. Industrialization appeals to few traditional pre-industrial societies as a desirable programme. To "national" pre-industrial societies, it may be a structural necessity, and in emergent nations, industrialization is always a national programme, even where its impact on local units is greatest.

THE PROBLEM OF STRATIFICATION

The nature of stratification is more complex and critical for our discussion. The common distinction between concrete and analytic structures, that is, between membership units and generalized aspects of social process,[1] suggests parallel distinctions between analytic and concrete concepts of stratification. Since the approach presented here differs from others in current use, I should try to indicate these differences at once.

Stratification is often conceived as the evaluative ranking of social units. Some theorists regard it as an abstract necessity of all social systems. Concretely, it refers to empirical distributions of advantages

---

[1] Marion J. Levy Jr., *The Structure of Society* (Princeton: Princeton University Press, 1952), pp. 88-89.

and benefits in specific societies.[2] Analytically, it connotes the abstract possibilities of evaluative rankings on any number of special scales.[3] As observers, we can construct as many stratification scales as we wish by employing any criteria we choose, separately or together; but we should not confuse these abstract possibilities or analytic artifacts with empirical systems of social stratification. The significance of any analytic scale depends on its meaningful correspondence with a concrete system of stratification; and, as Smelser and Lipset suggest in their introductory paper, these concrete stratifications may be identified by the differential distribution of social advantages.

Stratification is a process as well as a state of affairs. Of these two referents, the first seems more fundamental, since the state of affairs is both a product and condition of social process. As an institutional order, the process of social stratification must be regulated by some principles which can be derived by analysis of the social structure; and, on the basis of structural analysis, I shall argue that stratification consists in the principles that regulate the distribution of social advantages. Thus, the unit to which my argument refers is the society rather than its various components, the concept of society being the one presented by S. F. Nadel and Marion Levy, Jr.[4]

Being highly differentiated, modern industrial societies may accommodate considerable diversity of evaluative scales in their systems of stratification. Nonetheless, these scales must be functionally consistent and related if they are to be simultaneously institutionalized. In less differentiated pre-industrial societies, the theoretically possible variety of scales is severely restricted by structural stereotyping of social units and individual life-cycles. When the more complex pre-industrial systems institutionalize two or more stratification scales, relations between them are usually well defined.

Since the social evaluations reflecting stratification are neither random nor contingent, the criteria on which they rest must be institutionalized within the social structure, and for this reason evaluative rankings express underlying structural principles. The logical alternative involves such randomness, contingency and discord in the aggregate of evaluations that it cannot constitute a ranking system at all. But if the actual ranking of social units expresses structural relations, the differ-

[2] Neil J. Smelser and Seymour Martin Lipset, "Social Structure, Mobility and Development," in this volume.

[3] Levy, *op. cit.*, pp. 343-7, and Hilda Kuper, *An African Aristocracy: Rank among the Swazi* (London: Oxford University Press for International African Institute, 1947), pp. 8-7.

[4] S. F. Nadel, *The Foundations of Social Anthropology* (London: Cohen and West, 1951), pp. 187-188; Levy, *op cit.*, p. 113.

ential distribution of sanctions with which this rank order is identified will also be governed by structural principles. Such differential distributions of benefit and deprivation are no more random and contingent than the evaluative rankings that reflect them.

With these considerations in mind, while reviewing stratification in pre-industrial societies, I shall also explore relations between the prevailing distributions of advantage and the structural principles that regulate the processes of distribution. I shall also try to show why these principles are more significant for the analysis of social stratification than the mere distribution of advantages.

I approach this discussion of pre-industrial stratification systems as a social anthropologist, conscious of the divergences between sociology and social anthropology, especially in their conceptions of social structure and stratification. Despite personal involvement in a few small-scale societies, a social anthropologist is committed to comparative analysis; and in these comparisons his primary concern is with the particular combinations of structural principles underlying the observable variety of social processes and forms. For such analysis, the anthropologist's concept of social structure facilitates identification of these principles and their combinations. Thus, while the lineage principle is common to all lineages, these vary structurally as this principle is modified by others. In like manner, structural changes are modifications of structural units and relations that involve some rearrangement or alteration of the principles which constitute them. For this conception of social structure, the view of status as a bundle of rights and duties is critical. In static terms, structure can be conceived as an arrangement of such positions, some held by individuals, others by corporate units. Dynamically, structural change involves modification or rearrangement of the underlying principles. With this background, social anthropologists conceive societies positionally, as systems the key units of which are statuses, related to one another by their particular distributions of privilege, duty and right. Social action, change and stratification are understood by reference to the social structure.

In sociology, as I understand it, structure is often viewed as a set of "directional tendencies," or purposive processes of institutional action, which seek to satisfy the "functional prerequisites" of social order. In effect, the strategic concept for initial analysis is the role, usually defined by reference to normative expectations; and the society, as an action system with sufficient internal order to ensure its persistence, is identified as a normative consensual system. In analyzing congruent or incongruent role expectations, the sociologist relies heavily on such notions as norms, values, and value-orientations.

Many differences between sociology and anthropology flow from these divergent orientations; and some of these find expression in conflicting disciplinary approaches to the study of stratification. For many sociologists, "no society is 'classless' or unstratified"; [5] "social inequality in human society is marked by its ubiquity and its antiquity. Every known society, past and present, distributes its scarce and demanded goods unequally." [6] Stratification is "a particular type of role differentiation, that is a requirement for any society." [7] "Social stratification is a generalized aspect of the structure of all social systems." [8] This being so, sociologists attempt "to explain, in functional terms, the universal necessity which calls forth stratification in any social system. . . . The main functional necessity explaining the universal presence of stratification is precisely the requirement faced by any society of placing and motivating individuals in the social structure." [9] Though these views are not shared by all sociologists,[10] they represent the prevailing sociological approach to a theory of stratification. The point of view they express contrasts so sharply with the social anthropological approach that in preparing this paper I have had to seek some common ground between the two in order to relate anthropological materials on pre-industrial societies to the framework of current sociological theory.

One can contrast the assertion that "no society is classless or unstratified" with representative anthropological statements. For Landtmann, "one of the most remarkable facts ascertained and elucidated by sociology (is) that a condition of almost complete equality reigns among peoples in the lowest degrees of culture." [11] According to *Notes and Queries* (6th edition), "*some* societies are stratified in social classes or, where these are closed, castes. . . . Social classes entail differences in status and civic rights, often conditioned by descent, in the access to

[5] Kingsley Davis and Wilbert E. Moore, "Some Principles of Stratification," *American Sociological Review*, 10 (April, 1956), p. 242.

[6] Melvin M. Tumin, "Some Principles of Stratification: A Critical Analysis," *American Sociological Review*, 18 (August, 1953), p. 337.

[7] David F. Aberle, Albert K. Cohen, Allison K. Davis, Marion J. Levy Jr., Francis X. Sutton, "The Functional Prerequisites of a Society," *Ethics*, 60 (January, 1950), p. 106.

[8] Talcott Parsons, 'A Revised Analytical Approach to the Theory of Social Stratification, in Reinhard Bendix and Seymour M. Lipset (eds.), *Class, Status and Power: A Reader in Stratification*, (New York: Free Press of Glencoe, 1953), p. 93. See also Talcott Parsons, "An Analytical Approach to the Theory of Social Stratification," *American Journal of Sociology*, 45 (May, 1940), reprinted in Talcott Parsons, *Essays in Sociological Theory, Pure and Applied*, 165-184 (New York: Free Press of Glencoe, 1949).

[9] Davis and Moore, *op cit.*, p. 242.

[10] T. B. Bottomore, *Sociology: A Guide to Problems and Literature* (38-40, 195-196), London: Allen and Unwin, 1963), pp. 38-40, and 195-196.

[11] Gunnar Landtman, *The Origin of the Inequality of Social Classes* (London: Kegan Paul, Trench, Trubner and Co., 1938), p. 3.

positions of power, influence or wealth, and also in occupation and habitual modes of living." [12] For Nadel, stratification is identified by the presence of social strata. Only "when a society is divided into large aggregates of individuals who share, in relevant respects, the same status and are marked off from other such aggregates by different status (may) we speak of social strata. . . . Clearly, the various age-groups in a society, or the two sexes, may also be collectively differentiated by status; yet we should not in that case speak of social strata." [13] "Power and authority would seem to be more relevant criteria of social stratification than the varying access to other commonly valued benefits." [14] By status, Nadel understands "the rights and obligations of any individual relative both to those of others and to the scale of worth-whileness in the group. . . . 'Rank' is a more highly formalised version of status. . . . 'Prestige' . . . a more fluid version. By status we mean . . . status in the widest relevant group . . . the politically effective corporation, so that Status means political status." [15]

Sahlins, having asked, "What is egalitarianism and what is stratification?" replies

Theoretically an egalitarian society would be one in which every individual is of equal status, a society in which no one outranks anyone. But even the most primitive societies could not be described as egalitarian in this sense. There are differences in status carrying differential privilege in every human organisation . . . [but] the qualifications are not everywhere the same. In certain societies, e.g., Australian aboriginal communities, the only qualifications for higher status are those which every society uses to some extent, namely sex, age and personal characteristics. Aside from these qualifications, there may be no others. A society in which the only principles of rank allocation are these universals can be designated "egalitarian," first, because this society is at the stratification minimum of organised human societies; second, because, given these qualifications, every individual has an equal chance to succeed to whatever statuses may be open. But a society unlike this, that is, one in which statuses are fixed by a mechanism beyond the universals, e.g. [by] inheritance, can be called "stratified." [16]

For Bohannan, "stratification . . . implies not merely a ranked hierarchy, but also a homogeneous quality in each of the various strata. This quality . . . is certainly absent in . . . 'situs' systems . . . and minimal in 'caste' systems." [17]

[12] Royal Anthropological Institute, *Notes and Queries on Anthropology* (6th ed., London: Routledge and Kegan Paul, 1951), p. 93. My italics.
[13] Nadel, *op. cit.*, p. 174.
[14] *Ibid.*, p. 175.
[15] *Ibid.*, pp. 171-172, 174.
[16] Marshall Sahlins, *Social Stratification in Polynesia* (Seattle: University of Washington Press, 1958), pp. 1-2.
[17] Paul Bohannan, *Social Anthropology* (New York: Holt, Rinehart & Winston, 1963), p. 165.

While anthropologists conceive stratification concretely, as a feature of some, but not all, societies, sociologists tend to stress its universality as an abstract necessity of all social systems, whether these are conceived analytically or not. Underlying these differing orientations is the anthropologists's emphasis on status as the primary concept for analysis of social structure, and the sociologist's emphasis on role. I suggest that this difference also explains why sociologists are keenly concerned with a theory of stratification, while anthropologists are little concerned about it. Because anthropologists conceive social structure as a status structure, in their view an inclusive theory of stratification would represent a general theory of all forms of social structure. On the other hand, because sociologists regard societies as systems of roles, they need a theory of stratification to analyze the articulation of these roles.

No discussion of "pre-industrial stratification systems" that fails to resolve these differences can provide a useful basis for their comparison or for the study of their re-stratification. Any general comparative survey of social stratification presupposes an acceptable notion of stratification. In seeking to arrive at this, I shall have to deal with the following questions, among others: (1) In what sense does an unequal distribution of advantages indicate stratification? (2) Whether "functionally requisite" or not, is stratification universal and coextensive with society? (3) How useful is the dichotomy between ascription and achievement for an analysis and typology of status systems? (4) How valid is the assertion that stratification expresses normative consensus? (5) How valid is the thesis that "positions which are combined in the same family cannot be made the basis of stratification?" [18]

EQUALITY AND INEQUALITY

Various sociologists identify stratification with prevailing inequalities in the distribution of social advantages or benefits. "If the rights and prerequisites of different positions in a society must be unequal, then the society must be stratified, because that is precisely what stratification means. . . . Every society, no matter how simple or complex, must differentiate persons in terms of both prestige and esteem, and must, therefore, possess a certain amount of institutionalized inequality." [19] Being general, this formula neither attempts to distinguish types of social advantage, nor examines the distribution that identifies stratification. Here, the critical question is whether this distribution or the principles

[18] Kurt B. Mayer, *Class and Society* (New York: Random House, 1955), p. 5.
[19] Davis and Moore, *op. cit.*, p. 243.

which regulate it is the relevant object of study. Current social theory seeks to handle the second alternative by distinctions between systems in which status is ascribed and achieved; but the results are hardly satisfactory, first because all systems of stratification combine both principles, but more importantly because this device signally fails to answer the critical question, namely, in what sense is the unequal distribution of advantages evidence of stratification? Doubtless this obscurity is essential to the theoretical claim that stratification is a universal response of society to certain functional pre-requisites; but if this assumption obstructs discriminating analysis and comparison, it can scarcely provide a sound basis for the sociology of economic development. Especially, perhaps, because the theory based on it is said to represent such "a high degree of abstraction (that) . . . it is impossible to move directly from the kind of proposition we were making to descriptive propositions about, say, American society," [20] a more pedestrian but operational scheme is needed.

Inequality seems to be the heart of the matter. It is with this in one form or another that sociologists identify stratification; but they generally leave obscure the sense in which these unequal rankings or distributions of advantage are crucial for stratification. And though these inequalities are conventional and institutionalized, being regarded as necessary on theoretical grounds, all their forms are treated as equally appropriate and legitimate. "Social inequality is thus an unconsciously evolved device by which societies ensure that the most important positions are conscientiously filled by the most qualified persons." [21] It is difficult to show that the "most important positions" are always held by the "most qualified persons," or that they are always "conscientiously filled;" but if we accept these assumptions, the regimes of Adolf Hitler, Trujillo and Franklin Roosevelt are all equally appropriate and legitimate.

Since positional inequality is identified with stratification, it is useful to consider briefly what the diametrically opposite condition implies. Little effort has been made recently to see what such perfect equality involves.[22] A condition of perfect equality of social positions is admittedly hard to conceive, and its duration over any period of time even more so. The reasons are evident. Such perfect equality involves the

[20] Kingsley Davis, "Reply" (to M. M. Tumin), *American Sociological Review*, 18 (August, 1953), p. 394.

[21] Davis and Moore, *op cit.*, p. 243.

[22] For valuable discussions, see Jean-Jacques Rousseau, "Discourse sur l'Origine et Fondment de l'Inegalite parmi les hommes" (1753) in C. E. Vaughan, *The Political Writings of Jean-Jacques Rousseau* (London: Cambridge University Press, 1915, 2 vols.). Also R. H. Tawney, *Equality* (4th edn., New York: Capricorn Books, 1961).

systematic elimination of all socially relevant differences, biological or structural, with the result that, except perhaps for their differing locations, all persons simultaneously hold identical positions, rights, duties and relations. In consequence, none hold any. Child and father, ill and hale, sane and insane, all are positionally identical. Clearly no such aggregate could survive midsummer, since this perfect equality eliminates right, obligation and relation as well as individuation, and institutes the preconditions of the Hobbesian "war of all against all." Such total elimination of positional differences automatically dissolves society, since society can only be defined by reference to differentiation, whether this is conceived relationally or in terms of action.

In a condition of absolute positional identity, individual organisms are the only possible units, but despite their biological differences, they are *ex definitione* identical. Such total antithesis of differentiation is of course biologically impossible. Populations being biologically differentiated, societies inevitably consist in differentiated positions and roles, with their correlative rights and duties. Such differentiation inherently involves the differential distribution of rights and duties, simply because this is what the differentiation consists in; but clearly stratification is only one mode of social differentiation and not identical with all its forms.

The point here is simply that in any society, at any point in time, the current distribution of social positions and advantages must always be unequal, because they are differentiated; and not merely because these "advantages" are highly various, but because the members of any society are heterogeneous as regards age, sex and personal qualities. Even in social systems subsumed by kinship, this will be the case, since mother and child are an indispensable asymmetrical pair. Instead of simplistic references to the universality of unequal distributions of right, duty and advantage—that is, to social differentiation of status and role—we must seek to discriminate the principles regulating and institutionalizing varying modes of distribution. Some of these modes may constitute a stratification, others may not. Not inequality, but the modes of its institutionalization, its bases and forms, are the relevant materials for identifying and analyzing stratification systems. We have to take inequality for granted, since total equality in any indispensable relation such as parent and child is merely inequality once removed and intensified.

In studying institutionalized inequality, two questions are essential, and a third perhaps even more important. Descriptively, we must ask "In what does inequality consist? What is its form, degree and scale?" Analytically, we must ask "On what is this distribution based, and how does it relate to other features of the social order?" Historically, where data permit, we should ask, "How did the present system come into being? What changes has it recently undergone, or is currently undergoing?"

Whereas sociological theory regards answers to the first, descriptive question as proof of stratification, anthropologists generally rely on the second for the data by which they classify systems as "stratified" or unstratified. For them, simple inequality in the distribution of advantages is inevitable on grounds of biology and kinship, and therefore cannot provide sufficient evidence of stratification. In their view, the principles by which observable inequalities are institutionalized are the critical data. These principles differentiate systems in which inequalities are temporary, random or contingent from others in which access to advantageous positions is differentially distributed, so that, whatever the grounds, some persons are privileged and others disqualified. Systems of the latter sort may be stratified if the differential distribution of opportunities characterizes ranked strata having some internal homogeneity and external distinctness. Excluding biologically given differences—without which human society is of course impossible—inequality in the distribution of access to favored positions is decisive for societal classification as stratified; only some societies having differentially distributed opportunities may in fact be stratified; and stratification never consists in the mere existence or occupancy of these differential positions, but in the principles by which the distribution of access and opportunities is regulated.

Even when all members of a society enjoy equivalent opportunities to obtain positions of social precedence and advantage, at any given moment and over time, these must be distributed "unequally," in the sense that some persons hold them while others do not. "Photographic" accounts of current distributions fail to provide an adequate basis for social classification or analysis, simply because they assimilate sharply different types of society on the basis of superficial similarities.

Where access to the highest positions and advantages is equally open to all, these positions usually form an indefinite series, co-extensive in space and time with the society their dispersal identifies. They are accordingly highly standardized, and functional differentiation is limited thereby, the society concerned being typically acephalous. In intensity and span, integrative centralization corresponds with the degree of functional differentiation attained by a society; in form with its structural differentiation. Under conditions of centralization, equivalence of access to the highest positions and advantages will be limited in the first place by the small number of such positions relative to the size of the population. Since the chiefdom may only have one paramount at a

MICHAEL G. SMITH

time, and few in any individual life-span, most members cannot reasonably expect to be chief. In Athens, where offices were filled by lot, a conscious effort was made to maintain this ideal equivalence within a clearly defined stratum by devices combining the principles of divination and roulette.[23] Neither achievement nor ascription adequately describes this mode of recruitment.

UNSTRATIFIED SYSTEMS

Given the preceding discussion, it will be useful to describe various types of unstratified society, to clarify their variety and institutional mechanisms.

The political structure of many East African societies consists in a hierarchy of male age-sets. Organizational details vary widely as between societies; but in all, age-sets are ranked by seniority, and in most the different sets have differing roles, rights and duties. Age-mates are social and jural equals, and each set exercises jurisdiction over its members. Seniority regulates relations between successive sets. At regular intervals, new sets are instituted in tribal ceremonies that move all senior sets forward into the next higher grades. Rights to marry, to beget children, to establish a homestead, to participate in civil or judicial councils, to officiate at rituals, to go on raids, are all variably integrated with this age-stratification. At any given moment an unequal distribution of rights and advantages obtains among these peoples; but the mode of institutionalization guarantees the automatic transfer of positions and advantages to junior sets at determinate intervals, and thus ensures equality of access over time. The seniority principle, basic to age-set differentiation, regulates this distribution of social positions and access to them. Inequalities are always temporary, and each individual in turn automatically moves through the same series of positions by virtue of his compulsory identification with an age-set. Despite their internal homogeneity and external distinctiveness, given their ceaseless progression, it is patently ridiculous to designate these cohorts by the same term used for castes, estates, slavery or social classes. In age-stratification, mobility is identical with the system, in its rhythm and limits. The principles by which differential advantages are institutionally distributed in these age-systems are directly opposed to those constituting stratification. These conditions occur in varying form among the Galla, the Nandi, Kipsigi,

[23] H. Ward Fowler, *The City State of the Greeks and Romans* (London: Macmillan, 1952), pp. 166-167.

Terik, Masai, Turkana, Jie, Karimojong, Kikuyu, Kadara, Hidatsa, etc.[24] Stratification is scarcely possible below a certain minimum level of differentiation; but even where a number of asymmetrical roles and units are differentiated, these may be so distributed as to preclude stratification. According to Lauriston Sharp, this is the condition of the Australian Yir Yuront, where "a hierarchy of a pyramidal or inverted Y type to include all men in the system is an impossibility," [25] since each individual participates as superior and inferior in an exactly equal number of dyadic relations. Since the 28 Yir Yuront kinship relations embrace virtually all institutionalized roles, despite their asymmetry, their distribution enjoins social equality by restricting inequalities to individual relations, and by so distributing these that no individual lacks 14 superiors and 14 inferiors simultaneously. Few systems achieve this mathematical perfection. That of the Yir Yuront gives such extreme stress to specific asymmetrical relations that even the concept of *situs* seems excluded, much less stratification.

Different patterns appear among the Ituri pygmies and Bushmen, whose bilateral kinship institutions differentiate fewer roles and pattern them less strongly. These peoples are so weakly differentiated that stratification is impossible for them. Pygmy bands lack effective leaders and any differential distribution of sanctions or privileges among their members, above the level of the household. Individuals are free to leave or enter a band, unless members oppose their entry. Since all pygmy households are equally self-sufficient and interdependent, the distribution of household and inter-household roles is constant and

[24] G. W. B. Huntingford, *The Nandi of Kenya* (London: Routledge and Kegan Paul, 1953), and *The Galla of Ethiopia* (London: International African Institute, 1955); A. H. J. Prins, *East African Age-class Systems* (Groningen: J. B. Wolters, 1953); J. G. Peristiany, *The Social Institutions of the Kipsigis* (London: Routledge and Kegan Paul, 1939); Pamela Gulliver and P. H. Gulliver, *The Central Nilo-Hamites* (London: International African Institute, 1953); P. H. Gulliver, "The Age-set Organization of the Jie Tribe," *Journal of the Royal Anthropological Institute*, 83 (December, 1953), pp. 147-168, and "Turkana Age-Orientation," *American Anthropologist*, 60 (October, 1958), pp. 900-922; B. Bernardi, "The Age-Set System of the Nilo-Hamites," *Africa*, 22 (October, 1952), pp. 316-332; H. E. Lambert, *Kikuyu Social and Political Institutions* (London: Oxford University Press, 1956); N. Dyson-Hudson, "The Karimojong Age System," *Ethnology*, 2 (July, 1963), pp. 353-401; Robert A. LeVine and Walter H. Sangree, "The Diffusion of Age-Group Organisation in East Africa: A Controlled Comparison," *Africa*, 32 (April, 1962), pp. 97-110; Robert H. Lowie, *Primitive Society* (London: Routledge and Kegan Paul, 1949), pp. 273-282; and H. A. Fosbrooke, "An Administrative Survey of the Masai Social System," *Tanganyika Notes and Records*, 26 (1948), pp. 1-50.

[25] Lauriston Sharp, "People without Politics," in Verne F. Ray (ed.), *Systems of Political Control and Bureaucracy in Human Societies*, (Seattle: American Ethnological Society, University of Washington Press, 1958), p. 5. See also W. Lloyd Warner, *A Black Civilization: A Social Study of an Australian Tribe* (New York: Harper & Row, 1958).

uniform. Pygmies approach the Durkheimian model of the primitive undifferentiated society that excludes stratification, whether on grounds of ascription or achievement. Neither in ritual, hunting, kinship nor band relations do they exhibit any discernible inequalities of rank or advantage. In the familial sphere, the apparently unequal distribution of rights and duties has a simple biological basis in congruent inequalities of capacity.[26]

Pygmies are not unique. !Kung Bushmen evince similar patterns. !Kung live in bands, each with its component families and fixed resources of water rights, veldkos areas, mangbetti woods, etc. Each band has a headman, normally recruited by descent, who exercises symbolic custody of band resources. Among !Kung, bands cannot exist without headmen, but these may or may not reside in their bands. A "stranger" seeking water first asks the headman's permission before visiting the band's water-hole; but the headman will only refuse if the band members object—a rare event. Band headmen may be children or women, where men are unavailable for succession; apparently nobody wants the role. Headmen have no advantages that distinguish them from other !Kung. Band members hunt in small teams of their own choice; they are obliged by various institutions to distribute the meat of the hunt rather widely. Very few men are polygynists and these may or may not be headmen. When away from their bands, headmen have neither special statuses nor obligations. With the exceptions mentioned above, this is also their position within the band.

Certain devices of fictive kinship ensure the extension of kinship terms and behaviour to non-kin, so that in effect all !Kung are related to one another directly or indirectly in ways entailing specific rights and obligations; but the roster of differentiated relations is short by comparison with the Yir Yuront. In some relations, real or fictive, each !Kung will enjoy some advantage; in others his role is inferior; in the remainder the relation is symmetrical. The narrow bilateral kinship system by which kin are dispersed, mainly through marriage, provides no basis for gerontocracy; nor do !Kung allocate status on grounds of age. As among Pygmies and Andamanese, !Kung bands hold frequent rituals in which all adult members take part. All men are shamans. They share identical ritual status and collective duties. In no sense can the !Kung be said to exhibit stratification above the level of the family.[27]

[26] Colin Turnbull, The Forest People (New York: Simon and Schuster, 1961).

[27] Lorna Marshall, "The Kin Terminology System of the !Kung Bushmen," Africa, 27 (January, 1957), pp. 1-25; "Marriage among the !Kung Bushmen," Africa, 29 (October, 1959), pp. 335-365; "!Kung Bushmen Bands," Africa, 30 (October, 1960), pp. 225-355; "Sharing, Talking and Giving: Relief of Social Tensions among !Kung Bushmen," Africa, 31 (January, 1961) pp. 24-49; "!Kung Bushmen Religious Beliefs," Africa, 32 (July, 1962), pp. 221-252.

Descent provides another basis on which distributions of differential position and advantage may be so organized that equal access and automatic transfers prevail. Here also, societies vary: some trace descent through the male, others through the female line, and others through both lines, together or separately. In societies of the last type, all individuals simultaneously belong to their father's patrilineage and to their mother's matrilineage. In each, they hold different rights and obligations and enjoy a different status. These differences are balanced, and thus distinguish the complementary lineage forms.

Lineages, as these unilineal descent groups are called, vary widely in their depth, span, scale, form, functions and other attributes. Some incorporate sizable tribes, such as the Gusii, Tiv, Lugbara, or the issue of Abraham. Where this occurs, the component lineages are distinguished in a hierarchic series of corporations having an explicit segmentary organization corresponding to the genealogy. Social distance is then defined by the range of collateral kinship. Hierarchic relations of descent indicate jural identity. Close lineage kin share exclusive solidary obligations and identical jural status. As the range of kinship extends, jural differentiation increases, the relevant units being groups rather than individuals. The segmentary lineage is a system of corporate groups organized in a hierarchy of co-ordinate divisions of differing depth and span, and unified by an ideology of common descent.[28]

Long ago Radcliffe-Brown isolated the principles on which these corporate lineages are based, namely the unity of the sibling group as seen from without, and the equivalence of same-sex siblings.[29] Given the tradition of tracing descent through one sex to the exclusion of the other, these principles, if observed, inevitably promote corporate unilineal descent groups with a segmentary internal structure. Duplicated, they develop a system of double descent. Modifications that deviate from

[28] Max Gluckman, "Introduction," in J. C. Mitchell and J. A. Barnes, *The Lamba Village,* Communications of the School of African Studies, No. 24 (Capetown, 1948), pp. 5-8; Meyer Fortes, "The Structure of Unilineal Descent Groups," *American Anthropologist,* 55 (February, 1953), pp. 17-41; M. G. Smith, "On Segmentary Lineage Systems," *Journal of the Royal Anthropological Institute,* 86, part 2 (December, 1956), pp. 39-80; and Rosemary Harris, "The Political Significance of Double Unilineal Descent," *Journal of the Royal Anthropological Institute,* 92 part 1 (June, 1962), pp. 86-101. For an excellent collection of lineage studies, see J. Middleton and D. Tait (eds.), *Tribes Without Rulers* (London: Routledge and Kegan Paul, 1958).

[29] A. R. Radcliffe-Brown, "The Social Organization of Australian Tribes," *Oceania,* 1 (1930-31), parts 1-4, pp. 34-63, 206-246, 322-341, 426-456; "Patrilineal and Matrilineal Succession," reprinted in A. R. Radcliffe-Brown, *Structure and Function in Primitive Society* (London, Cohen and West, 1952), pp. 32-48; "The Study of Kinship Systems," reprinted in *Structure and Function in Primitive Society,* pp. 49-89; and "Introduction," in A. R. Radcliffe-Brown and Daryll Forde (eds.), *African Systems of Kinship and Marriage* (London: Oxford University Press, 1950) pp. 1-85.

these principles produce structures differing from the segmentary model in direct correspondence. Some illustrations of this are mentioned below.

For its emergence and continuity, the segmentary lineage presumes the jural, ritual and social equivalence of siblings in the direct line of descent. Accordingly, it classifies different sibling groups as units of co-ordinate status, each internally undifferentiated, therefore excluding jural inequalities among its members, even though at any given moment the senior men enjoy superior social and ritual advantages as family heads and custodians of lineage rights. The equivalence of lineage members really consists in the equal distribution of rights and access to such positions among them, as they mature. Thus, the segmentary lineage, a rather widespread social form, excludes internal stratification, despite the inevitable inequalities in the current distribution of advantages inherent in its generational and familial compositon. In place of horizontal strata, the lineage principle establishes vertical divisions between lineages as units of corporate status, as befits Durkheim's segmental model. The effect is to restrict lateral or inter-lineage mobility, while instituting vertical or intra-lineage mobility. The status system of the corporate lineage is thus diametrically opposite to hierarchic ranking; and all men are status peers in societies organized on these lines, since all lineages are co-ordinate at some level of the organization.

FAMILY AND STRATIFICATION

Despite the differential distribution of rights, duties and advantages within Pygmy or Bushmen families, I do not regard them as stratified, for two reasons. First, these differentiations do not go beyond what is essential for the definition and maintenance of the family as a unit of husband, wife and offspring. Second, the differentiated positions are equally open to all in due course. Without these differentiations, the family could not be constituted or identified. Children would have no fathers.

Whether the family everywhere exhibits this lack of internal stratification is surely an empirical matter. If we regard "hierarchical sex and age grading" [30] as stratification, then we must recognize the internal stratification of families in all societies where such grading occurs. Siblings who belong to different age-sets ranked as senior and junior are distinguished within as well as beyond the family. Conversely, if we do not regard families as internally stratified, these age and sex distinctions

[30] Aberle, Cohen, Davis, Levy, Sutton, *op. cit.*, p. 106.

should not be represented as stratification. Some writers, however, simultaneously hold that stratification is universal and deny that families are ever internally stratified. Since societies such as the Bushmen or Pygmies lack any supra-familial organization, if their families are unstratified, then they lack stratification also. Thus, the postulate of the unstratified family contradicts the asserted universality of stratification, both being advanced by the same writers, with relevant functional explanations. In fact, the data show that social stratification is not universal, and that families are not universally exempt from it, on any definitions of society and the family one cares to fashion.

For Kingsley Davis,

those positions that may be combined in the same legitimate family—viz., positions based on sex, age and kinship—do not form part of the system of stratification. On the other hand, those positions that are socially prohibited from being combined in the same legal family—viz., different caste or class positions—constitute what we call stratification. With reference to the class hierarchy the family is a unit: its members occupy the same rank. This is because one of the family's main functions is the ascription of status. It could not very well perform this function if it did not, as a family, occupy a single position in the scale. Children are said to "acquire their parents' status," with the implication that two parents have a common status to transmit, and that the child gets this status automatically as a member of the family. In the same way, husband and wife are treated as social equals.[31]

The convenience of this doctrine for the analysis of Western industrial society has encouraged its acceptance without much effort to check its validity. Evidently it refers mainly to the nuclear family in monogamous societies, but since the thesis is unqualified it is now being applied to polygynous societies also.[32] I shall therefore discuss its validity with reference to systems of either type. Even in monogamous societies, where siblings have differential rights to inheritance and succession, this generalization may not hold. The variety of organizational problems and solutions that such conditions present is illustrated by the coexistence of gavelkind, primogeniture, and "borough English" in medieval Britain.[33] Where wives and their offspring are differentially ranked in certain polygynous societies, these differences are often integrated with extra-familial stratification. Under such conditions the family functions

---

[31] Kingsley Davis, *Human Society* (New York: The Macmillan Co., 1949), p. 364; partly cited also in Davis, "Reply" (to M. M. Tumin), *op. cit.*, p. 394.

[32] See Bohannan, *op. cit.*, pp. 166, 180-182.

[33] Sir Paul Vinogradoff, *Common Sense in Law* (3rd ed., rev. by H. G. Hanbury, London: Oxford University Press, 1959), pp. 122-123; George C. Homans, *Sentiments and Activities: Essays in Social Science* (New York: Free Press of Glencoe, 1962), pp. 148-155, 161-165.

quite efficiently as a mechanism of status placement by meticulously differentiating members instead of assimilating them.

Among the Swazi,

the clans are graded into a rough hierarchy, and the rank of a clan is measured by its position in the national structure. The entire clan as such does not hold this position, but only certain lineages. . . . In every large clan there are a number of parallel lineages, . . . linked up with the senior lineage at irregular points of the family tree. . . . In every lineage members are graded by their distance from the head.[34]

Wives of a polygynist hold unequal status; during his lifetime they are graded primarily on the basis of seniority, the first taking precedence over the second, and so on, but after his death the children's rights to inheritance and succession are determined by their mother's rank and mode of marriage. . . . The fundamental principle underlying the selection of the main heir of a polygynist is that property and power are inherited from men and acquired by them, but are transmitted through women, whose rank, more than any other factor, determines the choice. "A ruler is ruler by his mother.". . . The tie between sons of the same father undoubtedly depends largely on the status of the wives, and it is over succession and inheritance that cleavages between half-brothers come out sharply and bitterly. . . . The main heir receives far and away the major share.[35]

Among the Tswana, there are "three separate classes, nobles, . . . commoners, . . . and immigrants, . . . Within each class there are further distinctions. Among nobles, the more closely a man is related to the chief, the higher does he rank. . . . Among commoners . . . the head of any group is senior to all his dependents, among whom his own relatives are of higher status than the others." [36] "The children of paternal uncles are differentiated according to the relative status of their father. . . . If senior to one's father by birth, they are entitled to obedience and respect; if junior, their services can be freely commanded. The saying that a man's 'elder brother' is his chief, and his 'younger brother' his subject, summarises adequately the accepted relation. . . . But disputes sometimes occur owing to arbitrary exercise of authority and rival claims to property and position, and it is not fortuitous that most accusations of sorcery are made against one's relatives in the same ward." [37]

Among the Zulu, "the closer a royal prince was (and is) by birth to the reigning king, the higher his social status. . . . The same rules

[34] Kuper, op. cit., p. 111.

[35] Hilda Kuper, "Kinship among the Swazi" in Radcliffe-Brown and Forde (eds.), African Systems of Kinship and Marriage, op. cit., pp. 93, 96, 98.

[36] I. Schapera, The Tswana (London: International African Institute, 1953), pp. 36-37, and "Kinship and Politics in Tswana History," Journal of the Royal Anthropological Institute, 93 (December, 1963), pp. 159-173.

[37] I. Schapera, "Kinship and Marriage among the Tswana," in Radcliffe-Brown and Forde (eds.), op cit., p. 104.

applied to the ruling families within the tribes."[38] "The status of sons depends on the status of their mothers in the compound family."[39]

Wives are graded. One, the chief wife of the great house, who may be married late in life, will produce the main heir. She has placed under her a number of subordinate wives. Another wife is head of the left-hand house, which also contains subordinate wives; and another group of wives, in very big families, form the right-hand huts. . . . The junior wife and her children are under the authority of the senior wife and her children. . . . The sons' rights and positions in their father's home and in their agnatic lineage are determined by the positions of their mothers. Some of the main sources of litigation among the Zulu are disputes between half-brothers about their rights arising from the respective status of their mothers. . . . The positions of the wives' huts in the village, their status in the tribe, the order of their marriage, their wedding ceremonial, the source of their marriage cattle, are all considered in evidence.[40]

Among the Kachins of highland Burma, few of whom have plural wives, ultimogeniture prevails and "elder sons to-day usually move to another village," to escape their high-ranking youngest brother. "A man's rank is in theory precisely defined by his birth," but since "an intolerable psychological situation is likely to arise" if he stays at home, the elder brother generally moves to his wife's village as "bond slave (*mayam*) to his *mayu* (wife's kin)." According to Leach, this "mechanism of lineage fission is closely linked with ideas about class status, and the process . . . is at the same time a process of social mobility up and down the class hierarchy. The choice that an individual makes about his place of residence affects the class status and prospects of his descendants."[41]

Polynesia provides some the most elaborate examples of a unitary stratification system that ranks family members as well as families.

The mode of succession is primogeniture; the eldest son succeeds to the position of his father. . . . Not only is he differentiated from his younger brothers, but so also is every brother differentiated from every other, in accordance with their respective order of birth and the consequent prospects of succeeding to the position of their father. . . . The seniority principle in the family is a microcosm of the ramified social system. . . . As a consequence of seniority, the descendants of an older brother rank higher than the descendants of a younger brother. . . . *Every individual* within this group of descendants of a common ancestor holds a differing status, one precisely in proportion to his

---

[38] Max Gluckman, "The Kingdom of the Zulu of South Africa" in Meyer Fortes and E. E. Evans-Pritchard (eds.), *African Political Systems* (London: Oxford University Press, 1940), p. 34.

[39] Max Gluckman, "Kinship and Marriage among the Lozi of Northern Rhodesia and the Zulu of Natal" in Radcliffe-Browne and Forde (eds.), *op. cit.*, p. 186.

[40] *Ibid.*, pp. 183, 195-196.

[41] Edmund Leach, *Political Systems of Highland Burma: A Study of Kachin Social Structure* (London: Bell and Sons, 1954), pp. 109, 160, 167-168.

distance from the senior line of descent in the group. . . . People descendent from remote collaterals of the common ancestor are lower in rank than those descendent from a more immediate relative of the chiefly line. People with the lowest status are those who have descended from younger brothers through younger brothers *ad infinitum*. The process of primogenitural succession and its consequent implication of seniority result in a ranking structure which encompasses the entire society. . . . In every ramified society one can recognise groups of statuses or status levels which are functionally significant in terms of differential socio-economic prerogatives. These different levels are normally present in all the larger ramages."[42]

Among the Moslem Hausa, besides his legal wives, a man could have slave concubines. Under Muslim law a concubine who bore her master a child became freed on the master's death, when her child inherited with those of the four legal wives. Several Hausa Emirs in the last century were born of concubines. In this case, free and slave, the master and the concubine, are joined in the same family; but only on the former's death is the latter freed.

In Hausa families, "differences of marriage order take precedence among co-wives over other differences, such as age or parentage, but outside the household these other differences may have more significance . . . . The average Hausa woman probably makes three or four marriages before the menopause. . . . Under such conditions of marital instability, spouses cannot share the same social status. Indeed, the status differentiation of co-wives by reference to marriage order precludes their status identity with the common husband. Legally and politically this identity is also impossible,"[43] since "authority over women is divided between their husbands, to whom they are subordinate, and their kinsmen, who are their legal guardians. Thus the wife is not identified with her husband as his ward."[44] In Hausa society, "the status gradient produced by rank and lineage is finite and steep. . . . Inheritance . . . facilitates the economic differentiation of descent lines, . . . lineages include descent lines of widely differing status."[45]

These data show that even within nuclear families, for example those of Hausa men and their concubines or wives, spouses may not share the same status, nor siblings the same rank, as among the Kachin, Polynesians or Bantu. In all the cases cited, the differential ranking of family members extends beyond the family to rank them and their descendants differently in the wider society. Thus the stratification

---

[42] Sahlins, *op. cit.*, pp. 140-142, 147 (his italics).

[43] M. G. Smith, "The Hausa System of Social Status," *Africa*, 29 (July, 1959), p. 244.

[44] M. G. Smith, "Kebbi and Hausa Stratification," *British Journal of Sociology*, 12 (March, 1961), p. 59.

[45] Smith, "The Hausa System of Social Status," *op cit.*, p. 241.

within the kin group supports and corresponds with that outside it, and this is an important feature of the political organization of these societies. For the Southern Bantu, Hoernlé generalizes, "among the children a strict hierarchy prevails, based on the seniority which serves as a fundamental principle of . . . Bantu society. The elder brother always takes precedence between brothers . . . and so too between sisters. . . . Outside the intimate circle of the immediate family, the same principles of kinship and seniority hold sway." [46] According to van Warmelo, "Bantu social structure knows no equals, as with whole sibs, so with individuals. The first-born of the same parents is always superior to those born after him, and this superiority is extended to his descendants, with varying consistency." [47] This is the type of rank-differentiated unilineal grouping that Kirchhoff identifies as the "conical clan." In his words, "it is precisely the nearness of relationship to the common ancestor of the group which matters. . . . (This) principle results in a group in which every single member, except brothers and sisters, has a different standing." [48] As our data show, Kirchhoff erred in ascribing equivalent status to siblings in these units. If siblings shared equivalent status, the conical clan could not emerge. In short, when societies rest their stratification on principles that differentiate descent lines in status by seniority, they do likewise with family members.

It is clear that many societies exhibit a stratification which differentiates family members as well as families. Thus, neither of the two general assumptions on which the functionalist theory of stratification rests are empirically valid. Neither is stratification universal, nor are families universally exempted from it.

If we ask why, given their inconsistency, these postulates of universal stratification and the unstratified family are combined, the answer seems to be that on this basis it is easy to distinguish different types of stratification system by reference to the family. The reasoning might be summarized as follows: (1) All societies are stratified. (2) In all societies, families are homogeneous units of status placement. (3) Stratification systems differ in the ways they treat families; some restrict opportunities to a limited number of families, others distribute them to all member-families equally. Systems of the first type are ascriptive and particularistic, while those of the second stress achievement and universalistic

[46] A. Winifred Hoernlé, "Social Organisation" in I. Schapera (ed.), *The Bantu-Speaking Tribes of South Africa* (London: Routledge and Kegan Paul, 1937), p. 71.
[47] N. J. van Warmelo, *Kinship Terminology of the South African Bantu* (Pretoria Department of Native Affairs, Union of South Africa, 1931), p. 11.
[48] Paul Kirchhoff, "The Principles of Clanship in Human Society," reprinted in Morton H. Fried, *Readings in Anthropology* (New York, Thomas Y. Crowell Company, 1959), vol. 2, p. 266.

criteria. (4) Since systems of both types exhibit both stratification and familial status unity, a single general theory is applicable to all.

Ethnographic data show that these assumptions, and the theory that seeks to justify them, are invalid. The "universal necessities" imposed by functional prerequisites are simple misapprehensions. If my argument holds, the critical sources of difficulty for this functional theory are twofold: first it seeks to explain structure by function, when the reverse is the wiser procedure. Structures are highly differentiated and complex, while functions tend to be generalized and rather abstract. Just as Malinowski failed adequately to account for the known range of variation in the family by his very general functional theory of the family, so it is probably impossible to "explain" the known variety of social structures by a single functional theory of stratification. Secondly, in seeking universality, this theory creates difficulties for itself by regarding any set of observable inequalities in the distribution of advantage as stratification, irrespective of the mode of their institutionalization. Given this, the errors regarding relations between family and stratification seem inevitable. But in segmentary lineages, which are political structures despite their familial components, and in age-set systems, though positions of unequal advantage and responsibility are general, the mode of their institutionalization involves an automatic serial rotation of these positions, since the modal life-cycle and life-chances are equal and standardized. Stratification consists in institutionalized differentiations of access to positions of differing advantage, rather than in the mere fact of social differentiation.

When unilineal descent principles are combined with internal differentiation of rank between siblings, on grounds of either matrifiliation or seniority by birth, the resulting internal stratification of the lineage group precludes the status equivalence of siblings, and the co-ordinate status of segments descended from them. As a direct effect of these principles of status differentiation, and in exact correspondence with their intensity, the structure of the unilineal descent group diverges from the pure model of the segmentary lineage as a hierarchy of levels, the members of which are all co-ordinate. In similar fashion, the ascriptive universalism of the age-set will be modified by principles that impose status inequalities among its members on other grounds. Similarly, band organization varies societally as a correlate of the differing principles on which the bands are constituted. However important, stratification—the differential distribution of access to advantageous positions—is only one of these modifying principles.

THE PROBLEM OF CONSENSUS

There are two sides to my argument. Negatively, I seek to show certain inadequacies in the current theory of stratification. Positively, I am suggesting that the principles that regulate access to positions of advantage also define political units such as age-sets, bands, segmentary lineages, ramages, etc. In short, I wish to stress the political basis of social stratification. Unstratified societies are acephalous, and in these units status consists of membership in the modal political units. Stratification is correlated with hierarchical political organization, which may or may not be fully centralized. Like other principles and modes of social differentiation, stratification has political bases and implications. Whether restrictive or egalitarian, differentiation is a condition of political organization. Some highly differentiated societies may not exhibit determinate strata; others do; but even systems with primary stress on situs will gravitate toward stratification unless certain principles prevent it. Stable situs systems may thus represent an arrested intermediate type between the formally stratified and the unstratified. The differences between the latter pair are fundamental.

I fail to see in what sense it is useful or accurate to describe personal status differences in bands, segmentary lineages or age-organized societies as either ascribed or achieved. Neither term seems meaningful here. The utility of either presupposes some hierarchic differentiation of positions and some principles by which access to them is differentially distributed. As these principles vary, status is usually said to be ascribed or achieved. The utility of this dichotomy is also doubtful on other grounds.

Munro Edmondson illustrates some of the operational difficulties in his distinctions betwen ascribed, achieved, and associational status. In his view, statuses differentiated on age, sex, and kinship are ascribed, while achieved statuses include differentiations based on religion, economy or politics. By associational status, he indicates differentiations based on membership in such voluntary or compulsory organizations as dance societies, ceremonial associations, fraternities, religious orders, clans or *gentes,* phratries, bands, villages, tribes, age-grades or stratified ranks.[49] The inconsistencies of this effort are apparent.

An important theme of the following paragraphs is that ascription and achievement of status are regularly concurrent in stratified societies.

[49] Munro S. Edmonson, *Status Terminology and the Social Structure of North American Indians* (Seattle: University of Washington Press, 1958), pp. 8-9.

Wherever secular stratification is overtly or formally ascriptive, positions are achieved or held by competitive struggles. Wherever the conditions of stratification formally stress individual achievement, ascriptive factors are crucial. Ideal-type analysis of these complex and very varied systems is not merely inadequate but misleading. Even an analysis in terms of dominant and subordinate value systems fails to deal adequately with their structural complexity and variety.[50] We must always seek the structural particulars, resisting reductionist temptations inherent in value theory until the essentials of a given system have been isolated as a particular complex of principles, and compared with others of similar and differing character. Quite probably such enquiries may require somewhat less ambiguous categories than ascription or achievement; attention to restriction, sponsorship, competition and personal or impersonal selection may be more useful.

Stratification consists in the restriction of access to positions of varying advantage. If uninstitutionalized, such "restriction" can only be random, unprincipled, contingent and temporary. Not to be so, it must be institutionalized on the basis of certain principles, whatever these might be. Such institutionalization always involves a historical selection of the relevant principles. Where the various principles that regulate this differential distribution of opportunities are mutually conflicting and obstructive, dissensus is generated, and the system may break down. Thus adequate institutionalization involves mutual accommodation of the relevant principles into a congruent scheme. These principles may and do vary widely; so do the positions and rewards to which they relate, and so does their mutual congruence and interdependence. Where the relevant principles regulating opportunities and defining the structural significance of positions are loosely integrated, a situs system may emerge, and such a system may enjoy adequate consensus. While the resilience of a stratification system depends on the consensus it elicits, this consensus itself depends on the character, congruence and inclusiveness of the principles that establish the stratification. Even though its constitutive principles are congruent and mutually reinforcing, a stratification may lack adequate consensus if these principles are not sufficiently inclusive. The political nature and implications of stratification are directly evident here.

To postulate a consensual normative basis for all forms of stratification is an unnecessary error which may be traced to the influence of

---

[50] Florence Kluckhohn and Fred L. Strodtbeck, *Variations in Value-Orientations* (Evanston, Ill.: Row, Peterson, 1961), pp. 32-35.

Weber and Durkheim.[51] It is also very common nowadays, and recurs at various levels of specificity as an indispensable premise for the analysis of society by reference to values. Thus, "regardless of the type of stratification and authority system, a normative scale of priorities for allocating scarce values (precedence, property rights, power, etc.) is . . . always vital." [52] "Human society achieves its unity primarily through the possession by its members of certain ultimate values and ends in common." [53] "Stratification *in its valuational aspect*, then, is the ranking of units in a social system in accordance with the standards of the common value system." [54]

Normative consensus expressed in agreement about standards relevant for ranking persons and positions is perhaps the most efficient basis for a system of differentiated access; but it is neither the only one, nor self-generating; and its principal conditions, ethnic homogeneity and identification by birth with a unit having a continuous history, are not general among underdeveloped nations currently engaged in industrialization. In consequence, as Shils observes, "consensus" may have to be "coerced." [55] This empties the notion of any positive meaning. Furnivall succinctly described some of these societies in their colonial phase as "plural societies." Perhaps this pluralism persists into early independence. In the plural society, "as a whole, there is no common social will. There may be apathy on such a vital point as defence against aggression. Few recognize that in fact all the members of all sections have material interests in common, but most see that on many points their material interests are opposed." [56] In these colonial and post-colonial societies, the system of stratification is one of the most fertile sources of discord. Its continuity often depends on constraint rather than consensus.

Schwab provides an illuminating application of consensualist theory and procedure in his discussion of stratification in Gwelo, a Rhodesian mining town of 7,000 Europeans and 25,000 Africans, mainly Shona,

[51] For representative statements by these writers, see Emile Durkheim, *Professional Ethics and Civic Morals*, trans. Cornelia Brookfield (London: Routledge and Kegan Paul, 1957) p. 61; Max Weber, *The Theory of Social and Economic Organization*, translated by Talcott Parsons and A. R. Henderson (London: William Hodge, 1947) Ch. 1, sec. 5 and p. 298.

[52] Aberle, Cohen, Davis, Levy, and Sutton, *op. cit.*, p. 106.

[53] Davis and Moore, *op. cit.*, p. 244.

[54] Parsons, "A Revised Analytical Approach to the Theory of Social Stratification," p. 93 (his italics).

[55] Edward A. Shils, *Political Development in the New States* (Gravenhage: Mouton, 1962), pp. 14, 16, 35, 58, 64, 70.

[56] John S. Furnivall, *Colonial Policy and Practice* (New York: New York University Press, 1956), p. 308. For comparative materials, see also International Institute of Different Civilisations, *Ethnic and Cultural Pluralism in Inter-Tropical Countries* (Brussels: INCIDI, 1957).

Ndebele, etc. Having defined social stratification as "the differential ranking of functionally significant roles in terms of a common set of values," he asks, quite correctly, "What are the functionally significant roles?" and "Is there a shared and common value system by which these roles are evaluated?" His answer follows immediately. "Clearly, in the African urban social system in Gwelo, which is marked by extreme heterogeneity and fluidity in norms and social behaviour, there is no single system of values by which individuals are ranked higher or lower according to their various roles and activities. Therefore what we must ask is whether there is one common set of values which predominates in the urban context, over all other value systems and which then may serve as a source of differential evaluation." In short, having failed to find evidence of a common value system, we must postulate one; and this follows duly in the next paragraph. "In any society, a person holds numerous roles, any one of which could be used as a basis for evaluation. Here I shall consider that the relevant roles for evaluation in the system of stratification in Gwelo are those that are socially functional within the urban context, and require . . . full-time participation. . . . In Gwelo, this means the roles an individual has within the urban industrial economic system." The illusory quality of this "common value system" is almost immediately apparent. "The most striking feature of the Gwelo social system is the discrimination in roles between Africans and Europeans. By custom and law, occupational categories have been stereotyped." [57] In short, the stratification is political in base and ultimately rests on force. Although among the Africans, "tribal affiliation is a primary category . . . of differentiation," Schwab regards such differentiation as secondary to "the socially functional roles in the urban industrial system which I have taken to be the primary basis for the system of social stratification." [58]

Schwab's frankness may be unique, but his assumptions and procedure are not. One major weakness of current sociological studies of stratification is their commitment to this postulate of a normative consensual basis and integrative function, even where the stratification is forcibly imposed. History is full of dead and overthrown stratification systems—e.g., that of 18th-century France.

Consensual normative bases can hardly be claimed for systems that were overthrown by popular revolt or subverted by new religious ideologies, or which provoked extensive withdrawal, such as the migra-

<hr>

[57] W. B. Schwab, "Social Stratification in Gwelo," in Aidan Southall (ed.), *Social Change in Modern Africa,* (London: Oxford University Press, 1961), pp. 128-129.
    [58] *Ibid.,* 131.

tions to America beginning in 1620, or a series of unsuccessful revolts, such as New World slavery. Simply to say that "stratification systems may in fact endure for considerable periods without causing rebellion or revolt, but because of the differential distribution of power (including knowledge), this is neither surprising nor to the point," [59] is merely begging the question. This confession admits that stratification may rest on other bases than "a common system of values;" and likewise social order. It is also a direct contradiction of the same writer's earlier thesis.[60] As I have pointed out elsewhere, "Social quiescence and cohesion differ sharply, and so do regulation and integration but, if we begin by assuming that integration prevails, it is virtually impossible to distinguish these conditions. . . . It is especially difficult to isolate the positive effects of common values in culturally split societies that owe their form and maintenance to a special concentration of regulative powers in the dominant group." [61]

The evidence shows that while some societies have integrated consensual normative systems, others are not, but depend on coercion for establishment and continuity. While stable acephalous societies lack stratification but are consensually integrated, stratified societies may or may not have consensual bases. Ubiquitous cleavages between groups labelled Conservative, Liberal, Communist, Fascist or other, indicate how widespread dissensus about the current stratification may be.

In the following sections, I shall therefore contrast stratification systems whose stability varies as an effect of differences in the inclusiveness and congruence of the structural principles which define them. All the systems discussed below are mixed in the sense that they combine institutional arrangements for the ascription and achievement of status. By considering their differing stablity, we can explore the relations between the structural principles on which these systems are based and the levels of consensus or dissensus that they exhibit.

This is not the place for a formal discussion of stability. By a stable system, I merely mean one that does not generate internal movements aimed at radical structural change. By an unstable system, I mean one with a history of violent internal movements for such change. By comparing systems of different degrees of stability, I merely wish to show how consensus varies as a function of the structural basis of their stratifications; and thus to suggest that instead of simply postulating

[59] Wilbert E. Moore, *Social Change* (Englewood Cliffs, N.J.: Prentice-Hall, 1963), p. 83.
[60] Davis and Moore, *op. cit.*, pp. 244, 246.
[61] M. G. Smith, "Social and Cultural Pluralism" in Vera Rubin (ed.), *Social and Cultural Pluralism in the Caribbean*, Annals of the New York Academy of Sciences, 83 (1960), pp. 775-776.

normative consensus as the basis of all social order and stratification, we should analyze the structural conditions that regulate its incidence, intensity and scope.

STABLE MIXED SYSTEMS

Opinion varies as to appropriate unit for stratification analysis. Some writers stress positions, others roles, others individuals, groups, or social categories. All agree that stratification consists in status rankings. Each of the statuses ranked has an absolute value, that is, its constitutive rights and powers; each also has a relative value in comparison to some or all others. This relative value varies with the units compared. The absolute value also varies as the right and powers of the status are latent or manifest. When these are latent, the absolute significance of the position or incumbent is of less interest than its relative significance in the system of positions. In a rigid, well-defined stratification, rankings are always constant and clear, despite the latency or relativism of the units, and this means that the system must observe certain laws of economy. It must be based on one or two very simple general principles, such as birth and ritual status, or birth and jural status. Where the system rests on several principles, ambiguities of relative status are almost unavoidable, and the system loses its rigidity as well as its definition. I can illustrate this by reviewing some familiar forms of stratification.

In a consensually based society, the unequal distributions of opportunities that constitute its stratification are accepted as part of the normal order of things, as for instance in Hindu India, medieval Japan or Europe. Such differential distributions of opportunity may have differing bases and may relate to ritual, material or social values. Several such systems of differentiation may co-exist without any single one being clearly primary. While some societies exhibit only one stratification scale, others exhibit more. In either event, the consensus on which the stratification rests also supports the political order. Systems lacking an adequate consensus differ in their properties, problems and potential.

Indian caste is an instance of a rigorously ascriptive system of ritual status, which enjoys such profound support that modernization makes limited headway against it. Caste being primarily ritual in its base, ranking and referents, it easily accommodates variable local secular rankings based on wealth, power, knowledge, etc. Its immutability simply means that ritual status is absolute, even when latent; and this condition restricts realignments and individual mobility to the secondary secular sphere. Although individual movement between castes is virtually nil, within limits people may change their occupation and residence and, by changing their ritual observance, they can also seek to elevate their ritual status and that of their issue. But since personal status is identical with caste status, individual mobility on this level is minimal, though *jati* (sub-castes) may change their relative status over the generations by internal fission, re-location, and by adopting new external ritual symbols. Given the deep consensual basis of caste, such enhancement of *jati* status corresponds to the more stringent observance of ritual norms. The system evokes this intense support through its identification of the social and religious orders. The religious principles that regulate caste differentiation legitimate the entire structure as a religious order.[62]

The feudal organization of medieval Europe and Japan also rested on fairly general consensus and habituation. Despite their institutional cleavages, these populations shared common cults and community membership, much as the Brahmans and *harijans* do. In differing places and periods, the rigidity of these feudal orders varied; but all based their differential distribution of opportunities primarily on birth. Some were born free, others serf, some noble, others villagers, merchants, and so on. Even guilds sought to restrict membership by descent from members. In both areas, only such religious structures as the Catholic Church or the Buddhist monasteries, by their celibacy rules, excluded recruitment by descent, thus implicitly presenting alternative structures. Nonetheless church recruitment for offices of varying rank was qualified by the candidate's birth status. In these systems, the principal avenue of individual mobility was physical transfer and re-location, usually in a town. Only thus could one escape the direct implications of one's birth status.

Nonetheless, these estate systems differ sharply from caste. Ritual heredity differentiates castes, but in estate systems, hereditary differences are secular in base and referents. While caste can accommodate

[62] J. H. Hutton, *Caste in India*, (London: Cambridge University Press, 1946); H. N. C. Stevenson, "Status Evaluation in the Hindu Caste System," *Journal of the Royal Anthropological Institute*, 84 (1954), pp. 45-65; M. N. Srivinas, Y. B. Dainle, S. Shahani, Andre Beteille, "Caste: A Trend Report and Bibliography," *Current Sociology*, Vol. 8, No. 3 (Oxford: Blackwells, 1959); A. L. Basham, *The Wonder That Was India* (New York: Grove Press, 1959) Ch. 5; Edmund Leach (ed.), *Aspects of Caste in South India, Ceylon and Northwest Pakistan*, Cambridge Papers in Social Anthropology, No. 2 (London: Cambridge University Press, 1960); Taya Zinkin, *Caste Today* (London: Institute of Race Relations, Oxford University Press, 1960); H. H. Gerth and C. W. Mills (eds.), *From Max Weber: Essays in Sociology* (London: Oxford University Press, 1947), pp. 396-615; McKim Marriott (ed.), *Village India: Studies in the Little Community* (Chicago: University of Chicago Press, 1955); Adrian Mayer, *Caste and Kinship in Central India* (London, Routledge and Kegan Paul, 1960); T. O. Beidelman, *A Comparative Analysis of the Jajmani System* (Locust Valley, N. Y.: J. J. Augustin, 1959); F. G. Bailey, *Tribe, Caste and Nation* (Manchester University Press, 1960); Pauline Mahar Kalenda, "Toward a Model of the Hindu Jajmani System," *Human Organization*, 22 (March, 1963), pp. 11-31.

secular ranking as a secondary local stratification, in medieval Europe, ritual stratification was itself indirectly dependent on birth differences of a secular nature. Under caste, secular relations among ranked castes are rather variable; and instances of Sudras acquiring Kshatriya status by virtue of their territorial and military dominance are well known. In the secular estate system, the political bases and correlates of stratification are fixed and clear. Members of superior strata exercise jurisdiction over members of inferior ones, individually and collectively. Short of rebellion, the only hope for the subordinate strata to improve their lot is by physical withdrawal—to the town. In Europe, besides strata differentiated by birth and political status, the nobility was also divided between Church and State. In the secular sphere, nobles competed for titles, land and power against rivals also qualified for this competition by birth; in the ritual sphere, birth status was qualified by secondary emphasis on learned clerical skills.[63]

This baronial competition has numerous parallels in other intermediate societies. In India, Kshatriyas were rivals or allies; in Buganda, Anuak, Zulu, Swazi, etc., royals fought for the throne while eligible commoners, recruited restrictively, competed for lesser offices open to them. Among the Hausa-Fulani, royals competed for the throne, noble lineages for reserved office, clerics for clerical office, slaves and eunuchs for theirs also. In Japan, *daimyo* were recruited mainly from *daimyo* and *samurai* competed with *samurai*. We cannot simply write off these combinations of restriction and competition as transitional phenomena, as Nadel would have us do.[64] The combination of competitive achievement and restricted eligibility is too variable and widespread to be glossed over lightly. Examination may show that it is in one form or

[63] Sir George B. Sansom, *Japan: A Short Cultural History* (New York: Appleton-Century-Crofts, 1962); John W. Hall, 'Feudalism in Japan: A Reassessment," *Comparative Studies in Society and History,* 5 (October, 1962), pp. 15-51; E. O. Reischauer, "Japan" in Rushton Coulborn (ed.), *Feudalism in History* (Princeton: Princeton University Press, 1956); Marc Bloch, *Feudal Society* (London: Routledge and Kegan Paul, 1961); Robert J. Smith, "Aspects of Mobility in Pre-Industrial Japanese Cities," *Comparative Studies in Society and History,* 5 (July, 1963), pp. 416-423; F. L. Ganshof, *Feudalism* (London: Longmans, Green, 1952); H. S. Bennett, *Life on the English Manor: A Study of Peasant Conditions, 1150-1400* (London: Cambridge University Press, 1960); Henri Pirenne, *Economic and Social History of Medieval Europe* (New York: Harcourt, Brace & World, 1963) and *Medieval Cities: Their Origins and the Revival of Trade* (New York: Doubleday & Company, no date); Max Weber, *General Economic History,* trans. by Frank Knight (New York: Free Press of Glencoe, no date); M. M. Postan, E. E. Rich and Edward Miller (eds.), *Economic Organization and Policies in the Middle Ages, The Cambridge Economic History of Europe,* Vol. 3 (London: Cambridge University Press, 1963); G. G. Coulton, *The Medieval Scene* (London: Cambridge University Press, 1959); John P. Davis, *Corporations* (New York: Capricorn Books, 1961).

[64] Nadel, *op. cit.,* p. 171.

another a universal feature of all stratification systems. Certainly such mixed systems vary widely in their particulars, and merit detailed study. Even modern industrial societies whose ideologies explicitly stress universalistic and achievement orientations exhibit restrictive particularisms which, despite their educational and financial bases, effectively preserve racial and social inequalities. Without this structured contrast with ideology, the conflicting interpretations of American stratification by such writers as Parsons, Mills and Warner are incomprehensible.[65]

Recent studies of the Chinese bureaucracy warn us against classifying mixed systems loosely as acriptive or open, and also against overlooking the critical analytic differences between ideal and actual patterns. Though in theory recruiting its officials by competition—and so encouraging social and economic mobility—positions in the Chinese bureaucracy were often acquired on other grounds; and though the Chinese stratification was notoriously static, movements between the gentry, bureaucrats, peasants and commercial class were apparently continuous. Despite Confucianism and these institutional provisions for social circulation, this stratification also lacked a religious ideology adequate to maintain general consensus, as the various revolts that punctuated Chinese history show.

In any centralized society of moderate scale, the number of highly rewarded positions will be small by comparison with the number of eligible candidates, however restrictive the conditions of eligibility. Technical qualifications may be stressed, but unless the opportunities to acquire them are uniformly distributed throughout the society, its stratification has a restrictive base, and the achievement of individual status by competition is qualified accordingly. Unequal distributions of educational and occupational opportunities may thus generalize ascriptions by birth and effectively maintain these long after they have been formally repudiated. Under such conditions, the stratification cannot be accurately represented either as an open system or an ascriptive one, or as a transitional form; its particulars require detailed analysis; and to distinguish the conditions and consequences of its combination of principles, we must ask what regulates the range and scope of the competition, and the recruitment of competitors, and what differential rewards and dis-

[65] Parsons, *op. cit.*; W. Lloyd Warner, Marcia Meeker and Kenneth Eells, *Social Class in America: A Manual of Procedure for the Measurement of Social Status* (Chicago: Science Research Associates, 1949); W. Lloyd Warner and Paul S. Lunt, *The Social Life of a Modern Community* (New Haven: Yale University Press, 1941); Irving L. Horowitz (ed.), *Power, Politics and People: The Collected Essays of C. Wright Mills* (New York: Ballantine Books, 1963), pp. 23-71, 305-323; C. Wright Mills, *The Sociological Imagination* (New York: Oxford University Press, 1959).

abilities are involved. In India, where inter-caste competition is ruled out, ritual heredity is the principle of recruitment, and differential ritual status the explicit reward. In feudal societies, descent is the basis of a differential distribution of jural status, including rights to land, jurisdiction and political office, these being the main rewards. In systems where "technical" qualifications prevail, such as Imperial China and the modern West, differential educational opportunities are the mode of restriction, and occupational status the main reward. Various combinations of these arrangements can be found in historical and contemporary societies, industrial or other.

UNSTABLE MIXED SYSTEMS

A consensualist theory of stratification tends to overlook conquest states, despotisms and slavery, which usually evince clear stratifications. Conquest and its consolidation establishes a stratification explicitly based on force, as for instance in Norman Britain, among the Swat Pathans, or in Aztec Mexico.[66] Accommodations developed during the process of consolidation may establish a solidary stratification on consensual or symbiotic bases,[67] or they may not. In Ruanda until recently, various writers believed that the subject Hutu accepted the "premise of inequality" on which Ruanda stratification was based. The introduction of democratic electoral processes has shown the error of this view.[68] Despite

[66] Fredrik Barth, *Political Leadership among Swat Pathans*, London School of Economics Monographs on Social Anthropology, No. 19 (London: University of London Press, 1959); Jacques Soustelle, *Daily Life of the Aztecs* (New York: The Macmillan Co., 1962); Manuel M. Moreno, *La Organizacion Politica y Social de los Aztecas* (Mexico: Instituto Nacional de Anthropologia, 1962); Ignacio Bernal, *Mexico before Cortez: Art, History, Legend*, trans. by Willis Branstone (New York: Doubleday, 1963).

[67] See S. F. Nadel, "Social Symbiosis and Tribal Organization," *Man*, 38 (June, 1938), pp. 85-90, and *A Black Byzantium: The Kingdom of Nupe in Nigeria* (London: Oxford University Press, 1941); and M. G. Smith, *Stratification in Grenada* (Berkeley: University of California Press, 1965).

[68] J. J. Maquet, "The Kingdom of Ruanda," in Daryll Forde (ed.), *African Worlds: Studies in the Cosmological Ideas and Social Values of African Peoples* (London: Oxford University Press, 1954), pp. 164-189; J. J. Maquet, *The Premise of Inequality in Ruanda* (London: Oxford University Press, 1961); A. Kagame, "Le Pluralisme ethnique et culturel dans le Ruanda" in *Ethnic and Cultural Pluralism in Inter-tropical Countries* (Brussels: INCIDI, 1957), pp. 268-293; Marcel d'Hertevelt, "Stratification Sociale et Structure Politique au Rwanda," *La Revue Nouvelle* 31 (Brussels: May, 1960), pp. 449-462, "Les Elections Communales et le Consensus Politique au Rwanda," *Zaire*, 14 (1960), pp. 403-438, and "Le Rwanda" and "Developpements Recents" in M. d'Hertevelt, A. Troubworst, J. Scherer (eds.), *Les Anciens Royaumes de la Zone Meridionale: Rwanda, Burundi, Buha* (London: International African Institute, 1962), pp. 9-112, 227-236.

a common ideology of divine kingship, Hutu expelled their Tutsi rulers with amazing efficiency and speed. In Hausaland (North Nigeria), where conditions are comparable, the ruling Fulani, whose power rests on conquest legitimated by Islam, are exposed to no such threat; the differences here are rather interesting. Tutsi consolidation in Ruanda instituted "caste endogamy" and a perpetual exclusion of Hutu from positions of social advantage in ritual, political, military and other fields. Fulani intermarried with Hausa, adopted their language and political institutions, and provided ample opportunities for mobility into important positions. Whereas the divine kingshp of Ruanda remained the property of the Tutsi "caste" and identified with it, in North Nigeria Fulani domination is expressly identified with Islam and its faithful observance. In line with this, Fulani stress Islam as an indispensable qualification for political office, descent being secondary though highly strategic. Hausa subjects accept this mixed regime, with its unequal opportunities, partly because it is legitimated by Islam, partly because the commercial context provides opportunities for the pursuit of compensatory values, and partly because the distribution of power discourages protest.[69]

Until 1900, slavery enjoyed official sanction in Hausaland; in some Hausa states, perhaps one-half the population were slaves, but to my knowledge the Hausa never experienced any slave revolt. In the West Indies and Brazil, where slavery was widespread, revolts were frequent and often serious.[70] Haiti owes its independence to such a revolt.[71] In Surinam, Jamaica and the Guianas, large groups of slaves withdrew to settle in inaccessible jungles or mountains, where their descendants presently remain. The contrasting responses in these Mohammedan and Christian slave systems illustrate how consensus may vary even in systems that are formally very similar. While some systems of slavery

[69] S. J. Hogben, *The Muhammadan Emirates of Northern Nigeria* (London: Oxford University Press, 1930); and M. G. Smith, "Historical and Cultural Conditions of Political Corruption among the Hausa," *Comparative Studies in Society and History*, 6 (January, 1964), pp. 164-194; *The Economy of Hausa Communities of Zaria Province* Colonial Research Publications No. 16 (London: H. M. Stationery Office, 1955), and *Government in Zazzau, 1800-1950* (London: Oxford University Press, 1960).

[70] Arturo Ramos, *The Negro in Brazil*, trans. by Richard Pattee (Washington, D.C.: Associated Publishers, 1939), pp. 25-43; J. H. Parry and P. M. Sherlock, *A Short History of the West Indies* (London: Macmillan, 1956), pp. 72, 151, 163, 186; Melville J. Herskovits, *The Myth of the Negro Past* (New York: Harper & Row, 1941); M. G. Smith, "Some Aspects of Social Structure in the British Caribbean about 1820," *Social and Economic Studies*, 1 (August, 1953), pp. 55-80; Stanley M. Elkins, *Slavery: A Problem in American Institutional and Intellectual Life* (New York: Grosset & Dunlap, 1963).

[71] James Leyburn, *The Haitian People* (New Haven: Yale University Press, 1941).

excite revolt, others do not. I have shown elsewhere how the assimilation of slave and free through religious and kinship institutions inhibits revolt, while the reverse obstructs satisfactory accommodations.[72]

The traditionalist Latin American societies present varied phenomena: revolts followed by acquiescence, competition within restrictively defined circles, political nullification of subordinate strata, and a universal Church identified with the social structure, both as critic and sanction. Systems of this sort may endure despite evident inequalities, dissent and apathy, partly through force, partly through inertia, partly because their organizational complexity and structural differentiation inhibits the emergence of effective large-scale movements with coherent programs. Castros are, perhaps, not only exceptional but limited in their effect.[73]

Latin American societies vary greatly in their particulars, but all display certain common features. Cultural and social pluralism prevails with racial stereotypes or classifications and correlative value divergences. Mobility is restricted, though individual "Indians can move, albeit slowly, into rural Mestizo classification." [74]

In general, South American countries impose fairly rigid barriers to both horizontal and vertical movement out of Indian society. . . . There is considerable reason to believe that some very distinctive rural Mestizo cultures are also plural societies, as rigidly demarcated as are Indian cultures. . . . In Mexico, large masses of rural Mestizos have substantially the same culture as many Indians, but do not form distinctive plural societies, although there is a high degree of localism and regionalism. The only countries where the feudal class system and, more particularly, feudal class attitudes have disappeared to any extent are the Europe-oriented countries and Mexico.[75]

The resilience or immobility of Latin American stratification may thus be in part a function of the cultural diversity of the large subordinate strata. This reinforces community closures among Mestizos and Indians alike, each community maintaining its distinctive status system. An individual's status is thus derived from his community. Such ethnic heterogeneity generates "racial" structures of discrimination which perpetuate the structure of inequality as a base for cultural and social differences, even where the populations thus segregated are overtly sim-

---

[72] M. G. Smith, "Slavery and Emancipation in Two Societies," Social and Economic Studies, 3, (October, 1954), pp. 239-280.

[73] Wyatt McGaffey, "Social Structure and Mobility in Cuba," Anthropological Quarterly, 34 (April, 1961), pp. 84-109; Richard N. Adams, John P. Gillin, A. R. Holmberg, Oscar Lewis, R. W. Patch, Charles Wagley, and L. Bryson, Social Change in Latin America Today: Its Implications for United States Policy (New York: Random House, 1961).

[74] Ralph Beals, "Social Stratification in Latin America," American Journal of Sociology, 58 (January, 1953), p. 338.

[75] Ibid., p. 336.

ilar in race, as for instance in Haiti or Guatemala.[76] Beals' conclusion that "the use of strictly economic or economic and political criteria for class analysis of Latin America is the least fruitful approach"[77] may hold for other societies in which "the significant feature of the stratification is its bifurcation,"[78] with many segments among the subordinate strata. Simple increases in market opportunity will not usually alter these stratifications, for two reasons. In many cases these economic differentiations are integrated with the system of stratification as conditional or dependent factors; in others, as India, they may be simply irrelevant. Geographical mobility, especially to the large anonymous cities, may offer an opportunity to escape one's given status; but this is only significant where one wishes to escape, or where ritual conditions permit it. In secular systems, unless individual levels of aspiration and expectation are adjusted to the conditions of stratification, dissent and protests are likely; but to be effective, these presume that the subordinate strata are not vertically divided into closed communities. In these unstable systems, with more or less dissensus, ascription and competition co-exist, and in the most extreme form of this system, the plural society, the closed community is often represented by occupationally specialized ethnic groups, such as the Jews, Chinese, etc., often represent closed communities.[79]

CONCLUSION

I summarize my argument as follows. Stratification is a mode of social differentiation, and though social structures may be viewed as

[76] Melvin M. Tumin, *Caste in a Peasant Society* (Princeton, N.J.: Princeton University Press, 1952), John Gillin, "Mestizo America" in Ralph Linton (ed.), *Most of the World* (New York: Columbia University Press, 1948), and *The Culture of Security in San Carlos* (New Orleans: Middle American Research Institute, Publication No. 16, 1951). For Haiti, see John Lobb, "Caste and Class in Haiti," *American Journal of Sociology,* 46 (January, 1940), pp. 23-24; Leyburn, *op. cit.,* and George E. Simpson, "Haiti's Social Structure," *American Sociological Review,* 6 (1941), pp. 640-649, and "Social Stratification in the Caribbean," *Phylon,* 24 (January, 1962), pp. 29-46.

[77] Ralph Beals, *op. cit.,* p. 339.

[78] Gideon Sjoberg, "Folk and Feudal Societies," *American Journal of Sociology,* 58 (November, 1952), p. 233.

[79] Leonard Broom, "The Social Differentiation of Jamaica," *American Sociological Review,* 19 (April, 1954), pp. 115-125, and "Urbanization and the Plural Society," in Vera Rubin (ed.), *op. cit.,* pp. 880-891; Burton Benedict, "Stratification in Plural Societies," *American Anthropologist,* (December, 1962), pp. 1235-1246, and *Indians in a Plural Society,* Colonial Research Studies No. 34 (London: H. M. Stationery Office, 1961); R. A. J. van Lier, *The Development and Nature of Society in the West Indies* (Amsterdam: Royal Institute for the Indies, 1950); and Furnivall, *op. cit.,* pp. 304-312.

status systems, only some of these are stratified. All such systems display observable unequal distributions of advantage, but they fall into quite distinct categories. Some societies institutionalize equal access to positions of advantage; this involves uniformity in the positions and in the modes of recruitment. Such societies lack stratification. Other societies institutionalize unequal access to positions of advantage, and display stratification in various forms and degrees. In all cases, unstratified societies are politically decentralized, and the political and status structures are coincident. Units, the members of which share an identical status, are the corporations on which political and administrative order rests. These units of public order and regulation are mutually distinguished and related by the same principles that regulate the distribution of status. Nor could it be otherwise, since status is a jural and political condition. These acephalous unstratified societies vary quite widely in structure, but if stable they all rest on general normative consensus.

Stratified societies also vary in many ways. Some, with diverse bases of distribution, emphasize situs to the virtual exclusion of ranked strata; others distinguish ranked strata of varying kinds, some being defined jurally, others ritually, yet others racially and culturally. In all cases, the principles that differentiate and regulate this unequal distribution of opportunities are identical with those that distinguish and regulate publics as corporate units of internal order and external articulation. That is to say, the principles of stratification are basic to the political order. Nor could it be otherwise, since the differentiated statuses have jural and political connotations, directly or indirectly, as Max Weber recurrently observed.[80]

The principal criteria of status differentiation are linked directly or indirectly with the various types of reward, and these criteria may vary from ritual or jural capacity, from race, culture or wealth to education and occupational qualifications; but in all cases the widest span of the status system coincides with the limits of the widest effective political unit, as Nadel points out; and its basis and significance lie in the political sphere. For this reason, stratification cannot be adequately studied in terms of underlying value-orientations; it represents an order interdependent with the political order, based on certain concrete structural principles. In consequence of these principles, people might develop adjustive value-orientations, or protestant ones; but we must explain the values by reference to the structural principles that generate them, rather than the reverse.

---

[80] Hans Gerth and C. Wright Mills, *From Max Weber: Essays in Sociology* (London: Oxford University Press, 1947), pp. 160-161, 163-164, 171, 179, 191-193, 259-260, 276, 283, 298, 300-301.

If my argument holds, economic variables cannot have unconditional priority in the allocation of status unless uniformly open conditions of occupational recruitment are institutionalized, so that expansive market opportunities will generate increased mobility. In such conditions, one would expect that market contraction would stimulate institutional barriers to mobility; in no society known to me, however, have economic or occupational differences served as unconditional criteria of status allocation. Restricted eligibilities are always important, though often covert. So far as economic and occupational opportunities or achievements are regulated by other principles of status allocation such as ritual, birth, race, cultural difference, etc., market fluctuations may leave the structure unaffected; but any general process of restratification is always political.

While stratification systems vary in stability as a function of their normative consensual structure, this consensus is itself dependent on the character, congruence and inclusiveness of the structural principles on which the stratification is based. Some stratified societies, despite high inequalities, develop a consensus that legitimates the order. Others, with similar or lesser inequalities, do not. The source of these differences seems to lie in the nature of the principles that regulate the systems rather than in the scale of inequalities as such. The wider the consensus and the more inclusive the legitimating ideology, the more absolute may be the tolerable differences between ranked strata and the wider the span of the stratification. India, China, feudal Europe, Japan, and Latin America illustrate this. Situs structures correspond to narrow spans of differential advantage and diverse or competing legitimating norms. History shows many examples of political orders, that is, status structures, which endure for more or less time despite popular dissent. European absolutism, New World slavery or peonage and modern colonialism are merely the most obvious examples. To regard stratification as universal, and as always based on common values, is doubly mistaken. In societies lacking consensus, stratification is explicitly political in base, function and form. In societies with consensual foundations, the status structure, whether stratified or not, is at least implicitly political in function, basis and form, and generally explicitly so. Where present, whatever its bases, stratification is a condition and focus of the political order as well as a product of political history. In societies with "bifurcated" or plural stratifications, such as Latin America, India, China, colonial Africa, South Africa, the Middle East, and the West Indies, the re-stratification requisite for adequate economic mobility to support industrialization may thus develop only though explicit political action that seeks to rearrange the relations and categories forming the structure.

If an industrializing "emergent nation" is a territorial association of diverse indigenous societies, the "national" stratification inevitably differs from that of these indigenous units; hence the generality and political basis of plural or "bifurcated" systems. Moreover, the process of industrialization pursued at the national level itself intensifies the differentiation of these two types of stratification. The local distribution of these industrializing efforts also differentiates their structures from the preindustrial systems around them. When tribesmen move to industrial towns, they may or may not lose their tribal identifications, wholly or in part; but in either event they enter a different milieu with its own logic and organization. In various urban industrial situations, such immigrants encounter differing structures of opportunity, incentive, restriction and sanction; and if they remain, they must accommodate to these as best they can. Normally, these structures of opportunity and restriction are politically determined and enforced; the events of this American summer (1964) or the processes of de-colonization are patent evidence. This constraint may also be true of the movement to town. While canalizing the accommodation of their urban proletariats, such social structures generate divergent responses according to the particulars of their situation. Amerindians in Tegucigalpa, Bantu in Johannesburg, Ibo in Enugu, Gonds in Orissa, Mende or Temne in Freetown, face rather different structures of opportunity and restriction, and, partly for this reason, they react differently.

5

INTERACTION BETWEEN

INDUSTRIAL AND PRE-INDUSTRIAL

STRATIFICATION SYSTEMS

BERT F. HOSELITZ, *University of Chicago*

A COMMON ASPECT of economic development, in societies that already have experienced it as well as those engaged in bringing it about, is the increase of the secondary and tertiary sectors in the economy. Although technical and other improvements of agriculture are being considered or carried out in all these societies, the major socio-economic change with which development is usually associated is the change from technically simple production to more complicated and often quite difficult modern production methods. With this change is associated an increase in the numbers of highly educated people and skilled and specialized workers, and an absolute or proportional decline of the rural, especially the small village population, as towns and urban areas grow.

I offer this crude description of economic advancement here, not in an attempt to describe economic development as a process, but to suggest the very general characteristics of change in economic practices, in residential patterns, and in the nature of economically and socially interacting groups, which are usually associated with economic development. In some countries these changes have been relatively rapid, in others slow, and in others they are just beginning. My purpose is to describe in rather general terms the characteristics of societies in which certain parts are still strongly influenced by the "old-fashioned" conditions of social structure and in which other parts, especially the industrialized urban sectors, have accepted or been forced into new forms of social organization and new relations between persons belonging to different and possibly new social classes.

DUALISM AND ECONOMIC DEVELOPMENT

In his doctoral dissertation, presented in 1910, J. H. Boeke set forth a theory of social and economic development founded on the concept of "dualism," and the present analysis is strongly influenced by his work. Boeke's extensive reading and research on Dutch practices and policies in Indonesia brought him to the conclusion that social and economic conditions and life patterns in Indonesia, and possibly in other tropical Asian territories, were so different from those prevailing in Europe that theories concerned with Western social and economic growth and development were an inadequate and unrealistic basis for interpreting socioeconomic relations in the less industrialized, economically non-rationalized societies of tropical Asia.

After concluding his dissertation Boeke spent some 19 years in the Netherlands Indies. When he returned to the Netherlands and joined the University of Leiden he expounded his theories of dualism in great detail and developed a set of propositions, based on the concept of social and economic dualism, which have played an important role in subsequent analyses of developing societies. His lectures and publications have stimulated a far-reaching discussion of dualism. Boeke himself presented his ideas in a slightly different manner in several of his later books,[1] and some of his colleagues in the Netherlands opposed his viewpoint. A very informative statement of the views supporting and objecting to Boeke's ideas was published recently,[2] and some economists have published a series of essays rather critical of dualism, even rebutting Boeke's views, although an anthropologically-inclined sociologist and a few economists concerned with some of the more interesting countries experiencing economic change and growth have adopted certain aspects of dualism.[3]

[1] Julius H. Boeke, *Dualistische Economie* (Leiden: S. C. van Doesburgh, 1930); *Oriental Economics* (New York: Institute of Pacific Relations, 1947).

[2] See the "Introduction" (writer's name not indicated) to *Indonesian Economics: The Concept of Dualism in Theory and Policy*, vol. 6 of *Selected Studies on Indonesia*, by Dutch Scholars (The Hague: W. van Hoeve, 1961), esp. pp. 30-64.

[3] Among the opposing essays are Benjamin H. Higgins, "The 'Dualistic Theory' of Underdeveloped Areas," *Economic Development and Cultural Change*, 4 (1956), pp. 99-115, and Yoichi Itagaki, "Some Notes on the Controversy Concerning Boeke's 'Dualistic Theory'; Implications for the Theory of Economic Development in Underdeveloped Countries," *Hitotsubashi Journal of Economics*, 1 (October, 1960), pp. 13-28. For a more positive treatment of dualism, see John H. Rex, "The Plural Society in Sociological Theory," *British Journal of Sociology*, 10 (June, 1959), pp. 114-124, and William J. Barber, *The Economy of British Central Africa* (Stanford: Stanford University Press, 1961), *passim*.

Dualism is one of the crucial issues concerning the difference between economically advanced and underdeveloped countries. For although much of the discussion of dualism is based on differences in economic performance and output, Boeke contended that dualism is a basic form of society. In his inaugural University lecture in 1930, he maintained that

Where there is no such unity, where instead of this inter-relationship there is a sharp, deep, broad cleavage dividing the society into two segments, many social and economic issues take on a quite different appearance and Western economic theories lose their relation to reality—and hence their value. . . . Such a segmented society may be called dualistic, and consequently the social sciences which concern themselves with it may also be indicated in brief by adding the adjective dualistic: dualistic law, dualistic sociology, dualistic economics.[4]

In principle these differences between "Western" and "Eastern" or dual societies, and their economic aspects, center around the following points. In advanced economies the main decisions on output, its magnitude and kind, are made by producers; the organization of economic action is centralized and based on the position of productive agencies within the whole nation, and the distribution of economic activity, as well as decisions as to which economic action is relevant, is based on the total penetration of monetary transactions and the use of money as the general economic measure. In other words, Western economies are monetary, centralized, nationally uniform, and producer-oriented. Moreover, they are characterized, or rather supported, by several general social factors. Economic and social decisions are made principally in towns or cities. These decisions, especially the social ones, are subject to the significance of industry, trade and associated services as conditions of economic performance, and decisions in the economic as well as the social realm are basically rational. Social mobility, due partly to changes in economic performance and partly to increased aspiration, characterizes an important sector of the society. In short, social mobility, rationality, and urbanism are the predominant sociological features of advanced societies.

Against these features the societies of tropical Asia have the following characteristics. They are—or were until quite recently—predominantly consumer-oriented economies. That is, a large portion of their agricultural output was produced not for the market, but primarily for immediate consumption. Moreover, peasant farming techniques were often based not on a desire to maximize marketable output, but to con-

4 Boeke's inaugural lecture at Leiden, "Dualistic Economics," reprinted in *Indonesian Economics, op. cit.*, p. 170.

form to traditionally imposed patterns of economic activity, often covered by religious or sacred sanctions.

Many years ago, Sombart distinguished the consumption-oriented medieval and pre-capitalist Western societies from the sales-oriented and profit-oriented advanced societies. Though Boeke does not completely accept Sombart's viewpoint, he is without doubt influenced by his description of the early phases of capitalism and follows, at least in part, the Sombartian analysis.[5] Hence his major distinction is between production and consumption orientation.

Once one recognizes that in the less advanced societies consumption and, in particular, productive organization for the agricultural household rather than for export or the market, is a leading factor, then it is clear that the significant economic entity, in terms of which major decisions are made, is not the centralized national state, but the local village community. The local village is not merely the most effective economic entity, but also the predominant political center; most of the traditional political arrangements in Asian tropical society have virtually no relation to the nation as a whole but refer at most to a series of closely associated villages.[6] This means that the significant social or political entity for the traditional "group" to which these men believe they belong is not a politically coordinated unit and does not rely on the power or privilege of certain persons and their capacity to control the others, but rests ultimately on some "organic" solidarity that has supernatural influence and significance.

Traditional Asian society as Boeke describes it, then, differs from western society not merely in its economic objectives but also in its political organization. And since consumption and small-scale village production predominate, money also has a much less important role than in advanced societies. Money is not entirely missing in the simple and traditional societies, but it is an adjunct to subsistence and merely incidental to productive processes.

To these, the major economic and political differences between the advanced Western and the traditional Asian or tropical societies, should be added certain sociological characteristics: the scarcity or sometimes complete absence of towns, the importance of tradition, and relative social immobility. In many Asian and African societies a very large

[5] On the relation between Boeke and Sombart, see Itagaki, *op. cit.*, p. 15.

[6] On the reality of small political entities, even where much larger groups are designated by one name and have certain general value identities, see the discussion by Lucy Mair, *Primitive Government* (Baltimore: Penguin Books, 1962), pp. 12ff. Mair's discussion refers to African societies, but up to the not very remote past, particularly under the European colonial powers, some Asian societies had similarly limited and narrowly confined village or tribal political entities.

proportion of the population is as yet engaged in agriculture, and though certain crafts are practiced in villages or small towns in the rural areas, large urban areas with industrial, administrative, and general service employment are a relatively new phenomenon that has not yet affected a sizable proportion of the population. For the most part, therefore, the social structure is based fundamentally on long-standing traditions. In other words, though certain structural relations in newly formed urban areas may resemble those characteristic of European societies, the lack of urban areas, the absence of high levels of secondary and tertiary production methods, and the dominance of various traditional occupations and forms of production create a social structure that is quite different from that typical of Western societies or of the few "modernized" localities in Asian and African countries where Western methods of production have been introduced.

Finally, in the rural and agricultural areas of the underdeveloped countries, traditional social relations and forms of social behavior prevail, so that the society as a whole is apparently (or allegedly) much more immobile and structurally stable than Western societies or areas affected by them. Production factors do not easily flow to optimum opportunity, and sometimes do not flow at all, and the allocation of economic as well as social and political positions reflects tradition rather than skill or actual power and influence. Transfers in social position occur in some less advanced societies, but these transfers are usually based not on skill or capacity, but on traditionally established transfer patterns.[7]

Boeke's ideal-type description of the Eastern or Dual society is a sort of *Gemeinschaft*, a "religious community of food-crop cultivators all belonging to the same clan or social unity. . . . It is . . . logical to assume as a principle that in the village economy economic laws are overshadowed by other, social laws, prescribed by religion, custom, and tradition."[8] The villagers have limited wants, exchange is minimal, families are the basic units, and production is socially subordinate to religiously inspired and traditionally influenced behavior patterns.

The central problem of dualism, as Boeke sees it, is that modern Western economic and social conditions have been imposed on the profoundly different conditions of agricultural peoples in Asia and Africa. As a result, the *Gemeinschaft* is laid bare; the organic unity of the traditional society and the meaning and basis of communal life are

---

[7] As an example, consider the conditions described in a simple Guatemalan society by Sol Tax in his *Penny Capitalism* (Chicago: University of Chicago Press, 1963), *passim*.

[8] Boeke, "Dualistic Economics," *op cit.*, pp. 190-191.

destroyed. It is not that two socioeconomic structures co-exist in the same country, but rather that one, capitalism, creates strains and stresses in the indigenous society that lead to continually decreasing social cohesion, deteriorating welfare and increasing misery for the population.

In almost all his works, Boeke expounds three main propositions on dualism. (1) Certain societies in tropical Asia (and probably also in Africa) are based on social principles antithetical to those of modern society. These tropical societies are somewhat like the ideal-type *Gemeinschaft*, an organic unity of peasant cultivators and in some instances simple craftsmen, whose social organization is founded on familial units and whose value system is rooted in a religious or sacred order. Social needs are dominant and the community is prior to and above the individuals who compose it.

(2) To such societies the principles of social analysis developed for Western social systems are inapplicable, for these tropical societies have their own dynamics, their own structural relations, and their own interaction patterns.

(3) Accordingly, policy prescriptions based on Western society and its dynamics are bound to miscarry in tropical societies. The Western principles tend to aggravate rather than alleviate the ills these policies were designed to treat.

These three propositions lay down an important challenge for social science, for they involve quite explicitly some of the most basic issues in understanding social and related change and in prescribing adequate means for adjustment, growth, and improvement in non-Western societies. As an expression of general principles, this statement of dualism is persuasive; if it is also an accurate description, it leads to questions as to whether, and to what extent, a balance between traditional and industrial sectors can be established in the developing countries of Africa and Asia, what implications for political stability or political movement such a balance may have, and whether particular kinds of social mobility may be regarded as characteristic of different sectors of these dual societies. In my opinion, however, Boeke's analysis is too abstract and too one-sided. Manning Nash has criticized this theory in a very significant statement, which I should like to summarize.

Nash's major points are the following: (1) Boeke's main error consists in describing tropical societies as much less varied than they actually are. Nash argues that Boeke's description even of Indonesian society is based on a "homemade typology" and that the possibilities for socioeconomic change and development in many tropical Asian and African societies need to be understood in their own terms, rather than in terms of the generalized conception of dualism developed by Boeke.

(2) To predict whether a given underdeveloped nation will make adjustments leading beyond the "dualist" system, one must observe its social and economic structure in full empirical detail. (3) Introducing Western socioeconomic elements into non-Western social systems will produce pluralistic or multiple social structures in which modification is inherent.[9]

In other words, whereas Boeke argued that the imposition of Western social, economic and political elements on non-Western societies would produce a structure permanently bifurcated into Western and non-Western systems, Nash insists that introducing Western social and economic conditions is likely to produce a plural system, subject to change and evolution, and that the more highly developed and the more traditional parts of the society may be interrelated to different degrees in different tropical countries. Since this criticism seems valid, I shall apply it in the following discussion of different patterns of economic growth and political change.

First, I shall outline the general changes that may take place under the impact of various Western economic and political institutions in underdeveloped societies. Let us assume that the societies not yet exposed to foreign technical or economic procedures are relatively well-integrated and functionally not highly differentiated, and that they can maintain themselves in their social and economic environment, in which some long-range changes may go on. These societies may appear to many foreign observers to be stable and essentially unchanging. Political activities tend to be hierarchical and probably not democratic in the modern sense. Minor disturbances can be handled without upsetting the social and economic equilibrium and without altering the nature of the society.

It may be argued that this description is too idealistic and that even societies that were observed before Western economic techniques or political institutions were introduced to any significant degree were in fact less stable and unchanging than earlier descriptions indicated. Of course, very important changes have occurred in Asia and Africa, but in both continents large areas have been relatively stable for a long time and change has been basically due to the intrusion of Western powers. Western intrusion produced changes often leading to economic development, which not only had different effects in different colonial or quasi-colonial areas, but which established quite different economic and social systems, sometimes even for a long period in different parts of the same country. Here is the basis of dualism, but as Nash pointed out,

[9] This is a somewhat modified presentation of ideas expressed by Manning Nash in "Southeast Asian Society—Dual or Multiple," *Journal of Asian Studies*, Vol. XXIII, No. 3, pp. 420-422.

this situation cannot be described simply as an instance of general dualism.

The imposition of Western institutions on a relatively stable, strongly tradition-oriented society may destroy the economically simpler society completely, and though its people may survive, they are either integrated with the more advanced population or maintained on a welfare basis. An example of this pattern of change is the destruction, absorption, or socioeconomic subjection of the American Indians during the settlement of the United States. Although quite a few Indian communities still exist on United States territory, their independent economic activity has ceased and their social and political systems have been destroyed. A number of Indians have been assimilated to some extent, but only those who settled in white American areas and completely gave up their associations with other members of the original societies.

A second pattern is the adoption of completely new forms of economic, social, and political organization. Although these non-Western social systems may have been relatively well developed, they become completely reoriented. The transformation of Japan in the last hundred years is perhaps the best example, but the same pattern has also occurred in geographically more limited areas such as Singapore and Hong Kong. There, colonial organization was politically limited by the boundaries between these urban populations and the much more stable populations in surrounding areas. The Japanese case is different, for here a large society adopted new methods of production—and as a result altered its political structure and social organization to produce a new social system. The latter cannot be said to exhibit dualism, for it is an integrated form of socioeconomic organization basically different from the form that existed before the major innovations took place.

In addition to complete destruction of the non-Western society and its complete reorganization, two other possibilities are substantively of greater significance and more closely related to the problem of dualism. One is the situation where an indigenous tribal or related group remains for a long time a self-centered, separate entity. For example, Barber argues that the Barotse tribe of Northern Rhodesia has remained socially and economically isolated and has scarcely interacted in any way with the remainder of the country.[10] Other instances of this type are known, though it is questionable how long these isolated communities can persist. The Indian societies in South America that survived Spanish colonialization belong in this class. Similarly, a number of separate tribal groups in India led a life of their own during all or most of the British colonial rule and did not interact with the part of the society that was

[10] See Barber, *op. cit.*, pp. 20 and 44.

under Western domination. Similar situations may exist in some Indonesian islands and elsewhere, and in some parts of Africa separate tribal groups have only minimal contact with non-tribal populations. These situations are probably not permanent, and changes occurring in the surrounding areas will eventually bring about some form of change in the relatively isolated groups. They may become integrated with the surrounding populations; this appears to be an important and powerful development in many parts of the world. Until a few years ago, for example, portions of Tibet formed a self-sustained, economically integrated social and political entity, whose connections with both the Indians and the Chinese were very limited. The Chinese invasion of Tibet altered this situation, and within the next few years the Tibetans will either be exterminated, essentially, or integrated with the Chinese people. Similar developments will probably take place in Africa and Asia, where independent and relatively isolated tribal groups still exist. In the Amazonian areas of Brazil a few very small, extremely isolated tribal communities still exist: they will be exterminated, completely subordinated like North American Indians, or incorporated in the wider Brazilian society. Similar patterns are likely to occur among Canadian and Alaskan Eskimos.

These are, in some ways, the most important and genuine examples of dualism, but modern communication methods, rising political aspirations, and the tendency toward unified political and social communities even among African and other still undeveloped societies, create conditions under which isolated communities can last only a relatively short time. At present, however, a good many such communities do exist, and research on them and their peculiarities during the past may be of some interest.

Finally I come to the fourth case, some form of integration of the more with the less westernized portions of a colonial area. Indonesia, India, Pakistan and many other areas in tropical Asia and Africa represent this situation. These, incidentally, were also the areas where integration took place so slowly and encountered so many obstacles that the concept of dualism was widely applied.

Furnivall, however, shows that the dualism may exist for a period but gradually breaks down and that western influence tends to produce changes outside social relationships, affecting the maintenance of indigenous social and economic systems. For example, he argues that in its initial impact on countries of southern Asia, "modern colonialism is an affair of capital and not of men." [11] He maintains, further, that within

[11] John S. Furnivall, *Colonial Policy and Practice* (New York: New York University Press, 1956), p. 5.

the indigenous populations all aspects of communal life were bound up with one another and with religion; that custom and not law regulated behavior; and that colonialism imposed on economic and social relations in the subject countries government by reason, impersonal law, and individual rights.[12] Economic laws and principles had a great impact on these countries, for the conquering western powers designated methods of direct and indirect rule principally to gain the economic objectives that attracted them to these countries. In Furnivall's opinion, colonialism is essentially economically oriented and governs principally by means supporting these economic interests.

In Western societies, the conditions that support profit motives, and make possible the survival of the cheapest producers, do not lead to individual anti-social tendencies because these tendencies are checked by a mass of social obligations, legal rules and the overall conditions of social life. But in traditional tropical societies, established customs and anti-individualistic principles have maintained integrated and stable social relations, at the cost of economic progress. Under colonial domination these customs were often abandoned, releasing anti-social forces; Furnivall describes this by saying that "these forces, liberated from the control of custom by the impact of the West, pursue their natural course, breaking down the social order, disintegrating organic society into individual atoms, and, thus, by depriving men of social protection against natural selfishness, operate more intensively, eliminating social values, and diffusing poverty."[13] It makes little difference whether the new economic principles and practices were introduced through direct or indirect rule. Under direct rule, contacts with the outer world occur only in the economic sphere, while for the most part the people's social life is steadily impoverished. Under indirect rule, chiefs and tribal authorities are used for purposes foreign to those to which their tradition accustomed them, so that native customs are weakened and the traditional sources of authority tend almost to disappear. Modern governmental rules, promoted as the ultimate force, are not socially or politically integrative. Hence, under either system the result is disintegration.

Furnivall's view is applicable to situations in which political and social change is caused by the economic interests and innovations of a dominating power. The result of these changes is not dualism, in any meaningful sense; yet the original societies persisted in some way, even when the original social organization was largely dissolved.

---

[12] *Ibid.*, p. 3.
[13] *Ibid.*, p. 293.

INTERACTION BETWEEN INDUSTRIAL AND
PRE-INDUSTRIAL STRATIFICATION SYSTEMS

In countries that have recently become independent and established new socio-political systems, the most significant social phenomenon is not dualism, but the fact that industrialization has created an urban, industrially-employed labor force, superimposed on or coordinated with a larger number of agricultural workers and producers. In many of these countries, particularly in Africa and Asia, by far the largest proportion of the economically active population—between 60 and 80 per cent or even more—is still in agriculture. Industries, as well as various services, are usually located in urban areas; hence agriculturalists differ substantially from persons in secondary and tertiary occupations, not only in terms of occupational activity but often in terms of the locality where it is carried out.

Where old cultures are well established, however—as, for example, in India—local differentiation between farming and other forms of productive activity is less important than it is in some of the African and Southeast Asian countries where persons in non-agricultural occupations are often foreigners or members of a linguistically or "nationally" distinct group. Examples are the Chinese in various Southeast Asian countries, the Lebanese and Syrians in parts of Africa, and the Indians in various parts of East Africa. Many of these people are in service and trade occupations, but to some extent modern industrial development has brought them into commercial activities as well. Thus, differences between urban and rural populations, between native and originally foreign persons, and between industrially and agriculturally occupied persons have tended to produce different processes of adjustment and change in different areas. Where important and apparently insuperable conflicts arose between two or more sections of the population, dualism or pluralism was discovered. But a more careful analysis of these changes shows that such contrasts and conflicts may not be insuperable and that gradual, if slow adjustment is possible and even probable.

Manning Nash has written a detailed description of the introduction of industrial production methods in a peasant society: Cantel, in Guatemala.[14] Cantel is a small Indian community, originally based entirely on agriculture, whose relations with other communities and other social groups clearly exhibited traditions prevalent among Central American

[14] This discussion is based on Manning Nash, "Introducing Industry in Peasant Societies," *Science*, 130 (November 27, 1959), pp. 1456-1462.

Indians. Though the different native communities in Guatemala possessed a variety of dialects, costumes, saints, and sacred ceremonies, their interrelations within a village and between villages created a culturally and sociologically stable system, changing little. Then a textile factory was set up in one community. The factory employed Indians from the neighborhood, some of whom had previously not earned money income, few of whom had lived close to the factory, and none of whom had been engaged in an economic activity requiring regular working hours, specific behavior at the work place, or other related forms of behavior.

Nash describes the whole process of change in the article cited and in a book dealing with the same problem; I shall not repeat this here, but I want to stress one point that he discusses, having to do with social relations in Cantel after the factory had been present for about 30 years. Nash discusses differences between the factory workers and those who remained traditional agricultural operators in Cantel and the surrounding area. Changes in industrial workers' houses and their furnishings have been minimal; similarly, foods and cooking arrangements have changed little. Above all, family relations have remained essentially identical. The factory workers share with the remaining peasants the same religious beliefs and practices and enjoy the same festivities. The closeness of personal relations in a number of important social areas is summed up by Nash as follows:

Unquestioning acceptance of folk ideas of reality is part of everyone's life, irrespective of his occupational role. In Cantel this includes acceptance of folk remedies, origin myths, modes of cure, and the belief that foods and persons are "hot" and "cold," that smoke from the candles carried one's prayer to heaven, that the sacrifice of a sheep keeps death from a household, and that an eclipse is a battle between good and evil. What is apparent in this matter of world view is the extent to which spheres of rationality and irrationality coincide among factory and non-factory workers.[15]

Yet, to some extent certain social differences did develop in Cantel, among them the new friendship clubs for factory workers—which previously did not exist at all—a sports club composed of bicycle riders and basketball players (sports introduced from more advanced societies), and labor union activity introduced by organizers from the outside.

In personal relations, in belief systems, in the more intimate behavior patterns, then, change has been negligible or nonexistent. Now, anyone looking at various developing countries in Asia and Africa will also have found that in many regions, personal, familial and other basic life patterns have changed least. Such changes as have occurred have involved new social groupings produced by the new work situation, new political

[15] *Ibid.,* p. 1460.

associations arising at least in part from the formation of new states or other new political entities, and new patterns of economic behavior resulting primarily from new and especially industrial methods of production rather than from altered social or cultural conditions.

In general, I think one can argue that the significant differences and patterns of change attributable to the introduction of new productive activities principally reflect changes in economic conditions, together with individual propensities to enter new and previously nonexistent social groups, rather than changes in attitudes or in family structure. It must be emphasized, however, that industrialization took place in Cantel only on a very limited scale. The factory was set up in a rural community, and though the population increased a bit and several new houses were constructed near the factory, and though other changes took place within the community, including the availability, to workers, of new and improved commodities that the peasants were too poor to buy, basic personal and even socio-cultural conditions altered not at all, or at most only very little. Dualism is absent from Cantel, because the new economic activities were fully integrated into the peasant community.

Now, industrialization often involves productive entities much larger than a small textile firm, and it usually occurs primarily in urban rather than in rural areas. Consequently, persons who enter the industrial enterprises leave their original place of work, move to an urban center, and lose contact with many members of their families and others with whom they have traditionally asociated. As observers of Indian or Indonesian cities have often reported, however, members of a given group (whether it is based on a common language, on caste, or on village of origin) try to associate with others from the same group and to maintain close relations with them. Moreover, urban residents in these countries, and in other newly industrializing nations in which urban areas have grown quickly and relatively recently, often return to the villages whence they came, when their urban employment ends. For example, in a survey of migration into and out of major urban centers in India, S. N. Agarwala found that in the older age groups emigration considerably exceeds immigration, an indication that these older people return to the villages or small towns from which they originally came.[16]

This implies that urbanization is an important factor in changes in social structure in the newly developing countries. For, although urban residents from similar social and geographical areas try to establish relations similar to those in the villages, these groups are often small, and

[16] See S. N. Agarwala, "A Method for Estimating Decade Internal Migration in Cities in India from Indian Census Data," *Indian Economic Review*, 4 (February, 1958), p. 71.

in many instances associations of this type are impossible. Workers moving to urban areas in which industrial employment is available often come without their families, and interaction among temporarily single men differs substantially from interaction among rural families in Asian and African countries.

Hence the increasing settlement of workers in cities, and the urban concentration of industrial establishments and related services are important factors in breaking up existing social relations and creating new forms of social interaction and social stratification. In short, alteration in stratification systems depends on the growth and increasing urban concentration of the population of developing countries.

Little research has been done on the changing stratification patterns in urban areas of developing Asian and African countries, partly because in many urban areas immigrant workers are still highly mobile. But studies of Indian cities,[17] for example, suggest that stratification in the urban areas of some developing countries generally resembles that of Western countries. Hence, the notion of "dualism" is mainly based on the observation that stratification in agricultural areas has changed little whereas in urban areas it has taken on many Western features. Changes in urban areas have been only partial, however, and without doubt have begun to affect rural areas in some parts of the world, though empirical knowledge on this is still very limited.

An additional problem involves the entry of foreign people, not through colonization, but through the immigration of ordinary people from other Asian or African societies at a similar level of development. The migration of Chinese into parts of South and Southeast Asia, the migration of Indians to parts of Africa and Southeast Asia, and that of various Middle Easterners to many parts of the world are examples. Where these immigrations involved large groups of foreigners, they usually concentrated on certain specialized economic activities, created their own residential centers in urban areas, and in general continued the social relations characteristic of their native countries.

But in a number of areas, as time goes on, changes have been taking place which are likely to increase interaction between the native inhabitants and the immigrants. European colonial powers did not interfere with or impose special rules on "colored" immigrants from Asian or African countries, but when these developing countries became politically independent, and political power was transferred to the natives, it became important to integrate these foreigners with the domestic social

---

[17] See for example, S. N. Sen, *The City of Calcutta* (Calcutta: Bookland, n.d.— ca. 1960), and C. W. Ranson, *A City in Transition: Studies in the Social Life of Madras* (Madras: The Christian Literature Society of India, 1938).

structure. Full integration cannot easily be achieved, and in the process the ethnically and linguistically distinct immigrants must choose whether to return to their home countries or to find a place in the social and economic life of the dominant and politically more powerful native population.

I do not regard the previous situation, which is now being altered everywhere in newly independent countries, as dualism. To be sure, substantial differences in personal associations and in stratification systems have divided immigrants from natives. But with one or two exceptions—Malaya being the principal one—the total number of foreign immigrants was too small to permit economic and political independence from the domestic majority. And with political independence and indigenous political leadership, any apparent elements of dualism in the relations between ethnic minorities and domestic majorities will gradually disappear.

In the United States, the gradual integration and "Americanization" of persons with very different linguistic and national origins, in the pre-World War I and pre-World War II periods, is clearly an instance of this tendency to form a national unity. And although the United States is still "dualistic" with respect to different racial groups, current policies are designed to bring about closer integration and ultimately perhaps, a complete eradication of various forms of dualism or "segregation."

The process of integrating ethnic groups does tend to produce a system of social stratification in which some difficulties and inconsistencies are inevitable. In many instances the ethnic minorities occupy positions in specialized secondary production, or in commercial activities, and therefore enjoy an income level higher than that of most of the indigenous population. For example, the income of the few thousand Indians who live in Nyasaland was estimated to be, on the average, 15 to 20 times higher than that of the indigenous Nyasas, and though the income differences may be smaller in Thailand between Chinese and Thais, or in Indonesia between Chinese and Indonesians, they still create an obstacle to the social and economic integration of the ethnic minorities. But as these countries achieve political independence, and take moderately successful steps toward modernization, economic growth will improve the social and economic positions of the indigenous people. More than any other factor, this tends to make possible the integration of foreign ethnic minorities into the social structure of newly developing countries. Some phases of the integration of ethnic minorities may be complex and difficult, however, leading to violence or other forms of serious social conflict. But in the long run ethnic "dualism" will disappear, as a structurally more simplified and better integrated society emerges.

CONCLUSION

Among the major issues I have raised, in connection with dualism as a feature of social stratification in societies containing both industrialized and non-industrialized sectors, one of the most important is the problem of social mobility, both between agricultural and industrial sectors and within each of them. As economic change of various kinds takes place in developing economies, the rural and urban, or agricultural and industrial sectors tend to become increasingly interdependent. With the growth of international commerce and the rise of internal markets, assisted by the extension of roads and railways, the old self-sufficiency of the village has been progressively worn down; the rigidity of the old village division of labor has softened; the old social barriers to economic mobility are slowly yielding, and in most villages—at least in most parts of Asia and probably within the next few years also in Africa—cash is replacing barter. At the same time the expansion of towns and the diversification of employment opportunities, the rise of new trades and the somewhat more limited decline of old ones, have been breaking down the formerly rather complete control exercised by the family, though in many developing countries the family is still a strong force. The spread of education, which has been very substantial in many developing countries, is working in the same direction. India, in particular, epitomizes these developments in many ways. There political independence, the formation of indigenous political movements, the formal abolition of large landed estates and the alleged and, in some cases genuine, increase of tenants' rights, have broadened village horizons. The substitution of a new social order for the old one has become concretely associated with more modern patterns of economic and social organization.[18]

In other words, the forms of social stratification characteristic of urban industrial and tertiary occupations have to some extent affected economic and related social patterns in the rural areas of developing countries. In some of the more isolated areas this change has not yet taken place, but with the growth of communication and transport systems the size and importance of these regions will decline. This is especially true in Asia, but it is beginning in Africa and will probably continue on both continents at a rapidly increasing rate.

Thus we may say that dualism either did not exist in the newly

[18] On India, and for other related aspects as well, see UNESCO, *Social Change and Economic Development* (Paris: UNESCO, 1963), esp. pp. 90-99, 110-118, and 157-163.

developing countries of Asia and Africa, or, where it did exist in some form, it is disappearing. For the changing social and economic conditions in these countries are making individuals in different productive activities more interdependent, and the major bases of social differentiation are increasingly confined to the more intimate spheres, to family relations, religious beliefs, and primary groups whose identity and composition have a long-standing and well-established significance. Changes in social structure are closely based, in my opinion, on changes in the nature and conditions of economic growth, and on the whole the basic processes of economic growth are very similar in all newly developing countries. What varies among these peoples are certain cultural conditions, most of which are inherited from a long past. Though in its intermediate phases the type of stratification associated with economic growth may appear to be dualistic, it is also compatible with quite different cultural conditions, and in the next few decades systems of stratification in different Asian and African countries should become increasingly similar.

6

CHANGES IN

OCCUPATIONAL STRUCTURES

WILBERT E. MOORE, *Russell Sage Foundation*

ONE OF THE most direct links between modes of economic production and social structure is, of course, in labor force participation and types of economic activity. As an economy shifts from decentralized "subsistence" production to interdependent production of a wide range of goods and services, the human or social counterpart is a series of shifts in work roles. Here I want to explore various facets of this transformation, identifying several interdependent but analytically distinct "processes" of change. I shall use the concept "occupational structure" in a broad sense to include a number of ways whereby economic performance roles are differentiated and organized.[*]

Since the focus will be on structural changes in the course of economic modernization, some introductory comments are in order regarding the view of social change that informs the subsequent discussion.

The degree to which changes in economic structure determine other changes in societies may have been exaggerated by analytical models that attend to interdependencies but not to autonomous variability in sub-systems. Thus attempts to generalize about the social consequences of economic development and to increase the precision of predictive generalizations, though laudable, may encounter some unbreechable barriers. Differences in pre-industrial social patterns do have lasting consequences, and there are options in politico-economic regimes. Precise replication of historic changes may not be expected in some aspects of contemporary modernization because the experience of the past may be forthrightly adopted or rejected, with resulting changes in both timing and sequence.

[*] I wish to express my thanks to W. Lee Hanson, whose written discussion of the original draft emphasized the economic bases for changes in labor demand; to Mrs. Karen Many, for helpful editorial suggestions; and to Neil J. Smelser, who pointed out the interdependence of processes of structural change.

These initial caveats are meant to be disarming, but they are less critical with respect to occupational structures than with respect to, say, the forms of the polity.

Specifically, I shall argue that several trends in occupational structures are closely associated with economic growth, as measured, say, by rising real income per capita. Thus some international cross-sectional data will be used for want of historical series, and the particular features of occupational structure examined are, inferentially, additional indicators of economic development.

A further implication of the use of cross-sectional and temporal data as direct or putative trends merits display. This implication is that economic growth may be properly treated as a continuous (and enduring) kind of transformation. Although some sharp transitions and discontinuities cannot be denied, they are generally exaggerated by "before-and-after" comparisons or by three-stage models that mark off modernization as a dynamic era distinct from pre-industrial or post-industrial economies.

My mission, then, is to examine structural changes in the disposition of human labor as a framework within which social mobility may be examined.

THE MOBILITY PROBLEM

Changes in social location or position are generally called by the general term mobility. (A semantic case can be made for the use of "mobility" to mean readiness to move, and some other term, say "movement," to refer to actual changes. This argument is likely to fall on deaf ears, and I shall continue to use the term conventionally and improperly.) Mobility thus comprises changes in location (locus), relative position (status), sector, industry, or "lateral" occupational segment (situs) or in employer (patronus).[1] Distinctions are also drawn for status mobility between intergenerational shifts and changes within a career. For reasons that probably could be traced to the intellectual history of their discipline, sociologists concerned with mobility trends have concentrated primarily on intergenerational movement, and have commonly espoused the view that the only significant question about such movement is the comparative "openness" of systems. Rogoff, for example, made a study of comparative mobility rates a generation apart, and

---

[1] See Arnold S. Feldman and Wilbert E. Moore, "The Work Place," in Moore and Feldman (eds.), *Labor Commitment and Social Change in Developing Areas* (New York: Social Science Research Council, 1960), Ch. 2.

"standardized out" changes in occupational structure—the "demand" side of the equation—by computing expected frequencies.[2] In fairness it must be added that she concluded that she had thereby eliminated the major factor in mobility changes between 1910 and 1940.

Now the analytical separation of mobility accounted for by changes in the distribution of occupations within the socioeconomic structure from that accounted for by changes in the distribution of opportunity or accessibility is a perfectly legitimate procedure. But there is no reason to say that only the second datum is interesting. Marsh, in fact, has suggested that the manifestly greater intergenerational mobility of industrial societies may be entirely explained by changes in occupational structures rather than in terms of values and norms that encourage mobility aspirations and merit recruitment.[3] For example, if a survey of current farmers reveals that virtually all had farmer fathers, it would be quite improper to conclude that there is very little mobility out of agriculture: the proportion of farmers in the total labor force may have declined by half in the course of a generation and a fair proportion of farmers' sons may thus be in some other economic sector and occupation.

The present discussion relates to changes in demand for types and grades of economic activity. Hypothetical directions of change will be noted, together with kinds of desirable data and, here and there, references to actual quantities.

SOURCES AND TYPES OF STRUCTURAL CHANGE

The demand for labor by industry, occupation, location, and employer may be viewed in economic terms as the resultant of two other classes of variables: the demand for goods and services, and the relevant factor proportions of capital, labor, and, especially, the state of the appropriate technology. Even at a given level of "available" technology, capital may within limits be substituted for labor—that is, machines for men. Though the occurrence is rare, the converse substitution of men for machines is of course theoretically possible. The supply and price of labor presumably influence employers' decisions on "factor mixes," including investments in technological change with the immediate or later aim of displacing some proportions of workers or avoiding dependence on certain skilled occupations in short supply.

---

[2] Natalie Rogoff, *Recent Trends in Occupational Mobility* (New York: Free Press of Glencoe, 1953).

[3] Robert M. Marsh, "Values, Demand and Social Mobility," *American Sociological Review*, 28 (August, 1963), pp. 565-575.

To these elementary principles of economic interdependence we should add that the supply of labor is affected not only by current demand but also by past demographic behavior of the relevant population, ease or difficulty of migration, by institutional determinants of labor-force participation, and notably by the efficacy whereby the schools and other training agencies produce the requisite manual skills or intellectual accomplishments. Thus the focus here on changing structures, on the "demand" for labor somehow filled by movement of individuals from the social or geographical or occupational origins, is not intended to make of occupational changes a sovereign determinant. It is only intended to redress the balance of customary discussion, which tends to view mobility solely as a sorting of persons into given positions.

The types of structural change attended to here are: the initial formation of labor market and its expansion at the "expense" of subsistence production or traditional modes of exchange; sectoral relocation, particularly the proportional growth of non-agricultural employments; specialization, or the process of subdividing complex skills but also multiplying the kinds and levels of skill needed; upgrading the long-term process of proportional shifts to higher skill categories, possibly accompanied by higher minimum skill levels; and finally, bureaucratization, the organization of specialized labor into large administrative units that secure "political" or disciplined coordination rather than relying solely on the impersonal controls of the market.

Although these processes will be discussed *seriatim*, they are all structurally related to economic growth, and to each other. It is hard to imagine, for example, extensive economic development without a great expansion of non-agricultural production and labor. The variety of goods and services that characterizes the advanced economy bespeaks specialization, but specialization also occurs because of considerations of efficiency and rationalized organization. Rationalized organization, plus the adaptation to change and its deliberate creation, demands increasing managerial, clerical, and technical services, and the coordination of the manifold specialties (most of which do not yield a single product but only a share in a complex productive and administrative process) could scarcely be effected without "political" coordination. But political coordination supplements rather than supersedes the market. The formation of a labor force paid in wages and salaries is the way specialized producers become generalized consumers for themselves and their dependents.

The interdependence of structural changes does not of course assure their perfect synchronization. For example, migrants from "subsistence" agriculture may swell the ranks of the urban unemployed, and the supply of "upgraded" aspirants turned out by the schools may exceed the rate at which the demand for their skills is expanding. Specialization may be carried to extremes that place complex processes in jeopardy from the failure of a single workman, and bureaucratization may add to the employment opportunities in "administrative" posts for otherwise unemployable scions of an archaic elite more than to efficient mobilization of human resources for productive tasks.

With respect to the interdependence of structural changes I shall have little more to say, but I shall attempt to note the implications of the several processes for occupational mobility.

MARKET PARTICIPATION

The first change in occupational structure associated with modernization is the creation of a labor force in the technical sense. That is, the separation of "work" from other, possibly useful, activities requires the operational definition of financial remuneration,[4] and thus the creation of a labor market or its indirect equivalent in a commodity market.

On this point national statistics are extremely unsatisfactory, for the category "agriculture" fails to distinguish between market production and "subsistence agriculture," with products and participants that are scarcely part of the market system. For many areas of Africa and Asia it would be helpful to have temporal trends in the assimilation of subsistence production into the national economy and of producers into the labor force. Some data on Sub-Saharan Africa indicate that less than half the potential male labor force may be actually involved in the labor market either as workers or commercial producers, though the ratios vary widely from place to place.[5] The African situation is further complicated by the well-established pattern of "temporary" labor migration, which for part of the actual labor force provides a bridge between otherwise incompatible economic systems. Though there is some dispute among Africanists about the stability of this "bridging" mechanism, it is my opinion that the "modernized sector" can be expected to make steadily greater inroads on the so-called "subsistence sector," both directly through regularized labor-force participation and indirectly through the increasing demand for manufactured products among tribal populations. Such data as are available, however, indicate that a minority of African

---

[4] Wilbert E. Moore, "The Exportability of the Labor Force Concept," *American Sociological Review*, 18 (February, 1953), pp. 68-72.

[5] Wilbert E. Moore, "African Labor Systems and Their Adaptation to Social Change," in Melville J. Herskovits and Mitchell Harwitz (eds.), *Economic Transition in Africa* (Evanston, Ill.: Northwestern University Press, 1964).

men at the time of a given enumeration or survey are engaged in wage labor, but these data (not very recent in most instances) leave out of account both commercial activities and self-employment in services, and give no hint at the extent of commercialization in agriculture.[6]

The African situation is interesting because it is probably the largest area of the world in which the commercialization of economies is recent and still incomplete. Regrettably, very little is being done in the way of analyzing the process as it takes place.

Trends in labor force participation rates by age and sex also warrant examination. Participation rates under age 18 are probably negatively correlated—cross-sectionally or temporally—with indicators of economic development. Put another way, the median age of labor force entry should be positively correlated with economic advancement. Labor force participation of the aged may also have a (probably low) negative correlation with advancement. (Though advanced economies offer a wider variety of employments that are physically not very demanding, they also generally afford institutionalized retirement systems.)

Female labor force participation is more strongly affected by institutional variation than is male participation, but the problem of cross-sectional or temporal comparison is further complicated by variations in concepts and statistical procedures. In particular, the "unpaid family worker" represents an attempt to represent statistically an economic role that the market itself does not record. Obviously such quasi-participants in the labor force are most numerous in economic activities where the family as such retains functions of production other than self-consumed services. This form of linkage between the family and the economy is most prominent in agriculture, and secondarily in various commercial services, though handicraft "putting-out systems" involving multiple participation by family members are not unknown. Unpaid family workers represented 19 per cent of agricultural workers in the United States in 1950, less than one per cent of non-agricultural workers. By 1962 the proportion had fallen to 16 per cent in agricultural but had risen to slightly over one per cent in non-agricultural employment.[7] Although the family inevitably retains many economic functions in an urban-industrial economy, including consumption decisions, major influence on vocational choice and occupational placement of the young, and various services that could be commercially evaluated, unpaid family workers are in a sense anachronistic, for they represent an incomplete development of an individualized labor market.

[6] *Ibid.*
[7] U.S. Bureau of the Census, *Statistical Abstract of the United States, 1962* (Washington: 1962), p. 226, Table 297.

With respect to direct, compensated female participation in the labor market, it may be hypothesized that rates will increase with economic growth, and that has been the American experience. If we take into account intrafamilial female work and the growth of non-familial production, it is somewhat more accurate to say that the initial impact of commercializing labor, an impact that may endure for a considerable period, is to *reduce* women's economic contributions, which are subsequently increased through rising rates of direct labor force participation. As far as release of married women from domestic household functions is concerned, it is clear that the major, and perhaps the only important labor-saving device has been the contraceptive, which permits limiting the number of children and especially the duration of childbearing. The increasing labor force participation rates of American women over the age of 45 are testimony to the combined effectiveness of family limitation and the school as the daytime custodian of children and youths.

SECTORAL RELOCATION

One of the best-established generalizations concerning structural changes related to modernization is the shift from agricultural to non-agricultural activities. Table 1 represents the proportions of the economically active populations in agriculture in various countries around 1950 (still the most recent data available for most countries). To show the cross-sectional progression from countries properly called economically backward to those that are advanced, I have arranged the countries in descending order of the agricultural labor force. The intermediate position of France, where "peasant" agriculture remains important, perhaps requires less comment than do Chile and Argentina. Though by no means truly "advanced" by many economic and social indicators, these South American countries do have highly commercialized farming, involving considerable mechanization especially in Argentina.

Actual historic trends in the decline of agricultural employment are also interesting. Table 2 presents for several countries the long-term changes in agricultural employment, with the final column representing the simple arithmetic mean annual rate of decline implicit in the before-and-after comparisons. This unsophisticated measure reveals some interesting differences between countries. It invites a somewhat speculative generalization to the effect that the later an economy enters on industrialization the more rapid is the shift from agricultural to non-agricultural occupations. The relatively rapid declines in Japan and the Soviet

TABLE 1

PROPORTIONS OF THE ECONOMICALLY ACTIVE POPULATION IN
AGRICULTURE, VARIOUS COUNTRIES, AROUND 1950 [1]

Country [1]	Date	Per Cent in Agriculture
Haiti [2,3]	1950	88
Thailand [2,3]	1947	81
India [2,3]	1951	69
Pakistan [4]	1951	62
Brazil	1950	58
Mexico	1950	58
USSR [5]	1950	56
Costa Rica [4]	1950	55
Ceylon [4]	1946	53
Egypt [4]	1947	51
Hungary	1941	50
Spain	1950	49
Japan	1950	48
Finland	1940	47
Italy	1954	41
France	1950	32
Chile [4]	1952	31
Ireland [4]	1951	31
Norway	1950	29
Argentina [4]	1947	25
Denmark	c. 1950	23
Canada	c. 1950	21
Sweden	1950	20
Switzerland	1941	20
Netherlands	1947	19
New Zealand [4]	1951	18
Australia [4]	1947	15
United States [6]	1950	12
Belgium	1947	11
United Kingdom	1951	5

[1] Source, unless otherwise indicated, is Simon Kuznets, "Quantitative Aspects of the Growth of Nations: II. Industrial Distribution of National Product and Labor Force," Supplement to *Economic Development and Cultural Change*, 5 (July, 1957), pp. 82-95. Table 4. Countries are arranged in descending order of last column.
[2] Men only.
[3] United Nations, *Statistical Yearbook 1955* (New York: 1955), Table 6 (men only).
[4] United Nations, *op. cit.* (both sexes).
[5] Warren W. Eason, "Labor Force," in Abram Bergson and Simon Kuznets, *Economic Trends in the Soviet Union* (Cambridge: Harvard University Press, 1963), pp. 38-149; data from p. 77.
[6] U.S. Bureau of the Census, *Statistical Abstract of the United States, 1962*, p. 215, Table 280.

Union at one extreme and the slow declines in France and the United
Kingdom at the other lend some credence to the generalization, but
effective confirmation or disproof would require more precise formulation of how the "onset" of modernization is to be measured and dated.

TABLE 2

LONG TERM RATES OF DECLINE IN AGRICULTURAL LABOR FORCE,
VARIOUS COUNTRIES AND PERIODS [1]

Country	Beginning Date	Per Cent in Agri- culture	Ending Date	Per Cent in Agri- culture	Mean Annual Per Cent Decline
USSR [2]	1925	85.5	1959	48.4	1.09
USA [2]	1820	71.8	1960	7.1	.46
France [3]	1846	57.0	1954	22.5	.32
U. K. [4]	1801	35.9	1951	5.0	.21
Denmark	1870	54.0	1940	29.0	.36
Ireland	1841	51.0	1951	31.0	.18
Sweden	1840	71.0	1940	27.0	.44
Japan	1872	85.0	1936	45.0	.63
Brazil	1872	78.0	1950	58.0	.26
Mexico	1900	70.0	1950	58.0	.24
Puerto Rico	1899	63.0	1948	39.0	.49

[1] Source, unless otherwise indicated, is Simon Kuznets, work cited in Table 1.
[2] Eason, work cited in Table 1, note 5.
[3] J-C. Toutain, La Population de la France de 1700 à 1959, Cahiers de l'Institut
de Science Economique Appliquée, Suppl. No. 133 (Paris, Janvier, 1963), pp. 54-55.
[4] Phyllis Deane and W. A. Cole, British Economic Growth, 1688-1959, (Cambridge: Cambridge University Press, 1962), p. 142.

Changes in trends through time within countries also hold some
interest. An inviting hypothesis alleges a height-slope relationship comparable to the temporal course of mortality rates, whereby high rates
decline rapidly and low rates decline slowly, with a resulting reverse
J-curve temporal trend. Again the Soviet or Japanese extremes as compared with British experience are consistent with the hypothesis, but the
joker is that no numerical magic is at work here. Real development has
to take place to permit the sectoral relocation to occur: witness the relatively slow decline from initially high levels in Brazil and Mexico.

An examination of somewhat shorter periods for the United Kingdom
does indicate some "coasting off" in the rate of decline (from the rather
low levels of agricultural participation *prior* to substantial industrialization). Had we started the comparison with 1851, when the proportion

in agriculture was down to 21.7 per cent, the annual rate of decline over the ensuing century would have been lower (0.17) than it was over the whole 150 years. The 1901-1951 decline, from a 1901 level of 8.7 per cent in agriculture, was even lower (0.07).[8]

On the other hand, the rate of decline of the agricultural labor force in the U.S. appears to have accelerated through time. For the 19th century the average annual rate of decline was 0.43 per cent, for the period 1900-1950 the annual rate of 0.51, and for 1950-1960 the rate was 0.67.[9] Nevertheless, unless we move to "automatic farms," a slowing rate of movement out of agriculture will eventually come about.

Cases may occur in which development, or at least early development, does not reduce the agricultural labor force. If the Indian data cited by Kuznets [10] are believable, the percentage in agriculture increased from 51 in 1881 to 63 in 1911, with perhaps no reduction thereafter. One possibility I suggested years ago in another connection is that cheap manufactured goods may displace the handicraft producers more rapidly than they can be absorbed by expanding employment opportunities in manufacturing.[11] Bauer and Yamey note the correlative possibility of rising unemployment rates in the cities.[12]

Descriptive materials and data relating to urbanization rates suggest that urban unemployment, or entrance into marginal "service" activities, is more probable than an increase in agricultural proportions. Thus an alteration of one historic pattern seems to be occurring. The Colin Clark formulation [13] was to the effect that economic growth is accompanied by a large proportional shift into secondary (manufacturing) production, followed by proportional increases in tertiary (service) production. It now appears in many developing countries that urbanization is proceeding at a more rapid pace than the expansion of manufacturing employment, resulting in a direct shift out of agriculture into services.[14]

"Industrial" classifications of the labor force appear to be more extensively available than other structural features of the labor force.

[8] United Nations, *Statistical Yearbook, 1955.*
[9] Eason, cited in Table 1, note 5.
[10] Kuznets, cited in Table 1, note 1.
[11] Wilbert E. Moore, *Industrialization and Labor* (Ithaca: Cornell University Press, 1951), p. 305.
[12] See. P. T. Bauer and B. S. Yamey, *The Economics of Under-Developed Countries* (London: James Nisbet, 1957), Ch. 6.
[13] Colin Clark, *The Conditions of Economic Progress,* 2nd ed. (London: Macmillan, 1951), pp. 395-439.
[14] Bauer and Yamey, noting similar points, miss completely the invariant association between economic development and transfers out of agriculture. This leads them to the idiotic statement that ". . . the thesis connecting changes in occupational distribution and economic progress is not established, and . . . occupational statistics are an infirm foundation for any generalization" (*op. cit.,* p. 42).

The changing proportions engaged, say, in construction and production of capital goods as compared with those engaged in consumer goods production may or may not show a uniform trend regardless of economic regime or historic era. Uniformity appears unlikely, but cannot be summarily denied, and a reliable and predictive typology is not quite at hand. Kuznets' analysis of international and temporal differences indicates, aside from the shift out of agriculture associated with economic growth, a probable increase in transportation and communication. Services as a whole are not highly unequal, though clearly changing in quality and type within the category.[15]

Though the shift from agricultural to non-agricultural activities may be hard to appraise in terms of status, it is a form of mobility of great significance for social organization and styles of life. It is a prime example of change of situs, missed by exclusive attention to changes of occupational rank. Most rural-urban migrants are youths and young adults. This pattern confirms what would be expected from the demand side: namely that occupational mobility between sectors favors the young, who can in general more readily acquire the unfamiliar skills. The transitional process will work "smoothly" only if the relocation is proportional to the rate at which the young can be spared form agricultural labor, or seek to leave it in any event. When technological displacement is very rapid, as in the contemporary United States, the young still provide most of the recruits to growing sectors (technical services, for example), but the older worker may lose his place in the labor market altogether.

SPECIALIZATION

The continuous expansion of the number of occupations is a widely noted dynamic feature of developing and industrial societies,[16] yet it remains unmeasured. For measurement one would need serial recording of the gross number of distinct occupations, though rate of change as distinct from total magnitude might be derived from successive sample surveys comparably drawn from the universe of the economically active. Grouping and reclassifying occupations inevitably appeals to census officials, and defeats calculations of trends. Even if one had, say, successive compilations in various countries such as the *Dictionary of Occupational Titles* prepared by the U.S. Employment Service, one would still have

---

[15] Kuznets. *op. cit.*

[16] See, for example, Neil J. Smelser, "Mechanisms of Change and Adjustment to Change," in Bert F. Hoselitz and Wilbert E. Moore (eds.), *Industrialization and Society* (Paris and The Hague: UNESCO and Mouton, 1963), Ch. 2.

to be cautious. A recorded increase in occupations might represent a mixture, in unknown proportions, of genuine increase and improved identification—a problem similar to the classic one of interpreting temporal trends in the incidence of diseases.

The sources of specialization are several: increased size of interdependent economic (and other social) units, making possible the classically recognized efficiencies of division of labor; technological changes, requiring new performance criteria; new products and services. It is useful to distinguish skill dilution—the subdivision of performance roles—from new skill combinations, often associated with the growth of knowledge.

The process of specialization makes *exact* occupational inheritance increasingly unlikely, a circumstance concealed by grouping occupations into white-collar and blue-collar,[17] or only slightly more elaborate classifications.[18] Specialization even invades occupations that appear to persist, such as various professions (which thus become in a sense occupational groups).

Assessing the relative importance of the sources of specialization is not likely to be possible from census data, for reasons noted, and even repeated surveys would have to collect data wisely and interpret them cautiously. Yet by taking into account the way various age groups may represent changes through time, a single survey might yield substantial additions to knowledge. This would, incidentally, permit testing the hypothesis that the historic "age" of an occupation is correlated with the mean age of its occupants, and conversely that genuinely new occupations tend to be filled by new or recent entrants to the labor force.

Were a moderately satisfactory "index of specialization" to be constructed, it would be possible not only to calculate long-term trends more precisely, but also to make certain other calculations: for example, the influence of labor-force size. And despite the hypothesis concerning the importance of youths in manning new occupations, it should be supposed that the index of specialization and within-career occupational mobility would be correlated when observed in appropriately fine detail. This should be true not only for the "mechanical" reason that rates of mobility are strongly associated with the number of categories distinguished, but for the somewhat more interesting reason that a highly specialized labor force presumably increases the chances of a fit between role requirements and individual aptitudes and interests. Since initial selective processes would not be perfect, further sorting would result,

[17] See, for example, Seymour M. Lipset and Reinhard Bendix, *Social Mobility in Industrial Society* (Berkeley: University of California Press, 1960).

[18] See S. M. Miller, "Comparative Social Mobility," *Current Sociology*, 9 (1960).

and as individual interests and capabilities change, further occupational mobility may occur.

Such attention to detail can scarcely be dismissed as trivial in the large sweep of socioeconomic changes, since the steady progress of specialization greatly increases the probability that individual careers will be marked by one or more changes in occupational role and associated social attributes.

UPGRADING

Economic growth appears to be accompanied by a long-term shift from manual to non-manual occupations in non-agricultural occupations. Data for constructing historic trends, however, are surprisingly scanty even for this dichotomous classification of "skill" categories. Incidentally, the increase in the number of engineers, and in such occupations as skilled service men for complex business machines, makes the manual, non-manual distinction a fuzzy one. I agree with Duncan's comments about the predominantly manual components of some white-collar occupations.[19] Just why a typist is a "head" worker and a linotypist, a "hand" worker, is by no means clear.

Despite these strictures, it is *generally* true that occupations commonly classified as non-manual require somewhat higher educational levels and—though with considerable overlapping of distributions—yield higher incomes.

Table 3 presents data for a number of countries representing a considerable range of economic advancement. The countries are arranged in the order of the proportion of white-collar workers in the labor force. Except for the anomalous, and unbelievable, figures for Burma, the order of the countries is not radically different from what one would expect. Varying degrees of census accuracy and varying statistical conventions impair the comparability of the data presented, and no confidence can be placed in the exact rank order.

The proportion of "professionals" in the labor force is probably subject to fewer errors and differences of definition, and the range presented in the last column of Table 3 perhaps produces a somewhat more accurate ordering of the countries involved. (The alleged "oversupply" of professionals in some developing areas is, I should think, less likely to be true of the category as a whole than of particular occupations, such as lawyers.)

[19] Otis Dudley Duncan, "Methodological Issues in the Analysis of Social Mobility," in this volume.

TABLE 3

WHITE-COLLAR AND PROFESSIONAL WORKERS AS PROPORTIONS OF
ECONOMICALLY ACTIVE POPULATIONS, SELECTED COUNTRIES,
AROUND 1950 [1]

| | | (In Thousands) | | | Per Cent | |
| | | Economically Active [2] | White Collar | Profes- sional | White Collar | Profes- sional |
Country	Date	(1)	(2)	(3)	(4)	(5)
Burma	1953	1,075	420	39	39	4
South Africa [3]	1946	889	321	......	36	......
Israel [4]	1958	319	111	37	35	12
U. S.	1950	60,037	21,213	4,736	35	8
Canada	1951	5,300	1,761	376	33	7
New Zealand	1951	740	235	53	32	7
U. K.	1951	22,578	6,447	1,387	29	6
Sweden	1950	3,120	843	219	27	7
Japan	1950	35,574	8,362	1,634	23	5
Chile	1952	2,188	445	92	20	4
Austria	1951	3,361	652	181	19	5
Denmark	1950	2,063	325	121	16	6
Mexico	1950	8,345	1,304	207	16	2
Costa Rica	1950	272	40	9	15	3
Paraguay	1950	437	55	13	13	3
Brazil	1950	17,117	2,107	286	12	2
Yugoslavia	1953	7,838	683	225	9	3
Pakistan	1951	22,393	1,765	224	8	1
India	1951	101,725	7,487	1,586	7	2

[1] Source is United Nations, *Demographic Yearbook,* 1956 (New York: 1956), pp. 388-418, Table 13. Percentages were computed prior to rounding population figures to thousands, and countries are arranged in order of magnitude of column 4.
[2] Excludes unpaid family workers.
[3] European population.
[4] Jewish population.

Even the "professional" category is remarkably heterogeneous in exact occupational composition. In American census practice, for example, not only are various "technicians" included, but also entertainers and other occupations that may have no formal educational requirements. The median number of years of school completed for all American male "professionals" 25 years of age and over in 1960 was 16.4, just beyond the college level, and 24.5 per cent of the group had less than a college education.[20]

Some examples of historic trends in "upgrading" occupational dis-

[20] U. S. Bureau of the Census, *U. S. Census of Population: 1960, Subject Reports, Educational Attainment* Final Report PC(2)-5B (Washington: 1963), Table 8, p. 136.

tributions are in order. White-collar workers represented 28 per cent of all non-agricultural occupations in the U.S. in 1900, 42 per cent in 1950.[21] By 1960 the percentage had almost reached 50, and for the white labor force had slightly exceeded that proportion.[22]

The rate of professionalization in the U.S. has been even more rapid. Professional and kindred workers represented 4.2 per cent of the total force in 1900, 8.6 per cent in 1950, and 11.2 per cent in 1960.[23] Though American non-whites had much lower representation in professional categories, the percentage increased from 3 per cent in 1950 to 4.7 per cent in 1960.[24]

In France, the "liberal professions" changed from 9.4 per cent of all services in 1856 to 11.9 per cent in 1936.[25] Though no later data are presented because of discontinuities in definitions, Toutain comments on the rapid growth of the professions after World War II.[26]

Eason presents data [27] showing that the Soviet "intelligentsia" with a higher education approximately doubled between 1926 (8.6 per cent) and 1956 (17.0 per cent) and the proportions with a technical secondary education more than doubled (10.6 per cent and 32.4 per cent, respectively). But Eason's data for workers in industry show virtually no decline between 1928 and 1959 in the proportions of "wage earners" (around 85 per cent), though a slight increase in engineering, technical, managerial, and salaried personnel (from 9 to 13 per cent); declines were registered in the initially small proportions of apprentices and service personnel.[28] Administrative personnel in industry showed an actual decline, 1954 to 1959, from 14 to 10 per cent, but Eason thinks this primarily represents some reduction in the governmental super-structure, and that the relatively low proportions of administrators as compared with American experience represents a genuine difference in the degree of "advancement" in the respective industrial structures.[29]

A rising average, and perhaps minimum, level of education of the labor force in the course of economic development appears probable in view of trends in education, but precise temporal comparisons for

[28] *Ibid.*, p. 89.
[21] U.S. Bureau of the Census, *Historical Statistics of the United States, Colonial Times to 1957* (Washington: 1960), p. 74.
[22] *Statistical Abstract of the United States, 1962*, Tables 297 and 299, pp. 226, 227.
[23] 1910 and 1950 figures from *Historical Statistics . . .* , *op. cit.*, p. 74; 1960 figure from *Statistical Abstract*, Table 297, p. 226.
[24] *Statistical Abstract*, Table 229, p. 227.
[25] Toutain, work cited in Table 2, note 2, at p. 147.
[26] *Ibid.*, p. 148.
[27] Eason, work cited in Table 1, note 5, at p. 64.
[29] *Ibid.*, p. 90.

particular occupations or occupational categories are not yet possible. Differing educational levels by age provide a reasonable basis of inference, however. In 1960 in the U.S., for example, male "operatives" aged 20-24 had a median educational level around the 12-year level—implying completion of secondary school. The medians then decline steadily with age to 7.9 years for the oldest group.[30] Virtually every occupational group displays a similar age pattern, with two notable exceptions: professionals have a median educational level at or just over the 16-year (college) level at all mature ages, and non-farm managers and officials have median levels under the 12-year (secondary) level only for ages 55 and over.[31]

Of course, it is impossible from these data to distinguish the relative influences of supply and demand. Does the labor market "require" rising educational levels, or merely "benefit" from the education provided for other reasons? The latter possibility cannot be rejected, as there are some grounds for suspecting that employers insist on educational specifications in recruitment that are not in fact required by the performance specifications of the positions to be filled. Educational levels by age and occupation for other countries and at successive periods would be a desirable check on the virtually unique American data.

If primary attention is paid to formal schooling of the young as the method of meeting the rising skill demands of the labor market, then the schools are clearly the principal agency of social mobility. The coordination of school curricula with *current* demand is quite unlikely to be perfect, since school administrators and counselors tend to get the vocational word tardily. As for prospective demand, a few years or a few decades after the completion of formal schooling, exact mobility preparation would be both unlikely and incorrect for the interim. The continuous capacity for learning, which is probably highly correlated with sheer level of education, is a prime requisite for multiple movements. Shortages of particular skills, which are an endemic feature of modernizing and advanced economies, are likely to lead to pressures on the regular schools to solve the mobility problem. Accumulated adaptive experience and formal adult retraining will probably be necessary if rapidly changing occupational demands are to be met without a built-in generational lag.

[30] U. S. Census report cited in note 19, at pp. 136-137.
[31] *Ibid.*

BUREAUCRATIZATION

Bureaucratization is a process of structural change in the labor force that may, over time, reduce certain kinds of mobility (for example, from manual to non-manual occupations via an independent business, or movement between employers) and increase others (such as promotion to higher levels of skill or responsibility and essentially "lateral" transfers within a "family" of related occupations). The simplest measure of bureaucratization is the proportion of wage and salary earners in the labor force. This proportion appears to show a long-term and relatively steady increase in "capitalist" countries,[32] but of course it is nominally complete in Soviet-type economies. Independent workers in non-agricultural occupations in the Soviet Union decreased from 28.3 per cent in 1928 to a mere 3.1 per cent in 1959.[33]

Table 4 presents for a number of countries the proportions of wage and salary earners among economically active men, the countries being ordered once more in terms of the magnitude of the percentages.[34] The proportions reflect in some degree the varying importance of "peasant" agriculture, and it might have been preferable, where possible, to confine the comparisons to non-agricultural participants in the labor force. This would of course have reduced the range of variation, but it would not have radically changed the order. In this connection, the sharp decline in U.S. agricultural employment, 1950-1960, from 7,507,000 to 5,723,000 was accompanied by an absolute *increase* (from 1,733,000 to 1,806,000) in wage and salary earners and a decline in the self-employed from 4,346,000 to 2,802,000.[35]

For France, Toutain [36] presents the following proportional distributions by "employment categories."

	1906	1936
Employers	30.3%	29.2%
Salaried	11.8	15.6
Workers	33.7	34.6
Self-Employed	20.1	13.7

[32] Hoselitz presents some data on this and on the increasing importance of large productive units. See Bert F. Hoselitz, "Some Problems in the Quantitative Study of Industrialization," Essays in Quantitative Study of Economic Growth, *Economic Development and Cultural Change*, 9 (April, 1961), pp. 537-549.

[33] Eason, work cited in Table 1, note 5, at p. 82.

[34] A somewhat comparable compilation for an earlier period, taking wage and salary earners as a proportion of males 15-64, is presented by Moore, "The Exportability of the Labor Force Concept," *op. cit.*

[35] *U. S. Statistical Abstract, 1962*, Table 297, p. 226.

[36] Toutain, work cited in Table 2, note 2, at Table 66 (p. 166, not numbered).

TABLE 4

WAGE AND SALARY EARNERS AS PROPORTION OF ECONOMICALLY
ACTIVE MALES, VARIOUS COUNTRIES AROUND 1950 [1]

(In Thousands)

Country [1]	Date	Men Economically Active [2]	Wage and Salary Earners	Per Cent Wage and Salary Earners
U. K.	1951	15,647.3	14,028.0	90
U. S.	1950	42,906.9	34,265.0	80
W. Germany	1950	13,483.0	10,831.0	80
Sweden	1950	2,188.0	1,673.0	76
Belgium	1947	2,525.8	1,903.0	75
Canada	1951	3,994.8	3,011.0	75
New Zealand	1951	567.0	423.2	75
Switzerland	1950	1,417.3	1,069.9	75
Australia	1947	2,454.8	1,827.0	74
Austria	1951	1,882.4	1,371.0	73
Netherlands	1947	2,757.0	2,025.0	73
Spain	1950	8,087.0	5,885.0	73
Czechoslovakia	1947	3,528.0	2,551.0	72
Argentina	1947	5,022.0	3,564.0	71
Denmark	1950	1,369.0	975.0	71
Portugal	1950	2,382.0	1,699.0	71
Costa Rica	1950	205.5	144.7	70
Norway	1950	1,010.0	708.0	70
France	1946	12,668.0	8,538.0	67
Bolivia	1950	360.6	234.0	65
Italy	1954	12,879.0	8,113.0	63
Ceylon	1946	2,042.0	1,206.0	59
Brazil	1950	12,209.0	7,064.0	58
Japan	1950	18,510.0	10,360.0	56
Venezuela	1950	1,273.9	696.0	55
Mexico [3]	1950	7,372.0	3,831.0	52
Philippines	1948	4,443.0	2,197.0	49
Yugoslavia	1953	3,940.0	1,914.0	49
Egypt	1947	5,957.0	2,626.8	44
Paraguay [3]	1950	364.3	144.4	40
Haiti	1950	635.1	129.9	36
Pakistan	1951	21,026.0	3,375.0	16

[1] Source is United Nations, *Statistical Yearbook*, 1955 (New York: 1955), pp. 56-61, Table 6. Countries are arranged in order of magnitude of last column.
[2] Excludes unpaid family workers.
[3] Both sexes.

In French manufacturing [37] the proportion of workers (*ouvriers*) appears to have risen from 56.0 per cent in 1906 to 66.8 per cent in 1931, then to have fallen to 60.0 per cent in 1936; but the rate of unemployment had markedly increased in 1936 and could be expected to bear

[37] *Ibid.*, Table 80 (p. 176, not numbered).

mostly heavily on this group. Salaried workers (*employés*) over the 1906-1936 period more than doubled in proportions (3.6 to 7.7 per cent) and the self-employed have been reduced by about half (25.3 to 13.9 per cent). On the other hand, the proportions of self-employed in services remained about constant at around 15.16 per cent.[38]

In the U.S. the proportion of self-employed workers outside agriculture was as low as 11.6 per cent in 1950, and fell to 10.4 per cent in 1955, but held virtually constant in 1960 and 1962.[39]

Shifts in type of self-employment should also prove instructive. In non-agricultural activities in the U.S., my impression is that self-employment is decreasing in construction and manufacturing, in financial operations and distribution, and even in the "liberal" professions, but perhaps increasing in repair and advisory services.

Whether bureaucratization in newly developing areas may be expected to accelerate is perhaps too hazardous a speculation. Yet the strong degree of governmental decision-making for the economy should lead to a fairly rapid extension of government services and perhaps a rapid reduction of self-employment, at least outside of agriculture.

A RETROSPECTIVE COMMENT

The processes of structural change in economic activity that I have discussed represent the "demand side" of various forms of occupational mobility. Though much ingenuity has been spent on detecting trends in the "supply" side, particularly the degree of openness of systems despite differences in social background, the studied neglect of structural changes is no longer tolerable. Surely no one would pretend that equal opportunity prevails in any advanced industrial economy, whatever the political regime. Yet to assert that mobility rates over the last half century or so have changed very little, as some researchers have done, or even that the American social structure has become more "rigid" since the turn of the century or after World War I, as is frequently asserted in sociology and social history texts, is to disregard totally the structural changes noted here, and particularly the process of upgrading. Whether the process can go on indefinitely, and at what cost for those left behind in the process, are theoretically interesting and practically significant questions. The lack of synchronization observable in areas newly emerging from a relatively slow-moving process of structural change has no prominent, tidy resolution in the course of continuing economic development. The stable future is surely as mythical as the stationary past.

[38] *Ibid.*, Table 90 (p. 184, not numbered).
[39] *U. S. Statistical Abstract, 1962*, Table 297, p. 226.

7

CHANGES IN RATES

AND FORMS OF MOBILITY

NATALIE ROGOFF RAMSØY, *Institute of Sociology, University of Oslo*

STUDENTS OF SOCIAL mobility in modern societies customarily make a great deal of the distinction between mobility connected with trends in technology and the division of labor, and mobility independent of such secular trends. The same distinction appeared in the late 19th-century studies by Italian and British researchers applying the ideas of statistics, especially the concept of statistical independence, to the phenomenon of "occupational heredity." It played a prominent role in the studies of the late 1940's and early 1950's under the heading of social distance mobility. And in the latest research, in which statuses are expressed in the form of continuous variables, the coefficient of correlation is used to evaluate the degree to which variation in sons' status is accounted for by variation in fathers' status. Since the coefficient of correlation standardizes for differences in means and standard deviations of fathers' and sons' occupational status—such differences being due to secular trends in the social and economic structure—this latest technique also follows the earlier ones in singling out for special attention mobility without the confounding effects of concurrent changes in the division of labor or the system of ranks.[1]

[1] Examples of the research carried out about the turn of the century are Federico Chessa, *La trasmissione erediteria delle professioni* (Torino: Fratelli Bocca, 1912) and Emily Perrin, "On the Contingency between Occupation in the Case of Fathers and Sons," *Biometrika*, 3 (1904), pp. 467-469. Of the studies of social distance mobility, Davis Glass (ed.), *Social Mobility in Britain* (London: Routledge and Kegan Paul, 1954), Gösta Carlsson, *Social Mobility and Class Structure* (Lund: CWK Gleerup, 1958) and Natalie Rogoff, *Recent Trends in Occupational Mobility* (New York: Free Press of Glencoe, 1953) are representative. Correlation analysis has been introduced in Otis Dudley Duncan and Robert W. Hodge, "Education and Occupational Mobility: A Regression Analysis," *American Journal of Sociology*, 68 (May, 1963), pp. 629-644.

The research based on techniques that take account of this distinction has taught us a good deal about social mobility as an indicator of the relative openness or penetrability of occupational statuses in a number of Western societies over the past, let us say, 60 years. So much has been said about these inquiries that little space need be given here to their major results. But at least two things need to be said about their relevance to the study of social mobility in non-Western societies undergoing more or less rapid social, technological, and economic change.

1. Research on the relative openness or permeability of social statuses has tended to stress the element of stratification in evaluating the amount of movement among unlike statuses. That is, instead of simply inquiring into the number of persons who move out of the status of their fathers, the research has attempted to evaluate that movement as occurring over a "long" or a "short" distance, as being "upward" or "downward" in direction, to give more point to overall judgments of the society's openness. Social mobility and social stratification have tended to be linked together as two quite inseparable sides of the same coin.

2. At the same time, virtually no attention has been devoted to what social mobility has to tell us about how the social structure changes, rather than about what it is. This is a difficult distinction to make. To express it roughly and approximately, we have, in all of our research on social mobility, observed that large numbers of sons occupy positions different from those occupied by their fathers. This information we use to describe the social structure of a particular society at a particular time: It *is* a "mobile" society, or it *has* a "permeable" set of statuses. But we do not ask whether the considerable amount of turnover in persons or families occupying diverse statuses is itself an indicator of structural change.[2] In initiating the study of social mobility in developing societies, it may be better to ask what the amount and types of turnover of personnel suggest about structural change, for it is precisely this kind of change we should like to "capture" as it occurs in these societies.

In fact, in the present analysis I shall all but drop the element of stratification, giving the study of change more attention than it ordinarily receives. My object is to see whether a fresh examination of con-

²Harry Johnson has attempted to come to terms with the problem of specifying indicators of structural change, by ordering them from the more important to the less important kinds. His list begins with change in social values, institutional change, change in the distribution of possessions and rewards, and ends with change in personnel and change in the abilities and attitudes of personnel. Johnson's discussion is provocative because it points up the difficulties in distinguishing among types of change—that is, in following up all of the consequences of a unique trend or event —and in deciding where to draw the line between changes that keep things intact and those that do not. See Harry M. Johnson, *Sociology: A Systematic Introduction* (New York: Harcourt, Brace & World, 1960) pp. 626-631.

ventional data on social mobility will uncover some of the processes it would be desirable to observe in developing societies.

THE "STARTING POINT"

The first thing to consider is the "starting point:" the occupational distribution of the previous generation. Elsewhere in this volume, Duncan criticizes the use of conventional data on social mobility to estimate this distribution. Information collected from a sample of the present generation, representing a cross-section of the population, about the occupational status of their fathers is admittedly heterogeneous and inadequate to the task of estimating the occupational structure at a particular time in the past. Some of the major sources of error: not all members of the previous generation produced sons who survived to adulthood; those who did produce surviving sons had unequal chances of being represented proportional to their fertility rates; the fathers are so varied in age that not all of them were in the labor force at a given time; some sons were immigrants whose fathers never participated in the occupational structure of the society of which the sons now are members.

The occupational distribution of the fathers of members of the current generation is indisputably a poor indicator of the true occupational distribution a generation earlier. When we use such data, we are in much the same position as the historian forced to reconstruct the past in a biased fashion because only some of the past, and that not a fair sample, survives into the present. Just *how* unfair a sample is not clear. Systematic comparisons of the true with the estimated distributions have not been made. The fact that this analysis begins with data derived from conventional social mobility studies does not mean that the errors involved are considered small, but rather that one uses the data available, being willing to accept the loss of accuracy arising from that convenience.

Relatively little attention has been paid to the profile of the division of labor at the starting point in research on social mobility. Reexamination of many of the inquiries suggests far more diversity among the so-called modern societies than has hitherto been mentioned. It is particularly interesting to note just how much diversity exists in the proportion of the active population engaged in agriculture and related occupations. In France, no less than 43 per cent of the men represented in the father's generation were farm owners, tenants, or laborers. In Sweden, the corresponding figure was 42 per cent, in Japan 43 per cent, in the United States

32 per cent and in Germany three different studies report 11, 22 and 24 per cent.[3] For Britain and Denmark no corresponding figures are available, since fathers' and sons' statuses are reported in terms of prestige categories, rather than occupations. Nonetheless, the proportion of men engaged in agriculture in Britain is clearly lower than that for any of the other societies just mentioned, and would probably be on the order of 5 to 10 per cent in the kind of retrospective distribution given in mobility research.

It is among precisely this set of societies that relatively little difference has been observed in mobility or permeability of occupational statuses. Evidently the openness of the social structure may be constant even when the distribution of persons over a set of significantly different locations in that structure varies. Of course, the variation in occupational structure among these seven societies is small in comparison with the variation among all contemporary societies. Nonetheless, examination of the "starting points" suggests that even when a large proportion of a society's population—perhaps as much as 40 per cent—work in agriculture, the stratification system may still be typical of modern urban industrial societies.

Just as the division of labor at the starting point was not identical in the various societies studied by investigators of social mobility, so were changes in the division of labor from one generation to the next quite diverse, both in degree and in kind. On this point, the studies in question are extremely difficult to compare, because the techniques used to sample and classify the population vary. But a few remarks can be made. The proportion of farmers in the sons' generation in France was 36 per cent, Japan 25 per cent, and in Sweden 22—despite the fact that in all three countries, 43 per cent of the fathers' generation were engaged in agriculture.[4]

---

[3] The figures for France, Japan, and Germany are in Seymour M. Lipset and Reinhard Bendix, *Social Mobility in Industrial Society* (Berkeley: University of California Press, 1959), pp. 19-21. The Swedish data are in Carlsson, *op. cit.*, p. 98. For the United States, a 1947 NORC study reported 31 per cent, but the latest study, conducted in 1960 by the University of Michigan Survey Research Center, reported that no less than 32 per cent of the sample were sons of farmers. The two American studies give the proportion of fathers in agriculture by the age of the sons; the age-specific proportions are identical in the two studies despite the passage of 13 years between them. In 1900, 42 per cent of the American male labor force were in agricultural occupations; 60 years later, 32 per cent of the current generation said they were the sons of farmers. The Survey Research Center study reported an occupational distribution of the sample of sons that squares with the current census distribution, but its occupational distribution of fathers does not fit any of the decennial distributions back to 1900 and the proportion in farming is the most deviant of all categories. See James N. Morgan *et al.*, *Income and Welfare in the United States* (New York: McGraw-Hill, 1962), pp. 331-337.

[4] Sources for these figures are the same as in footnote 3.

But if we are to make anything out of the relationship between various starting points and rates of change on the one hand, and social mobility on the other, more detailed analysis of more strictly comparable exhibits of data will certainly be required. It is to this I now turn.

The data concern the occupational origins and destinations of a cohort of young Norwegians.[5] On the whole, Norway began at the same starting point as France, Sweden, and Japan: 43 per cent of the men in the fathers' generation were engaged in farming and related occupations (forestry and fishing). The occupational distribution changed to the extent that only 22 per cent of the sons were in these statuses. But it is not the experience of the age cohort as a whole that is of concern here. Fortunately, information was available on the nature of the locality where the young men had grown up—whether urban or rural—with additional detail on the size of urban localities and the type of economic base prevailing in rural communities.[6] This makes it possible to compare the mobility of young men coming from places that differ greatly in their division of labor at the starting point.

Some 37 per cent of the Norwegians in the younger generation grew up in communities where the division of labor is not unlike what one might expect in a peasant agricultural society. Of their fathers, 70 per cent were farmers or fishermen or combined these two occupations or, in inland districts, combined farming and forestry. Fifteen per cent of the fathers' generation in these rural communities were either day laborers or practiced one of the traditional skilled crafts. Only the remaining 15 per cent, consisting of about equal numbers of white-collar workers and

[5] The data were collected in 1950, in the course of interviews conducted by psychologists in the Norwegian armed services with young men called for military service. In principle, the interviews take place during the year when young men reach the age of 19, and no man is exempt. In practice, the 19,300 men interviewed include some men born before 1931 (8 per cent of the total) and a few born after 1931 (1 per cent of the total). And of those born in 1931, only 84 per cent are included, the remainder consisting almost exclusively of merchant seamen whose ships were at sea during the interviewing period. Their loss is partly made up by the older men, many of whom had been in the merchant marine earlier. For fuller descriptions of the sample, as well as analyses of the data concerning their education and intelligence, see Vidkunn Coucheron Jarl, "Skolegang og naeringsmiljø," *Skole og samfunn*, 1958, pp. 227-232; "De unge menns utdanning," *Norsk Pedagogisk Tidskrift*, (1953), No. 3, pp. 1-27; and Natalie Rogoff Ramsøy, "Evner, utdannelse, og yrkesvalg i norsk samfunnsstruktur," *Tidsskrift for Samfunnsforskning*, 2 (December, 1961), pp. 217-237.

[6] The classification of communes pertains to their status at the time of the 1946 census of population. For rural communes, that is, all communes except those designated as cities through an act of the Norwegian Parliament, the classification according to type of economic base consisted originally of nine categories, representing various combinations of agriculture, forestry, fishing, and industry. The predominance of each occupation was judged according to the proportion of the total population dependent on it.

manual workers in industry, earned their living in occupations typical of contemporary developed societies. Thus, about one-third of the young generation of Norwegians grew up in communities where modern industry, commerce and professional services were all but missing from the local occupational scene.

Another 27 per cent of the young men grew up in rural communities with a more complex division of labor. Here, while farming was still the occupation of somewhat over half—56 per cent—of the fathers, industry and service occupations were more prevalent. But industry was still on a small and relatively unskilled basis. About 20 per cent of the fathers were laborers or in traditional skilled crafts, 12 per cent were industrial workers, and the remaining 12 per cent were in white-collar and service occupations.

A few rural communities had gone much farther in the direction of industrialism. Large-scale production of metals, and hydroelectric installations where proximity to raw materials far outweighs proximity to the market in production costs, are often located in isolated rural settings in Norway, and they naturally make great inroads on the local division of labor. Farming has virtually disappeared in these settings (only 18 per cent of the fathers are in agriculture) while industrial workers and white-collar workers together account for some 42 per cent of the members of the fathers' generation. But day laborers and traditional craftsmen are still present in large numbers, comprising 40 per cent of the total. Large-scale industry in a rural setting is not a very frequent combination. Only 8 per cent of the young men grew up in such communities.

The remaining 28 per cent of the young generation grew up in Norway's cities and suburbs, and here the division of labor is typical of urban communities in modern societies. About 5 per cent of the fathers were engaged in farming, fishing, or forestry. Another 25 per cent were day laborers or in traditional skilled crafts. The great majority were connected with modern industry or in professional or service occupations. These two major sets of occupations, blue-collar and white-collar, each employed some 35 per cent of the fathers of young men who grew up in urban and suburban communities.

In short, four different occupational distributions characterize what has been called the starting point. The first is overwhelmingly agricultural, with no more than one father in seven associated with modern industrial and service occupations. In the second, agriculture is combined with small-scale industry, but the population aggregates are so small that professional or commercial service occupations are not yet required. The third, large-scale industry in the countryside, includes industrial establishments large enough to absorb most of the working population, but the full range of modern industrial and professional occupations is still not present. Only in urban communities does the occupational distribution approach a fully developed division of labor with the majority of adult male workers in occupations connected with industry, or in professional and commercial services.

NET MOBILITY

So much for the starting points. By how much do the occupational distributions of sons differ from those of their fathers, and does the dissimilarity between fathers and sons itself vary from one type of locality to another? The proportion of fathers in each type of occupational status was compared with that of their sons,[7] and a simple index of dissimilarity

	White-Collar Upper	White-Collar Lower	Trades- men	Crafts- men	Labor; Industrial	Agriculture & related	Total
Sample: Plans	15.9	9.0	3.6	12.0	38.0	21.5	100.0
1950 Census: Age 25-29	13.0	9.8	1.4	12.1	40.7	23.0	100.0

For census data, see *Population Census, 1950,* Vol. 4 (Oslo: Central Bureau of Statistics, 1959), p. 66, Table 42.

was computed by calculating the proportion of members of one generation who would have to change their occupational status if the two distributions—that of fathers and that of sons—were to match one another.[8] When applied to the diverse types of communities, this indicator of change in the occupational structure presents a clear trend, as shown below. (The classification of communities in Table 1 is more detailed than that discussed in the text.)

The more urbanized and industrialized their place of residence, the greater was the similarity in the occupational distributions of fathers

[7] The young men were asked what their current occupation was and what their occupational plans were. Problems arise in the use of either set of answers. About 15 per cent of the sample were still attending school, and therefore had no current occupation. On the other hand, some 16 per cent could not say what their plans were. After much preliminary analysis, the responses concerning plans were selected as the more realistic indicator of the sons' occupational statuses. The data on plans include the category of professionals and technicians, entirely absent as the current occupation of 19-year-olds, and also correctly anticipate the drastic reduction of unpaid family farm workers (a status that many farmers' sons fail to resume after they return from military service). The distribution of the sample according to occupational plans (omitting those without plans) corresponds to the actual distribution of 25-29 year-olds in the 1950 census as follows (in percentages):

[8] See Otis Dudley Duncan and Albert J. Reiss, Jr., *Social Characteristics of Urban and Rural Communities, 1950* (New York: John Wiley & Sons, 1956) p. 99, where the index is defined as the "percentage of nonoverlapping of two distributions."

and sons. The index values, measuring the degree of nonoverlapping or dissimilarity between fathers and sons, increase noticeably from the most to the least urbanized localities. Since the two distributions refer to persons separated by the time span of a generation, it is not inappropriate to consider the index values as indicating net change or net mobility in occupational status. The tendency, therefore, is toward a higher rate of net occupational mobility in localities where agriculture and other nonindustrial occupations predominate. In other words, the amount of change was correlated with the occupational distribution at the "starting point:" the larger the proportion of fathers who were engaged in farming and related occupations, the greater the intergenerational shift in occupational status.

Furthermore, each occupational category changed size in the same direction in virtually all types of community. The proportion of sons in professional, technical, clerical, and sales occupations everywhere exceeded the proportion of fathers; the proportion of sons who were proprietors of retail and service establishments was lower than the proportion of fathers in all communities except agricultural villages (where there was a barely noticeable increase). The proportion of sons who were farmers, fishermen, and day laborers was everywhere lower, and the proportion of skilled- and semi-skilled industrial workers everywhere

TABLE 1

OCCUPATIONAL DISTRIBUTION OF 19-YEAR-OLD MEN * AND THEIR FATHERS,

| | Place of Residence | | | | | |
| Occupational Status | Capital city | | Smaller cities | | Suburbs | |
	Father	Son	Father	Son	Father	Son
Professionals, managers, & technicians	24.3%	27.6%	16.7%	24.8%	21.8%	25.4%
White collar workers	6.8	17.8	6.1	15.1	4.5	12.1
Tradesmen	10.9	5.2	11.6	5.2	7.5	4.2
Craftsmen	9.3	10.7	12.9	12.2	8.7	11.6
Industrial workers	32.0	33.0	31.3	35.0	27.8	35.8
Unskilled labor	14.2	4.6	17.2	6.1	12.5	3.3
Farming, fishing, forestry	2.5	1.1	4.2	1.6	17.2	7.6
Total	100.0	100.0	100.0	100.0	100.0	100.0
INDEX OF DISSIMILARITY, FATHERS TO SONS	16.7		20.8		22.1	
No. of cases	1,310		2,911		1,146	

* See footnote 7.

higher, in the sons' generation. The only traditional occupational status that increased in size over time was that of skilled craftsmen, in six of the seven types of community.

No matter what the starting point, then, there was a general shift toward industrial jobs, skilled crafts, white-collar and professional occupations. The rate of net movement into these occupations, however, seems to have varied negatively with the size of these occupations at the starting point. This notion could be tested by relating the percentages involved in the net change to the percentages of fathers in the "traditional" occupations, but such a test runs up against the difficult question of what is meant by "modern" occupations, and what is meant by "pre-industrial," or "traditional" occupations. The provisional classification offered earlier, in the description of the occupational distributions prevailing in the various types of community at the starting point, includes the status of skilled craftsman under the category of "traditional" occupations. But this category did not diminish in size over time. Clearly, such a rough division of occupational positions cannot stand up to detailed examination. And to use the terms "modern" and "traditional" in anything but the roughest sense is beyond the scope of this study.

Another principle of classification, which avoids these difficulties, is based on the fact that some occupational statuses attracted more sons

ACCORDING TO PLACE OF RESIDENCE, NORWAY, 1950

Place of Residence									
Industrial villages		Mixed villages		Agricultural villages		Fishing villages		All communities	
Father	Son	*Father*	Son	*Father*	Son	*Father*	Son	*Father*	Son
7.2%	17.2%	5.9%	12.3%	4.7%	10.2%	3.5%	8.8%	9.3%	15.9%
2.1	7.0	1.2	6.3	1.1	6.6	0.7	5.0	2.5	9.0
4.7	2.9	4.1	3.3	2.9	3.0	4.0	2.8	5.5	3.6
12.4	14.7	8.4	11.3	7.0	12.6	3.1	9.4	8.8	12.0
27.8	40.0	12.2	34.3	8.8	27.2	3.8	25.9	17.1	32.5
27.6	9.6	13.2	5.7	9.2	4.8	5.5	4.3	13.3	5.5
18.2	8.6	55.0	26.8	66.3	35.6	79.4	43.8	43.5	21.5
100.0	100.0	100.0	100.0	100.0	100.0	100.0	100.0	100.0	100.0
29.4		36.5		35.1		38.0		31.7	
1,469		5,199		6,469		695		19,199	

than fathers, while others attracted fewer sons; some categories grew, others contracted in size. And the same occupations—professional, technical, managerial, white-collar, and industrial—increased in the proportion of sons relative to fathers, no matter in what type of community the young men lived, while the occupations of tradesman, unskilled laborer, farmer and fisherman declined.

The index values of net occupational change may therefore be compared with the proportion of fathers in occupations that contracted in size. This comparison allows one to evaluate the extent to which each set of young men moved "ahead" (i.e., into growing occupational statuses) from the baseline of their fathers' occupational distribution. In the capital city, for example, some 72 per cent of the fathers were engaged in occupations that attracted even larger proportions of their sons; in fishing villages, only 11 per cent of the fathers were in these growing occupations. Clearly, more of the young men who grew up in fishing villages could move into professional, industrial, and related occupational statuses, since fewer of them had social origins in these categories.

For the young men who grew up in urban communities, the direction in which they moved, occupationally, represents an ever greater concentration in the occupational statuses already dominant in their local environment. Industrial, commercial, and professional occupations were typical there, before the young men entered the labor force. But for the young men who grew up in rural communities, where the local occupational structure was typically agricultural, the direction in which they moved occupationally represents a discontinuity with local conditions. Instead of extending the prevailing local tendency, they have disrupted it.

Under the assumption that the local occupational structure usually exerts something of a pull when the new generation enters the labor force, the behavior of young men who grew up in predominantly agricultural communities is far more problematic than that of their contemporaries who grew up in cities. If the prevailing occupational structure alone were important, then the young men in rural communities should have become more concentrated than their fathers in the locally prevailing occupations. Clearly, something other than locally prevailing conditions must be taken into consideration to explain the occupational distribution of young men in rural communities. Instead of responding to local conditions, they are responding to the "national economy" or the "total occupational structure." At least we may infer this from the uniformity of direction of net occupational movement among young men living in all types of communities. However diverse the local conditions,

TABLE 2

NET OCCUPATIONAL CHANGE RELATIVE TO MAXIMUM NET CHANGE,
BY PLACE OF RESIDENCE, NORWAY, 1950.

Place of Residence	Per Cent in Growing Occupations *		Net Change/ Maximum Net Change,† or B — A/100 — A
	Fathers (A)	Sons (B)	
Capital City	72.4	89.1	60.5
Smaller Cities	67.0	87.1	60.9
Suburbs	62.8	84.9	59.5
Industrial Villages	49.5	78.9	58.2
Mixed Villages	37.7	64.2	50.5
Farming Villages	21.4	56.6	44.8
Fishing Villages	11.1	49.1	42.8

* Occupational statuses that grew in size include professional, technical, and managerial, white-collar, craftsmen, and industrial workers. Retail and service trades, unskilled labor, and farming and related occupations decreased. (The percentages of fathers in the latter occupations is equal to the denominator of the standardized index in the last column.)

† The index of net occupational change or mobility was defined earlier as the proportion of sons who would have to shift occupation if the distribution of sons were to match that of fathers. Here it is defined as the surplus of sons in the occupations that show a larger proportion of sons than fathers. The two definitions are identical, but because the otherwise standard list of occupations that increased in size differed slightly in the smaller cities and in the farming villages, the index values for these two types of community differ slightly in Tables 1 and 2.

as indicated by their fathers' occupational distributions, the sons' behavior suggests that they are all responsive to socio-economic tendencies present all over Norway.

One other point concerning the indices of net occupational mobility affects their significance for the changing occupational structure of the society as a whole. The occupational distributions of young men brought up in cities, towns, and villages do not bear the same relation to the local economic base as do the occupational distributions of their fathers. For the younger generation, the localities where they were raised are not necessarily the localities where they will live later on.[9]

[9] In their interviews the young men were asked where they were born, where they attended elementary school, and where they lived currently (that is, at age 19). This analysis is based on their residence while attending elementary school. We have examined the migration that occurred between that period and the time of the interview, but since migration among the 15-19-year-old men does not resemble migration among 20-29-year-old men, either in extent or in direction, it was not used to study the point at issue here.

Unfortunately, the later occupational and residential histories of the sample were not obtained. But an idea of the role of migration in reshaping the local occupational structure may be gained from Boalt's well-known study of social mobility in Stockholm.[10]

TABLE 3

OCCUPATIONAL DISTRIBUTIONS OF STOCKHOLM FATHERS,
STOCKHOLM SONS, AND MIGRANT "SONS"

Occupational Status	Stockholm Fathers	Stockholm Sons	Migrants Same Age as "Sons"	All "Sons"
	(A)	(B)	(C)	(B+C)
I (Upper white collar)	12.8%	12.1%	4.3%	7.9%
II (Lower white collar)	32.6	54.1	27.2	39.6
III (Manual)	54.6	33.8	68.5	52.5
	100.0	100.0	100.0	100.0

INDICES OF DISSIMILARITY:

A — B:	21.5
A — C:	13.9
A — (B + C):	7.0

Between the young men brought up in Stockholm and their own fathers, the major difference in occupational status involved a smaller proportion of sons in manual work, and a correspondingly larger proportion in lower white-collar work. The extent of the difference between the two distributions is represented by the dissimilarity index value of 21.5 (a value roughly comparable with the corresponding figures for Norway's cities and suburbs). But Stockholm's population of young men (the sample consisted of 24-year-olds living in the city) included a considerable number of migrants in addition to the native sons. The occupational distribution of the migrants resembled that of the Stockholm fathers more than did the distribution of the native sons, the index of dissimilarity between columns A and C being 13.9. Finally, the index value comparing the distribution of all young men in Stockholm, native and migrants, with that of the native father is only 7.0. The last figure indicates the degree to which the occupational structure in the city

[10] See Gunnar Boalt, "Social Mobility in Stockholm: A Pilot Investigation" in *Transactions of the Second World Congress of Sociology* (London: International Sociological Association, 1954) Vol. 2, pp. 67-73.

changed in the course of one generation, after both migration and inter-generational occupational mobility took place.

Boalt's results have previously aroused a good deal of attention because of their implications for the stratification system: the urban working class is apparently recruited primarily from rural and small-town migrants, while the sons of urban working-class families move up into middle- or lower middle-class positions. But the data appear to have equal bearing on the development of the occupational structure in the diverse "parts" or ecological units of a differentiated and complex society. Migration may have a combination of effects on net changes in the occupational structure. On the one hand, the possibility of migration may increase the likelihood that young men will choose occupations deviating from the local structure of opportunities. On the other hand, by "draining off" deviants to other localities where their occupational choice is more typical, migration allows each type of local structure to preserve its occupational distribution (although not necessarily its size).[11]

Under extreme conditions, differential migration might result in perfect stability in the occupational structure of diverse types of communities, at the same time that the occupational structure of the society as a whole changed considerably with the growth and decline in the sizes of various types of locality. The Stockholm data do not correspond to this extreme, since the occupational structure in the city did not remain stable, but the change was far smaller than that indicated by the net occupational mobility of native sons.

The data in Tables 1 and 2 suggest that the sons in various types of localities resemble one another in their occupational distributions more than do their fathers. If it were possible to add a new set of distributions of sons, however, after they had migrated, the sons' distributions would probably be more dissimilar, from place to place, than they were before they moved. But at least some of the growing homogeneity evident in the premigration phase should still be evident.

In 1950, the labor force in over half of Norway's non-urban com-

---

[11] Donald Bogue has considered the same problems concerning migration, mobility, and local industrial structure in his study of workers in Ohio and Michigan in 1947. His research design is so different from the present one that the two analyses are not directly comparable, but a few lines from his results may stimulate interest in the problem. He notes, ". . . contrary to what might be expected, the great influx of male workers from other states was not to the automotive, primary and fabricated metals, machinery and rubber products industries which are major sources of employment in [Michigan and Ohio]. Instead, 'other manufacturing,' . . . the finance and service industries, contract construction, wholesale trade, retail trade, and transportation provided employment for the net gain." Donald J. Bogue, *A Methodological Study of Migration and Labor Mobility* (Scripps Foundation Studies in Population Distribution, No. 4, 1952), p. 44.

munes was predominantly agricultural (including forestry and fishing).[12] But in the short space of ten years, the proportion in extractive industries shifted from over 50 per cent to less than 50 per cent in no less than a third of the previously agricultural communes. As noted earlier, young men in these localities were most likely to shift away from the occupations prevailing locally. But net outward migration might leave the local occupational structure about the same in shape, if not in size. Clearly this was not the case, for the local structure in previously agricultural communes has *not* remained intact. It is becoming less and less agricultural and it has changed at what we may permit ourselves to call a rapid rate.

In the same decade, predominantly agricultural communities declined in population by 3 per cent, while in all other communities the population increased by more than 11 per cent.[13] Many of the young men from agricultural communities who chose non-agricultural occupations apparently found their way to places with a non-agricultural structure. In sum, by no means all of the change in the shape of the division of labor in diverse types of locality suggested by the father-son comparisons is cancelled out by net migration, but some of it undoubtedly is.

It is well to consider just how much these conclusions concerning net mobility rates depend on the classification schemes selected for comparing occupations and communities. Simon Kuznets pointed out that the systematic decrease in net mobility rates from the least to the most urbanized and industrialized types of community vanishes when occupations are simply divided between manual and non-manual.[14] Nor would a more detailed set of occupational categories, where the principle of classification consisted exclusively of occupational prestige, necessarily duplicate the results given here. For example, the social prestige classification developed for the British study of social mobility combined in one category certain types of routine clerical occupations with manual occupations, since they were all accorded about the same amount of prestige by a cross-section of the British population.[15] The variations reported earlier among communities in net mobility rates might not appear if a prestige-graded set of occupational categories were the basis of the mobility measurements. In that event, it would follow that occupa-

[12] The discussion in this paragraph is based on a table from the 1960 population census of Norway, appearing in preliminary form in *Statistisk Ukehefte*, No. 52 (December, 28, 1962).

[13] Based on unpublished tabulations from the 1960 census.

[14] Kuznets' observation was made in his discussion of the original draft of this paper. According to his computation, the range of variation in net mobility rates shrinks to practically nothing when only a manual-non-manual classification is used, and the little variation remaining is unrelated to type of community.

[15] Glass, *op. cit.*, Ch. 2.

tions sharing the same amount of prestige are not necessarily changing in size homogeneously, for the net mobility rates presented here simply indicate the degree to which the occupational structure is changing in shape. In effect, the present occupational classification attempts to catch as much of the "modernization" of the work force as is possible within the limits of the original data. Modernization does not necessarily imply changes in the prestige hierarchy or shifts across the white-collar-blue-collar line, and the results should be evaluated in the light of the specific trends that the classification scheme aims to emphasize.

The occupational classification used here, as well as the classification of communities, do not find their counterparts in official Norwegian census data. The typology of communities was developed by a geographer using data from the census of 1946; [16] the classification was changed in 1950 and only since about the middle of the 1950's has it led to the use of a functional classification of communities in Norwegian official statistics. It is, in other words, impossible to compare the occupational distributions of fathers and sons in the diverse types of communities with census data for the working force as a whole in those communities, because the classification according to place of residence is simply not to be found in the published data.

The same holds for the occupational classification. Only in 1960 has the Norwegian census reported what deserves to be called an occupational distribution. Before then, workers were classified only according to industry, with an occasional table reporting the number of manual and white-collar workers in each industry, or the number of independent workers and the number of wage and salary workers. Although we have estimated the occupational distribution of men aged 25-29 from 1950 census data (see footnote 7), more refined estimates, especially according to place of residence, are not warranted by the amount of occupational information in the original census data.

This discussion began by casting doubt on the use of intergenerational mobility data to estimate the distribution of occupations in the previous generation—the "starting point" for the observation of mobility. But unless adequate data are collected at the time, the *only* available source of this retrospective information may be the conventional kind of intergenerational mobility data. This is certainly a point to remember with respect to underdeveloped countries whose many lacks and insufficiencies include a shortage of information, especially concerning the past.

---

[16] Øivind Rødevand in Isachsen and Ellefsen, *Verdens land og folk etter annen verdenskrig* (Oslo: Halvorsen og Larsen, 1950), Vol. 4, pp. 613-34.

GROSS MOBILITY AND OCCUPATIONAL EXCHANGE

The analysis thus far has been based on comparisons between the occupational distributions of fathers and sons, without reference to the degree of correspondence between the occupational status of each father and that of his own son. From the point of view of conventional analyses of social mobility, only the two sets of marginal distributions have been taken into account, while nothing has been said about the various occupational destinations of sons coming from each parental (origin) category. But the index of net change derived from the comparison of the marginals has been used previously, because it turns out to have considerable value in making the difficult decision as to whether an observed mobility rate is "high" or "low": the net mobility rate, or index of net change, represents a floor below which the observed mobility rate cannot go.

When the occupational distribution changes from one generation to the next, it is impossible for all sons to remain in the occupational statuses of their fathers. In the terms of a mobility matrix, some cell frequencies must be located off the main diagonal, since a minimum number of cases must move out of the parental occupational category to produce the change in the marginal distributions. Therefore, the index of net occupational change may be defined in still another way: it is the smallest proportion of the total population of sons who could have moved from their father's occupational status, given the change in the occupational structure between succeeding generations.[17]

Among the various types of Norwegian localities, net occupational mobility varied inversely with the degree of industrial-urbanism characterizing the locality. The question now is whether the total proportion of sons who moved from their fathers' occupational status, or *gross* mobility, varied from one type of community to another in corresponding fashion.

What is called in Table 4 the "gross mobility rate" is perhaps the most widespread and simplest index of occupational mobility: the percentage of sons whose occupations differ from their fathers'. Variation among the community types in the general tendency of sons to move out of their fathers' occupational status does *not* run parallel to the

[17] Gösta Carlsson made use of net mobility rates, or rather the mathematical complement of net mobility rates, in his analysis of occupational mobility in Sweden. Dividing his sample into nine sets of cases according to year of brth, he notes that net mobility rates were highest for the youngest age cohort. See Gösta Carlsson, *op. cit.*, 103-4.

variation in the net mobility rate. Instead, the gross rates are quite similar in all communities except farming and fishing villages, where they are somewhat lower than elsewhere, despite the fact that the "floor" of mobility is highest in such villages.

TABLE 4

GROSS AND NET OCCUPATIONAL MOBILITY RATES, BY PLACE OF RESIDENCE, NORWAY, 1950

Place of Residence	Gross Mobility Rate	Net Mobility Rate	Exchange Mobility Rate
	(A)	(B)	(A) — (B)
Capital City	64.2%	16.7%	47.5%
Smaller Cities	67.0	20.8	46.2
Suburbs	64.1	22.1	42.0
Industrial Villages	64.5	29.4	35.1
Mixed Villages	61.0	36.5	24.5
Agricultural Villages	54.6	35.2	19.4
Fishing Villages	51.6	38.0	13.6

To social scientists steeped in the results of mobility research of the past decade, this finding must surely appear anomalous. It has been assumed that the total mobility rate is positively correlated with the rate of change in the occupational structure, that the more the occupational structure changes, the greater the proportion of men in occupational statuses different from those of their fathers. Yet the data in Table 4 belie this supposition. The gross mobility rate is about the same in all types of community except the most agricultural, despite the variations observed in the net rate. And it is precisely where the occupational structure is changing most markedly—in the farming and fishing villages—that the *smallest* proportion of men are occupationally mobile. Common sense insists that the more the occupational structure changes, the more men must be in occupations other than their fathers. But this need not be so, provided the gross rate exceeds the net by so much that there is considerable "free play" in the arithmetical relation between the two.

To go one step further in analyzing gross and net mobility rates, the net rate, representing a minimum or a floor, can be used to facilitate comparisons in mobility among populations that differ in the degree of change in their occupational structures. This kind of standardization is carried out in the last column of Table 4 simply by subtracting the gross from the net mobility rate. But instead of calling the difference a standardized index value, I have named it the exchange mobility rate.[18]

The data in Table 4 suggest that exchange mobility is more prevalent, the more urbanized and industrialized the locality. Most of the occupational movement in urban centers does not contribute to changes in the occupational structure. Instead, it involves a rearrangement of the members of the younger generation within a relatively stable structure. In the least urban and industrialized communities, most of the mobility that occurs is directly involved in the shift of the sons' occupational distribution away from that of the fathers. While a larger proportion of sons in farming and fishing villages remain in their fathers' occupational status than is true of sons elsewhere, the moves that do occur are more likely to represent a net change in the occupational structure.

In urbanized and industrialized localities, occupational movement tends to be reciprocal. Men move from their occupational origins to other statuses, but their movement is reciprocated by others who take the positions the first would have occupied had they remained in their fathers' statuses. In rural, non-industrial localities, however, individual shifts are primarily uni-directional. Those who move are not replaced by others. Occupational mobility in agriculture communities does involve the well-known tendency for many to move out of farming and few to move into it, but this frequently identified phenomenon has a corollary to which little attention has been given: it therefore takes a lower gross mobility rate among farmers' sons or young men from predominantly farm communities to produce a noticeable shift in the occupational structure than is required where movement is not uni-directional, but reciprocal. The character of occupational mobility gradually shifts from the most to the least urban localities. At the urban-industrial extreme, it consists predominantly of mutually reciprocating moves with little effect on the total distribution of positions in the occupational structure, but considerable effect on the composition (at least the social origins) of persons in diverse occupational positions. At the rural-agricultural extreme, mobility consists primarily of unreciprocated moves, tending to represent a wholesale departure from agriculture and other extractive occupations and a corresponding recruitment into industrial, clerical, and professional occupations previously represented in far smaller num-

[18] After completing this manuscript, I found a reference to a study published five years ago, of mobility in Sao Paulo. It was cast in terms of the same distinction between occupational exchanges and net occupational shifts. See Bertram Hutchinson, "Structural and Exchange Mobility in the Assimilation of Immigrants to Brazil," *Population Studies*, 12 (November, 1958), pp. 111-120. Judah Matras has used the same measure extensively to compare net, exchange, and gross mobility rates in a number of modern societies: see "Differential Fertility, Intergenerational Mobility and Change in the Occupational Distribution: Some Elementary Interrelationships," *Population Studies*, 15 (July, 1961), pp. 187-197.

bers in these localities. Here it is far less the case that the men who move away from their fathers' status are replaced by and themselves replace men from other occupational origins; instead, the moves add up to pronounced changes in the occupational structure itself.

The distinction between occupational exchanges and net mobility may evoke, for sociologists, assertions about two major consequences of a high rate of social mobility. First, that a high mobility rate indicates adaptability to technological and other "external" changes, such that the occupational or industrial composition of the working force can be altered by recruiting new workers where and when they are needed. Second, that mobility indicates change and, presumably, improvement in the relation between individual qualifications and occupational position. A high rate of *net* mobility suggests a labor force adaptable to changes in the demand for workers in diverse occupational positions. A high rate of *occupational exchange* suggests intensive competition for positions according to personal qualifications, with the result that occupational statuses are distributed more efficiently and, at the same time more fairly, than they would be if men remained in their fathers' statuses.

DISCUSSION

The analysis presented above has been set forth in the hope that it will enrich discussion of the way social mobility and socio-economic development are involved with one another. Its results suggest the following comparative inquiries.

1. *Comparing rates of mobility in diverse "parts" of a society.* The comparison between the sons' occupational distribution and that of their fathers in different communities led to two conclusions:

(a) The *direction* of change in the occupational structure, that is, the types of occupations that grew or contracted, was uniform from one type of locality to another.

(b) The *rate* of change in the occupational structure varied inversely with, and more or less proportionally to, the level of urban-industrialism in the locality.

In the absence of material from other societies, it is difficult to know whether these tendencies are typical, or whether they are correlated with rates of change in societies as a whole. Nonetheless, they open the way for a number of significant questions concerning the way in which socioeconomic development moves out from a point of origin to include ever larger sectors of a society. While this analysis has been concerned only with diverse types of communities, the techniques are, of course, equally appropriate for examining other socially significant categories, such as ethnic, religious, or racial groups (all of which are distinguished by their absence in Norway).

It is, I take it, one of the core problems of underdeveloped societies that efforts to induce social change are quickly blocked because they cannot be made to affect the entire population. The problem may be attributed to one or some combination of such difficulties as extreme poverty, illiteracy, suspicion, or inability to identify with the innovators. But the point to be stressed here is that a society's capacity for economic development may depend as much on the relations among different population groups as on such aggregate properties as its total wealth or resources.

This is not to say that modernization, requires that change be spread at a uniform rate throughout the population. This has probably never happened, and indeed there is no reason for thinking that it is necessary. For example, during America's extremely marked economic expansion from 1880 to 1930, the disparities in degree of industrialization prevailing among the different regions of the country became more marked, rather than less. In 1880, the Far West and the region north of the Mason-Dixon line and east of the Mississippi had already become predominantly non-agricultural in occupational composition, while the South, Midwest, and Southwest were still mainly farming regions. Yet it was in the former sections of the country that industrial and service occupations grew most rapidly in the ensuing 50 years, thereby widening the early differences.[19]

If systematic data were available on the degree of evenness of socioeconomic structural change within societies, they would probably show that anything approaching homogeneous rates of change among diverse population categories has been proved the rare exception. In this most general sense, the principle of uniformity in direction or rate of occupational change is of little use in explaining variations among societies in their capacity to modernize or develop. Examined more concretely and in more detail, however, the principle may prove useful in casting light on the significance for structural change of the extreme social heterogeneity in many underdeveloped societies. This heterogeneity may be based on differences in language, tribal affiliation, ethnic, racial, or religious status, or it may stem from the enormous gap between the few rich and the many poor, but in all its forms, extreme internal heterogeneity limits stringently the possibility of change in the economic

[19] See National Resources Committee, *The Problems of a Changing Population* (Washington: U.S. Government Printing Office, 1938), pp. 43-45.

and occupational structure of the society as a whole. The Norwegian data, for instance, do not indicate that the various types of community are alike, but they do suggest that the capacity of the society as a whole to develop has not been blocked by the existing social differentiation.

2. *Occupational exchanges.* The second part of the empirical analysis began with an examination of gross mobility rates, or the overall proportion of sons who moved out of their fathers' occupational statuses. This proportion is more often called the actual mobility rate, since it has frequently been compared with the expected or theoretical rate—that is, the proportion of sons who would occupy statuses other than their fathers' if statuses were allocated independently of paternal origins. But in the present context, the term gross mobility rate seems more appropriate, since it calls attention to the discrepancy between the total number of men who change their occupational status and the smaller number who could have accounted for all of the observed shift in the occupational structure. The size of this discrepancy, the difference between the gross and the net mobility rates, was by no means a constant in the Norwegian data. It was largest among young men raised in the capital city, and decreased with increasing distance from the urban-industrial complex. The reciprocal movement of men who exchange occupational statuses, each taking the position another would have occupied had he remained in his status of origin, occurs frequently where the occupational structure is changing little, but infrequently where it is changing a great deal.

The analysis of gross, net, and exchange mobility rates is perhaps most valuable because it enables one to develop a differentiated typology of mobility, based on the observation that net and exchange mobility rates may vary independently of one another. Societies, or parts of societies, may be classified as having a high rate of net mobility but a low rate of exchange mobility, or as high with respect to both types of mobility, and so on.

This in turn generates a set of empirical problems concerning mobility, the answers to which may improve our understanding of the way mobility and modernization are interrelated. For example, the data in Table 4 may be expressed in a slightly different way, namely in the form of a simple equation, which states that gross mobility is an additive function of net and exchange mobility. This functional relationship immediately suggests two things. First, what we have called the openness or permeability of positions in the stratification structure may be defined as the sum of (a) the tendency of the structure itself to undergo change and (b) the prevalence of mechanisms that open positions to individuals according to their talent or inclination. Now a caste society, as it is described in the textbooks of sociologists, is occupationally neither adaptive nor open, while modern Western societies are presumably both. Classical Chinese society may have been open but not adaptive; it would then have had a high exchange mobility rate but a low net mobility rate. Paradoxically, the same configuration may occur at a time of major social upheaval or revolution, when the energies of the leadership are directed primarily to replacing the elite.

On some occasions, the net mobility rate has been high and the exchange mobility rate, low. A discovery, or a major technological development, may lead to great changes in the occupational structure, but without inducing new institutional provisions for free movement of individuals into positions in the changing structure. Or, two societies may have the same gross mobility rate, but in one case primarily by virtue of a rapidly shifting occupational structure and in the other, by virtue of an open pattern of allocating individuals to occupations.

So the gross mobility rate is a heterogeneous measure, consisting of two components that may vary independently. At least, the Norwegian data call attention to this possibility. And some of the most general problems concerning the process of modernization may be specified in terms of the supposition that modernization of the occupational structure has at least two sides: flexibility and adaptability on the one side, permeability and selectivity on the other. How have modern societies achieved a high degree of openness and permeability of status positions, as well as a capacity to modify the roles making up the occupational structure when it is adaptive to do so? Have the two tendencies developed at the same pace, and through the same set of social arrangements? Does one of them appear before the other historically, do they mutually reinforce one another, and are the institutional arrangements fostering one of them ever at odds with those fostering the other?

The distinction between exchange mobility, whereby men make reciprocal changes in occupational status, and net mobility, where the moves are in keeping with changes in the distribution of occupational positions, took precedence in this analysis because we did not follow the same ground rules as previous analyses. Instead of being isolated or "held constant" on the grounds that it might mask underlying variation in the tendency toward an open system of ranks, mobility due to structural changes—net mobility—was examined in full light. This led to a systematic analysis of the relation between net and gross mobility, out of which the notion of exchange mobility developed. To the extent that the disinction between net and exchange mobility brings out new aspects of the role of mobility in modernization and economic development, the shift in ground rules will justify itself.

8

RURAL-URBAN BALANCE AND MODELS
OF ECONOMIC DEVELOPMENT *

GIDEON SJOBERG, *University of Texas*

RELATIONS BETWEEN the urban and rural sectors lie at the core of many of the ideological, economic, and political dilemmas that beset nations currently striving to build an industrial-urban order. In this context rural-urban patterning emerges again as a significant area of sociological inquiry at the very time it has lost favor among researchers living in advanced industrial orders where traditional rural-urban differences have largely disappeared.

This essay is divided into two parts: In the first, or background section, I address myself to the more narrowly "demographic" aspects of rural-urban relations, notably the nature and extent of rural-to-urban migration in underdeveloped countries and the consequent growth of metropolitan centers in these societies. In the second part I shall put this rural-to-urban movement in broader perspective by examining the question implicit in the title of this paper: What is the optimum balance between the rural and urban sectors during the course of economic development? The answer to this, I believe, has manifold implications for the study of both individual and group mobility in any modernizing society.

To examine the matter of optimum balance between the rural and urban sectors, one must necessarily study rural and urban communities as sub-systems in a larger socio-cultural context. What is viewed as optimum balance between these two sectors is a function of the ideological, economic, and political orientations toward rural-urban relations in the society involved.

* I am indebted to Leo F. Schnore for his detailed criticisms of an earlier version of this paper. I have incorporated a number of his suggestions, particularly with respect to the typology of change in rural-urban ratios.

THE SHIFT FROM RURAL TO URBAN COMMUNITIES

Rural-to-urban movement is one dimension of social mobility. At a minimum this migration represents a form of horizontal mobility and is a precondition for many kinds of vertical mobility. Throughout history cities have been more prestigeful than rural communities as centers of residence. Not only does urban living enhance interpersonal communication but, because cities are the foci of transportation routes, it facilitates intra-societal communication as well. Cities have long supported activities that have been absent in the rural environment, particularly in the small villages. Significantly, the upper socio-economic groups—including political rulers, the chief educational and religious leaders, and large landowners—have traditionally been urban-based.[1] A relatively close association has always existed between place of residence and position in the class structure.

Today the traditional relations between rural and urban sectors in many societies are being overturned as nations seek to abandon their largely agrarian past in favor of an industrial-urban tomorrow. This modernization process demands that vast numbers of people move from rural to urban communities.

Unfortunately, the study of this rural-to-urban migration is hampered by several methodological barriers. Not only are certain materials unavailable but the existing data are at times of questionable validity and reliability. Moreover, theoretical issues, notably those relating to the definition of key terms, confront the researcher. Especially troublesome is the variety of definitions of "rural" and "urban;" often different nations use different cutting-points in their census definitions of these "entities." Some employ administrative criteria; others use an arbitrary dividing line of 2,500, others 5,000 and so on, severely limiting the utility of these census data for comparative purposes.[2]

Adding to the confusion are the disagreements among sociologists concerning the definitions of rural and urban. Some, like Duncan and Reiss, Schnore, and Davis, all of whom follow Hope Tisdale Eldridge,[3] employ a single criterion—size—to distinguish rural from urban commu-

---

[1] Gideon Sjoberg, *The Preindustrial City: Past and Present* (New York: Free Press of Glencoe, 1960).

[2] For the various criteria employed see United Nations, *Demographic Yearbook, 1960* (New York: United Nations, 1961), pp. 391-395.

[3] E.g. Hope Tisdale, "The Process of Urbanization," *Social Forces,* 20 (March, 1942) pp. 311-316; Otis Dudley Duncan and Albert J. Reiss, Jr., *Social Characteristics of Urban and Rural Communities, 1950* (New York: John Wiley & Sons, 1956); Leo Schnore, "The Statistical Measurement of Urbanization and Economic Development," *Land Economics,* 37 (August, 1961), pp. 229-245.

nities: a procedure that is especially convenient for analyzing census materials. Nevertheless, the use of size poses difficulties in cross-cultural study; communities in, say, the 2,500-to-5,000 category may differ considerably in their social organization across cultures and over time. The other orientation, developed by Sorokin and Zimmerman, Redfield, and Wirth, among others, divides rural and urban communities according to multiple criteria.[4] My own perspective is more in line with this tradition.[5]

Change in the Rural-Urban Ratio

Economic development, it seems clear, demands expansion of the urban sector. In less-developed countries this involves today, as it will in the future, far greater numbers of people than the sizable rural-to-urban movement in 19th-century Europe. The ever-expanding populations of most modernizing societies have added a new and significant variable to the study of rural-to-urban migration. Moreover, the urbanization process, at least in some societies, will probably be compressed in a far shorter time span than was the case in Europe during the past century.

The extent of out-migration from rural communities varies considerably among modernizing societies—affected as it is by the current size and distribution of the population, the pace of industrialization, and so on.[6] The sheer number of people involved can be significant. In India during recent decades, millions of persons have exchanged a rural for an urban mode of existence. Bogue and Zachariah, on the strength of their analysis of data on India for the period 1941-1951, concluded that during this interval almost 9 million people participated in the movement to the cities; the number of migrants involved amounted to 20 per cent of the urban population and 3 per cent of the rural population in 1941.[7]

The figures for China are even more dramatic. Orleans' studied

---

[4] Pitirim Sorokin and Carle Zimmerman, *Principles of Rural-Urban Sociology* (New York: Holt, Rinehart & Winston, 1929); Robert Redfield, *The Folk Culture of a Way of Life," American Journal of Sociology,* 44 (July, 1938), pp. 1-15.
a Way of Life," *American Journal of Sociology,"* 44 (July, 1938), pp. 1-15.
These authors differ among themselves as to the criteria for distinguishing between rural and urban communities. Wirth, for example, used size, heterogeneity, and density, whereas Redfield used isolation and heterogeneity.

[5] I distinguish urban from rural communities by their greater size and density and the presence of a significantly large number of persons employed in a wide range of non-agricultural occupations (including some requiring literacy).

[6] Methodological and theoretical difficulties, combined with the paucity of certain kinds of data, force me to rely on illustrations to support many of my tentative generalizations.

[7] Donald J. Bogue and K. C. Zachariah, "Urbanization and Migration in India," in Roy Turner (ed.), *India's Urban Future* (Berkeley: University of California Press, 1962), p. 31.

guesses, based upon admittedly questionable data, suggest that about 20 million Chinese left the countryside for the cities during the years 1949-1956. This figure is equivalent to about 4 per cent of China's estimated rural population in 1949 and over 30 per cent of the estimated urban population for that year.[8]

Although the absolute numbers of migrants involved in rural-to-urban movement are of interest in their own right, the relative changes in rural-urban composition often are of greater sociological significance. To cope with the variety of patterns that have emerged in the process of industrialization, I have constructed a simple typology based on the relation of relative to absolute changes in rural-urban composition.

TYPES OF CHANGE IN RURAL-URBAN RATIO IN DEVELOPING SOCIETIES

| | | RELATIVE CHANGES | |
		Rural < Urban	Rural ≥ Urban
ABSOLUTE CHANGES	Rural Loss	*Type I*	*Type IV*
	Rural Gain	*Type II*	*Type III*

Type I. In this case the rural population, primarily as a result of out-migration, declines in absolute as well as relative terms. In recent decades, such a pattern has been relatively uncommon. It seems to have occurred in North Korea just after the Korean War (that is, if we can trust the official statistics): ". . . the proportion of peasants in the population declined from 74.1 per cent in 1946 to 66.4 per cent in 1953 and to 44.4 per cent in 1960."[9] This represented a net loss of about 85,000 persons between 1953 and 1960.

The Soviet Union also seems to have experienced an absolute decline in its rural population during the era of rapid change, 1926-1939.[10] In most countries, however, even in periods of advanced industrialization, the decline in absolute numbers of persons in agricultural occupations

[8] Leo A. Orleans, "The Recent Growth of China's Urban Population," *Geographical Review*, 49 (January, 1959), pp. 43-57.

[9] Chong-Sik Lee, "Land Reform, Collectivisation and the Peasants in North Korea," *China Quarterly*, 14 (April-June, 1963), p. 75.

[10] Frank Lorimer, *The Population of the Soviet Union* (Geneva: League of Nations, 1946), pp. 106-110.

(the largest element in rural communities) has so far been moderate.[11]

Type II. This is the most common type of underdeveloped country today. The rural community experiences a significant increase in absolute number of inhabitants, while the proportion of ruralities in the total population declines significantly. Many Latin American countries belong in this category, at least during the decade 1940-1950.[12] And the data for Tunisia evince a similar pattern. In 1931 the total population was 2.14 million but it rose to 3.44 million in 1956. During this period the proportion of ruralites declined from 83 to 71 per cent, while the rural population increased in numbers from 1.79 million to about 2.45 million.[13]

Type III. This pattern appears to be relatively uncommon in underdeveloped countries. Yet, in Ceylon during the period 1946-1953 the absolute number of ruralites increased, and the proportion rural remained constant despite considerable out-migration, for the urban areas (defined vaguely as "municipal or urban council areas") were expanding at a relatively slow rate.[14]

India also approximated this type during the period 1951 to 1961. The rural sector grew from 294.1 million in 1951 to 358.6 million in 1961, whereas the urban population only expanded from 61.9 to 77.8 million. The proportion of the population resident in cities was 17.38 per cent in 1951 but only 17.84 per cent in 1961.[15] Unfortunately, the data for 1951 and 1961 are not strictly comparable. Although in general a community of 5,000 or more can be viewed as urban, the greater strictures in the 1961 census regarding the definition of "urban" make it likely that the stability in the proportion of the total population living in urban centers is to some extent an artifact of the changing classification system.

Type IV. Although I have not been able to document the occurrence of this type, it may have existed in a few societies at times when, for example, large-scale disasters engulfed the countryside.

Up to this point I have focused the population shift from rural to

[11] F. Dovring, "The Share of Agriculture in a Growing Population," *Monthly Bulletin of Agricultural Economics and Statistics* (August-September, 1959); pp. 1-11; Wilbur Zelinsky, "Rural Population Dynamics as an Index to Social and Economic Development: A Geographic Overview," *Sociological Quarterly*, 4 (Spring, 1963), pp. 99-121.

[12] T. Lynn Smith, "Rural-Urban Demographic Differences in Latin America," *Genus*, 16 (1960), p. 6.

[13] Mahmoud Seklani, "Villes et campagnes en Tunisie: Evaluations et prévisions," *Population*, 15 (Juin-Juillet, 1960), pp. 485-512. Here "urban" refers to localities with 1,000 or more inhabitants and local self-government.

[14] H. E. Peries, *Census of Ceylon, 1953*, Vol. I (Colombo: Department of Census and Statistics, 1957), p. 152.

[15] "Preliminary Report on Census," *Economic Weekly*, 13 (April 8, 1961), pp. 571-574.

urban areas largely from the perspective of the rural sector and in societies experiencing little international in-migration. In a few countries —e.g., Israel—international migration has had considerable impact on the proportion of people living in cities.

As for cities, many of them owe their existence and rapid expansion to heavy rural out-migration, at least in the early stages of economic development. Data from various Latin American countries allow one to contrast the growth of urban populations by natural increase with their expansion by in-migration. For example, in Venezuela 71 per cent of the urban growth (1941-50) resulted from in-migration, 29 per cent from natural increase. In Nicaragua (1940-50) migration accounted for 65 per cent of the urban growth, whereas in Brazil (1940-50) the figure was 49 per cent and in Mexico (1940-50) 42 per cent.[16]

Other, more specific data on Latin American cities underline the significance of migration (usually from rural areas) in urban growth,[17] and similar patterns have been documented for nations such as Morocco [18] and India. Jamshedpur, India, is an especially dramatic instance. Only 6.35 per cent of the heads of families were non-migrants—i.e., were born in Jamshedpur. Of the in-migrants about 44 per cent arrived before 1940, about 55 per cent 'after that date (the survey was conducted in 1954-55). Eighty-three per cent came from rural areas.[19]

Within any developing society, cities are likely to differ considerably in their proportion of in-migrants: this generalization is supported by Hutchinson's data on Brazil.[20] For many types of sociological investigations, it is profitable to follow Taeuber who, in studying migration in Japan, distinguished between "migrant" and "stable" cities.[21]

As large urban centers mature, they not only tend to become more "stable" but their in-migrants are more frequently drawn from similar

[16] Philip M. Hauser (ed.), *Urbanization in Latin America* (Paris: UNESCO, 1961), p. 110. Except in Venezuela, the proportion of foreign-born immigrants, or in-migrants, was small.

[17] E.g. Louis J. Ducoff, "Población Migratoria en un Area Metropolitana de un País en Proceso de Desarrollo: Informe Preliminar Sobre un Estudio Experimental Efectuado en El Salvador," *Estadística*, 20 (Marzo, 1962), pp. 131-139; José Francisco de Camargo, *Exodo Rural No Brasil* (Rio de Janeiro: Conquista, 1960).

[18] Dr. Benhima, "Les problèmes d'urbanisation posés par le développement des des agglomérations," *Bulletin Economique et Social du Maroc*, 26 (Décembre, 1962), pp. 163-192.

[19] B. R. Misra, *Report on Socio-Economic Survey of Jamshedpur City* (Patna: Patna University Press, 1959), pp. 69-71.

[20] Bertram Hutchinson, "The Migrant Population of Urban Brazil," *América Latina*, (Abril-Junho, 1963), pp. 43-44.

[21] Irene B. Taeuber, *The Population of Japan* (Princeton: Princeton University Press, 1958), pp. 150-151.

cities rather than from rural communities.[22] In many societies the first move is from the countryside to a small or meduim-sized city and thence to a large one. Sometimes individuals engage in this stair-step migration; in other instances, one generation leaves the rural community for small cities, and the next generation migrates to the larger urban centers.[23] The first move (or moves) provides the experience necessary for survival in the metropolis.

Social Characteristics of Rural-Urban Migrants

Urban in-migrants can be classified in two broad categories: the permanent and the temporary. Membership in the latter category, however, is difficult to ascertain, in part because definitions of "temporary" vary among research reports. For instance, is a visitor to the city a temporary migrant? To resolve this problem the researcher frequently falls back upon the migrant's own definition of the situation, asking him, for example, Do you expect to remain in the city?

Clearly, in modernizing societies a great deal of the movement into the cities involves temporary migrants.[24] This movement to and fro is encouraged by the dearth of specialized skills among the villagers and among the low-income groups in the cities. In underdeveloped countries, unskilled workers often must depend on temporary work, and even in more permanent jobs they usually profit little from length of service. Moreover, some urban in-migrants arrive with the idea of staying, but for various social and economic reasons they fail to establish themselves. Others arrive with the definite intention of returning after a time to the village.

On the other hand, many avowedly temporary migrants become permanent urban residents. Rather meager data indicate that although a person may move to the city with the intention of returning sooner or

---

[22] One can infer this from such data as appear in S. N. Sen, *The City of Calcutta: A Socio-Economic Survey, 1954-55 to 1957-58* (Calcutta: Bookland Private Ltd., 1960). In-migrants to Calcutta are increasingly from urban rather than rural areas.

[23] Some crude data indirectly bearing on the stair-step migration of individuals are presented by George W. Hill, "The Adjustment of Rural Migrants in an Urban Venezuelan Community," *Migration News*, 12 (March-April, 1963), pp. 2-3. Also, see Jane Moore, *Cityward Migration* (Chicago: University of Chicago Press, 1938), p. 126, and Dorothy S. Thomas, "Internal Migration in Sweden: A Recent Study," *Population Index*, 29 (April, 1963), pp. 125-129, for discussions of these patterns in a somewhat more industrialized setting.

[24] This has been documented for Bangkok by M. R. Meinkoth, "Migration in Thailand with Particular Reference to the Northeast," *Economics and Business Bulletin* (Temple University), 14 (1962), pp. 3-45.

later to the village, his expectations—both economic and social—may, and often do, undergo marked change. Often an individual fails to notice such change until after he returns to the village and discovers how urban-oriented he has become. He soon looks for a way back to the city. Then too, every new foray into the city augments an in-migrant's capacity to survive therein. And this horizontal mobility is a necessary precondition, or at least is highly advantageous, for eventual vertical mobility.

Although temporary movement to the cities is prevalent in preindustrial orders, it is especially marked in the tribal societies of Africa south of the Sahara. Various reasons for this pattern have been advanced, including the rudimentary division of labor among rural and lower-class urban occupations. Elkan [25] argues that the migrant's identification with the land and, often, special land-tenure patterns keep him from becoming a full-fledged urbanite. My own tentative hypothesis is that because tribal peoples, unlike peasants, lack any long-standing normative tie with urban living, and because their "world view" tends toward closure more than the peasants, it is more difficult for tribal peoples to adapt themselves to the urban milieu.

Still other characteristics of rural-to-urban migrants—age, sex, and education—merit attention. Young adults move in proportionally greater numbers than do older persons, no doubt because people in their late teens and early twenties have comparatively few encumbrances and responsibilities. In most underdeveloped countries of Africa and Asia, men have been far more mobile than women [26]—at least during the early stages of industrial-urbanization. In more extreme cases, cities have contained one and one-half to two times as many men as women.[27] Yet, this greater mobility of men is far from universal. In Latin America women appear to migrate in greater numbers than do men.[28] Some writers ascribe this to special cultural values, perhaps correctly. Nonetheless, the greater movement of women in Latin America may be due partially to the fact that urbanization has proceeded farther than in most nations of Asia or Africa. As urbanization proceeds in Asia and Africa, the divergency between the migration of men and that of women appears to narrow considerably. Once a man becomes established in the city he tends to bring the women of the family from the village to live

[25] Walter Elkan, *Migrants and Proletarians* (London: Oxford University Press, 1960), pp. 135ff.

[26] See, e.g., Edwin Eames and William Schwab, "Urban Migration in India and Africa," *Human Organization*, 23 (Spring, 1964), pp. 24-27.

[27] See e.g., Kingsley Davis, *The Population of India and Pakistan* (Princeton: Princeton University Press, 1951), pp. 140-141.

[28] Hauser, *op. cit.*, pp. 100ff.

with him. In addition, economic opportunities for women are more numerous in industrializing cities.

Education is another variable in rural out-migration. The more highly educated apparently leave in relatively greater numbers than do the more poorly educated.[29] On the surface, this seems to conflict with the argument that rural poverty drives people to the city, but both generalizations may be valid. Even the more highly educated villagers are relatively worse off than the majority of urbanites. At the same time, they are most sensitive to the limited opportunities in the village (including the absence of advanced educational facilities) and are best equipped to succeed in the urban environment. The very poor and illiterate ruralites not only lack the resources to escape from their misery but, if they do migrate to the city, they are the least likely to survive. The economic and social problems of rural communities are, of course, exaggerated by these patterns of out-migration.

Reasons for Rural-Urban Migration

Students of rural-to-urban migration continually write about "push" and "pull" factors. Yet it is exceedingly difficult to separate the forces that drive people out of the rural setting from those that draw them to the city. For one thing, villagers may well modify their reasons for moving, *after* the fact. Eames writes:

> The most frequent causes of initial migration are: to pay debts, to build a new house, to buy bullocks and pay for marriage. . . . However, once established in the city, other needs are discovered, and very often these needs replace the primary ones which caused the migration to the city. . . . Thus it can be seen that in twenty-five responses individuals went to the city to obtain money for building a new house, or for building a new house in conjunction with some other reason or reasons. However, when asked about the uses to which the money earned was presently being put, only four responses showed that it was being used to build a new house.[30]

Social scientists, in discussing underdeveloped countries, tend to stress the push factor, especially the economic one. Consider the conclusions of a report issued in 1960 by the International Labour Office.

> The main push factor causing workers to leave agriculture is the lower level of incomes. In almost all countries incomes in agriculture are lower than in other sectors of the economy. Wages in agriculture are also, as a rule, below the average level. The difference in wages between agriculture and other occupations is the most significant aspect of the general income contrast, since

[29] See, e.g., Bogue and Zachariah, *op. cit.*, pp. 51ff.

[30] E. Eames, "Some Aspects in Urban Migration from a Village in North Central India" *Eastern Anthropologist*, 8 (September-November, 1954), pp. 21-22.

it influences hired workers and members of farm families in their decision to find other employment.[31]

Various factors operate to reduce the level of agricultural income in underdeveloped countries and thus heighten out-migration.

In the advanced countries labour leaves the land because agriculture is growing in efficiency. Income per head in agriculture tends to fall in relation to incomes in other occupations because food production increases more rapidly than the demand for food. In the less developed countries, however, incomes from agriculture tend to fall relative to other incomes because (a) population on the land increases more rapidly than food output; (b) new investment is concentrated in industrial production and urban development generally; and (c) the prices of primary products in world markets are falling. These income-depressing factors may operate singly or together.[32]

Still other variables, besides the economic one, affect this country-to-city movement. The emphasis given them varies considerably among research reports, in part because of the difficulties in separating push and pull factors, and in part because of differences in the manner in which migrants are questioned. Certainly one cannot ignore the greater prestige and freedom that urban life offers. Once having experienced the wider range of social services available in the city—including easier access to mass communication media—migrants find it difficult to reconcile themselves to a village existence.

Another factor—often neglected in studies of rural-to-urban movement—is social power.[33] Many sociologists assume, unrealistically, that this migration takes place in a laissez-faire political and economic structure. In my discussion (below) of the Soviet model, I shall try to clarify the impact of broader societal forces on the movement from the land.

We must also recognize that rural-to-urban migration is sustained by a complex network of social interaction. Migrants to the cities tend to cluster in neighborhoods or communities with others from their own region of origin or with fellow members of their particular ethnic or minority group. This urban sub-system reinforces its members' ties with the rural world. Periodic visits to the village, especially on national or religious holidays, are common, and create occasions for recruiting urban in-migrants. Siguan observes that in Spain returned urbanites frequently dazzle friends and relatives in the village with descriptions of their

[31] International Labour Office, *Why Labour Leaves the Land* (Geneva: International Labour Office, 1960), p. 208.

[32] *Ibid.*, pp. 209-210.

[33] Some sociologists have discussed this to some extent: e.g., Wilbert E. Moore, *Industrialization and Labor* (Ithaca: Cornell University Press, 1951), pp. 59ff.

life in the urban milieu.[34] Misra,[35] in his study of Jamshedpur, India, indicates that approximately 75 per cent of the migrants came to this community because they had relatives or friends there. After all, in many underdeveloped countries one usually secures employment through a chain of personal contacts.[36]

Regrettably, we know little about the role of formal organizational structures in recruiting ruralites for the urban labor force and socializing them in the norms of city life. Certainly formal educational and military structures channel ruralites into the city. In Communist countries the Party is (and will continue to be) as a significant organizational link between the rural and the urban sectors.

RURAL-URBAN BALANCE AND THE SOCIO-POLITICAL CONTEXT

The preceding discussion provides a basis for analyzing rural-urban relationships in developing societies. Although we can learn much from a detailed survey of the literature on rural-to-urban migration, most of the reach in this area has been cast in too narrow a framework, one that ignores the broader socio-political setting.

To be sure, certain rural-urban patterns—e.g., the age, sex, and educational differentials between migrants and non-migrants—can be studied without adopting a societal perspective. But if we are to grasp the social implications of these differentials or of the four types of change in rural-urban ratio, or if we are to explain massive movements from rural to urban areas, a societal frame of reference is mandatory.

The rural-to-urban movement, and the relative importance of the rural and urban sectors in developing societies, are increasingly being determined by political decision-makers. More specifically, the "balance" between the rural and urban sectors during the period of modernization is a function of three variables—the ideological, the economic, and the

---

[34] M. Siguan, *Del Campo al Suburbio* (Madrid: Consejo Superior de Investigaciones Científicas, 1959), p. 207.

[35] Misra, *op. cit.*, p. 78. Cf. D. N. Majumdar, *Social Counters of an Industrial City* (Bombay: Asia Publishing House, 1960), p. 75. Here the role of relatives and friends seems to have been less important. For a discussion of the rather ambiguous role of friends and relatives in the migration process in another cultural setting, see Hutchinson, *op. cit.*, pp. 60ff.

[36] E.g., Richard D. Lambert, *Workers, Factories, and Social Change in India* (Princeton: Princeton University Press, 1963), p. 77.

GIDEON SJOBERG

political—which, as I seek to demonstrate, are not always in harmony.[37] Ideologies (specifically, pro-urban and anti-urban values) can and do conflict with economic and political (or social power) considerations (internal or external). In any society contradictory pressures of this sort must somehow be balanced.

Most modernizing societies are committed to some kind of social planning. Inherent in any such plan are judgments concerning the proper, or optimum, rural-urban balance and, ultimately, the type of change in the rural-urban ratio that best serves the needs of the society. Thus, developing societies make a host of assumptions as to which sector is to receive the major share of attention. The resulting economic and social policies strongly influence status relations between ruralites and urbanites, and these in turn affect the movement of people from country to city.

Models of Economic Development and Rural-Urban Balance

Several different models of economic development are currently competing for favor on the world scene. The following rather simple typology (relating political structure to the society's ideology concerning rural-urban relations) will serve as the basis for discussion.

MODELS OF ECONOMIC DEVELOPMENT

		POLITICAL STRUCTURE	
		"Totalitarian"	"Democratic"
IDEOLOGY	Anti-Urban Pro-Rural	Type I	Type IV
	Pro-Urban Anti-Rural	Type II	Type III

Although "industrialization" and "urbanization" are not synonymous, large-scale urbanization is both a precondition for and a result of large-scale industrialization. For this reason I shall employ the term "industrial-urbanization" as the occasion demands.

[37] Even though one can distinguish among these dimensions analytically, they overlap in many complex ways on the empirical level. Moreover, other dimensions are also important.

The term "ideology" requires explanation. The economic and political dimensions have an ideological component; however, "ideology" herein refers primarily to the values and beliefs associated with rural and urban residence.

We begin with the *Type I* totalitarian model. A number of nations in recent decades have taken rather strong stands against any major expansion of the industrial and urban sectors. Portugal, and to a degree Spain, seem to be in this category (although we have no detailed study of the effect of ideology on industrial-urbanization in these countries). Paraguay also appears to fit this type: the totalitarian power structure, supported by an anti-industrial-urban ideology, has sought to maintain the traditional preindustrial order.

Nazi Germany approached this type in several respects and is an instructive case study. Frieda Wunderlich has summarized the attitudes of the National Socialist leaders toward the rural and urban sectors:

> National Socialism had come into power with a well-defined romantic agrarian program. De-urbanization and repopulation of rural districts were to restore physical and mental health for the degenerated nation and provide a sound breeding place for the future generation. Rootedness in the soil, stabilization instead of mobility, security of land tenure, would result in a new aristocracy of blood and soil, the rise of a peasant class of highest prestige.[38]

These anti-urban values and ideals could not be sustained, however, for they ran counter to the political requirements—above all the demands for an effective war machine, which required an expanded industrial base, with emphasis upon heavy industry. This fostered urban groth (rather than decline.).

In the Union of South Africa today the situation is somewhat analogous. The ideology of apartheid calls for the concentration of natives in special areas, where they are to engage in agricultural pursuits and eventually build up a very limited industrial system.[39] Yet, if the Europeans are to sustain their social power within the country and the political power of the Union vis-à-vis the rest of the continent, they must maintain and even expand the industrial-urban base. And this requires a large native population living in cities.

But what about the kind of totalitarian model that has encouraged economic development in recent decades—that formulated by the Communists? This model (*Type II*) has been, and is being, applied within the Communist sphere, and it is an alternative approach to development for nations in the "third world" as well.

The model, as it has evolved, is a complex one, less unified and

---

[38] Frieda Wunderlich, *Farm Labor in Germany, 1810-1945* (Princeton, Princeton University Press, 1961), p. 351.

[39] See, e.g., Sheila T. van der Horst, "A Plan for the Union's Backward Areas: Some Economic Aspects of the Tomlinson Commission's Report," *South African Journal of Economics*, 24 (June, 1956), pp. 89-112.

self-consistent than some would suppose. Not only does policy zigzag over time within a given society—as in the Soviet Union—but the patterns pursued by the Chinese Communists on the one hand and the Yugoslavs on the other indicate significant differences among Communist nations.

At the same time, the totalitarian Communist approach to economic development displays certain characteristic features.[40] One of these is negation of the peasant way of life. The title of Mitrany's work, *Marx Against the Peasant*,[41] expresses it well. Although Mitrany dealt primarily with Europe, much of his discussion can be applied more broadly. But at this point, for clarity's sake, a digression is in order.

As is well known, the Communists have prospered in certain heavily agrarian, largely preindustrial, settings, contrary to Marx's predictions. Mao Tse-Tung flouted the traditional Communist doctrine and the admonitions of Stalin when he used the peasantry as a means to a revolutionary end: destruction of the older order.[42] Earlier efforts to establish the revolution in China with cities as the bases of operation had come to naught, so the Communist leaders turned their attention to the peasantry. By exploiting the peasants' traditionally anti-urban orientation (an antagonism that stems in part from the traditional identification of urban residence with the large landlords and the broader ruling class), they rallied the peasants and the inhabitants of the smaller towns and villages to the cause. A similar performance is now center stage in South Viet Nam: the Viet Cong are attempting to turn to their advantage the peasants' fear of, and antagonism toward, the urban ruling element.[43] In Latin America, too, particularly in Cuba, some of these patterns have been in evidence.

Yet, even where the Communists have employed the peasants as a means of acquiring power, once in control they have shifted their atten-

[40] See, e.g., Barrington Moore, Jr., *Terror and Progress: USSR* (Cambridge: Harvard University Press, 1954); Naum Jasny, *Essays on the Soviet Economy* (New York: Frederick A. Praeger, 1962); A. Nove, "The Soviet Model and Under-Developed Countries," *International Affairs*, 37 (January, 1961), pp. 29-38; N. Spulber, "Contrasting Economic Patterns: Chinese and Soviet Development Strategies," *Soviet Studies*, 15 (July, 1963), pp. 1-17.

[41] David Mitrany, *Marx Against the Peasant* (London: George Weidenfeld and Nicholson Ltd., 1951). Cf. Adam B. Ulam, *The Unfinished Revolution* (New York: Random House, 1960), Ch. 5.

[42] See Donald Gillin, "Peasant and Communist in Modern China: Reflections on the Origins of the Communist-led Peasant Movement," *South Atlantic Quarterly*, 60 (Fall, 1961), pp. 434-446.

[43] The significance of the rural-urban hiatus and its relation to the present revolutionary ferment was stressed in a rather informative letter to the editor by Alfred Hussey, "Buddhists in Vietnam," *New York Times* (September 22, 1963), p. 10E.

tion and come to emphasize the construction of an industrial-urban order. Heavy industry and scientific advances within urban centers are the ideals, as leaders strive to maintain power internally and on the world scene. The priority attached to industrial-urbanization is in keeping with the Marxian glamorization of the proletariat. So great is the glorification of the industrial-urban sector that the Soviets, in particular, have for some time talked in terms of destroying all distinctions between rural and urban areas. Such an ideological stance was reflected in Khrushchev's proposals (in the early 1950's) calling for the establishment of agrogorods, or city farms, and in the Program of the Communist Party of the Soviet Union set forth in 1961.[44]

The pro-urban, anti-rural ideology of the Communists has been reflected in various programs of action. They have stressed investment in urban centers, especially in heavy industry; capital investment in the rural, or more specifically agricultural, sector has been sharply limited. Moreover, they have sought, through the collectivizing agricultural enterprise, to restructure and reorganize the social and economic fabric of rural life. The drive to collectivize agriculture has served a number of functions relative to the overall industrial-urban effort.

Collectivization has given the state more direct control of the agricultural sector. Farmers scattered about the countryside or living in small villages can more readily evade the rulings of the state apparatus than those who are herded into collective farms and kept under close surveillance. Now the peasant can more easily be told what to plant and when, when to harvest, and how much of the produce to turn over to the state. That is, collective farming makes it easier, from an organizational standpoint, for the state to channel the farmer's labor along certain lines and to appropriate the "surplus" foodstuffs for consumption in the city. This may produce, as it did in Russia in the 1930's, a decline in the rural standard of living. But it is, in effect, one means of utilizing the labor and products of the rural population to pay part of the cost of industrial-urbanization. Lower-class urbanites also assume a heavy share of the social and economic costs, but the urban managerial group, as well as some politicians and intellectuals, tend to gain special advantages even during the early period of industrialization.

Collectivization not only permits tighter control of the economic surplus but, particularly in the USSR, it has been a prime means for industrializing the agricultural sector—of extending the industrial order into the countryside. In theory at least, collectivization signifies a factory-like organization of the rural labor force. In turn this mechanization and

[44] *The Communist Blueprint for the Future* (New York: E. P. Dutton & Co., 1962), pp. 170-179.

industrialization frees labor for, or even forces labor into, urban employment. This process has been more significant in the Soviet Union than
in China, for the former has traditionally suffered from a shortage of
urban labor.

The collectivization of agriculture has also been a major vehicle for
attacking the traditional social structure—one of the main goals of the
Communist revolution. In preindustrial civilized orders, the elite (composed of leaders in the educational, religious, and political spheres),
though typically resident in cities, have controlled landed property
either directly as landlords, or indirectly through their positions in the
key political or religious organizations of the society. Land, after all,
has been one of the few stable forms of wealth in traditional preindustrial societies, which were subject to all manner of social and natural
catastrophes. Collectivization thus destroys one traditional base of the
elites. So too, it tends to undermine the traditional family, or the com-
munity-centered structure of village life, and to orient rural people
toward urban centers.

Quite in contrast to the totalitarian model stands the "democratic"
one. We shall be concerned not with *Type III*—the pro-urban, anti-rural
democratic model of development (which has few, if any, effective
champions on the world scene)—but with *Type IV*—the anti-urban,
pro-rural democratic model. This latter type is difficult to analyze. First,
its specific assumptions are, almost by definition, vaguer than those
underlying the totalitarian model. The very conception of "democratic
planning" permits more variation within a particular society over time
and among societies as well.

Second, the main sponsors of this democratic approach are the advanced industrial-urban societies of the West who are applying the model
not to their own development but to underdeveloped countries under
their "sphere of influence." [45] The assumptions of this model are most
clearly stated in the proposals and activities of the U.S. government
and the various semi-official agencies under its domination. These prem-
ises have also been ardently supported by most American intellectuals.
At the same time, the anti-urban, pro-rural model seems to be consistent
not only with the dominant orientation of the countries within the

[45] A strongly anti-urban (even anti-industrial) tradition has persisted in the
U.S. and in Europe for over a century. For a discussion of this tradition among
American intellectuals, see: Morton White and Lucia White, *The Intellectual Versus
the City* (Cambridge: Harvard University Press and The M.I.T. Press, 1962). But
these anti-urban values and ideas appear to have been exaggerated in the ideology
and policies that are now advocated for underdeveloped countries.

Still other contradictions exist: for instance, European countries during the
early period of industrial-urbanization were less democratic than they now expect
developing societies to be.

Western Alliance but with that of the United Nations as well, and the ideology and policies of a number of key nations in the "third world"— e.g., India—approximate its assumptions.

A strategic feature of this democratic model is its *relatively* greater emphasis on the rural, especially the agricultural, sector and its relative de-emphasis of heavy industry and of industrialized cities in general. Although advanced industrial-urbanization may be considered a goal for some distant tomorrow, it is not an end to be stressed in the immediate present. Keep in mind that this model carries both anti-urban and anti-industrial overtones.

There are at least two major justifications for emphasizing the rural sector during the early stages of economic development. The first is the humanitarian one: the hope is to reduce the social and economic burdens that individuals must bear. It is frequently assumed that greater investment in the rural sector in the short run will not only sustain the existing standard of living for the whole society but perhaps enhance it. Note, for instance, the report of the mission of the International Bank of Reconstruction and Development with respect to Jordan:

> In years of good harvests, agriculture accounts for approximately one-half of total production in the private sector. Rural productivity is low and unless it can be raised there is no hope of improving the lot of a sizable section of the population. The mission therefore gives first priority to agricultural development.[46]

A second justification for the priority given the rural sector runs something like this:

> Industrialization is not necessarily equivalent to development in any setting and at any given time. Industry may, to be sure, yield a greater output per capita than, say, agriculture, but the same amount of capital invested in agriculture may yield a far greater total return to the economy.[47]

The Alliance for Progress has been rationalized on these grounds: So far, at least, attention has been focused upon land reform and other policies intended to build up the rural economy. Surprisingly few formal programs have been devised for promoting industrial-urbanization or coping with its consequences.[48] To be sure, the role of education in economic

---

[46] International Bank of Reconstruction and Development, *The Economic Development of Jordan* (Baltimore: The Johns Hopkins Press, 1957), p. 12.

[47] Louis J. Walinsky, *Economic Development in Burma, 1951-1960* (New York: Twentieth Century Fund, 1962), p. 496. Cf. Robert Dorfman, "An Economic Strategy for West Pakistan," *Asian Survey,* 3 (May, 1963), pp. 217-223.

[48] On this point see C. M. Haar, "Latin America's Troubled Cities," *Foreign Affairs,* 41 (April, 1963), pp. 536-549.

development has been played up; still, no compelling stress has been placed on science and scientific technology.

One of the main programs for rural development has been land reform. With reform of the tax structure, land reform offers the greatest challenge to the traditional preindustrial order, wherein economic and political power resides chiefly in the ownership or control of large landed estates.

With respect to the urban sector, the democratic model assumes that light industry is a more effective means of absorbing the underemployed or unemployed than is the construction of heavy-industry complexes. The experience of Japan, with its rapid development and economic growth, is often invoked to support this point of view. It is also widely assumed that the rise of cities, especially large industrialized cities, threatens the stability of underdeveloped countries.[49] Intellectuals and many policy-makers in the West (as well as in a number of under-developed countries) have, consciously or not, adopted the Wirth frame of reference which assumes that the growth of urban agglomerations leads to secularization and disruption of the normative order. The vast proliferation of slums in industrializing cities—from the *favelas* of Brazil to the *bidonvilles* of North Africa—reinforces the belief that mass migration from the countryside, as well as, for instance, the unbalanced sex ratio (see above), leads to many undesirable social conditions and that, in fact, people are worse off, in terms of economic and personal well-being, in the city than in the countryside.

Then too, large urban agglomerations are often viewed as fundamentally uneconomic in that the society is forced to invest considerably more in social services, including housing and sanitary facilities, than is necessary in medium-sized cities. The megalopolis absorbs the scarce capital that could more rationally be employed in developing industry or raising the standard of living of the entire populace. A preference for medium-sized cities articulates well with programs emphasizing light over heavy industry and with those that divert rural out-migrants from the larger urban centers.

Again, though Western industrial-urban orders, particularly the U.S., have strongly supported the democratic model, numerous other countries outside the Communist bloc have, as part of their official policy, en-

[49] Western intellectuals, social scientists, and policy-makers are committed to a rather well-defined anti-urban position. See e.g. William Petersen, "On the Concept of Urbanization Planning," *Population Review*, 6 (July, 1962), pp. 100-108. Intellectuals and policy-makers in underdeveloped countries such as India hold a similar view. Consult various issues of the *Economic Weekly*, for example.

dorsed the ideology and policies inherent in this model.[50] Of course, many of these societies are "democratic" in name only, but India, a developing country genuinely committed to a democratic political structure, adheres to this anti-urban, pro-rural model of economic development. In its first five-year plan, priority was given expanding agricultural productivity. Emphasis on the urban sector and heavy industry was to be postponed until a later date.

Evaluation of the Contrasting Models

We can now address ourselves to the question that initiated this discussion: Is there some optimum balance between a society's rural and urban sectors during the course of economic development?[51] To answer this question, I shall advance several arguments. Both the totalitarian (or Communist) and the democratic (or Western) models are fraught with internal inconsistencies stemming from the fundamentally contradictory demands they must meet. For one thing, an objective conflict of interests between city and countryside appears to emerge during the early stages of economic development.[52] Consequently, both the Communist and the Western models, what is considered optimum balance depends on whether the criterion is ideological, political, or economic.

First, the ideology of the Communist model stresses an industrialurban tomorrow; to argue otherwise is to deny that ideas or beliefs have consequences. This accent on industrial-urbanization as a kind of utopia focuses attention on the need for economic growth and justifies sacrifices demanded at the present moment. It supplies the incentive for large-scale investment in heavy industry and for shaping an educational system committed to modern science and technology. Furthermore, an avowed purpose of the Communist revolution has been to destroy the agrarian base of the traditional order and, with it, the

[50] See, e.g., Vu Van Thai, "Vietnam's Concept of Development," in Wesley R. Fishel (ed.), *Problems of Freedom: South Vietnam Since Independence* (New York: Free Press of Glencoe, 1961), pp. 69-74; International Labour Office, *Employment Objectives in Economic Development* (Geneva: International Labour Office, 1961), Appendices.

[51] The problems of an optimum rural-urban balance and of optimum city size have been discussed by Walter Firey, "The Optimum Rural-Urban Population Balance," *Rural Sociology*, 12 (June, 1947), pp. 116-127, and Otis Dudley Duncan, "Optimum Size of Cities," in Paul K. Hatt and Albert J. Reiss, Jr. (eds.), *Cities and Society: The Revised Reader in Urban Sociology* (New York: Free Press of Glencoe, 1957), pp. 759-772. These studies focus on modern American society, however.

[52] Nathan Keyfitz, "The Political Economy of Urbanization in Developing Countries: The Southeast Asia Case," in Philip Hauser and Leo Schnore (eds.), *The Study of Urbanization* (New York: John Wiley & Sons, 1965).

traditional power structure and family-centered village organization. The widespread terror and bloodshed that characterized the Stalinist regime may be minimizing present-day opposition to the industrial-urban emphasis in Soviet planning.

These efforts to undermine the traditional status system and social organization are perhaps easier to understand in the context of social change in developing nations. On the one hand, as industrial-urbanization proceeds, members of the upper socio-economic groups, typically urban-based, are usually the first to adopt the ideas, values, and techniques of advanced industrial orders. On the other hand, the researches of Friedl,[53] among others, suggest that the lower socioeconomic groups, notably in rural areas, not only lag behind others in emulating the industrial model but first adopt the ideals of the traditional preindustrial order. Their somewhat increased standard of living (though lower than that in the cities) permits them to uphold some of the ideal norms that were previously sustained only by the elite, so that they can now maintain larger families (even within single households); for one thing, modernization results in a decline in mortality. Also, many ruralites command more adequate means for performing certain traditional rites; and with greater access to formal education their understanding of the ideal norms of the traditional order is enhanced. The available evidence indicates that this pattern was typical of the early period of industrial-urbanization in Europe, too.

The counterforces to industrial-urbanization that sustain "conserva-tive" or traditional patterns are themselves reinforced by the fact that all systems undergoing change, even revolutionary ones, must employ the past (or some idealized version of it) as the basis for shaping a utopian future. Even in the Soviet Union the leaders have sought to glorify certain traditions as a means of ensuring support for future ventures.

Yet the Communist model, as I indicated, embodies some striking contradictions. The ideological and political compulsion to industrialize and urbanize has on a number of occasions led to serious misallocation of resources available. Then too, the Communists, especially in China, though intent on demolishing traditional social organization, have yet to face up to the runaway population growth that threatens to cancel any economic advance. A society committed to industrial-urbanization, rather than to a rural way of life, however, does possess potentially more effective means for resisting the population explosion.

---

[53] Ernestine Friedl, "Lagging Emulation in Post-Peasant Society: A Greek Case," *American Anthropologist*, 66 (June, 1964), pp. 569-586.

Galbraith and Nove,[54] among other writers, perceive as the major weakness of the Comunist model its inability to deal effectively with agriculture. Its very strength, emphasis on industrial-urbanization, has actually compounded the problems of agricultural production. To this day, advances in the rural sector continue to lag far behind those in the cities of the Soviet Union. China and North Vietnam have also experienced grave difficulties as a result of economic and social failures in the rural sector.[55] After the disaster that befell China as a result of the "Great Leap Forward," the priority of investment and attention given the rural areas was increased relative to the industrial-urban areas.

Why should the rural sector pose such a barrier to economic growth in these societies? Apparently, generally harsh treatment of the peasants, combined with limited capital investment in agriculture, has stifled any real incentive to produce. In addition, the discrepancy in socioeconomic status between rural and urban communities—evidently greater in Communist systems than in other developing societies—has done much to inhibit economic advances in agriculture. Anti-rural policies have, so it seems, exaggerated the otherwise "normal" movement of the more skilled and educated persons to the cities. Consequently, agriculture has been left in the hands of the less able and least motivated—with further depressing effects on productivity. All this has been intensified by efforts to obliterate the traditional social order in the rural areas.

Poland since Gomulka's rise to power is a significant "control" case to support this reasoning. Of all the East European countries, Poland seems to have been the most successful in increasing its agricultural productivity. This has occurred as the peasants' ideological, economic, and political conditions have improved. Certainly, the peasants now have more "freedom" than formerly—so much so that de-collectivization has been permitted.[56]

Another aspect of rural-urban balance has been brought to the fore by the Chinese Communist experiment. Here "blind infiltration" of rural

[54] John Kenneth Galbraith, "The Poverty of Nations," *Atlantic Monthly*, 210 (October, 1962), pp. 47-53; Alex Nove, *The Soviet Economy* (New York: Frederick A. Praeger, 1961).

[55] Philip P. Jones and Thomas T. Poleman, "Communes and the Agricultural Crisis in Communist China," *Food Research Institute Studies*, 3 (February, 1962), pp. 3-22; Choh-Ming Li, "China's Industrial Development, 1958-63" *China Quarterly*, 17 (January-March, 1964), pp. 3-38. A number of other articles in this issue of the *China Quarterly*—e.g., that by Franz Schurmann—deal directly with this topic. For the difficulties experienced by North Vietnam see R. J. Honey, "Food Crisis in North Vietnam," *Far Eastern Economic Review*, 41 (August 15, 1963), pp. 493-495.

[56] R. H. S. Crossman, "The Polish Miracle," *Commentary*, 35 (March, 1963), pp. 210-219.

peoples into the cities became so rampant that in the later 1950's political controls were instituted to stem the tide.[57] For even a society whose ideology stresses industrialization and urbanization may be unable to support, economically and politically, a very rapidly burgeoning urban population.

The zigzag course of economic planning in the Soviet Union and now in China—with respect to the relative priority given the rural and urban sectors—may well reflect certain contradictory requirements.[58] The pro-urban ideology, along with power considerations—especially on the international level—may dictate policies for a time, but when these run counter to such vital economic conditions as an insufficient food supply, chaos will result unless some retrenchment occurs, with a temporary shelving of the major goals. "Two steps forward and one step back" may well describe the actual situation.

With the Communist model as a backdrop, we can now evaluate the Western model, which emphasizes the rural sector at least during the early stages of economic development.

The ideals of "freedom," "democracy," and "humanitarianism" loom large for those who favor the Western model. But these ideals are exceedingly difficult to attain in a peasant-dominated society, and the political leaders in many underdeveloped countries do little more than give them lip-service. Nor do these ideals elicit sacrifices from the populace —sacrifices that may be necessary if the society is to build a better tomorrow. In fact, these ideals of freedom and humanitarianism may exaggerate the "revolution of expectations" in economic and other spheres. As a result the society may be forced to concentrate upon immediate, rather than long-range, goals of economic development.

The stress on the rural sector also conflicts with the realities of a rapidly expanding population—a problem which is exasercbated by maintaining a high proportion of the population in rural communities. In addition, intellectuals and politicians in these societies are more and more apt to challenge the priority given to the rural sector,[59] if only because industrial-urbanization is essential if the society is to attain political power and "respectability" on the world scene.

Several facets of the Western model require careful empirical scrutiny.

[57] Leo A. Orleans, "Population Redistribution in Communist China," in *Population Trends in Eastern Europe, the USSR and Mainland China* (New York: Milbank Memorial Fund, 1960), pp. 144ff.

[58] For an elaboration of this idea see Gideon Sjoberg, "Contradictory Functional Requirements and Social Systems," *Conflict Resolution*, 4 (June, 1960), pp. 198-208.

[59] Fleeting references to this issue appear in John J. Johnson, "The Political Role of the Latin-American Middle Sectors," *The Annals*, 334 (March, 1961), p. 23, and Frank Golay, *The Philippines: Public Policy and National Economic Development* (Ithaca: Cornell University Press 1961), p. 241.

One is the belief that ruralites are better off economically if they remain in the village than if they crowd into the teeming city slums. The general invisibility of even the more extreme rural povetry, combined with a romantic image of the rural past, has led many policy-makers, and not a few social scientists, to view the city dweller's setting as a more unfavorable one than the villager's. But the available data indicate otherwise: urbanites have a higher standard of living than do ruralites.[60] Even the urban poor seem to be better off than the villagers, especially those in the more isolated areas. We must not overlook the services available in the city: medical help (completely lacking in the isolated rural community),[61] schools, running water—these are only some of the potential gains that accrue from residence in the city. To be sure, one tap may have to serve an entire city block, but even that is a luxury compared to the situation in some rural areas where one may have to trudge miles every day to obtain water for the family's needs. As one economist, a specialist on Latin America, has put it: "for millions . . . already living in urban slums, . . . petty commerce and an occasional day's work represent better economic alternatives than can be found in the rural sector." [62]

Even the matter of increased personal and social disorganization in the city bears extensive re-thinking. If certain family structures, traditional religious patterns, and so on on must be re-arranged to fit the needs of industrial-urbanization (an assumption most sociologists make) some degree of social and personal disorganization may be helpful, even essential, to rapid industrialization and urbanization. For instance, how can population growth be slowed unless fundamental changes occur in the traditional patriarchal family organization? [63] The evidence indicates that such changes may be well-nigh impossible to achieve without extensive industral-urbanization.

We must also recognize that urban agglomerations make possible a more rational deployment of certain vital but scarce facilities and personnel (especially those in education) than does a population scattered

[60] Ansley J. Coale and Edgar M. Hoover, *Population Growth and Economic Development in Low-Income Countries* (Princeton: Princeton University Press, 1958), pp. 131 ff.; D. Maulit, "Income Ratio Between Rural and Urban Workers in the Philippines," *Economic Research Journal*, 6 (September, 1959), pp. 83-95.

[61] Gwendolyn Z. Johnson, "Health Conditions in Rural and Urban Areas of Developing Countries," *Population Studies*, 17 (March, 1964), pp. 293-309.

[62] Calvin P. Blair, "Introduction to Forum on Latin American Resource Problems," *Business Review*, University of Houston (Spring, 1962), p. 1.

[63] Felicia J. Deyrup, "Family Dominance as a Factor in Population Growth of Developing Countries," *Social Research*, 29 (Summer, 1962), pp. 177-189; Leo Schnore, "Social Problems in the Underdeveloped Areas: An Ecological View," *Social Problems*, 8 (Winter, 1960-61). pp. 186-189.

about in villages and small towns. More specifically, we must test some of the propositions that assume the superiority of medium-sized cities over large ones.[64] We need much more data to verify the contention of some that large cities represent an irrational allocation of resources in terms of economic development. But we must be prepared to maintain a broader perspective in our analysis than is usually the case. My own hypothesis is that very large urban concentrations (in contrast to medium-sized ones) permit groupings of scarce specialists (teachers, scientists, managers, and so on) in sufficient numbers to engage in effective pursuit of particular types of organizational, notably scientific, activities. The function of cities in heightening interpersonal communication[65]—as a necessary condition for sustaining various kinds of social activity—is usually ignored by those who perceive the large metropolis as a hindrance to economic development.

Of course, that the association between urbanization and industrialization is not perfect—some nations are not as highly urbanized as they are industrialized (and vice versa).[66] Nevertheless, in nations at the extremes of the industrialization scale, industrialization and urbanization are closely associated indeed; discrepancies are most marked in the "middle range." One reason is that some nations can sustain a high level of urbanization at a disproportionately low level of industrialization, because they have economic ties with the major industrial-urban complexes.

Overall, a major weakness of the Western model is its attempt to achieve economic growth by concentrating first on rural development and then on industrial-urban expansion. Land and tax reforms and stress on education are not sufficient to topple the walls of tradition or to hurdle the barriers to "progress" created by a rapidly expanding population. An ideology favoring the rural sector not only does little to demolish the traditional power structure but runs counter to the establishment of a viable democratic political system which, after all, has been alien to agrarian-dominated societies.

The anti-urban values, in themselves, may well slow the process of industrialization. Although large metropolitan centers may not be a

[64] For a defense of the medium-sized city, see John P. Lewis, *Quiet Crisis in India* (Washington, D.C.: The Brookings Institution, 1962).

[65] Edgar M. Hoover and Raymond Vernon, *Anatomy of a Metropolis* (Cambridge: Harvard University Press, 1959).

[66] See, e.g., T. O. Wilkinson, "Urban Structure and Industrialization," *American Sociological Review*, 25 (June, 1960), pp. 356-363. Nonetheless, the association with industrialization as well as the relation of urbanization to other indices of economic development, have been noted by Simon Kuznets, "Quantitative Aspects of the Economic Growth of Nations: VII. The Share and Structure of Consumption," *Economic Development and Cultural Change*, 10 (January, 1962), pt. 2, pp. 36ff.

sufficient condition for advanced industrialization, they are, in general, a necessary one, for modernization of the rural sector requires a certain level of industrial-urban organization, with concomitant skills and knowledge.

CONCLUSIONS

First I discussed certain rural-to-urban migration patterns in developing societies; then I attempted, in a more speculative vein, to lay bare the relations between various models of economic development and the matter of rural-urban balance.

My primary concern has been with the totalitarian (or Communist) and democratic (or Western) models of development, the former stressing the industrial-urban, the latter the rural sector, during the early stages of economic development. Both models are beset by internal contradictions. The ideological criteria for determining the optimum balance between rural and urban areas do not necessarily produce the optimum balance defined by political or economic criteria, and vice versa. These functional contradictions are most evident during the initial period of a nation's economic development.

At this point the relations between the two models of economic development and rural-to-urban migration can be made more explicit, for both the model and the prevailing definition of the proper balance between the rural and urban sectors affect the flow of people from rural to urban centers—in qualitative as well as quantitative terms.

The social characteristics of rural out-migrants may in part reflect the ideology and the political and economic policies of the state. Available data permit only speculation, but some of the difficulties inherent in the Communist model (in contrast to the Western one) appear to stem from the relatively greater movement of educated (or able) persons from countryside to city as well as an increased status discrepancy between rural and urban communities. The anti-peasant value system thus inhibits rural development.

More significant still, changes in the number and proportion of people in rural and urban areas are closely related to the society's orientation toward economic development. Underdeveloped countries committed to the democratic (or Western) model have done little to encourage rural residents to move to cities. Nor have they exerted any major effort to expand the industrial-urban sector so as to absorb the growing number of people in rural communities. Such countries as India and Ceylon (where the rural population exceeds the urban) are likely to experience increased difficulties in bringing about sustained economic growth—as the flames of the population explosion are fanned by the very rapid increase of persons living in small towns and villages. It is a paradox that Communist societies, which deny the existence of a population problem, adopt policies that may prove to be more effective in overcoming the handicaps posed by a runaway population than those adopted by nations oriented toward the Western model.[67] At the same time, in Communist societies economic and political factors limit the extent and rapidity of rural out-migration.

Ultimately, we cannot explain the vast movement of rural peoples to urban areas merely by studying the motives of individual migrants. We must analyze the structural changes in the society—changes that are products of broad ideological and economic policy considerations. In this context, we must examine the impact of political (the Party in Communist societies), military, and educational organizations on rural-to-urban migration and the ultimate assimilation of the migrants into the mainstream of the society.

I shall end on a rather personal note. Committed as I am to a democratic, industrial ideal, I find one of the implicit conclusions of this essay disturbing. This is the conclusion that totalitarianism is functionally related to *rapid* economic development. One major difficulty in interpreting the literature on underdeveloped nations arises from the ideological commitments of social scientists; scientists in industrial-urban countries frequently reflect the ideals of the system that nurtures them.[68]

At the very least, open debate concerning the assumptions that influence one's research findings is in order. A researcher's ideals and beliefs may blind him to the reality of change in underdeveloped countries, which increases the possibility of a widening rift between social scientists reared in modernizing societies and those reared in advanced industrial systems.[69]

[67] Such an inference might be drawn from the statements of Zelinsky, *op. cit.*, p. 117.

[68] An interesting question is whether Soviet social scientists will, in time, come to share the ideology of their counterparts in industrial-urban Western societies, in opposition to that of social scientists in underdeveloped countries? That is, will the main rift be between the "haves" and the "have-nots"—irrespective of current ideology?

[69] To some extent the debate concerning the industrialization and urbanization of underdeveloped countries is analogous to the disagreements among scholars regarding actual conditions during the Industrial Revolution in Europe. See, e.g., E. J. Hobsbawm and R. M. Hartwell, "The Standard of Living During the Industrial Revolution: A Discussion," *Economic History Review*, 16 (August, 1963), pp. 120-148.

Surely, the pressures for social change on the world scene are bound to intensify. The population explosion, the sharp rise in social expectations, and the emergence of fervent nationalism—these and other factors will shape future policies toward rural and urban sectors. One urgent need of our time is an ideology that will reconcile the ideals of a democratic society with the revolutionary changes that seem likely to remake underdeveloped nations in the decades immediately ahead.

9

A CASE STUDY IN CULTURAL

AND EDUCATIONAL MOBILITY:

JAPAN AND THE PROTESTANT ETHIC

REINHARD BENDIX, *University of California, Berkeley*

"CULTURAL-EDUCATIONAL mobility and development"—the topic assigned to me in this Conference—suggests that education and mobility are positively related to economic development. This positive relationship exists only, I believe, where the value of economic development is already accepted as a *sine qua non* of individual and national advance. It is true that this ideology is widespread in the many countries which since World War II have been transformed by a turn of phrase (and often by little else), from "underdeveloped" into "developing" nations. But in what general sense is it meaningful to link culture with mobility and economic development? To speak of development is to imply that at one time a given society was not developing or was "underdeveloped." With regard to that contrast culture typically maintains the established social structure; education helps to transmit and uphold the received tradition. Accordingly, the extensive literature on development contrasts—at least implicitly—tradition and modernity, and much of it is focused on the problem of how a non-industrial society can give rise to an industrial society. Each type has cultural and educational attributes of its own. It is, therefore, necessary to distinguish between the cultural *preconditions* of development and the cultural and educational *changes* that occur once development is under way, difficult as it may be to pinpoint this distinction. In the present case the question will be how cultural patterns supporting tradition can give rise to cultural patterns supporting modernity. I am concerned with the cultural preconditions of development.

Japan, in contrast with England and France, experienced rapid economic growth, especially in the industrial sector, only after 1868. She borrowed heavily from abroad in a conscious effort to benefit from the advanced technology and the political institutions of other countries.

Today, she is among the most industrialized nations of the world. My principal emphasis will not be on economic development itself, but on its "cultural-educational" preconditions. Since the classic study in this field is still Max Weber's famous essay on *The Protestant Ethic and the Spirit of Capitalism*, I shall begin with a brief, critical discussion of that essay. A comparative consideration of that essay and the Japanese development yields a perspective that illuminates "cultural-educational mobility" as a condition of development in both cases.

II

Max Weber's study of this problem in his *Protestant Ethic and the Spirit of Capitalism* begins with the observation that societies develop differentially and that "capitalism" originated in certain areas of Western Europe. Within these areas the traditional Catholic approach to economic pursuits tended in practice to condone what it could not prevent. Continuing a moral and religious posture that condemned usury, monopolistic practices, and generally the dance around the golden calf, the Church allowed erring men to obtain, through indulgences and the confessional, sanctioned release from whatever pangs of conscience or religious tribulations their worldly activities induced in them. In their explicit teachings the great Reformers opposed the money-changers and all their works as clearly as had Catholic doctrine. Here no change is discernible, unless it be the greater ethical rigor that reformist zeal imparted to pastoral practice. But the religious doctrines of the Reformers—above all the Calvinist doctrine of predestination—introduced a basic anxiety into the believer's relation to his God, and this anxiety, so Weber's argument runs, introduced a decisive change.[1] In lieu of the permissive pastoral practice by which Catholicism softened the psychological impact of its doctrine, the Protestant believer had to face the Divinely ordained uncertainty of his salvation without aid or comfort from anyone. Only his actions could allay that uncertainty, whether through inward contrition and an abiding faith as in Lutheranism, or through self-discipline and an active life in the service of God as in Calvinism.

Weber points out that for analytical purposes he presents the ideas of the Reformers "in their most consistent and logical forms." In this

---

[1] No one who has examined some of the personal documents of the period, will want to minimize that anxiety. Especially impressive in this respect is the fear induced in children as documented in Sanford Fleming, *Children and Puritanism* (New Haven: Yale University Press, 1933).

way he hopes to bring out the drift of these ideas, the direction in which a sincere believer would move. The gist of the argument is to posit an intensified motivation. All men of that time were concerned with their salvation, but the pastoral practice of Catholicism had diminished that concern. It had been greatly heightened, on the other hand, by the religious zeal of the great Reformers and by the unintended implications of their theological doctrines as these were revealed in the sermons of Puritan Divines. The economic actions consistent with the "Spirit of Capitalism," were in significant measure efforts to relieve religious anxiety—at any rate during the 16th and 17th centuries.

It is difficult, however, to infer the intensification of a motive (the quest for salvation) from the logical implications of a theological doctrine (the believer's uncertainty concerning his salvation, as a corollary of the doctrine of predestination). For all its subtlety and learning, Weber's text contains evidence that he himself remained uncertain concerning the relation between doctrine and conduct.[2] In this case analysis of the text can help us understand the difference between cultural and behavioral analysis.

Weber writes:

> We are naturally not concerned with the question of what was theoretically and officially taught in the ethical compendia of the time, however much practical significance this may have had through the influence of the Church discipline, pastoral work, and preaching. We are interested rather in something entirely different: the influence of those *psychological sanctions* which, originating in religious belief and the practice of religion, gave a direction to practical conduct and held the individual to it.[3]

Since this passage states the specific focus of attention, it is all the more significant that the key word "sanction" is ambiguous. If discipline, pastoral work and preaching are *not* relevant for understanding the impact of doctrine on conduct, then what of the "psychological sanctions" that are? In the original, Weber uses the German word *Antrieb* or impulse; he thus posits psychological impulses originating in the religious beliefs evoked by a theological doctrine. His use of the term "impulse" suggests that a propensity to act in accord with the implications of the doctrine of predestination has already been internalized. But this begs the question, since he is investigating and not presupposing the impact of doctrine on belief and conduct. (The translation unfortunately

    [2] Cf. the related points made by Paul Lazarsfeld and Anthony R. Oberschall, "Max Weber and Empirical Social Research," *American Sociological Review*, 30 (1965), pp. 191-93. Cf. also the discussion in Reinhard Bendix, *Max Weber, An Intellectual Portrait* (Garden City, N.Y.: Anchor Books, 1962), Ch. 7.
    [3] Max Weber, *The Protestant Ethic and the Spirit of Capitalism* (New York: Charles Scribner's Sons, 1958), p. 97. My Italics.

obscures the passage further, since the word "sanction," which corresponds to German words like *Bestätigung, Genehmigung* or *Zwangsmass-nahme*, refers to external controls. "Psychological sanction" is a contradiction in terms—in addition to being a wrong translation of *Antrieb*.) To be clear on this point, Weber would have had to use the word *Anreiz* or incentive. Thus he would have stated what indeed he shows in brilliant fashion, that the religious beliefs of the Puritans contained incentives encouraging a personal conduct of "innerworldly asceticism" *to the extent that these beliefs were internalized*—clearly a conditional assertion. Yet his whole analysis rests on the thesis that Puritan believers differed from Catholics by their *greater internalization* of religious precepts, their anxious concern with the uncertainty of salvation unrelieved by indulgences or the confessional, each man facing the stern and inscrutable majesty of God alone and unaided. In his responses to critics Weber declared that this intensified motivation had been a causal factor of great, but uncertain magnitude, because men of that day were more deeply affected by abstract religious dogmas than a more secular age can readily understand.

This reply, it seems to me, does not resolve the issue I have raised, nor does it do justice to the profundity of Weber's analysis. That profundity consists in Weber's paradoxical assertion that the Reformers continued to adhere to the traditional, Christian devaluation of mundane pursuits, that Christian believers of this period continued to be concerned with their fate in the hereafter (though in a more intense fashion than hitherto)—but that Western civilization shifted from a predominantly otherworldly to a predominantly innerworldly orientation nonetheless. In other words, the "Spirit of Capitalism" represents a direct outgrowth of the earlier, anti-materialistic tradition of Christianity and, as Weber shows, was all the more powerful for that reason. Was this due in part to the intensified motivation that Weber analyzes?

Questions of this kind have given rise to a large, controversial literature which seems to have resolved very little. One reason for this failure is probably that both critics and defenders have discussed Weber's thesis entirely in the context in which he first formulated it. It may be worthwhile, therefore, to pursue this unresolved problem in Weber's analysis in the different context of the cultural-educational preconditions of Japanese development.[4]

---

[4] This is made possible for me by Ronald Dore's volume, *Education in Tokugawa Japan* (Berkeley: University of California Press, 1965). I am indebted to Professor Dore for making the manuscript of the book available to me before publication.

III

To do this, I must enumerate some background factors concerning Tokugawa Japan. That background, I shall suggest, militated *against* the self-disciplined vigor in action that the samurai displayed in the decades following the Restoration of 1868. There is evidence that under the Tokugawa the education of samurai and of commoners continued to inculcate the traditional ethic of the samurai, but there is evidence also that such education was at best partially successful. If one distinguishes clearly between cultural incentive and internalized, psychological impulse (as I believe one should), then the evidence of the Tokugawa regime appears to point to a partial decline (rather than the increased vigor) of the samurai ethic.[5] The post-Restoration experience suggests, on the other hand, that the Western challenge arrested that decline by providing an opportunity for the leading groups of samurai and of commoners to live up to their ideals in modified form, and thus to overcome the discrepancies between ideal and conduct in the pre-Restoration period.

Following a long succession of internecine wars lasting until the end of the 16th century, Japan underwent a massive, political and administrative consolidation, at the local as well as the national level. By 1560 Japanese fiefs had been amalgamated into large territorial units, and seignorial rights were usurped by the locally dominant daimyo families. In this process smaller lords (samurai) were deprived of their seignorial rights and forced to reside, as retainers and officials of the daimyos, in castle-towns, whose construction in the period from 1580 to 1610— together with the destruction of all other fortified places—outwardly symbolized the new dispensation. This transformation of the samurai from rural landholders into urban retainers under the authority of the daimyos occurred when the Tokugawa Shogunate was consolidating its own position at the national level by a determined policy of isolation, the expulsion or extermination of Christians, and the imposition of the alternate-residence system (*sankin-kotai*) which made all daimyo families personally and politically dependent on the Shogunate in Edo. Within

[5] The reiteration of the phrase "cultural incentive" in this altered context calls for an additional comment. In his analysis of Calvinist and other Reformed doctrines Weber was not concerned with their explicit moral injunctions but with their implicit effects. The following discussion of Japanese materials is similar in the sense that explicitly the official code called for militancy, while official practice discouraged certain forms of it, and this discrepancy provided the "cultural incentives" of the Tokugawa period.

this general context the samurai were transformed from an estate of independent, landed, and self-equipped warriors into one of urbanized, aristocratic retainers, whose privileged social and economic position was universally acknowledged. They remained attached to their tradition of ceremonious conduct, intense pride of rank and the cultivation of physical prowess. The problem to be explained is how this demilitarized aristocracy could retain, for some two centuries, its individualized military stance and its cult of disciplined action in a thoroughly pacified society in which differences of hereditary rank were strongly emphasized but all forms of military aggression suppressed. For at the time of the Meiji Restoration it was against this improbable background that the samurai not only provided the active political and intellectual leadership of the nation, but pioneered in modern entrepreneurial activities as well.[6]

Why is this background improbable? The demilitarization of the samurai, the employment of some of their number as daimyo officials, the opportunities, at least among the better-off samurai families, for corruption in an urbanized, retainer existence, the emphasis on rank and the discouragement of competition, and among many lower samurai families, the sheer necessity to supplement rice stipends by some employment, often menial: these were so many reasons why the samurai could be expected to lose their militancy and self-discipline. No doubt some of them did, especially among the highest-ranking samurai and daimyo, for whom the Shogunal court at Edo provided additional opportunities for corruption. But this weakening of "moral fiber" was intensely resented among many samurai, especially during the last decades of the Tokugawa regime, and so the puzzle remains. Dore's analysis of education provides an answer to these questions and enables us to pinpoint the "functional equivalents" of Puritanism in Japan.[7]

With private tutors and, since the end of the 18th century, in an increasing number of fief-schools, the samurai families who could afford it, appear to have educated their sons.[8] In addition, a significant propor-

[6] See the data reported by Ronald Dore, "Mobility, Equality and Individuation in Modern Japan" (mimeographed paper presented to Second Conference on Modern Japan, Bermuda, January, 1963). Dore notes that until well into the 20th century it remained customary for a man to declare himself a commoner or aristocrat on every legal document or hotel register.

[7] The following summary does not do justice to the richness of Dore's materials, but it attempts to make a contribution by singling out the issues that appear critical in a comparative perspective.

[8] In 1703 only 9 per cent of all daimyo fiefs had schools, but the unbroken continuity of the samurai-ethic makes it probable that a significant proportion had private instruction. By 1814 about one half of all daimyo fiefs and almost all of the large fiefs had schools; by the time of the Restoration only the smallest fiefs remained without them.

tion of townsmen and well-to-do farmers sent their sons to temple-schools or private tutors, where they learned the rudiments of reading, writing and arithmetic. The private schools for commoners were in large part responsible for the fact that at the time of the Restoration some 40 per cent of Japanese boys and about 10 per cent of the girls were receiving formal education; the sons and daughters of aristocratic families probably did not constitute more than 6 per cent of the school-age population.[9]

What were the aims of samurai education? In 1786 Hayashi Shihei formulated these aims in a manner that Dore considers representative:

With the eight virtues as your basis [his list is filial piety, respect for elders, loyalty, trust, courage, justice, straightforwardness, and a sense of honor] cultivate a boldness of spirit without losing self-discipline; acquire wisdom and wide learning without despising other people. Do not become weak and feeble; do not lose your dignity; do not sink stagnantly into mere logic-chopping, nor allow yourself to be carried away by prose and poetry. Do not lose your courage; do not become introverted. Do not become an admirer of China who sees no good in Japan. Do not fall in love with novelty or with pleasures of the eye. Practice your military skills with devotion and at the same time learn something of astronomy and geography, of the tea ceremony and of No drama.[10]

Avoidance of book-learning as such, of novelty and pleasure, behavior appropriate to the samurai's rank with proper dignity of bearing and respect for elders, above all self-discipline, wisdom and an active way of life: these appear to be the principal themes in this orientation. The literary arts are of secondary significance; their importance lies primarily in providing a medium of instruction through which the pupil can acquire the proper frame of mind, conscious of his duties and earnest in his practice of military skills.

Apparently, the same ideals of conduct were instilled in pupils of commoner orgin. To be sure, military skills were the exclusive prerogative of the aristocracy, while the high rank, strutting arrogance and

[9] This inference is based on a comparison between Dore's estimate of formal schooling and literacy and Abegglen and Mannari's estimate that all ranks of the aristocracy comprised 460,000 out of 7 million households or about 6.1 per cent of the total population in 1872. Cf. James J. Abegglen and Hiroshi Mannari, "Japanese Business Leaders, 1880-1960" (mimeographed paper presented to the Conference on the State and Economic Enterprise in Modern Japan, Estes Park, Colo.: June, 1963), pp. 9-11. It is of course, speculative to identify the proportion of children from aristocratic households with the proportion of aristocratic households, since this assumes that the number of children per aristocratic household was identical with the national average. But a sizable proportion of Japanese boys with formal education must have come from households of commoners, since aristocratic households could hardly have made up in excess of children what they lacked in total numbers.

[10] Quoted in Dore, Education in Tokugawa Japan, op. cit., p. 64.

rentier-existence of the samurai were in turn objects of emulation, envy and ridicule among the commoners. But temple-schools and private tutors taught the sons of commoners the art of writing with a single-minded emphasis on proper manners and the right frame of mind. Dore has translated a set of Terakoya (temple-school) precepts from which I quote two paragraphs, to illustrate the link between literacy, social structure and the ideology of self-discipline:

To be born human and not be able to write is to be less than human. Illiteracy is a form of blindness. It brings shame on your teacher, shame on your parents, and shame on yourself. The heart of a child of three stays with him till he is a hundred as the proverb says. Determine to succeed, study with all your might, never forgetting the shame of failure. . . . Cooperate with each other to behave yourselves as you should, check in yourselves any tendencies to be attracted to evil ways, and put all your heart into your brush-work.

At your desks let there be no useless idle talk, or yawning or stretching, or dozing or picking your nose, or chewing paper, or biting the end of your brush. To imitate the idle is the road to evil habits. Just concentrate whole-heartedly on your writing, giving each character the care it deserves.[11]

There is much more of the same with special enumeration of all the careless or undisciplined ways that the students are admonished to avoid, incidentally giving a pretty graphic picture of the pranks, misdemeanors and bad habits that Japanese schoolboys seem to have in common with their peers all over the world. Apparently, neither the social aspiration of commoners nor hereditary privilege with its pride of rank were sufficient in themselves to inculcate self-discipline.

In the fief schools as well as in schools for commoners, instruction became a highly formalized affair which was intrinsically dull and meaningless, as Dore points out. Without holding the individual's interest, the teachers apparently insisted on writing and reading as media through which the student should learn proper behavior and the right frame of mind. Tedious repetition under conditions in which the student's bearing and attitude were subjected to the most detailed scrutiny and control, were the means used to teach self-discipline. It must remain uncertain how far these educational methods succeeded in inculcating the habits of thought and action that proved highly suitable for the rapid modernization of Japan after 1868. All we really know is that the educational system helped to maintain the ideals of the samurai. One might also say that the teachers had a vested interest in these ideals and that daimyos and Bakufu officials encouraged their educational endeavors, because they considered these ideals suitable supports of domestic stability. If one goes beyond these statements to the con-

[11] *Ibid.,* p. 323 ff.

clusion that in the schools of the Tokugawa period students internalized ideals of conduct and hence actually acquired the drive and discipline that were in evidence later on, one is guilty of the same confusion between cultural prescription and psychological impulse noted earlier.[12]

Certainly, Tokugawa education put a high premium on self-discipline, filial piety and an activist way of life. But there is evidence that many samurai students did not take to this education with alacrity. Fief edicts frequently deplored the lack of diligence among samurai students and admonished them to greater effort. Moreover, it is difficult to imagine that the personal militancy of the samurai remained unimpaired under a regime that sought to control all manifestations of aggressive or competitive behavior. The fief schools discouraged all forms of rivalry between different schools and strictly prohibited contests or simulated combat among their pupils, even though the ideology and practice of swordsmanship continued unabated. One result of this double-edged policy was that, as Dore comments, "combat was less and less practiced, and swordsmanship and the use of the lance became increasingly a matter of formal gymnastics, and disciplined choreography."[13] Presumably this applied to those pupils who put dignity, respect for elders, self-discipline and wisdom above the "cult of action." There were others, however, whom circumstances and temperament prompted to make the opposite choice. As *ronin* or masterless samurai they lived a wayward life by the sword at the expense of most other tenets of the samurai ethic. One can gauge the tensions inherent in Japanese culture before the Restoration when one observes that the Tokugawa regime did not abandon its praise of militancy despite its policy of pacification and the apprehensions aroused by the activities of the *ronin*.

The famous story of the 47 *ronin* exemplifies many of these themes. At the Shogunal Court a daimyo has drawn his sword and wounded a high Court official, to avenge an insult. As a penalty the daimyo is asked to commit suicide, because by his act he has jeopardized Tokugawa supremacy and the policy of pacification on which it rests. The daimyo's retainers are now without a master; they acknowledge that he had to die, but out of loyalty to him they make every effort to preserve their Lord's fief for the members of his family. This effort fails. For two years the 47 *ronin* (the original number is larger, but many withdraw)

---

[12] This confusion is widespread because all cultural values have such *possible* psychological correlates. In the field of psychological drives or patterns, the *post-hoc-ergo-propter-hoc* fallacy is especially hard to avoid, because observation of such drives or patterns invites inquiry into their antecedents, and in most instances it is impossible to document that these antecedents did *not* exist.

[13] Dore, *Education, op. cit.*, p. 151.

secretly plan to avenge their Lord. After successfully eluding the ubiquitous Tokugawa police, they kill the Court official who had provoked their master. As penalty for this violation of the Tokugawa peace the Shogun demands that the 47 commit suicide in turn. The conduct of these men exemplifies unconditional loyalty to their master, self-discipline in guarding their secret plans, and complete devotion to the cult of action in the successful consummation of their endeavor. The 47 *ronin* epitomize the priorities and contradictions of the ideals of Tokugawa culture. They divorce their wives or have their wives and daughters turn to prostitution so that they can fulfil their pledge of loyalty to their master; and they combine this act of upholding the hierarchy of rank with the unconditional commitment to action that the Bakufu simultaneously encouraged and suppressed. The hierarchy of rank is more important than the family while the peace of the Tokugawa is still more important than the hierarchy of rank. Both these priorities are here exemplified by actions which can be turned against others only at the price of turning against oneself in the end.

This true story of the early 18th century instantly became the cultural epitome of the samurai ethic, but in retrospect it reads more like an epitaph than an apotheosis. Its heroes serve their master by their deaths, since they can no longer serve him in their lives. Such symbolic consummation of the cult of self-disciplined action points insistently, albeit by implication, to the discrepancy between this cult and the daily round of a retainer's life that characterized the lives of most samurai under the Tokugawa settlement. One would suppose that many of these men, for whom militancy was the mark of rank, were aware at times of the emptiness of that pretense. While the story of the 47 *ronin* certainly upheld the ideal, did it not also underscore the pettiness of militancy without war? At any rate, the ideal heroism of these *ronin* does not explain whether and how such ideals could be harnessed to meet the contingencies of everyday life, which developed precipitously following the Restoration of 1868.[14] In the Japanese case we certainly have an instance of the discrepancy between cultural ideals and behavior; perhaps we can infer—for the decades preceding the Restoration—a growing ambivalence and even a diminished adherence to these ideals. The

---

[14] In 1867 payments in rice to the samurai amounted to 34.6 million yen, while in 1876 the value of yearly interest paid on a commutation basis had fallen to 11.5 million. For a relatively short time the Meiji government cushioned this precipitous decline by allocating a sizable portion of its budgets for stipends to dispossessed samurai, as well as by the more intangible method of ideological support for their high rank. But these short-term methods only delayed for a little the stark necessity of going to work.

question is how such evidence and the more tentative inferences based on it can be related, however provisionally, to the intense and disciplined effort of many samurai immediately following the Restoration.

Historical instances are numerous in which discrepancies of this kind lead to a decline of an ideal. Under the Tokugawa regime the peaceful existence of most samurai was increasingly at odds with their militant stance, a condition hardly conducive to the vigor and self-discipline that the samurai displayed during the Meiji Restoration. Here some allowance must be made for the accident of timing: we will never know whether the samurai ethic would have become an empty sham in spite of teaching, official propaganda and increased education of commoners, *if* the Western challenge to Japanese independence had come much later. All we know is that this challenge brought into the open a capacity for self-disciplined action that had been jeopardized (and may well have been diminishing) by the discrepancy between ideal and conduct under the Tokugawa regime.

Before 1868 the samurai ethic was maintained in its entirety by the educational system and by the officials of the Bakufu. There is evidence that the militant ideal of self-disciplined and vigorous action could be "domesticated" through the educational system. Dore shows how this ideal was incorporated in the teaching of reading and writing as well as in the "demilitarized" practice of military skills. The spread of Tera-koya education and the high level of literacy by the time of Restoration suggest that samurai ideals gradually became ideals for commoners as well.[15] Moreover, the samurai tradition of militancy was kept alive in several ways despite the increasing discrepancies between cultural ideals and behavior. In response to the contrast between high social rank and low economic position the samurai who turned *ronin* chose to act out the militant aspects of their ethic at the price of neglecting other aspects of its code. For their part, samurai retainers adopted the alternative way of emphasizing rank-consciousness and stylized behavior at the price of turning militancy into "disciplined choreography," a pattern also followed by the samurai whose way of life became hardly distinguishable from that of commoners. One imagines that subjectively samurai of every description adhered to their ideals with that "sensitive pride and the fear of shaming defeat" (Dore) which most experts consider the exem-

---

[15] The "demilitarized" teaching of the samurai-ethic probably facilitated its general applicability, especially among commoners. Dore emphasizes that there is hardly any evidence in Tokugawa Japan of assertions that commoners should be barred from the acquisition of literacy, while such assertions were frequent in Europe on the ground that such a skill would make the lower orders unruly. In this sense the adoption of samurai-precepts in the instruction of commoners was a move in the direction of equality despite the rank-consciousness instilled by these precepts.

plary motivational pattern of the Japanese people.[16] In this they were greatly aided by the Bakufu officials, who always upheld the ideal of samurai militancy, even though they suppressed the aggressive conduct that was an essential part of this ideal. Thus, before 1868, formal education and official ideology supported ideals some of which it disavowed in practice.

Since after 1868 the samurai implemented their ideal of disciplined action in economic, political and intellectual pursuits, one can infer that the Restoration provided the opportunity to overcome the long-standing, internal contradictions of the Tokugawa regime. Paradoxically, the same qualities that had sustained a quiescent and internally contradictory regime for so long, now found a new outlet. As Dore puts it in a telling summary:

Sensitive pride and fear of shaming defeat, the strength of which probably led the majority of samurai to avoid competitive situations and certainly prompted most educators and teachers of military skills deliberately to refrain from creating them, also meant that—once competition was declared and the race was on, the self-respecting samurai really did go all out to win.[17]

Thus, the release of pent-up energies was decisive and there is little doubt that it was occasioned not by internal structural changes but by an external event, the arrival of Commodore Perry's ships and the challenge to national preservation that it symbolized. During the critical period from 1853 to 1868 (the so-called Bakumatsu period) the national goals of Japanese society were defined unequivocally, perhaps for the first time, the "ethic" of filial piety, self-discipline and an activist way of life was greatly reinforced by the external threat, and the intense social conflicts that ensued turned primarily on how best to meet the Western challenge.[18]

IV

From the perspective of Japanese development one gains a clearer view of the cultural preconditions of development from tradition to modernity. For our purposes the central fact of Tokugawa Japan is the

---

[16] For a telling description of this pattern, illuminated by evidence from Japanese history, cf. Edwin O. Reischauer, *The United States and Japan* (New York: The Viking Press, 1957), pp. 99-177.

[17] Dore, *Education, op. cit.*, p. 212.

[18] For a masterly exposition of these conflicts over policy and their compatibility with a basic agreement on national goals, see W. G. Beasley, "Introduction," in W. G. Beasley (ed.), *Select Documents—Japanese Foreign Policy, 1853-1868* (London: Oxford University Press, 1955) pp. 1-93.

contradiction between official support of the traditional ideal of militancy and official suppression of warlike actions which accord with that ideal. The Bakufu officials who upheld the ideal of militancy surely did not wish to encourage the outlawry of the *ronin*, and they may have had misgivings concerning the increasingly empty pretense of samurai-retainers. Yet in effect they encouraged both, and the contrast between official ideology and practice would have undermined the ideological support of the Tokugawa regime in the long run. It is reasonable to suppose that this support was weakening in the decades preceding the Restoration.

Apparently, then, an event external to the society, the sudden jeopardy in which Japan was placed by the Western challenge to her isolation, was responsible in large measure for defining national goals and the redirecting and intensifying actions based on unchanged motivational patterns and unchanged cultural ideals. The Western challenge redefined the situation for large numbers of Japanese, and while it is true that for a time Westernization was "the rage," a wave of Japanization followed in turn, leading to a reaffirmation of cultural ideals and to a reenforcement of filial piety and the sense of hierarchy, which were now compatible with more national unity and economic development than had existed before 1868.

With this interpretation in mind we can turn once again to the problems raised by Max Weber's analysis. That problem consists, as stated earlier, in the hiatus between doctrine and conduct, between the *incentives* implicit in religious ideas and the internalized *impulses* that prompt groups of men to act in the manner Weber defined as "inner-worldly asceticism." An attempt to elucidate this unresolved question by reference to the Japanese development may appear far-fetched. After all, how is it possible to find points of comparison or even analogy between the Western challenge to Japanese isolation and, say, Calvin's or Luther's challenge of Catholic orthodoxy? Yet at an abstract level we deal here with rather similar phenomena. Both cases have to do with the process by which cultural ideals supporting tradition give rise to cultural ideals supporting modernity.

The discrepancy between official ideology and practice in Tokugawa Japan finds its analogue in the pre-Reformation spokesmen of the Catholic church who upheld the traditional faith but condoned religious practices, like the indiscriminate sale of indulgences, at variance with the ideals of that faith. The same spokesmen also condemned and at times suppressed individuals and movements that appeared to challenge the supremacy of the Church. It is common knowledge that the immediate antecedents of the Reformation were only the past phases of a century-long development in which the Church had had to grapple again and again with the doctrinal, pastoral and organizational consequences of the hiatus between faith and secular involvement. It is reasonable to suppose that in the course of this development orthodox spokesmen found themselves time and again in a situation similar to that of Tokugawa officialdom. Whatever the differences in culture and social structure, the task of upholding an orthodox doctrinal position while prohibiting and suppressing actions in consonance with orthodox principles is similar in an abstract sense.[19]

For present purposes it is most relevant to note the probable collective effect. Confronted with a patent discrepancy between official doctrine and sanctioned behavior, a large population—whether of Catholic believers or Japanese samurai—becomes divided into hypocrites and true believers. We know too little about this process, but there is ample evidence from both medieval Europe and Tokugawa Japan that the discrepancy between doctrine and practice was welcomed by some and condemned by others. Some used the occasion as an excuse for moral laxity, others became moral rigorists as a reaction against official dishonesty. The proportions of the population responding in one way or the other may never be known. Perhaps no more can be said in the end than that Catholic Europeans had to live with this discrepancy between doctrine and sanctioned behavior for a much longer period than the population of Tokugawa Japan. Prio to *the* Reformation, the number and intensity of movements for internal reform of the Church probably exceeded the analogous stirring of reform-movements in Tokugawa Japan prior to the Restoration. It is conceivable that this longer history of spiritual and psychological unrest indicates a greater attenuation of the moral code in Europe than in Japan. Speculative as such reasoning is, it suggests that we must look for some massive cause, affecting large numbers, if we are to explain how a considerable part of a population could turn for a significant period from the hypothesized vacillation between laxity and rigorism to self-disciplined action in this world, to inner-worldly asceticism. The venturesome analogue of the Japanese development suggests that this massive cause may well lie in events external to that self-contained world of religious ideas and moral precepts that Weber analyzed with such insight.

[19] This similarity can be analyzed in several ways. Cf. for example, the analysis of this parallelism in the case of Catholic and Communist orthodoxy in Zbigniew Brzezinski, "Deviation Control: A Study in the Dynamics of Doctrinal Conflict," *American Political Science Review* 56 (1962), pp. 5-22.

What was the context in which the incentives implicit in religious doctrines became linked with the impulses that prompt men to action? [20] In the case of the Lutheran Reformation it is noteworthy that around 1500 Wittenberg was located in a German frontier region, bordering on areas inhabited by people of Slavic descent. The town had 2,500 residents, of whom 550 were liable to pay taxes; composed primarily of artisans and local traders, the community provided little opportunity for the development of an urban patriciate. During the crucial years of Luther's work, Wittenberg had to accommodate between 1,500 and 2,000 students, and Schoeffler shows that under Luther's influence the faculty of the university rapidly became very young indeed. Men in their twenties and thirties predominated while older professors retired or left the university altogether. Surely, Luther was a very powerful and courageous innovator, who attracted students from far and wide, and who succeeded in transforming the bulk of the faculty into a group of loyal collaborators and followers.[21] Thus, Luther created some of the community support he enjoyed. But in the larger context, he could do so because Wittenberg provided cultural and political opportunities for his reorientation of established traditions. Located in a linguistic and cultural frontier area, Wittenberg was a natural setting for a cultural and religious appeal based on the vernacular and the original: the translation of the Bible into German, the use of German in religious ceremonies, and beyond this, recourse to the texts of classical antiquity in the original rather than dependence on commentaries. This link between religious reform and a revival of humanistic learning also appealed to other regions and universities lacking in tradition, in striking contrast to areas with more established traditions and older universities where these innovations were bitterly opposed for cultural as well as for religious reasons. Schoeffler examines the signatories of the Augsburg confession (1530) and suggests that they represent "outposts" of German settlement and areas of relatively late Christianization, which either lacked universities altogether or had universities bereft of the scholarly traditions of that period.

On the Continent the Lutheran Reformation became stabilized through the Articles of Schmalkalden (1537) which distinguish between the coercive, legal authority of the temporal power and the spiritual

---

[20] The following observations are based on the work of Herbert Schoeffler, *Wirkungen der Reformation* (Frankfurt: V. Klostermann, 1960), containing essays originally published in 1932 and 1936. My brief statement cannot do justice to the subtlety of Schoeffler's analysis.

[21] Both directly and indirectly Luther had special influence with the Elector Friedrich of Saxony, who used his authority to effect these changes of personnel at the university.

authority of the church, but then place a certain authority over affairs of the Church in the hands of the prince. His duty is to "diligently further God's glory." To this end he must place his authority in the service of the Church, which at the time meant the right and duty to defend correct doctrine and superintend preaching and worship. Henceforth, acceptance of established, secular authority became an integral part of Lutheran piety—a link which to this day has had repercussions in German society especially. In this instance it is easy to see that to the extent that the incentives implicit in Luther's theological doctrines were internalized, they were internalized in a political context—however difficult it may be to disentangle the religious from the political incentives or to analyze the interweaving of both in a socialization based on Lutheran precepts.

The context of the English Reformation differs greatly from that on the Continent. Schoeffler points to the absence of a religious leadership in any way comparable to that of Luther or Calvin. Initiated under political auspices the English Reformation lacked a great religious ethos. During several decades of the 16th century the government was markedly unstable. Yet each new government gave rise to new, authoritative decisions on Church policy. As a result the English people were exposed to the whole gamut of religious disputes characteristic of the period, an experience which in Schoeffler's judgment created considerable religious anxiety while providing no prospect of a new consensus on religious questions. In this case religious anxiety is attributed to the uncertainties introduced into Church affairs by a vacillating government which has assumed authority over these affairs but proves unable to develop a consistent approach to the organizational and spiritual problems of the Church. Yet each approach to Church policy found its passionate advocates, leading eventually to the formation of sects whose members adhered to their religious convictions all the more stubbornly, the more the authorities continued to vacillate. As Schoeffler puts it:

> The English nation is the only great people, which in all its segments was really led into a state of religious need or anxiety (*Not*). Everyone had to make his own decision among several and eventually among many doctrinal systems and principles of church organization, while the state was in no position to take this decision into its own hands.[22]

Having made such decisions under conditions of special uncertainty the new sectarian communities were anxious to preserve the faith they had had to discover for themselves, and the unity of the congregation which had been forged in the midst of political conflicts and religious disputes. Thus, the political context of the English Reformation helps us to inter-

[22] *Ibid.*, p. 324.

pret the link between the incentives implicit in religious ideas and the internalization of these religious precepts, which Weber has analyzed in part.

There is no need to examine the manifest dissimilarities between the English Reformation and the Japanese response to the Western challenge. In both instances motivation was intensified along established lines, apparently because the context stimulated a heightened concern with the supreme value of personal salvation or national integrity, respectively. The two cases suggest that the cultural-educational preconditions of economic development can be understood more clearly, if the internal structure of a society is analyzed in relation to its political structure and international setting.

V

To answer the question of how cultural patterns that support tradition can give rise to cultural patterns that support modernity, I have explored two different settings. The question is especially difficult to answer because such patterns are accessible to the scholar only so far as they are reflected in documents, and documents which do that tend to be "projections" of a cultural minority. Hence, the meaning of cultural patterns for large numbers remains inevitably speculative. And yet, without some answer to the question of what these patterns mean, at least to leading strata of a society numbering in the thousands, we cannot expect to understand the cultural preconditions of economic development. This essay has advanced two suggestions in this respect.

One is that the mass effect of cultural patterns can be understood better if their political context is observed. In the Japanese case the evidence points unequivocally to a massive redirection of effort as a response to the Western challenge. The evidence from the Reformation is much more complex. Yet, if it be true as Weber argued that men of that time were very directly concerned with abstract theological doctrines, then it seems just as plausible to suggest that this concern with personal salvation was hard to separate from political controversy at a time when theological and political differences went hand in hand. Political involvement, I suggest, is another side of that devotional piety or innerworldly asceticism that Weber analyzed in Lutheranism and Calvinism, and I believe that the intensification of motives which he emphasized cannot be understood without attention to this aspect.

The other suggestion is more abstract, but perhaps more important. Throughout his work Weber was concerned with the uniqueness of

Western civilization, from Greek philosophy and Roman jurisprudence to the Protestant Ethic, capitalist enterprise and modern science. Since his day a few other countries have accomplished a transition to modernity, aided by the preceding developments of Europe and America but also contributing cultural elements of their own. Japan is an outstanding example. But the number of such countries is quite limited, and the question seems warranted whether across all the differences among them this "capacity for development" points to some common element. I noted that both Tokugawa Japan and Catholic Europe were characterized by protracted discrepancies between orthodox doctrine and practical accommodations, giving rise to moral "tokenism'" on one hand and moral "rigorism" on the other. The tensions imparted to both cultures as a result may have prepared the ground for the innovating impact of political challenges and religious ideas.

10

PSYCHOLOGICAL ORIGINS

OF MOBILITY *

HARRY J. CROCKETT, JR., *University of North Carolina*

EMPIRICAL STUDIES of psychological factors contributing to mobility are rare; studies suggesting the relevance of these factors to mobility, while more frequent, are not abundant.[1] This paper will focus on recent treatments of the subject, highlighting works based on empirical data, but noting also relatively recent non-empirical contributions. Because most students of mobility have neglected personality factors, I shall begin by urging the necessity for such concern, going on to discuss alternative conceptions of motivation, and to examine the impact of personal factors in mobility, as alleged in or demonstrated by the literature, in different structural contexts.

The study of mobility in modern societies has been undertaken almost exclusively by sociologists and economists. Inevitably, therefore, social structural and demographic factors—social class or stratum of origin, region of origin, education, race, age—have been prominent in analyses of mobility. The major concern of such inquiry has been to describe, and sometimes predict, shifts in occupational or social status distributions within a population. From this admittedly useful point of view, the potential contributions of personality factors to mobility appears irrelevant. Not much "variance" remains to be explained by

* Ralph H. Turner's excellent critique of the draft of this paper presented to the Conference enabled me to make a number of changes in this version, and I regret that I have not been able to incorporate more of his discussion in the paper. The extent to which my perspective on the matters under discussion has been shaped, and my understanding of them enhanced by John W. Atkinson is cheerfully and gratefully acknowledged. I also wish to acknowledge the careful criticisms of the earlier draft by Robert L. Carroll, Richard L. Simpson, Neil J. Smelser, Carleton W. Smith, and Mrs. Karen Many.

[1] For a thorough review of such research in modern societies through 1958, see Seymour M. Lipset and Reinhard Bendix, *Social Mobility in Industrial Society* (Berkeley: University of California Press, 1959), pp. 227-259.

personality factors when mobility is studied from an over-all societal point of view. But this is so, in modern societies, precisely because the conditions under which personality factors may contribute to mobility are somehow controlled for, partialled out, or obliterated in such analyses. (Data presented below on pre-modern societies indicate psychological factors exert greater influence on mobility there than in modern industrial societies.) When one asks why, given the presence of certain social structural conditions, particular persons rise, fall, or remain stationary in the status system, personality characteristics immediately become relevant and important. Some sons of laborers become skilled workers, others do not; some sons of professionals descend into slightly skilled white-collar jobs, or into manual occupations, others do not. This variation in mobility among persons sharing similar social positions and influence requires attention to personality factors in mobility even in modern societies.[2]

Three classes of personality factors may be usefully distinguished as potential sources of mobility: capacities, e.g., intelligence, learned skills; cognitions, e.g., attitudes, beliefs, values; and motivations. Terminological or conceptual problems do not seem likely in the case of capacities or cognitions, but it does seem well at the outset to discuss, albeit briefly, the concept of motivation. For although the difficult conceptual problems familiar to students of motivation [3] surely cannot be reviewed in detail here, it would be foolhardy not to acknowledge their existence, and less than fair to the reader not to state my own theoretical preference. All theories of motivation are concerned with why behavior starts, persists with greater or less vigor through time, and terminates when some end-state or goal is reached. The position on this matter most congenial to a plurality of sociologists, I suppose, is that of the symbolic interactionists,[4] who ignore unconscious strivings and do not emphasize the lasting effects of early learning experiences while stressing conventional

---

[2] The conjoining of personal and social factors in the study of mobility has been urged by Alex Inkeles, "Personality and Social Structure," in Robert K. Merton, Leonard Broom and Leonard S. Cottrell, Jr. (eds.), *Sociology Today* (New York: Basic Books, 1959), pp. 249-276, and by Lipset and Bendix, *op. cit.*, pp. 255-259. For a conceptual scheme of occupational choice that unites personal and structural variables, see Peter M. Blau, John W. Gustad, Richard Jessor, Herbert S. Parnes and Richard C. Wilcock, "Occupational Choice: A Conceptual Framework," in Neil J. Smelser and William T. Smelser (eds.), *Personality and Social Systems* (New York: John Wiley & Sons, 1963), pp. 559-571.

[3] For an excellent treatment of these problems, see Richard S. Peters, *The Concept of Motivation* (London: Routledge and Kegan Paul, 1958).

[4] A representative statement is that of Alfred R. Lindesmith and Anselm L. Strauss, *Social Psychology* (New York: Holt, Rinehart & Winston, 1956), especially pp. 297-310. See also Nelson Foote, "Identification as the Basis for a Theory of Motivation," *American Sociological Review*, 16 (February, 1951), pp. 14-21.

understandings acquired through verbal interaction in specific, especially current, situations. Motives, in this view, enable people to "understand" their own and others' behaviors by attaching conventionally given linguistic labels to them, by "naming"; rather than "explaining" behavior, in the sense of "causing" a given sequence of action to occur, they are merely convenient "fictive" descriptions enabling people to make sense of their world.

In contrast, the general position informing this paper is that presented by McClelland,[5] wherein motives are learned, internalized, persisting dispositions that are activated when appropriate situations (those containing the pleasureful or painful characteristics that accompanied past learning) recur. The importance of early learning is assumed, as is the tendency for motives to be more unconscious than open to conscious awareness, and motives are taken as "causal" variables in the sense that prior knowledge of motive strength permits relatively accurate prediction of behavior under relevant conditions.

Obviously, one's basic view concerning the nature of motives affects significantly one's evaluation of empirical studies of motivation and mobility. I hope that readers radically at odds with the position taken here will be able to suspend their disbelief until the data have been presented.

NON-LITERATE, PRE-INDUSTRIAL SOCIETIES

Nowhere are data on mobility more scattered and difficult to assess than in the literature on pre-industrial societies. Fortunately, some of these settings are systematically considered by my colleague, Gerhard Lenski, in a manuscript now nearing completion.[6] In hunting and gathering societies,[7] stratification, and hence mobility, is chiefly in terms of honor and prestige. Age and sex, of course, are generally bases for differential allocation of honor, with the aged frequently enjoying high prestige, sometimes not, and with men typically more honored than women. More important for present purposes are Lenski's conclusions that "in primitive hunting and gathering societies, power, privilege, and

[5] David C. McClelland, *Personality* (New York: William Sloane Associates, 1951), pp. 466–475. Some evidence relevant to the assumptions of this position is reviewed later in the paper.

[6] Gerhard Lenski, *Power and Privilege: The Theory of Social Stratification* (New York: McGraw-Hill, forthcoming). Since the work is in manuscript form, page references for quotations cannot be given.

[7] Lenski is aware of the important structural distinctions which obtain among "hunting and gathering" societies. The generalizations compactly presented below are carefully qualified in his work.

honor are largely a function of personal skills and ability," and that intergenerational mobility is likely to be very high because "there is little to prevent the talented son of an untalented father from rising to a position of leadership in his community." Honor accrues disproportionately in these groups to persons proficient in hunting, warfare, or magico-religious endeavors; [8] and personal characteristics—such as intelligence, energy and other physical endowments, and the distinctive personality traits appropriate to the shaman role [9]—are functional to the achievement of such proficiency. Chiefs or headmen, as well as shamans, frequently inherit their positions, but remaining in these roles as powerful and honored incumbents is fundamentally contingent on personal competence.

Granting the validity of these conclusions, it is important to ask why personal factors so heavily determine mobility here. Lenski's answer is that provisions for the transmission of advantage between generations are lacking in these societies. Little wealth exists to be inherited; inherited roles carrying power and honor irrespective of the incumbent's competence are generally absent; and class subcultures do not provide differential advantages to children because these groups are too small to support class differentiation.

Lenski considers two other types of primitive societies, "simple" and "advanced" horticultural societies.[10] Simple horticultural societies are more highly developed in social, political, and economic organization than are hunting and gathering societies, while advanced horticultural societies, in turn, are much more specialized and complex along these dimensions. In simple horticultural societies, some institutionalized offices emerge, as well as some capital goods (e.g., women) that can be monopolized. In advanced horticultural societies, institutionalized offices are numerous, hereditary status groups develop, the concept of property rights appears, and readily transferable forms of wealth (money, cattle) are present. Lenski finds distinctive shifts in the rates and determinants of mobility accompanying these alterations in social structure. In the simple horticultural societies, high rates of mobility are still common, and personal characteristics still underlie much mobility. But in the

[8] Downward mobility as a function of personality factors is strikingly illustrated by the berdaches found among some of the American Plains Indian groups. Here, men lacking the attributes essential to success as warriors adopt the role of women.

[9] The charismatic and "deviant" qualities so frequently attributed to shamans in the literature are probably not sufficient in themselves to account for success in the shaman role. It is Richard Lieban's view, on the basis of his work with shaman informants in contemporary Cebu City (Philippines), that successful shamans are also highly intelligent. Personal communication.

[10] Again, as in the material on hunting and gathering societies, structural variations within these categories are acknowledged and seriously considered by Lenski.

advanced horticultural societies, the rates of both inter- and intra-generational mobility are slowed, and personal qualities count for much less. Here also, different personal characteristics than in the other two societal types are relevant to mobility:

". . . talent and ability alone are not enough for men to rise high at court. They must also be willing and able to be submissive, cringing and fawning in the presence of their superiors, and skilled in the subtle arts of manipulation and dissimulation.

Lenski's findings, based on an exhaustive reading of the ethnographic literature, may be summarized in the following formulation: Assuming that in any population ability and other personality characteristics are distributed unevenly between and within generations, then where social structural constraints on mobility are lacking (1) mobility between and within generations will be relatively frequent and (2) individual personality factors will play the most important part in determining who will be mobile.[11] It is in the advanced horticultural societies, apparently, that social structural factors assume the dominant role in mobility so familiar to students of modern societies, while personality factors retain importance mainly with regard to differential mobility among those from similar structural positions.

Data nicely complementing Lenski's findings are reported in Barry, Child and Bacon's [12] study of the relation of subsistence economy to child training in a sample of 104 societies. These authors reason that in agricultural and animal husbandry economies, where traditional routines of crop-growing and herd-control assure the future food supply, individual initiative will not be stressed and adults will tend to be "conscientious, compliant, and conservative." On the other hand, in hunting and gathering, and fishing economies, where food cannot generally be stored over extended periods, individual initiative in the essential subsistence activities should be stressed and "adults should tend to be individualistic, assertive, and venturesome." [13] Assuming that parents try to rear their children so that the children will function effectively as adults, quite different patterns of child rearing ought to prevail in the two types of societies. Content analysis of the ethnographies with regard to train-

[11] Turner suggests that societies vary in the distributions of personality characteristics related to mobility, and that these variations are a function of social structural factors. "Hence the explanation in terms of personality distribution is never adequate by itself since there might also be a direct connection between the one social structural factor and another." Ralph H. Turner, "Comments on Crockett," unpublished critique of the present paper presented to the Conference, p. 3.

[12] Herbert Barry, III, Irvin L. Child and Margaret K. Bacon, "Relation of Child Training to Subsistence Economy," *American Anthropologist,* 61 (February, 1959), pp. 51-63.

[13] *Ibid.,* p. 53.

ing for obedience, responsibility, nurturance, achievement, self-reliance, and general independence revealed strong evidence favoring the authors' hypotheses. Agricultural and animal husbandry societies tended to stress compliance in child rearing, while in the hunting and gathering, and fishing societies, child rearing tended to stress assertion. Whether or not these differences stem primarily from variations in economic organization, they are what one would expect if Lenski's analysis of the differential contribution of personality factors to mobility in these diverse types of societies is correct.

A final type of pre-industrial society considered by Lenski is the "agrarian" society which, in comparison with the advanced horticultural type, is much more advanced technologically, exhibits extensive specialization of labor, involves much larger populations, and features marked social inequality associated with a more highly differentiated social class system. Formidable problems in developing a generic type from the diversity of historical instances (e.g., China, India, Russia, the Roman Empire) are acknowledged and carefully handled by Lenski. Societies sharing many of the features of this type but based more on maritime than agrarian economic activities are excluded.

Mobility in the agrarian society is more structurally determined than in any of the previous types discussed. This point is well illustrated by the tendency for downward mobility to be much more frequent in the long run than upward mobility, a tendency arising from the production of more offspring than available occupational positions in all but the lowest strata (Lenski differentiates eight overlapping classes here). New positions (e.g., merchant positions when commerce is expanding) afford some opportunities for upward mobility, as does the vacating of positions by men who leave no heirs and by men who lack the skills required to retain their positions. Lenski finds the emergence of new positions less common a source of upward mobility than the latter two factors. In keeping with class differentiation, which provides for differential socialization and built-in privileges and disadvantages, upward mobility is generally one-step rather than extreme, rags-to-riches movement. The contribution of various factors to mobility here is difficult to estimate because of the paucity of data, but it is clear that variation in personal abilities and skills plays some part in differential mobility. Equally clear, however, is the predominant role of social structural factors in determining both the total amount of mobility and the various rates of mobility between the several social classes.

TRANSITIONAL SOCIETIES

With respect to moving toward modern industrial status, specific concern with personality factors related to mobility is again infrequently met in the literature.[14] A burgeoning array of data concerns personality factors in relation to economic growth from which, perhaps, valid inferences relevant to personality and mobility are derivable. But mobility bears no simple relation to economic growth. Miller and Bryce,[15] in a sample of 18 nations, fail to find consistent and clear-cut relations between indicators of economic growth and rates of upward and downward mobility.[16] The ensuing discussion of transitional nations, then, incorporates only that portion of the literature on economic growth in which the linkage to personality factors and mobility is fairly direct and explicit.

The extensive work on psychological factors and economic development undertaken by McClelland and his associates [17] may serve as a

[14] Moore states the situation aptly: "Many of the bits and fragments of 'evidence' on what causes native workers to work in unfamiliar surroundings have been gleaned from chance comments and explanations introduced *ad hoc* to explain particular circumstances that fell under the observer's eye while his primary attention was devoted to other questions." Wilbert E. Moore, *Industrialization and Labor* (Ithaca: Cornell University Press, 1951), p. 148.

[15] S. M. Miller and Herrington Bryce, "Social Mobility and Economic Growth and Structure," mimeographed paper reprinted from *Kolner Zeitschrift für Soziologie und Sozialpsychologie* (Special Issue 5, 1961), pp. 303-315.

[16] Whiteford's detailed evidence on mobility in two small Latin American cities, one undergoing rapid industrialization, the other relatively stable, also reveals a mixed picture. Higher rates of both upward and downward mobility are found in the growing city as compared to the stable one among persons of middle-class or higher status; but upward movement within the lower class is greater in the stable city, and movement out of the lower class occurred with equal frequency in the two cities. See Andrew H. Whiteford, *Two Cities of Latin America* (Beloit, Wisconsin: The Logan Museum of Anthropology, 1960), pp. 119-138.

[17] Much of this work is reported in David C. McClelland, *The Achieving Society* (Princeton: D. Van Nostrand Co., 1961). For a concise summary of this book, see David C. McClelland, "The Achievement Motive in Economic Growth," in Bert F. Hoselitz and Wilbert E. Moore (eds.), *Industrialization and Society* (Paris: UNESCO, 1963), pp. 74-95. McClelland's stress on motivation in economic development should not be dismissed as an isolated instance of a psychologist turning his attention to societal phenomena; motives have also been deemed important to economic development, although usually not studied in empirical detail by economists, sociologists, and anthropologists. Among the many writers who might be cited here, the diversity of interest is illustrated by the following: Charles J. Erasmus, *Man Takes Control* (Minneapolis: University of Minnesota Press, 1961); George M. Foster, *Traditional Cultures and the Impact of Technological Change* (New York: Harper & Row, 1962); William Arthur Lewis, *Theory of Economic Growth* (London: Allen & Unwin, 1955); Wilbert E. Moore, *op. cit.;* and Eugene Staley, *The Future of Underdeveloped Countries: Political Implications of Economic Development* (New York: Harper & Row, 1954).

point of departure for this discussion. McClelland assumes that societal values guide parents in rearing their children, varying value systems or ideologies thus giving rise to varying motivational dispositions, which persist as instigators of behavior when the children become adults. His major thesis is that parents who embrace an ideology stressing diligent work, self-reliance, and personal autonomy are apt to rear their children so as to inculcate in them strong motives to achieve.[18] Societies where the general level of achievement motivation is high, in comparison with societies in which it is low (and "other things being equal"), should show higher rates of economic development, then, for two reasons. First, economic activity is frequently, perhaps typically, perceived in success-failure terms by those who engage in it. Hence, the effort expended in economic activities should generally be greater in societies where the level of achievement motivation is high than where it is low, and this should lead to greater economic growth, "other things equal." Assessing the general level of achievement motivation by analyzing the content of children's readers, in a sample including both transitional and modern industrial societies, McClelland found statistically significant relations between strength of achievement motivation in both 1925 and 1950 and subsequent economic growth, in both 1925 and 1950.[19]

The second way in which the achievement motive is linked to economic development is via entrepreneurial activity. Assuming that entrepreneurial activity is an important factor in economic growth, McClelland relates experimental and other data on the behavior of persons with high n Achievement to a conceptual model of the entrepreneurial role, and concludes that:

. . . high n Achievement leads people to behave in most of the ways they should behave if they are to fulfill the entrepreneurial role successfully as it has been defined by economists, historians and sociologists.[20]

---

[18] The achievement motive, or n Achievement, is conceived as an enduring personality disposition to strive for success in situations where performance is to be evaluated in terms of some standard of excellence. The disposition, is assumed to be learned, so that its strength may vary as between individuals. I shall defer discussion of the measurement of n Achievement, its roots in social structural arrangements, and certain problems raised by critics regarding its use in the study of mobility and development until the next section of the paper dealing with modern industrial societies.

[19] McClelland, *op. cit.*, pp. 70-105. See also Rosen, who argues that "the relatively low levels of achievement motivation and achievement values among Brazilians, we believe, has been an adverse factor in Brazil's economic development, since the competitive, work-oriented, achievement motivated individual provides much of the human drive and direction on which economic growth depends." Bernard C. Rosen, "The Achievement Syndrome and Economic Growth in Brazil," *Social Forces*, 42 (March, 1964), pp. 341-54, quoted from p. 342.

[20] *Ibid.*, p. 238. I shall consider these findings in more detail in the next section of the paper.

To supplement the foregoing rather common-sense notions with some theoretically-based hypotheses concerning variation among societies in the relation between achievement motivation and mobility, a brief review of Atkinson's model of achievement motivation is necessary.[21]

In the Atkinson model, strength of performance in a situation, or aroused motivation, is conceived as a product of strength of achievement motive multiplied by the values of two situationally-given factors, "expectancy of success" and "incentive value of success." One's subjective expectancy of success in a given task is largely set by past experience, being higher or lower according to the relative frequency of success or failure in similar past situations. These past experiences also produce an inverse relation between expectancy of success and perceived difficulty of task: the lower the expectancy of success, the more difficult the task. The incentive value of success is conceived as the degree of satisfaction one attaches to the attainment of some goal. The model specifies an inverse relation between expectancy of success and incentive value of success, since goals seen as difficult to attain are likely to provide stronger satisfaction when reached than are goals seen as relatively easy to accomplish. Letting expectancy of success take values from 0 to 1.0, and setting incentive value of success equal to 1.0 minus the expectancy of success, the model generates two predictions: (1) for any given level of motive strength, aroused motivation to achieve is strongest for tasks in the middle range of apparent difficulty; (2) prefence for tasks perceived as intermediate increases with increments in strength of achievement motive.[22]

Empirical justification for applying this model to occupational mobility in industrial societies has been set forth in detail elsewhere.[23] Suffice it to say here that the properties of the model are present in the occupational prestige systems of such societies: occupations having higher prestige typically hold higher incentive values in the eyes of the

[21] John W. Atkinson, "Motivational Determinants of Risk-Taking Behavior," *Psychological Review*, 64 (November, 1957), pp. 359-372. Most critics of the achievement motive find the scheme too simple to produce much understanding of relations between personality and social structure or to explain much of the variance in mobility. The Atkinson model begins to meet these criticisms by tying together personal and situational factors in a scheme that generates predictions not immediately given in common sense.

[22] The model also takes account of the effects of striving through "fear of failure," conceived as a negative motive to avoid failure, as well as the positive motive to approach success (the achievement motive) discussed here. The full statement of the model cannot be given in the present sketch; interested readers are referred to Atkinson's original paper, cited in footnote 22.

[23] Harry J. Crockett, Jr., "The Achievement Motive and Differential Occupational Mobility in the United States," *American Sociological Review*, 27 (April, 1962), pp. 191-204.

population, and at the same time the difficulty of attaining specific occupations is typically perceived to increase with increments of prestige.

Now the degree to which the occupational prestige systems of transitional societies possess the properties specified in the Atkinson model is an open question. Assuming the model to be applicable, however, it is possible to identify different types of societies in terms of different combinations of expectancy of success and incentive value of success. If expectancy of success is interpreted here as the chance of rising very high in the occupational system, as viewed by the mass of the population,[24] then the low-expectancy-of-success situation is characteristic of more "closed" societies, and the middle expectancy of success situation, characteristic of more "open" systems.

For any given level of achievement motive strength, then, aroused motivation to achieve should be higher in "open" than in "closed" societies. Hence, if effort expended is positively related to goals attained, with average strength of achievement motive held constant, the relation between strength of achievement motive and mobility ought to be stronger in "open" societies than in "closed" societies. Second, the relation between strength of achievement motive and mobility should be stronger in "closed" than in "open" societies *only* when the average level of achievement motive is much higher in the "closed" than in the "open" society. Finally, within both "closed" and "open" societies, the relation between strength of achievement motive and mobility should increase with increments in average levels of achievement motive.[25]

As was the case with motives, evidence relating more or less consciously held values and attitudes to mobility in transitional societies must be garnered from studies of economic growth. The importance of these psychological factors in development, urged by many students,[26] is succinctly put by Ayal: [27]

. . . for economic development to come about, it is essential that the value system fulfill two functions. First, it has to provide goals, either public or

---

[24] Societies may well vary widely in the degree to which their members share similar perceptions of potential occupational mobility. Oversimplifying empirical reality here is essential, however, due to limitations of both knowledge and space.

[25] Although it has been necessary in this truncated discussion to make a number of assumptions that must be checked empirically in future research, enough has been said to indicate how Atkinson's theory of motivation may be used to generate testable and non-obvious propositions in the study of mobility in transitional societies as well as in industrial societies.

[26] See especially the excellent discussions of problems in this area in Ralph Braibanti and Joseph J. Spengler (eds.), *Tradition, Values, and Socio-Economic Development* (Durham, N.C.: Duke University Press, 1961).

[27] Eliezer B. Ayal, "Value Systems and Economic Development in Japan and Thailand," *Journal of Social Issues*, 19 (January, 1963), pp. 35-51.

private, which can be promoted by increased production. The ultimate goals may, but do not have to, be economic, but economic activity must be a path toward the achievement of the ultimate goals. They could be, for example, greater power and prestige, greater social welfare, etc. Second, the value system must generate, include, or at least sanction the means—namely, the propensities and the activities associated with them. The degree of fruition of the propensities in actual performance depends upon the environment, such as physical conditions, institutions, availability of knowledge, etc. But without the appropriate value system a favorable environment would not bring about development.[28]

Since different value configurations may be conducive to economic growth in different cultural contexts, the search for a general set of value-attitude configurations universally associated with development may be fruitless. Among the many cognitive factors deemed important to development by one writer or another, however, many have urged an important role for expanding knowledge of lines of action other than those traditionally given. Lerner [29] proposes that the spread of "empathic ability"—skill in perceiving and identifying with new experiences and roles—stemming from urbanization, the rise of literacy, and exposure to mass media influences, is essential in the modernizing of traditional societies. For accompanying the increase in empathic ability is a rise in curiosity and imaginativeness in dealing with life's problems, and this promotes innovation and change.[30] Lerner's thesis is developed by McClelland,[31] who finds "other-directedness"—a set of values and attitudes similar to Lerner's empathy concept—significantly related to economic growth. Similarly relevant here is Hagen's [32] emphasis, shared with numerous other writers, on "creativity" as a factor in development.[33]

[28] Ibid., p. 39.

[29] Daniel Lerner, The Passing of Traditional Society (New York: Free Press of Glencoe, 1958), especially pp. 48-73.

[30] This process is strikingly illustrated in the differential response of American Indian groups to subjugation by the white man. Comparative analysis of economic development of the Cherokee versus the Creek Indians subsequent to contact with whites shows that the Cherokees far outstripped the Creeks economically, over a period of more than a century. Closely bound up with the Cherokees' greater development was the major innovation, by Sequoyah, of a syllabary permitting these people to become literate, early in the 19th century, in their own language. The differential development of the two groups seems also to be linked with certain social structural differences in indigenous culture, but that is too complex a matter to pursue here. See Harry J. Crockett, Jr., "American Negro Relationships with the Cherokee and Creek Indians, 1540-1915," unpublished paper.

[31] McClelland, op. cit., pp. 192-197.

[32] Everett E. Hagen, On The Theory of Social Change (Homewood, Ill.: Dorsey Press, 1962), especially Chs. 7, 8, 9, 11 and 12.

[33] See for example Erasmus, op cit., pp. 11-12, 173-174; Bert F. Hoselitz, "Entrepreneurship and Economic Growth," American Journal of Economics and Sociology, 12 (October, 1952), pp. 97-110; Edward Shils, "The Concentration and Dispersion of Charisma: Their Bearing on Economic Policy in Underdeveloped Countries," World Politics, 11 (1958), pp. 1-19.

Much work remains to be done before the main sources of empathic ability, other directedness, and creativity may be confidently stated,[34] more before their relations to mobility are established. The works cited advance the hypothesis that persons with greater empathic ability, other-directedness, and creative capacity ought to evince greater upward mobility and less downward mobility in transitional societies. Research on these matters, to my knowledge, has yet to appear.

MODERN INDUSTRIAL SOCIETIES

The extensive analysis of the literature on psychological factors and mobility in industrial societies presented by Lipset and Bendix [35] provides a framework for organizing much of this portion of the paper. Their work permits me to emphasize materials published after 1958, and at the same time, it provides a base from which to assess the degree of cumulativeness and the extent of new developments revealed by research during this relatively short period.

Differential socialization in social class subcultures continues to affect mobility, especially by establishing different valuations of higher education among youths.[36] Darley [37] reports from both national sample data and studies of four separate states that proportionately fewer low-status than high-status persons, including those with superior abilities, actually enter college; while he does not assess the factors producing this result directly, differential motivation is presumably an important determinant. With regard to plans to enter college, as distinct from actual matriculation, Bordua reports significant differences by socio-economic background, among high school youths in two Massachusetts cities.[38] Other subcultural differences are also reported by Bordua: Men

[34] In addition to the factors cited from Lerner above, various writers have pointed to the importance of the nuclear family (versus extended family organization), peer groups, family power relations, and the nature of early socialization evaluated in terms of some standard of excellence. The disposition is assumed to experiences in the generation of these qualities. For a richly suggestive account relevant to many of these factors, see Hamed Ammar, *Growing Up in an Egyptian Village* (London: Routledge and Kegan Paul, 1954).

[35] Lipset and Bendix, *op. cit.*, pp. 227-259.

[36] Anderson's demonstration that education has less impact on mobility than typically assumed in the literature does not invalidate this point. For while education may be less important in determining the total amount of mobility than heretofore thought, increments of education continue to differentiate the mobile from the non-mobile among those starting from similar social positions. See C. Arnold Anderson, "A Skeptical Note on the Relation of Vertical Mobility to Education," *American Journal of Sociology*, 66 (May, 1961), pp. 560-570.

[37] John G. Darley, *Promise and Performance: A Study of Ability and Achievement in Higher Education* (Berkeley: University of California Press, 1962).

[38] David J. Bordua, "Educational Aspirations and Parental Stress on College," *Social Forces*, 38 (March, 1960), pp. 262-269.

more frequently than women plan to enter college, while Jews exceed Protestants who in turn exceed Catholics in plans to enter college. These socioeconomic, sex, and religious differences, while independent of one another, are all materially affected by parental stress on college attendance—another factor found important in the earlier studies reviewed by Lipset and Bendix. Within each social class, and among Jews, Protestants, and Catholics, the greater the parental stress on college attendance, the higher the proportions of youth planning to enter college.

Socioeconomic differences in ambition and mobility aspirations, and the effect of parental advice, are also reported in recent studies of high school youths in Los Angeles, Boulder, Colo., Kansas City, and the urban South.[39] Additionally, support for the effects of anticipatory socialization is reported in the Colorado study, where boys with high aspirations interacted with boys higher in status more than did those with low aspirations, and in the Southern study, where working-class boys with high mobility aspirations, compared with those with low aspirations, were more similar to ambitious middle-class boys in their tendency to name only middle-class boys as friends and to belong to more clubs and organizations. Thus, national sample data and independent studies in widely dispersed parts of the U.S. attest to persisting differences in aspiring to and attending college, arising from socioeconomic and religious background, parental advice, and peer-group influence.

Feldmesser's [40] comparative analysis of data for the Soviet Union and the United States suggests how a coercive system may alter these effects of status background. While Soviet youths from non-manual backgrounds were over-represented in college attendance to much the same extent as their counterparts in the United States, Soviet youths from manual backgrounds attended college in considerably greater proportions than did American youth from manual strata. Feldmesser concludes that the priority of the State over other agencies of socialization (class subcultures, families, the schools, and the mass media) produces a lower degree of cultural diversity in the Soviet Union than in the U.S., which is reflected in less variation throughout the Soviet status system

[39] Ralph H. Turner, "Some Family Determinants of Ambition," *Sociology and Social Research*, 46 (July, 1962), pp. 397-411; Gerald D. Bell, Processes in the Formation of Adolescents' Aspirations," *Social Forces*, 42 (December, 1963); pp. 179-186; Noel P. Gist and William S. Bennett, Jr., "Aspirations of Negro and White Students," *Social Forces*, 42 (October, 1963), pp. 40-48; and Richard L. Simpson, "Anticipatory Socialization and Social Mobility," *American Sociological Review*, 27 (August, 1962), pp. 517-522.

[40] Robert A. Feldmesser, "Social Status and Access to Higher Education: A Comparison of the United States and the Soviet Union," *Harvard Educational Review*, 27 (Spring, 1957), pp. 92-106.

in attitudes and motivations regarding higher education.[41] It is consistent with this position to suppose that intelligence may play a greater role in mobility in the Soviet Union and other coercive states than in the U.S. and the free industrial nations. This bald hypothesis of course requires qualification, one direction being offered by Turner's [42] comparison of "sponsored" with "contest" mobility in the educational systems of Britain and the U.S., respectively. Intelligence ought to affect mobility in Great Britain, where the state systematically selects candidates for college preparatory schooling in part on the basis of periodic intelligence tests, more than in the U.S., where such selection is generally lacking. As Lipset and Bendix [43] indicate, however, British youths from manual strata are heavily underrepresented in college attendance. More recently, Jackson and Marsden [44] have shown the extraordinary importance of motivation in determining the academic success of British working-class youth. Thus, while intelligence probably counts for more in college attendance in Britain than in the U.S., attitudinal and motivational differences stemming from class subcultures probably play a greater role in college attendance, and hence in mobility, in Great Britain than in the Soviet Union.[45]

For the relation between motivation and mobility, studies of achievement motivation assume primary importance. At the outset of this discussion, two themes running through the comments of most of my critics must be confronted. Turner states the first matter forcefully:

> One must ask whether so simple a concept as the achievement motive is psychologically meaningful. Has not the study of personality proceeded far enough that formulations can be made of a more complex character and based upon some conception of the nature of personality? The concept of need for achievement incorporates no conception of personality except as a bundle of motives which are inferred from the evidence of socially relevant behavior.[46]

[41] As to the nature of motivation here, Korol observes that in the competition for entry into Soviet schools of higher education "the ambition to get ahead is far stronger than motivations deriving from natural aptitudes or intellectual curiosity." Alexander G. Korol, *Soviet Education for Science and Technology* (Cambridge: Massachusetts Institute of Technology Press, 1957).

[42] Ralph H. Turner, "Sponsored and Contest Mobility and the School System," *American Sociological Review*, 25 (December, 1960), pp. 855-867.

[43] Lipset and Bendix, *op. cit.*, pp. 231-232.

[44] Brian Jackson and Dennis Marsden, *Education and the Working Class: Some General Themes Raised by a Study of 88 Working-Class Children in a Northern Industrial City* (New York: Monthly Review Press, 1962).

[45] While selection into Soviet schools of higher education on the basis of intelligence is blunted to some extent by such factors as State-administered admission quotas and special privilege for the children of the Party elite, intellectual capacity and performance remain the fundamental criteria of selection. See Korol, *op. cit.*, pp. 167-190.

[46] "Comments on Crockett," *op. cit.*, p. 6.

It is true that in the McClelland-Atkinson "school" motives are seen to "constitute the core of what is called personality." [47] Similarly, an explicit research strategy from the beginning of work on the achievement motive has been to abstract motives from the complex whole of personality for empirical study. [48] More complex schemes relating personality to mobility are also available. [49]

What reasons, then, may be given for my emphasis on achievement motivation? First, as an article of faith (although this "faith" seems to me far more supported than contradicted by available evidence), I believe the achievement motive, especially when considered as part of Atkinson's theoretical model of aroused achievement motivation, is highly relevant to differential mobility in industrial societies. Second, the major task attempted in this paper is to pull together the empirical research on personality factors and mobility; as it happens, not much empirical work exists on factors other than achievement motivation. [50]

The second common theme appearing in criticism of the work on achievement motivation concerns the measurement of n Achievement. Strenth of achievement motive is assessed through content analysis of stories written in response to relatively unstructured pictures (the thematic apperceptive, "TAT," technique) according to a standard scoring scheme. [51] This mode of measurement was originally tried out on the assumption that motives are largely unavailable to conscious awareness, hence might best be tapped through an indirect procedure.

Objections to this procedure are, essentially, that it yields an impure,

[47] John W. Atkinson, "Thematic Apperception Measurement of Motives Within the Context of a Theory of Motivation," in John W. Atkinson (ed.), Motives in Fantasy, Action, and Society (Princeton: D. Van Nostrand Co., 1958), pp. 596-616, quoted from p. 601.

[48] "In personality theory there is inevitably a certain impatience—a desire to solve every problem at once so as to get the "whole" personality in focus. We have proceeded the other way. By concentrating on one problem, on one motive, we have found in the course of our study that we have learned not only a lot about the achievement motive but other areas of personality as well. . . ." See David C. McClelland, John W. Atkinson, Russell A. Clark, and Edward A. Lowell, The Achievement Motive (New York: Appleton-Century-Crofts, 1953), p. vi.

[49] For two recent examples, see Hagen, op. cit., and John H. Kunkel, "Psychological Factors in the Analysis of Economic Development," Journal of Social Issues, 19 (January, 1963), pp. 68-87.

[50] Systematic study of achievement motivation by McClelland, Atkinson and their associates has provided a theoretical base and a fund of experimental and other empirical knowledge far beyond that available for any other motives that might be relevant to mobility. The cumulative record of this work is documented in McClelland, et al., op. cit. (1953); Atkinson, op. cit. (1958); and McClelland, op. cit. (1961).

[51] For details of the procedure and practice materials, see Charles P. Smith and Sheila Feld, "How to Learn the Method of Content Analysis for n Achievement, n Affiliation, and n Power," in Atkinson, op. cit. (1958), pp. 685-735.

imprecise measure of motive strength, and that it is not valid in diverse cultures. Regarding the first point, Turner notes that while thematic content may reveal what a person wants, it may also reveal what a person is anxious about or simply what he frequently experiences in day-to-day life. Unquestionably, these sources of error are present in the measure. Moreover, numerous other factors are relevant to the story-collecting situation and, if not controlled, they may confound measurement.[52] In fact, the measure is relatively crude, and this is reflected in the practice of employing median breaks, rather than statistically stronger classifications, in most research in this area. But measurement difficulties are endemic in social research, and I believe the evidence to be reviewed demonstrates the adequacy of the procedure for research purposes.

Assuming motives to be largely unconscious and hence assessing motive strength through a projective test seems to me to have been fruitful in a number of ways. First, the procedure avoids the circularity inherent in postulating the existence of some internal disposition after the behavior supposedly instigated by the disposition has occurred—the sort of fallacious reasoning that brought about the demise of instinct theory. Instead, motive strength is assessed separately from the situational context in which performance is to be predicted. Second a wealth of evidence shows that consciously held values and attitudes concerning achievement are not significantly related to motive strength as tapped by thematic apperception; people are not especially good judges of their own or others' achievement dispositions.[53] Continuing efforts to devise paper-and-pencil tests to substitute for the relatively costly TAT procedure have been generally unsuccessful.[54] Finally, where measures

[52] See Charles P. Smith, "Achievement-Related Motives and Goal-Setting Under Different Conditions," *Journal of Personality*, 31 (1963), pp. 124-140.

of both n Achievement and achievement values were used to predict

[53] See Michael Argyle and Peter Robinson, "Two Origins of Achievement Motivation," *British Journal of Social and Clinical Psychology*, 1 (June, 1962), pp. 107-120; Richard C. de Charms, H. William Morrison, Walter R. Reitman, and David C. McClelland, "Behavioral Correlates of Directly and Indirectly Measured Achievement Motivation," in David C. McClelland (ed.), *Studies in Motivation* (New York: Appleton-Century-Crofts, 1955), pp. 414-423; Herbert H. Meyer, William B. Walker, and George H. Litwin, "Motive Patterns and Risk-Preferences Associated with Entrepreneurship," *Journal of Abnormal and Social Psychology*, 63 (1963), pp. 570-574; Fred L. Strodtbeck, "Family Interaction, Values, and Achievement," in David C. McClelland, Alfred L. Baldwin, Urie Bronfenbrenner and Fred L. Strodtbeck, *Talent and Society* (Princeton, D. Van Nostrand Co., 1958), pp. 135-194.

[54] For a recent review and extension of this work, see John W. Atkinson and Patricia O'Connor, "Neglected Factors in the Study of Achievement-Oriented Performance: Social Approval as an Incentive and Performance Decrement," unpublished paper.

achievement behavior, the former was the better predictor, as should be the case if effort is instigated by unconscious motivation.[55]

On the question of cross-cultural validity, critics say that achievement-related themes vary from culture to culture, and hence no single measure of achievement motive is valid for all cultures. Here I believe we have an open question, which will not be quickly resolved. The wisest course seems to me the pragmatic one: try the measure out in many cultures.

What now may be said concerning achievement motivation and mobility? The evidence concerns (1) relations between n Achievement, educational and occupational aspirations, and school performance: (2) relations between n Achievement and entrepreneurial behavior; and (3) relations between n Achievement and occupational mobility.

Rosen [56] found strength of n Achievement unrelated to aspirations for college education among New England high school youths. As he points out, strong achievement motive may induce persistent striving for "success," but the definition of success-relevant situations is a function of cognitive factors—attitudes and values. Thus in Rosen's sample, while many youths, especially those from working-class backgrounds, may be strongly motivated to achieve, they may not value success in the educational system; consequently, strength of achievement motive is unrelated to educational aspirations. Burnstein, Moulton and Liberty, following Rosen's suggestion that both n Achievement and achievement values are important in predicting behavior, show that college students scoring high on both variables prefer occupations requiring high competence relative to prestige conferred, while students low in n Achievement and achievement values prefer occupations bestowing high prestige relative to competence demanded.[57] Similarly relevant here is Mahone's study, employing a measure of the motive to avoid failure as well as the n Achievement measure.[58] Mahone found that the occupational aspirations of college students with strong achievement motive

[55] See deCharms et al., op. cit.; Bernard C. Rosen, "The Achievement Syndrome: A Psychocultural Dimension of Social Stratification," American Sociological Review, 21 (April, 1956), pp. 203-211. But see also Strodtbeck, op. cit., who reports significant, independent relations between both n Achievement and achievement values on the one hand, and achievant behavior on the other. Turner's reminder that present evidence does not demonstrate better prediction of upward mobility by strength of achievement motive versus more direct measures of aspiration and achievement strivings must also be entered here.

[56] Rosen, "The Achievement Syndrome: A Psychocultural Dimension of Social Stratification," op. cit., pp. 208-210.

[57] Eugene Burnstein, Robert Moulton and Paul Liberty, Jr., "Prestige Versus Excellence as Determinants of Role Attractiveness," American Sociological Review, 28 (April, 1963), pp. 212-219.

[58] Charles H. Mahone, 'Fear of Failure and Unrealistic Vocational Aspiration," Journal of Abnormal and Social Psychology, 60 (March, 1960), pp. 253-261.

and weak motive to avoid failure were commensurate with their own estimated ability, while students weak in achievement motive and strong in motive to avoid failure aspired significantly more often to occupations either much above or much below their own estimated ability level. These studies taken together suggest that to the degree that aspirations and preferences are translated into action, persons with strong n Achievemen may well strive harder for more realistic goals, than those weak in achivement motive.[59] In terms of mobility, then, persons from comparable social positions with strong n Achievement should be upwardly mobile more often than those weak in motive to achieve.

As noted in connection with aspirations, a strong positive relation between n Achievement and academic performance should be expected only among those who conceive school as a domain in which they should excel. Since none of the studies of n Achievement in relation to school performance control for this factor, it is not surprising that the expected relationships are not always observed.[60] Students who do not define the academic domain as one in which to do well, however, are probably numerous only in high school and grammar school; most college students, no doubt, would affirm that academic success in college is a relevant concern. Yet many of the studies in which the expected relation between achievement motive and academic performance was not found were studies of college students. There is an important point to consider here.

Differences in intelligence might depress the relation between achievement motive and school performance; some of the studies in which I.Q. is controlled find no relation between strength of achievement motive and college grades. But in making this inference, as McClelland and his colleagues have noted,[61] one must assume that n Achievement is not one of the determinants of measured intelligence. Fortunately, longitudinal data bearing on this assumption are available.

Kagan *et al.*[62] hypothesized that performance on an I.Q. test is a function of abilities and skills plus the motivation to learn and to do

---

[59] Experimental confirmation of differential task-persistence as a function of n Achievement versus motive to avoid failure is presented by Norman T. Feather, "The Relationship of Persistence at a Task to Expectation of Success and Achievement Related Motives," *Journal of Abnormal and Social Psychology*, 63 (1961) pp. 552-561, and "The Study of Persistence," *Psychological Bulletin*, 59 (1962), pp. 94-155.

[60] See Rosen, "The Achievement Syndrome: A Psychocultural Dimension of Social Stratification," *op. cit.*; and studies reported in Atkinson, *Motives in Fantasy, Action, and Society*, *op. cit.*, pp. 521, 605, and McClelland, *et al.*, *The Achievement Motive op. cit.*, pp. 237-242.

[61] McClelland, *et al.*, *The Achievement Motive, op. cit.*, p. 238.

[62] Jerome Kagan, Lester W. Sontag, Charles T. Baker, and Virginia L. Nelson, "Personality and I.Q. Change," *Journal of Abnormal and Social Psychology*, 56 (1958), pp. 261-266.

well on tests. In a sample of boys and girls whose I.Q. scores at age six were roughly similar (all were above 115), they found a significant positive relation between n Achievement (measured for most subjects at ages 11 and 12) and increase in I.Q. test score. They concluded that "high motivation to achieve, competitive strivings, and curiosity about nature may motivate the acquisition of intellectual skills and knowledge which, in turn, facilitates increases in tested I.Q."[63] Kagan and Moss report in addition that change in I.Q. between ages six and ten is not a function of initial intellectual capacity.[64] These studies support the interpretation that the achievement motive is not identical with measured intelligence, but rather seems to be one of the determinants of increases in measured intelligence.[65]

Further light on these matters is afforded by Eckland's unique data on the relations between intelligence, social class background and college education, and occupational mobility.[66] Assessing the college performance and subsequent occupational attainments over a ten-year period of an age-cohort of men entering a large midwestern university in 1952, Eckland shows that gaining a college degree has more effect on upward occupational mobility than does either social class background or intelligence (as measured by the A.C.E. college entrance tests). Moreover, among those who take more than four years to attain the college degree (the majority of all graduates), social class background is more predictive of college graduation than is ability. Eckland suggests, then, that persistence to the college degree among these men is primarily a function of class-linked motivation and values, rather than intelligence.

Among persons who value success in school, then, strength of achievement motive should be related to academic success, and hence, so far as education determines mobility, to subsequent mobility. Strength of

---

[63] *Ibid.*, p. 266.

[64] Jerome Kagan and Howard H. Moss, "Stability and Validity of Achievement Fantasy," *Journal of Abnormal and Social Psychology,*" 58 (1959), pp. 357-364. Evidence extending these effects into adulthood is reported in Jerome Kagan and Howard H. Moss, *Birth to Maturity* (New York: John Wiley & Sons, 1962), pp. 148-152.

[65] Given these results, Robinson's finding that among British school children with similar I.Q. scores, those selected for grammar school were stronger in n Achievement than those rejected probably means that strong n Achievement led to harder work in school and hence to selection for grammar school. See Peter Robinson, "The Measurement of Achievement Motivation," unpublished doctoral dissertation (Oxford University, 1961).

[66] Bruce K. Eckland, "Social Class and College Graduation: Some Misconceptions Corrected," *American Journal of Sociology,* 7 (July, 1964), pp. 36-51, and "The Relative Importance of Class, Intelligence and Higher Education in Determining the Occupational Achievement of College Dropouts and Graduates," paper given at the annual meeting of the American Sociological Association, 1964.

achievement motive should also be related to mobility among those who do not value success in school; many occupations representing upward movement for working-class youth do not require much formal education, although the effects of education are such that even those with strong achievement motive in this group should be less upwardly mobile than those with weak achievement motive in the group valuing (and presumably in goodly proportion obtaining) higher education. Finally, these data underscore the need for complex research designs, incorporating measures of intelligence, values, and motivations, in future studies of differential mobility.

Atkinson and Hoselitz have analyzed motivational factors in entrepreneurship, explicitly recognizing that basic skills, intelligence, and relevant values and attitudes are important factors in entrepreneurial success, but choosing to begin work in this area by stressing motivational factors. They reason that "if, as is generally supposed, individuals differ greatly in the strength of their motives for certain kinds of satisfaction, the person whose motives correspond to the kinds of satisfaction that are to be experienced in meeting the demands of entrepreneurship should be attracted to it and should perform the role with great efficiency and satisfaction." [67] McClelland carries this interest forward by linking entrepreneurial success with strong achievement motive:

> The achievement motive should lead people to seek out situations which provide moderate challenges to their skills, to perform better in such situations, and to have greater confidence in the likelihood of their success. It should make them conservative where things are completely beyond their control, as in games of chance, and happier where they have some opportunity of influencing the outcome of a series of events by their own actions and of knowing concretely what those actions have accomplished." [68]

A few beginning studies of achievement motive and entrepreneurship suggest that mobility and stability in entrepreneurial occupations may be in part a function of strength of n Achievement.[69] And future research should incorporate the work of economic historians, whose analyses have stressed the importance, in successful entrepreneurship,

[67] John W. Atkinson and Bert F. Hoselitz, "Entrepreneurship and Personality," *Explorations in Entrepreneurial History*, 10 (1958), pp. 107-112; quoted from p. 110.

[68] McClelland, *The Achieving Society, op. cit.*, p. 238.

[69] *Ibid.*, pp. 260-266. These studies also support the cross-cultural validity of the TAT in measuring n Achievement, as do James T. Tedeschi and Mohamed Kian, "Cross-Cultural Study of the TAT Assessment for Achievement Motivation: Americans and Persians," *Journal of Social Psychology*, 58 (December, 1962), pp. 227-234; and Tamotsu Hayashi and Kaoru Habu, "A Research on Achievement Motive: An Experimental Test of the 'Thought-Sampling' Method by Using Japanese Students," *Japanese Psychological Research*, (April, 1962), pp. 30-42.

of group affiliations and motivations arising from the total social structure.[70]

Occupational mobility has been related to strength of achievement motive in a sample representing men of non-farm background in the U.S.[71] Strength of achievement motive was associated with upward mobility among men from the lower portion of the occupational prestige hierarchy (NORC prestige scores below 69) but not among men from the upper portion of the hierarchy (NORC prestige scores above 68).[72] These results persisted in trend, although with some reduction in strength, under controls for age, education, marital status, and the presence of children in the home.[73] Moreover, the results could not be attributed to strong general motivation, since separate analyses of affiliation and power motives in relation to mobility disclosed only slight and inconsistent relationships.[74] With regard to downward mobility, no strong differences attributable to achievement motive were found.

[70] See, for example, William Miller (ed.), *Men in Business* (Cambridge: Harvard University Press, 1952).

[71] Crockett, "The Achievement Motive and Differential Occupational Mobility in the United States," *op. cit.* Additional analyses of data for sons of farmers and for women are presented in Harry J. Crockett, Jr., "Achievement Motivation and Occupational Mobility in the United States," unpublished doctoral dissertation (University of Michigan, 1960), pp. 182-203. For assessment of the validity of the TAT measure of n Achievement in a national sample survey, see Joseph Veroff, John W. Atkinson, Sheila C. Feld, and Gerald Gurin, "The Use of Thematic Apperception to Assess Motivation in a Nationwide Interview Study," *Psychological Monographs,* 74 (Whole Number 499, Fall, 1960). The data were obtained in a Survey Research Center study conducted in 1957 and reported in Gerald Gurin, Joseph Veroff and Sheila Feld, *Americans View Their Mental Health* (New York: Basic Books, 1960). In the sub-sample discussed here, N=368.

[72] Occupational prestige was scored on the basis of the scheme developed by Paul Hatt and Cecil C. North reported in "Jobs and Occupations: A Popular Evaluation," in Reinhard Bendix and Seymour M. Lipset (eds.), *Class, Status and Power* (New York: Free Press of Glencoe, 1953), pp. 411-426. Re-examination of these findings in the light of the methods developed by Duncan, and by Duncan and Hodge, has not been possible, but I believe the findings would persist using the methods presented by these authors. See Otis Dudley Duncan, "A Socioeconomic Index for all Occupations," and "Properties and Characteristics of the Socioeconomic Index," in Albert J. Reiss, Jr., *Occupations and Social Status* (New York: Free Press of Glencoe, 1961), pp. 109-161; and Otis Dudley Duncan and Robert W. Hodge, "Education and Occupational Mobility: A Regression Analysis," *American Journal of Sociology,* 68 (May, 1963), pp. 629-644.

[73] In addition, relations between strength of achievement motive and region of birth, rural-urban residence, race, religion and nativity were examined, in each case with occupational prestige level of origin controlled. These analyses did not indicate that positive results regarding strength of achievement motive and occupational mobility had been inflated. See Crockett, "Achievement Motivation and Occupational Mobility in the United States," *op. cit.,* pp. 64-72.

[74] Only among men from the upper middle portion of the prestige hierarchy (NORC scores from 69-77) was a marked relationship observed; here, men strong in affiliative motive were considerably more likely to be upward mobile than those weak in affiliative motive. Crockett, "The Achievement Motive and Differential Occupational Mobility in the United States," *op. cit.,* pp. 199-200.

These initial data, showing that strength of achievement motive is related to upward mobility in a national sample, are taken to indicate that n Achievement is one determinant of such differential mobility in industrial societies. Since these results stem from cross-sectional data, however, they could be interpreted quite differently; one could argue that the experience of upward mobility (or stability, among those with higher-status origins), i.e., success in the occupational sphere, gives rise to strong n Achievement. This position is taken by Littig [75] on the basis of data from a recent sample survey in Corning, N.Y. While Littig finds evidence supporting the relations between n Achievement and mobility reported above, he also reports a tendency for strength of n Achievement to be related to present class position more strongly than to class of origin. This latter trend, however, is marked only among women, and occupational mobility via strong achievement motive is theoretically expected only for men.[76] The issue cannot be decided in the absence of longitudinal data, but the evidence regarding acquisition of strong achievement motive (to be considered shortly), together with the absence of evidence supporting other explanations for differential mobility, favors the position taken here.[77]

McClelland's summary of the child-rearing literature related to n Achievement through 1960 affords a convenient point of departure for considering the sources of achievement motivation:

To begin with, let us list the "extremes" that do not develop n Achievement. First, father-dominance is one extreme in which the son develops low self-reliance and n Achievement because the father makes the decisions and little pressure is put on the son to work out high standards for himself. Secondly, another extreme is simply low standards of excellence and an indulgent attitude toward the son that obviously should not promote his n Achievement. Still a third "extreme" is very early achievement demands . . . , where the son

---

[75] Lawrence W. Littig and Constantine A. Yeracaris, "Effects of Motivation on Intergenerational Occupational Mobility," *Journal of Abnormal and Social Psychology,* forthcoming.

[76] The achievement motive seems to be engaged for women by situations in which concern over social approval is paramount, a concern which is essentially irrelevant to arousal of the motive among men. See the summary of studies presented in Crockett, "Achievement Motivation and Occupational Mobility in the United States," *op. cit.,* pp. 188-189.

[77] Morgan and his associates report data from a national sample study of heads of households that support the present interpretation. They find that children of persons with strong achievement motive obtain more schooling than children of persons with weak achievement motive. Since it is highly unlikely that parents' n Achievement would be formed after their children had completed their schooling; parental n Achievement must precede children's education. If these parents pass on their achievement concerns to children, strength of achievement motive should be antecedent to mobility among the children. See James N. Morgan, Martin H. David, Wilbur J. Cohen, and Harvey E. Brazer, *Income and Welfare in the United States* (New York: McGraw-Hill, 1962), pp. 376-378.

is, so to speak, thrust out of the nest before he is ready to fly. What lies in the middle of all these extremes is reasonably high standards of excellence imposed at a time when the son can obtain them, a willingness to let him attain them without interference, and real emotional pleasure in his achievements short of overprotection and indulgence.[78]

While low n Achievement is associated in these studies with father-dominance in the family, it is equally associated with father-absence; mothers in father-absent households apparently are more frequently indulgent and less rewarding of achieving behavior than those in intact families. Strodtbeck suggests, in addition, that the development of strong n Achievement in boys is probably facilitated by adequate identification with the male role.[79]

Turner has an alternative explanation for these relationships:

If we consider the character of a family in which the mother takes the primary responsibility for training a boy, although a father is present, we seem to have exactly the configuration that would be expected when the father is himself busily pursuing achievement in the conventional fashion. The father is head of the household but he is much too busy with his business and professional activities to take the primary responsibility for handling the child. Consequently, there is every reason to suppose that these correlations might simply be an artifact of the fact that those families in which preoccupation with achievement is already strong will tend to transmit the same preoccupation with achievement to their children. Only if we could hold constant these relevant variables could we have evidence which supported in an important way the achievement motive formulation.[80]

Turner's own study of ambitions among Los Angeles high school seniors illustrates the importance of watching out for artifactual relationships in this area.[81] His data show that boys whose mothers have more education than their fathers are more ambitious than boys where this is not the case, suggesting that disparagement of the father's attainments by the mother raises the son's level of ambition. But higher ambition is also found among boys whose fathers have more education than is necessary for their occupational positions leading Turner to conclude that the hypothesis of the special influence of the mother washed out in favor of the more parsimonious principle that any element in the family situation which introduces a higher class component contributes to mobility." [82] While the hypothesis of the mother's special influence is

[78] McClelland, The Achieving Society, op. cit., p. 356.
[79] Strodtbeck, op. cit., p. 148.
[80] Turner, "Comments on Crockett," op. cit., p. 16.
[81] Turner, "Some Family Determinants of Ambition," op. cit.; and Ralph H. Turner, The Social Context of Ambition (San Francisco: Chandler Publishing Co., 1964).
[82] "Comments on Crockett," op. cit., p. 17.

not clearly refuted (when the father's educational attainments exceed his occupational attainments, the mother may belittle his occupational performance and hence increase her son's ambition), the necessity for controls minimizing the possibility of artifactual findings is established.

Several recent studies bear on the supposed familial sources of variation in n Achiement. The negative relation between father-absence and n Achievement is reported by Nuttall among a sample of Boston Negroes.[83] Rosen finds average strength of achievement motive significantly lower among a sample of Brazilian boys in comparison with an American sample, and relates this difference to two of the factors discussed above: Brazilian mothers less frequently than American mothers train their sons to be self-reliant, autonomous, and achieving, and Brazilian families are much more frequently dominated by an authoritarian father.[84] Additional cross-cultural data supporting the same general picture are presented by Prothro:

> On the whole it may be concluded that those Lebanese groups which show outstanding achievement are characterized by mothers who reward successful accomplishment, who foster independence, and who predominate over the father in the control of the young child.[85]

The data reviewed by McClelland [86] also link these familial sources of variation in achievement motive strength to such social structural factors as social class, ethnicity, and religion. Of these, class subcultures, through their effect on socialization practices, produce more variation in n Achievement than do either ethnic or religious subcultures; only the effects associated with the Jewish subculture were commensurate with those of social class.[87] Typically, middle-class families exhibit more of the features thought to give rise to strong achievement motive than do working-class families, and middle-class children score higher, on the average, in achievement motive than working-class children. Variations among cultures in average strength of achievement motive, associated with variations in value configurations at the total cultural level, are

[83] Ronald L. Nuttall, "Some Correlates of High Need for Achievement among Urban Northern Negroes," *Journal of Abnormal and Social Psychology*, forthcoming.

[84] Bernard C. Rosen, "Socialization and Achievement Motivation in Brazil," *American Sociological Review*, 27 (October, 1962), pp. 612-624.

[85] E. Terry Prothro, *Child Rearing in the Lebanon* (Cambridge: Harvard University Press, 1961), esp. pp. 141-152; quoted from p. 152.

[86] McClelland, *The Achieving Society, op. cit.*, pp. 356-383.

[87] Differences between Jews and non-Jews in values and family authority relations are considered responsible for this result, and to have produced the notably greater upward mobility of American Jews in comparison with non-Jews. A detailed exposition subsequent to the studies reviewed by McClelland is Nathan Hurvitz, "Sources of Motivation and Achievement of American Jews," *Jewish Social Studies*, 23 (October, 1961), pp. 217-234.

also apparent in the studies reviewed by McClelland. These results are affirmed by Rosen's comparative data for Brazil and the United States: American boys from the lowest class group score significantly higher in achievement motive than do boys in any of the class groups in Brazil.[88]

Passing now to other psychological factors affecting mobility in modern societies, Straus offers additional evidence supporting the importance of deferred need-gratifications (evidence both for and against this proposition was reviewed by Lipset and Bendix [89]) from his study of Wisconsin high school boys.[90] Deferral of need gratifications (using a combined scale of needs for affiliation, aggression, consumption, economic independence, and sex) was significantly related to both high school grades and occupational aspirations. Moreover, these results were maintained under controls for socioeconomic status and intelligence.

Although it does not deal directly with the deferral of need-gratifications, Ellis and Lane's [91] panel study of college youths from lower socioeconomic strata may be cited here to illustrate probable connections between personality characteristics and social structural factors in mobility. Lower-class college students, compared with students from higher social strata, were more influenced by adults outside their families (especially high school teachers) both in deciding to enter college and in choosing an undergraduate major. It may be obvious to suggest that personal characteristics of lower-class students—including superior intelligence,[92] as well as such factors as the deferred gratification pattern—lead adults outside their families to befriend and guide them. It may be less obvious to suggest that this process of selection by adults is *most* influenced by the non-intellective personality factors; that is, given a pool of highly talented lower-class youth, those who possess additional positively-valued personality attributes will receive extra-familial adult support and assistance. My hypothesis is that by the time this selection occurs, socialization by parents and peers has crystallized the non-intellective personality components of these students, and support from extra-family adults is then largely determined by degree of conformity to middle-class personality preferences. Thus, those selected for encouragement are far more likely to exhibit such factors as deferral of gratification than those passed over. Simultaneous study of personality and social

[88] Rosen, "Socialization and Achievement Motivation in Brazil," *op. cit.*, especially pp. 617-618, 622-623.

[89] Lipset and Bendix, *Social Mobility in Industrial Society, op. cit.*, pp. 247-249.

[90] Murray A. Straus, "Deferred Gratification, Social Class, and the Achievement Syndrome," *American Sociological Review*, 27 (June, 1962), pp. 326-335.

[91] Robert A. Ellis and W. Clayton Lane, "Structural Supports for Upward Mobility," *American Sociological Review*, 28 (October, 1963), pp. 743-756.

[92] Lower-class students scored higher on college entrance tests, on the average, than did the other students in the sample. *Ibid.*, p. 754.

structural factors in this aspect of mobility process seems long overdue.[93] McGuire has suggested that mobility may be motivated for some by anxiety and neurotic strivings,[94] a suggestion supported in some but by no means all of the studies of aspirations and mobility reviewed by Lipset and Bendix.[95] Recent studies continue to provide evidence supporting as well as contradicting the proposition. Morrow and Wilson, analyzing self-reports by high-achieving and low-achieving high school boys matched on I.Q., grade in school, and socioeconomic status, find that the high-achieving boys have more friendly, positive, non-stressful relations with parents than the low achievers do.[96] On the other hand, Bieri, *et al.*, assessing psychological factors in mobility in a small sample of New York City men, report less "dominance" and less "acceptance of authority" (factors probably linked to neurotic striving) among upwardly mobile Jewish men than among the non-mobile, but this finding does not hold among Catholic men.[97] It seems fair to conclude from research to data that neurotic, anxious motivations stemming from unresolved resentments and conflicts in early socialization are not important determinants of differential mobility.

Some widespread ideas concerning personality factors in mobility, found in the work of such diverse thinkers as Miller and Swanson, Mills, Riesman, and Whyte, should be noted in concluding this section.[98] The common thread in these works is something as follows. Fundamental change in occupational structure and work setting occurs as societies achieve full industrial status. The proportions of independent farmers and unskilled laborers in the occupational system are sharply reduced, while the proportions of professionals and especially of minor white-collar

[93] Lipset and Bendix suggested a similar hypothesis in 1959: "Thus, lower-class individuals who exhibit good work habits, cleanliness, concern for personal appearance, and generally follow the established rules of "middle class morality" are much more likely to move up in the social structure than those who reject these norms." The empirical work on this matter, however, remains to be done. See Lipset and Bendix, *Social Mobility in Industrial Society, op. cit.,* p. 258.

[94] Carson McGuire, "Social Stratification and Mobility Patterns," *American Sociological Review,* 15 (April, 1950), pp. 195-204.

[95] Lipset and Bendix, *Social Mobility in Industrial Society, op. cit.,* pp. 249-254.

[96] William R. Morrow and Robert C. Wilson, "Family Relations of Bright, High-Achieving and Under-Achieving High School Boys," *Child Development,* 32 (1961), pp. 501-510.

[97] James Bieri, Robin Lobeck and Harold Plotnick, "Psychosocial Factors in Differential Social Mobility," *Journal of Social Psychology,* 58 (October, 1962), pp. 183-200.

[98] Daniel R. Miller and Guy E. Swanson, *The Changing American Parent* (New York: John Wiley & Sons, 1958); C. Wright Mills, *White Collar* (New York: Oxford University Press, 1951); David Riesman, Nathan Glazer, and Reuel Denney, *The Lonely Crowd* (New Haven: Yale University Press, 1950); and William H. Whyte, *The Organization Man* (New York: Simon and Schuster, 1956).

workers (the "new middle classes") are sharply increased. The work setting, in turn, shifts from one in which most individuals work on their own or in firms of small size to one in which most individuals work in large-scale organizations. Where individuals were previously led to compete occupationally with others, they are now called on to blend their personalities harmoniously with the personalities of others working in the same organization and to fit their efforts co-operatively into the complicated activity through which some group-product is achieved. Changes in occupational structure and work setting, then, alter the terms on which occupational success and upward mobility are widely available. Rather than rewarding the self-reliant, competitive, risk-taking individual (Riesman's "inner-directed" man) as before, the present social arrangements reward the friendly, affiliative person whose greatest satisfactions are derived from effective performance as a member of a team (Riesman's "other-directed" man).

While there is some evidence that the structural changes just described have affected child-rearing ideology and practice,[99] almost no evidence regarding the hypothesized shift in the personality bases of mobility has appeared.[100] This is a highly promising line of inquiry for future study.

CONCLUDING REMARKS

Since I have summarized the substantive findings reported in this paper at appropriate points throughout, I shall devote this section to some promising next steps for research in this area.

A prime necessity is the discovery and theoretical explication of additional personality factors systematically related to mobility within diverse

[99] In addition to the works cited above, see Urie Bronfenbrenner, "Socialization and Social Class Through Time and Space," in Eleanor E. Maccoby, Theodore M. Newcomb, and E. L. Hartley (eds.), *Readings in Social Psychology* (New York: Holt, Rinehart & Winston, 1958); Alex Inkeles, "Social Change and Social Character: The Role of Parental Mediation," *Journal of Social Issues*, 11 (1955), pp. 12-23; Celia B. Stendler, "Sixty Years of Child Training Practices, *Journal of Pediatrics*, 36 (1950), pp. 122-134; Murray A. Straus and Lawrence J. Houghton, "Achievement, Affiliation, and Co-operation Values as Clues to Trends in American Rural Society, 1924-1958," *Rural Sociology*, 25 (December, 1960), pp. 394-403 and Martha Wolfenstein, "Trends in Infant Care," *American Journal of Orthopsychiatry*, 23 (1953), pp. 120-130.

[100] National sample data discussed earlier revealed no *general* tendency for strength of affiliative motive to affect mobility, but strong affiliative motive was significantly related to upward mobility among sons of fathers in the upper middle portion of the occupational prestige hierarchy. See Crockett, "The Achievement Motive and Differential Occupational Mobility in the United States," *op. cit.*, pp. 199-200.

societies. One strategy for discovering such factors may be outlined as follows. First, assess the major values of a given society—personality factors relevant to mobility ought to vary as a function of such values. Second, estimate the fit between the received cultural values and the actual behavioral possibilities and requirements laid down by structural arrangements, especially in regard to occupational roles. Where rapid social change is taking place, the fit between ideology and social structure is apt to be loose, so that variables presumed important from an examination of ideology may prove less fruitful when viewed in the light of changing structural arrangements. Third, from the basic values plus the role-requirements, deduce the types of behavior that logically should enhance or impede mobility, and finally, infer the personality attributes that logically should lead individuals to behave in the ways indicated by the preceding analysis. At this point, personality theory may provide the necessary concepts, but it is likely that the researcher will have to develop both personality concepts and adequate measures thereof. In any case, however, this procedure should discover personality variables related to mobility more efficiently than studies employing variables selected intuitively or variables that happen to be convenient. One example of this procedure is the work on achievement motive and mobility reviewed earlier in the paper.[101]

Turner's valuable suggestions on this procedure merit quoting in full:

There is an important distinction to be made between what we might call *favored personality* [102] and *exemplary personality*. The exemplary personality refers to the configuration which is held up as an example to be emulated and whose components are deliberately taught in the society. It does not necessarily follow, however, in the simple fashion that Ruth Benedict proposed, that the characteristics which fit the valued model are necessarily those which equip the individual for succeeding in the society. Accordingly, the term favored personality had best be reserved for those characteristics which actually pay off in the light of social structure and which often do not correspond with the exemplary personality. Indeed, it is a major function of the journalist and the publicity agent and the myth-maker to create an image of the successful individual which corresponds to the exemplary personality, even though in fact the correspondence is not there. It does not then follow automatically that personality characteristics which lead to behavior which is con-

---

[101] This general research strategy for relating personality variables to social structure is of course not novel. For excellent examples of similar procedures, apart from studies of mobility, see Miller and Swanson, *The Changing American Parent, op. cit.*; and Guy E. Swanson, "Determinants of the Individual's Defenses Against Inner Conflict: Review and Reformulation," in John C. Glidewell (ed.), *Parental Attitudes and Child Behavior* (Springfield, Ill.: Charles C. Thomas, 1961).

[102] The notion of favored personality is developed in Don Martindale and Elio D. Monachesi, *Elements of Sociology* (New York: Harper & Row, 1951), pp. 321-333, 359-376.

sistent with the values and ideology of the society will necessarily facilitate mobility.[103]

High priority should also be assigned to studies of personality factors in the mobility of women through marriage. Do women who marry above or below their original social positions have distinctive personality attributes? What about women who marry men of similar social positions, whose husbands in time rise or fall considerably in social status? If personality factors are related to mobility through marriage among women, do the mobile women differ from the majority in their strata of origin or destination with regard to socialization practices they themselves underwent or now employ? Given that personality factors affect mobility among men, and that socialization is fundamental to personality formation, answers to questions of this sort may be of considerable practical importance, apart from their intrinsic theoretical interest. For even in the most advanced industrial societies, women continue to have the major responsibility for rearing children. Thus for example, if women marrying upward have personality attributes leading them to do so, as a group they may have had similar socialization experiences as children and share distinctive socialization practices as parents. In turn, these procedures may tend to encourage in their own children propensities for further mobility-striving. Thus, study of women's mobility through marriage leads back to study of the conditions under which personality factors conducive or detrimental to mobility may be formed through socialization within the family.

Comparative studies among societies obviously merit attention. Perhaps one or a few personality factors may be more strongly related to mobility than others, in societies that are quite diverse in culture and social structure. That is, while the degree to which personality factors affect mobility must vary widely among societies, because of varying socio-cultural arrangements, the same few personality variables may be most closely related to mobility everywhere. It is most probable that in societies relatively similar in culture and social structure, similar personality factors are relevant to mobility, an outcome that should yield new theoretical generalizations regarding relations between socio-cultural and personality factors. It is also possible that patterned relations between personality factors and mobility across societies will *not* be found. Any of the foregoing results would represent new knowledge, and the odds are that it would be suprising.

Finally, scant attention has been given in research thus far to personality factors in intra-generational mobility. Work in this area should

---

[103] Turner, "Comments on Crockett," *op. cit.*, p. 18.

be especially valuable in determining whether or not personality factors are typically antecedents or consequents of mobility experience, an important question that cross-sectional studies of intergenerational mobility cannot answer. And as Turner suggests, certain personality characteristics are probably more relevant to "career" mobility, or orderly progression within the pestige ranks of some stratum (e.g., in academic institutions), than to "true" mobility, in which the person moves between sharply different strata (e.g., from mechanic to large-scale manufacturer).[104] I suggest further that different personality factors are important in career mobility within different occupational categories (e.g., among corporate executives, M.D.'s, academicians, craftsmen), and that one or a few factors might be of general importance across these different occupational types. An exciting prospect is that structural factors affecting the impact of personality factors on mobility in these smaller social systems may turn out to be isomorphic with those making for important differences among total societies.

[104] "Comments on Crockett," *op. cit.*, pp. 18-19.

11

THE DISREPUTABLE POOR

DAVID MATZA, *University of California, Berkeley*

SHIFTING TERMS to designate the same entity is a familiar practice in social science. The terms used to refer to backward nations are a notorious example. What used to be called savage societies came to be called primitive, then backward, then preliterate, then non-literate, then undeveloped or "so-called underdeveloped" and now, in an optimistic reversion to evolutionary theory, the emerging and even expectant nations. A similar process of word-substitution has occurred with reference to backward and immobilized enclaves within advanced and mobilized societies. I refer to the portion of society currently termed "hard-to-reach."

Though there is no great harm in such an exercise, the names we apply to things do, after all, matter. To say that a rose by any other name is just as sweet is to reckon without the findings of modern social psychology. Calling a rose an onion would under certain very special conditions provoke tears instead of delight. But this startling reversal does not mean that a rose is an onion; it only means that the perceiver can be deceived. Accordingly, word-substitution is consequential, not because the referents of concepts are thereby transformed, but because it is a deception of self and others.

The intellectual price we pay for this deception is more apparent perhaps than the social harm. When terms referring to essentially the same entity shift rapidly, and with so great a sense of orthodoxy, intellectuals and researchers, and the practitioners who depend on them for ideas, remain largely unaware of the historical continuity of the referent to which these shifty concepts apply. Moreover, word-substitution obscures and ultimately suppresses the underlying theories, especially in value-laden or offensive names.

The historical continuity of disreputable poverty has been obscured by the obsessive shifting of terms. One predictable consequence has been the continual rediscovery of the poor—an example of what Sorokin called the Columbus complex. The poor, it seems, are perennially hidden and the brave explorers of each decade reiterate their previous invisibility and regularly proclaim the distinctive and special qualities of the "new poor." Dr. John Griscom, commenting on the wretchedness of slum life in the 1840's, said, "one half of the world does not know how the other half lives."[1] Griscom's language and viewpoint were echoed almost a half century later by Jacob Riis, and now, more than another half century later, Michael Harrington again rediscovers a heretofore invisible class of submerged poor and again stresses the novelty of their predicament.

Disreputable poverty has gone under many names in the past two centuries. The major thrust and purpose of word-substitution has been to reduce and remove the stigma, and perhaps the reason for its obsessiveness is that the effort is fruitless. The stigma inheres mostly in the referent and not the concept. In five years or so, if not already, the term "hard-to-reach" will be considered stigmatizing and relegated to the dead file of offensive labels. The culmination of this process is not hard to predict since it has already occurred in a discipline even more addicted to word-substitution and mystification than ours—the field of education. Doubtless we shall eventually refer to the disreputable poor as "exceptional families."

In referring to the disreputable poor, I mean disreputable in the distinguishing rather than the descriptive sense. Though there is considerable variation, at any given time only a portion of those who can reasonably be considered poor are disreputable. In the term disreputable I mean to introduce no personal judgment; but to reckon without the judgments made by other members of society, to ignore the stigma that adheres to this special kind of poverty, is to miss one of its key aspects.

The disreputable poor are the people who remain unemployed, or casually and irregularly employed, even during periods approaching full employment and prosperity; for that reason, and others, they live in disrepute. They do not include the majority of those who are unemployed or irregularly employed during a period of mass unemployment such as we are currently experiencing in a relatively mild way. To locate the section of the able-bodied poor that remains unemployed or casually employed during periods of full employment is a difficult task, particularly in the American setting where the number unemployed is subject to frequent and relatively drastic fluctuations. The economist

[1] Robert H. Bremner, *From the Depths* (New York: New York University Press, 1956), pp. 5-6.

Stanley Lebergott finds that, "No decade [in the 20th century] has passed without severe unemployment (over 7 per cent the labor force) occurring at least once. And none, except for that of the 1930's has passed without seeing at least one year of what we may call minimal unemployment (3 per cent or less.)" [2] Consequently, the line between those who are unemployed only during periods of depression or recession and those who are permanently unoccupied is especially difficult to draw in America.

Despite the difficulties in identifying and locating it, however, one may plausibly assert the existence of a small but persistent section of the poor who differ in a variety of ways from those who are deemed deserving. These disreputable poor cannot be easily reformed or rehabilitated through the simple provision of employment, training or guidance. They are resistant and recalcitrant—from the perspective of the welfare establishment, they are "hard-to-reach."

CONCEPTIONS OF DISREPUTABLE POVERTY

Concepts are both instructive and limiting. Each conception of disreputable poverty harbors some measure of wisdom and thus illuminates the referent; each makes us one-eyed and thus obscures it. Thus a sample of conceptions of disreputable poverty will serve to introduce consideration of its persistent features.

The current conception, "hard-to-reach," considers and defines the disreputable poor from an administrative vantage point. Implicit in the concept is a view of the disreputable poor as human material that can be worked on, helped and hopefully transformed.[3] Reasonably enough, this conception implies that one crucial difficulty is that the material cannot even be got hold of. It is hard to reach, at least without great expenditures of time and effort. Only a short step is required to transform the concept from one rooted in administrative perspective to one suggesting an important insight. Surely, they are not hard-to-reach only because the welfare establishment is deficient. Rather, the elusiveness resides at least partially in the stratum itself. The disreputable poor are disaffiliated: they exist in the crevices or at the margins of modern society. This empirical wisdom inherent in the concept "hard-to-reach"

[2] Stanley Lebergott, "Economic Crises in the United States," in Special Committee on Unemployment Problems, *Readings in Unemployment* (Washington: U.S. Government Printing Office, 1960), pp. 86-87.

[3] For a brief discussion of the administrative-welfare perspective, see Thomas Gladwin, "The Anthropologist's View of Poverty," *The Social Welfare Forum* (New York: Columbia University Press, 1961), pp. 73-74.

represents a considerable insight. The disreputable poor are probably the only authentic outsiders, for modern democratic industrial life, contrary to romantic opinion, has had a remarkable capacity for integrating increasingly larger proportions of the population. For this reason, perhaps, they have been consistently romanticized, glamorized and misunderstood by intellectuals, especially radicals and Bohemians who frequently aspire to be outsiders but never quite make it.

Beyond this, the concept "hard-to-reach" tells us little. We should not be discouraged, however, since one insight per concept is doing well. Many concepts are completely nondescript, being the bland and neutral labels best exemplified in the usage of British and American sociologists when they refer as they do to Class 5 or Class E. There is nothing wrong with this. Indeed, from the viewpoint of science it is meritorious. Strictly speaking, concepts should not contain implicit theories since this permits one to smuggle in hypotheses better left to empirical investigation. But concepts that imply specific theories are a boon, providing the theory is empirically sound rather than romantic foolishness. The theory implicit, for instance, in a concept of the "happy poor" is mostly romantic foolishness.

Almost nondescript but not quite is the phrase initiated by Warner and still fashionable among sociologists—the lower-lower class. In repeating the term lower and in distinguishing it from the upper-lower class, the concept is suggestive. Since Warner's categories were ostensibly supplied by members of the community, it implies that from their perspective, the distinction between two sections of the lower class is meaningful. The difference between lower-lowers and upper-lowers above all pertains to reputation—the one disreputable, the other reputable.

More suggestive is the British term, "problem-family." Implicit in this concept are two points. First, to refer to problem families is to observe with typical English understatement that the disreputable poor are a bit of a pain in the neck. They are bothersome, they are disproportionately costly in terms of the amount of care, welfare and policing they require. Second, and more important, the term suggests that these families collect problems. They contribute far more than their share to the relief recipients, to crime and delinquency rates, to rates of alcoholism, to the list of unmarried mothers and thus illegitimate children, to divorces, desertions, and to the mentally ill. The idea of plural problems, reinforcing and nurturing each other in the manner of a vicious circle was well stated and developed in the English notion, but the American adaptation, "multi-problem" family, unnecessarily reiterates. Moreover, the American term loses the *double-entendre* implicit in the British formulation.

The remaining concepts, unlike those already discussed, were not attempts to reduce stigma, but, on the contrary, are decidedly offensive terms developed outside the circle of sociologists, social workers and psychiatrists. The first term, *lumpenproletariat*, which despite its wide usage among Marxists was never really clarified or developed systematically, refers to the dirt or scum that inhabits the lower orders, nearby, but not of the working class. The *lumpenproletariat*, according to Bukharin was one of the "categories of persons outside the outlines of social labor" and barred from being a revolutionary class "chiefly by the circumstance that it performs no productive work." [4] For the Marxist, this stratum was fundamentally reactionary, and in the revolutionary situation, it would either remain apathetic or become mercenary in the service of the bourgeoisie. Bukharin maintains that in the *lumpenproletariat* we find, "shiftlessness, lack of discipline, hatred of the old, but impotence to construct or organize anything new, an individualistic declassed 'personality,' whose actions are based only on foolish caprices." [5]

Frequently, *lumpenproletariat* was used as a derogatory term in the struggles for power among various revolutionaries. If an opponent could be associated with the *lumpenproletariat*, his stature might be lessened. Despite frequent abuse, the term maintained some distinctive meaning. It continued to refer to the disreputable poor, and implicit in the Marxian conception are a number of suggestive insights regarding their character, background and destiny. The description given by Victor Chernov, a Russian social revolutionary, is typical since it is garbed in highly evaluative language and since he uses the designation to attack an opponent, Lenin.

Besides the proletarian *"demos"* there exists in all capitalist countries a proletarian *"ochlos,"* the enormous mass of *declasses*, chronic paupers, *Lumpenproletariat*, what may be termed the "capitalistically superfluous industrial reserve army." Like the proletariat, it is a product of capitalist civilization, but it reflects the destructive, not the constructive aspects of capitalism. Exploited and down-trodden, it is full of bitterness and despair, but has none of the traditions and none of the potentialities of organization, of a new consciousness, a new law, and a new culture, which distinguish the genuine "hereditary" proletariat. In Russia the growth of capitalism has been strongest in its destructive, predatory aspects, while its constructive achievements have lagged. It was accompanied by a catastrophic growth of the *"ochlos,"* a tremendous mass of uprooted, drifting humanity. Wrongly idealized at times, as in Gorky's early works, this mob supplied the contingents for those sporadic mass outbursts, pogroms, anti-Jewish and others, for which old Russia was famous. During the war, the personnel of industry had . . . been completely trans-

---

[4] Nikolai Bukharin, *Historical Materialism* (New York: International Publishers, 1925), pp. 284 and 290.
[5] *Ibid.*, p. 290.

formed. . . . The ranks of factory workers, severely depleted by indiscriminate mobilizations, were filled with whatever human material came to hand: peasants, small shopkeepers, clerks, janitors, porters, people of indeterminate trade. . . . The genuine proletariat was submerged in a motley crowd of Lumpenproletarians and Lumpenbourgeois.[6]

What may we infer from this description? First, the *lumpenproletariat* differs in economic function from the proletariat. It is not an industrial working class; instead, it consists of a heterogeneous mass of casual and irregular laborers, farmworkers, artisans, tradesmen, service workers and petty thieves. They work in traditional and increasingly obsolete jobs rather than, in the Marxian phrase, in the technologically advanced sectors of the economy. They are not of stable working-class stock, but include declassed persons of every stratum. Because of its background and character, the *lumpenproletariat* is not easily amenable to organization for political and economic protest. It is apathetic. It has been "hard-to-reach" for agitators as well as for social workers, or at least so thought the Marxists. In point of fact, it has frequently been amenable to political organization, but as soon as it was organized it was no longer *lumpenproletariat*, at least not by Marxian standards.

Another concept worth exploring is one suggested by Thorstein Veblen: the notion of a spurious leisure class. It too was never fully developed. Veblen intimated that at the very bottom of the class system, as at the very top, a stratum that lived in leisure developed, given to predatory sentiments and behavior.[7] The resemblance between the genuine and spurious leisure class was also noted by George Dowling in 1893. He wrote in *Scribners*, "The opulent who are not rich by the results of their own industry . . . suffer atrophy of virile and moral powers, and like paupers, live on the world's surplus without adding to it or giving any fair equivalent for their maintenance."[8] The spurious leisure class, like Veblen's pecuniary masters of society, lived in industrial society but temperamentally and functionally were not of it. Because they were not dedicated to the spirit of industrial workmanship, they never evinced the matter-of-fact, mechanistic and sober frame of mind so admired by Veblen. Instead, this class, like the genuine leisure class, was parasitic and useless, barbaric and military-minded, and given to wasteful display and frequent excess. The major difference was that its leisure was spurious, bolstered by neither aristocratic right nor financial where-

[6] Victor Chernov, *The Great Russian Revolution* (New Haven: Yale University Press, 1936), pp. 414-415.
[7] Thorstein Veblen, *The Theory of the Leisure Class* (New York: Huebsch, 1919), Ch. 10.
[8] Bremner, *op. cit.*, p. 22.

withal.[9] A spurious leisure class, then, must be peculiarly embittered and resentful. It is dedicated to luxury without the necessary finances, and thus its members are given to pose, pretense and bluster. Veblen's caricature is as harsh as anything he had to say about the pecuniary captains of society. Though it has a ring of truth, there is just as surely distortion.

A final conception pertaining to disreputable poverty was that of pauper. The distinction between paupers and the poor, maintained during the 19th and early 20th centuries, is a useful one, and its demise was one of the major casualties of obsessive word-substitution. Harriet Martineau, commenting on England in the early 19th century, observed that "Except for the distinction between sovereign and subject, there is no social difference . . . so wide as that between independent laborer and the pauper." [10] Paupers as distinguished from the poor were often characterized as apathetic regarding their condition. While they were not romantically deemed happy, they were considered less miserable or unhappy than the poor. They had adapted to their poverty, and that was their distinctive feature. Robert Hunter said:

Paupers are not, as a rule, unhappy. They are not ashamed; they are not keen to become independent; they are not bitter or discontented. They have passed over the line which separates poverty from pauperism. . . . This distinction between the poor and paupers may be seen everywhere. They are in all large cities in America and abroad, streets and courts and alleys where a class of people live who have lost all self-respect and ambition, who rarely, if ever, work, who are aimless and drifting, who like drink, who have no thought for their children, and who live more or less contentedly on rubbish and alms. Such districts are . . . in all cities everywhere. The lowest level of humanity is reached in these districts. . . . This is pauperism. There is no mental agony here; they do not work sore; there is no dread; they live miserably, but they do not care.[11]

Of all the conceptions reviewed, pauperism comes closest to what I wish to convey in the term, disreputable poverty. Though there are differences,[12] many of the features of disreputable poverty are implicit

---

[9] In like manner, Boulding has referred to "poor aristocrats" who pass easily into the criminal and purely exploitative subcultures which survive on "transfer of commodities and . . . produce very little." See Kenneth Boulding, "Reflections on Poverty," *The Social Welfare Forum* (New York: Columbia University Press, 1961), p. 52.

[10] Cited in Karl Polanyi, *The Great Transformation* (New York: Holt, Rinehart and Winston, 1944), p. 100.

[11] Robert Hunter, *Poverty* (New York: The Macmillan Co., 1912), pp. 3-4.

[12] For instance, a pauper, strictly speaking, depends on public or private charity for sustenance while in my conception, the disreputable poor are sometime recipients of welfare. They also work casually or irregularly, and occasionally engage in petty crime.

in the conception of pauperism. The concept of pauperism harbored the ideas of disaffiliation and immobilization which, taken together, indicate the outcasting from modern society suggested by Thomas and Znaniecki. Pauperism, like vice, "declasses a man definitely, puts him outside both the old and new hierarchy. Beggars, tramps, criminals, prostitutes, have no place in the class hierarchy." [13]

Despite the shifting conceptions held by intellectuals, social scientists and practitioners, a relatively stable conception of pauperism has persisted among laymen, insisting throughout on a distinction, radical or measured, between the deserving and undeserving poor. Ordinary members of society still maintain the views expressed in 1851 by Robert Harley, the founder of the New York Association for Improving the Condition of the Poor. The debased poor, he said, "love to clan together in some out-of-the-way place, are content to live in filth and disorder with a bare subsistence, provided they can drink, and smoke, and gossip, and enjoy their balls, and wakes, and frolics, without molestation." [14] One need not concur with Harley's sentiment, still pervasive today, that the debased poor do not deserve sympathy, to concur with the wisdom in the common understanding of the differences between pauper and independent laborer. A distinction between the two, measured instead of radical, refined rather than obtuse, is a preface to understanding the working classes and especially the unemployed among them.

THE SITUATION OF DISREPUTABLE POVERTY

Disreputable poverty has been conceived in many ways. Each conception is illuminating, but also obscuring, since each stresses certain elements of disreputable poverty at the expense of others. To understand disreputable poverty, and to appreciate its complexity, one must distinguish among the various components that constitute its milieu. Disreputable poverty and the tradition it sustains are a compote, blending together the distinctive contribution of each ingredient.

Dregs

The core of disreputable poverty consists of dregs—persons spawned in poverty and belonging to families who have been left behind by otherwise mobile ethnic populations. In these families there is at least

---

[13] William I. Thomas and Florian Znaniecki, *The Polish Peasant in America* (New York: Dover Publications, reissued 1958), p. 136.

[14] Bremner, *op. cit.*, p. 5.

the beginning of some tradition of disreputable poverty.[15] In America, the primary examples include immobile descendants of Italian and Polish immigrants, and the remnants of even earlier arrivals—German, Irish, and Yankees and Negroes who have already become habituated to the regions in which disreputable poverty flourishes. The situation of dregs is well described in a Russell Sage Foundation report on Hell's Kitchen in New York shortly before the first World War.

The district is like a spider's web. Of those who come to it very few, either by their own efforts or through outside agency, ever leave it. Usually those who come to live here find at first . . . that they cannot get out, and presently that they do not want to. . . . It is not [just] that conditions throughout the district are economically extreme, although greater misery and worse poverty cannot be found in other parts of New York. But there is something of the dullness of these West Side streets and the traditional apathy of their tenants that crushes the wish for anything better and kills the hope of change. It is as though decades of lawlessness and neglect have formed an atmospheric monster, beyond the power and understanding of its creators, overwhelming German and Irish alike.[16]

The above statement refers to the dregs of the mid-19th century Irish and German migrations, to those who did not advance with their ethnic brethren. Only a small proportion of the Irish and Germans living in New York at the time were trapped in the "spider's web" of Hell's Kitchen. Putting Hell's Kitchen in its proper context, Handlin says:

From 1870 onward the Irish and Germans were dynamically moving groups. . . . [however] some remained unskilled laborers. They stayed either down-town or in the middle West Side, beyond Eighth Avenue and between 23rd and 59th streets, where the other shanty towns were transformed into Hell's Kitchen, a teeming neighborhood that housed laborers from the docks and from the nearby . . . factories, and also a good portion of the city's vice and crime.[17]

Rural immigrants to urban areas in the U.S. and other nations usually entered the system at the very bottom, but in the course of a few generations—depending on the availability of new ethnic or regional replacements and numerous other factors—their descendants achieved conventional, reputable positions in society. But some proportion of each cohort, the majority of which advanced to the reputable working class or the lower rungs of the middle class, remained behind. Each experience of

[15] Boulding suggests that there is perhaps some cause for alarm when "the dependent children who have been aided ask for aid for *their* dependent children," i.e., when a sort of tradition is formed. See Boulding, *op. cit.*

[16] *West Side Studies*, Vol. 1 (New York: Russell Sage Foundation, 1914), pp. 8-9; also see Richard O'Connor, *Hell's Kitchen* (Philadelphia: J. B. Lippincott Co., 1958), p. 176.

[17] Oscar Handlin, *The Newcomers* (Cambridge: Harvard University Press, 1959), p. 31.

ethnic mobility leaves a sediment which appears to be trapped in slum life, as a result of insistence on maintaining traditional peasant values, family disorganization, relatively lower intelligence, more emotional problems, or just plain misfortune. These are the dregs who settle into the milieu of disreputable poverty and maintain and perpetuate its distinctive style. Neighborhoods in which this style flourishes possess diversified populations which, like the layers of a geological specimen, reflect its dim history. Handlin describes a single tenement in such an area.

The poor and the unsuccessful [of each ethnic group] were generally lost in the characterless enclaves scattered throughout the city, in part of the West Side, in Greenwich Village, in Brooklyn, and later in Queens where they were surrounded by communities of the foreign born. The very poorest were left behind, immobilized by their failure, and swamped by successive waves of immigrants. In the notorious "Big Flat" tenement on Mott Street, for instance, lived 478 residents, of whom 368 were Jews and 31 Italians, who were just entering the neighborhood. But there were also 31 Irish, 30 Germans, and 4 natives, a kind of sediment left behind when their groups departed.[18]

Dregs are the key component of the milieu of disreputable poverty because they link new cohorts entering the lowest level of society and the old cohorts leaving it. In the conflict between new and old ethnic arrivals, the unseemly traditions of disreputable poverty are transmitted. These traditions are manifested in a style of life distinctive to disreputable poverty and apparently similar in different parts of the world. What are the main features of this style?

Income in this stratum is obviously low, but "more important even than the size of income is its regularity." [19] Unemployment and underemployment are common. When work can be found it is typically unskilled or at best semi-skilled. Job duration is relatively short; hiring is frequently on a day-to-day basis. Child labor lingers on,[20] and in many of these families, the wage earner, if there is one, suffers from frequent ill health resulting in intermittent employment. Savings even over a very short time are virtually unknown and as a result, small quantities of food may be bought many times a day, as the need arises. Also evident is "the pawning of personal possessions, borrowing from local money lenders at usurious rates, and the use of second-hand clothing and furniture." [21] The Brock Committee in England indignantly observed that "an important feature of this group is misspending." "Misspending," the committee asserts, "is the visible expression of thriftlessness and improvidence." The Brock Committee was impressed with the frequency

---

[18] Handlin, *op. cit.*, p. 29.
[19] Tom Stephens (ed.), *Problem Families* (London: Victor Gollancz, 1946), p. 3.
[20] Oscar Lewis, *The Children of Sanchez* (New York: Random House, 1961), p. xxvi.
[21] *Ibid.*

with which "money is squandered on gambling, drinking, cigarettes, and unnecessary household luxuries when bare necessities are lacking." [22] Available resources are frequently mismanaged. "Rent is typically in arrears . . . and similar irresponsibility is shown towards bills and debts." [23]

To British investigators, the most obvious common feature of these families is the disorder of family life.[24] People frequently resort to violence in training children and in settling quarrels; wifebeating, early initiation into sex, and free unions or consensual marriage are common, and the incidence of abandoned mothers and children is high.[25] "The children play outside until late in the evening . . . and are sent to bed, all ages at the same time, when the parents are tired. . . ." In many of these homes there is no clock, and "one may visit at ten in the morning to find the entire household asleep." [26] Relations between parents are often characterized by constant dissension and an absence of affection and mutual trust.[27] As a result, family dissolution is frequent and there is a distinct pressure toward a mother-centered family—a rather disorganized version of what anthropologists call serial monogamy with a female-based household.[28] Though family solidarity is emphasized, it is an ideal that is rarely even approximated.[29] The disposition to paternal authoritarianism is strong, but since paternal authority is frequently challenged, its implementing requires a show of power or force. The discipline of children has been described "as a mixture of spoiling affection and impatient chastisement or mental and physical cruelty." [30] Moreover, the household is extremely complex. It may contain "in addition to the joint off-spring, . . . children of diverse parentage. There may be children from previous marriages, illegitimate children, and children of near-relatives and friends who have deserted, died, or been imprisoned." [31] Thus, the normal manifestations of sibling rivalry are perhaps heightened.

The disreputable poor are "the least educated group in the popula-

[22] Cited in C. P. Blacker (ed.), *Problem Families: Five Inquiries* (London: Eugenics Society, 1952), p. 3.

[23] Stephens, *op. cit.*, p. 3.

[24] *Ibid.*, p. 4.

[25] Lewis, *op. cit.*, p. xxvi.

[26] Stephens, *op. cit.*, p. 4.

[27] *Ibid.*, p. 5.

[28] Some, like Walter Miller, are so taken by the durability of this style that, straight-faced, they hold the adjective "disorganized" to be an unwarranted ethnocentric imputation. See *Delinquent Behavior: Culture and the Individual* (Washington: National Education Association, 1959), pp. 94-97.

[29] Lewis, *op. cit.*, p. xxvi.

[30] Stephens, *op. cit.*, p. 5.

[31] Blacker, *op. cit.*, p. 32, and for a perceptive documentation, Lewis, *op. cit.* in its entirety.

tion and the least interested in education." [32] Returning to the Brock Committee, we learn that this group suffers from "an intractable ineducability which expresses itself in a refusal, or else an incapacity to make effective use of the technical advice available." [33] To the uncritical and the indignant these families seem content with squalor,[34] a misunderstanding that obviously arises from failure to distinguish between satisfaction and apathy.

The disreputable poor "react to their economic situation and to their degradation in the eyes of respectable people by becoming fatalistic; they feel that they are down and out, and that there is no point in trying to improve. . . ." [35] Their life is provincial and locally oriented. "Its members are only partly integrated into national institutions and are a marginal people even when they live in the heart of a great city." [36] Typically, they neither belong to trade unions nor support any political party.[37] They are immobilized in that they do not participate in the two responses to discontent characteristic of Western working classes— collective mobilization culminating in trade unions, ethnic federations or political action, and familial mobilization culminating in individual mobility. Members of this group are attracted episodically to revolutionary incidents [38] or at the individual level to criminal behavior in the form of a quick score or hustle.[39] Both are best viewed as forms of quasi-protest, however, since they contemplate quick and easy remedy without recognizing the onerous necessities of sustained and conscientious effort. Except for episodic manifestations of quasi-protest, the characteristic response of the disreputable poor, especially the dregs, is apathy.

Thus, the style of disreputable poverty apparently transcends national boundaries. Transmission of this style from one cohort to the next is a major contribution of dregs, but it is not the only mark they make on the texture of disreputable poverty. Just as important, perhaps, is the unmistakable tone of embittered resentment emanating from their immobility. Dregs are immobile within a context of considerable mobility in their ethnic reference groups, consequently they are apt to see

[32] Joseph A. Kahl, *The American Class Structure* (New York: Holt, Rinehart and Winston, 1953), p. 211.

[33] Blacker, *op. cit.*, p. 16.

[34] Hunter, *op. cit.*, pp. 3-4.

[35] Kahl, *op. cit.*, p. 211.

[36] Lewis, *op. cit.*, p. xxvi.

[37] Genevieve Knupfer, "Portrait of the Underdog," *Public Opinion Quarterly* (Spring 1947), pp. 103-114.

[38] E. J. Hobsbawm, *Social Bandits and Primitive Rebels* (New York: Free Press of Glencoe, 1960).

[39] Walter Miller, "Lower Class Culture as a Generating Milieu of Gang Delinquency," *Journal of Social Issues*, 14 (1958), pp. 5-19.

the good fortunes of ethnic brethren as desertion and obsequious ambition. Their view of those who have been successfully mobile is likely
to be jaundiced and defensive. How else explain their own failure?
What the reputable applaud as sobriety and effort must seem to those
left behind an implicit, if not explicit, rejection of their way of life, and
thus a rejection of themselves as persons.

From their resentful assessment of successful ethnic brethren, and
also from the peculiarly seamy view of law enforcement agencies afforded slum denizens, another distinctive element emerges. A cynical
sense of superiority appears based on the partially accurate belief that
they are privy to guilty knowledge shared only with influential insiders.
In a word, they are "hip," free of the delusions regarding ethics and
propriety that guide the "square" citizenry. Thus, for instance, "hip" slum-
dwellers in New York knew or claimed to know of the incidents underlying the famous basketball scandals years before the public was shocked
by exposés, just as "hip" slum dwellers in Chicago knew or claimed
to know of the incidents underlying the police scandals there a few
years ago.

Newcomers

Recent arrival is the second component of disreputable poverty. Not
all newcomers gravitate to these regions—mostly, those without marketable skills or financial resources. Irish newcomers escaping to America
even before the great famine settled in neighborhoods already infamous
and in disrepute. Ernst describes one of the most notorious of these
neighborhoods in New York.

To live in the lower wards required some money. The penniless stranger,
wholly without means, could not afford the relative luxury of a boardinghouse.
His search for shelter led him to the sparsely populated sections north of the
settled part of town. In the twenties and thirties Irish immigrants clustered
around the "five points," a depressed and unhealthy area on the site of the
filled-in Collect swamp in the old Sixth ward. Here, at little or no cost, the
poorest of the Irish occupied dilapidated old dwellings and built flimsy
shanties. . . . In the heart of the Five Points was the old brewery, erected in
1792. . . . Transformed into a dwelling in 1837, the Old Brewery came to
house several hundred men, women and children, almoset equally divided
between Irish and Negroes, including an assortment of "thieves, murderers,
pickpockets, beggars, harlots, and degenerates of every type" . . . . As early as
1830 the Sixth ward, and the Five Points in particular, had become notorious
as a center of crime. . . . The criminality of the area was usually overemphasized, but poverty was widespread, and thousands of law-abiding
inhabitants led wretched lives in cellars and garrets.[40]

[40] Robert Ernst, *Immigrant Life in New York City, 1825-1863* (New York:
King's Crown Press, 1949), p. 39.

Numerically, newcomers are probably the largest component of the disreputable poor, but it is important to recall that except for a small proportion their collective destiny is eventually to enter reputable society. Thus, the new ethnics do not fully exhibit the features of disreputable poverty described above nor do they manifest the embittered sense of defeat and resignation characteristic of dregs. They are more apt to express a sort of naive optimism, especially since their new urban standard of life is, if anything, higher than standards previously experienced.

Newcomers contribute an exotic element, whether they are European, Latin American, or indigenously American as in the case of Southern Negroes and whites. Typically backward peoples, they season the streets of the metropolis with peasant traditions. It is this element of the exotic that has excited the imagination of Bohemians and other intellectuals and led to the persistent romanticizing of life among the disreputable poor. Unfortunately, however, this exotic quality is double-edged, and one of the edges is considerably sharper than the other. Admiration from intellectuals was of little consequence for newly-arrived ethnics especially compared with their persistent humiliation and degradation by resident ethnics.

The style of disreputable poverty was transmitted in the context of humiliation and victimization. The newcomers are, in the folklore of slum traditions, and to a considerable degree in reality, untutored in the ways of slum sophistication. "Greenhorns," "banana boaters," whatever they were called, they learn the style of disreputable poverty primarily through being victims of it. They learn not by doing but, initially, by being had. This traditional pattern is neatly summarized in an older description of the environment of newcomers in American slums, a description refreshingly free of the contrived relativism that currently misleads some anthropologists and sociologists.

The moral surroundings are . . . bad for them. In tenement districts the unsophisticated Italian peasant or the quiet, inoffensive Hebrew is thrown into contact with the degenerate remnants of former immigrant populations, who bring influence to bear to rob, persecute, and corrupt the newcomers.[41]

Transmission of the style of disreputable povety in the context of humiliation and victimization helped to dampen the optimism with which newcomers frequently arrived, and thus facilitated its adoption by a segment of them. Optimism and other cultural resistances were never completely obliterated, however, and only a small though variable proportion succumbed to the temptations of disreputable poverty. Ethnic

[41] *United States Industrial Commission on Immigration,* Volume XV of the Commission's Report (Washington: Government Printing Office, 1901), p. xlvii.

groups entering America and other nations have varied considerably in their vulnerability,[42] but in each one at least a few families became dregs.

Why have the newly arrived ethnics been so persistently humiliated and degraded by the old ethnic remnants? At one level, the answer seems simple. Despite all their failings, those who were left behind could lord it over the new arrivals for they at least were Americanized, though not sufficiently Americanized to be confident. Embittered and resentful on the one hand, and anxious and uncertain about their Americanism on the other, the ethnic dregs suffered from the classic conditions under which groups seek out scapegoats.

Skidders

Skidders are a third component in the milieu of disreputable poverty. These are men and women who have fallen from higher social standing. They include alcoholics, addicts, perverts and otherwise disturbed individuals who come, after a long history of skidding, to live in the run-down sections of the metropolis. To a slight extent, low-cost public housing has concealed skidders from immediate view, but it still serves only a small proportion of the poor, and at any rate tends to be reserved for the deserving poor. Among the disreputable poor, the visibility of skidders remains high.

Occasionally, along with the skidders, one finds some especially hardy Bohemians who take their ideology seriously enough to live among their folk. But it is the skidders rather than Bohemians who contribute importantly to the culture of disreputable poverty. Even when they live in sections of this sort, Bohemians tend to be insulated, partly by their clannishness but primarily because they are ungratefully rejected by the authentic outsiders they romanticize.

Skidders contribute a tone of neuroticism and flagrant degradation. They are pathetic and dramatic symbols of the ultimate in disreputable poverty. Perhaps more important, they are visible evidence of the flimsy foundations of success and standing in society and as such, furnish yet another argument against sustained and conscientious effort. These are the fallen; they have achieved success and found it somehow lacking in worth. Skidders are important not because they are very numerous among the disreputable poor, but rather because they dramatically exemplify the worthlessness of effort. While their degradation may sometimes goad others, particularly the new ethnic, to conscientious ef-

---

[42] The reasons for this variability are complicated; some of them will be suggested in the final section on "The Process of Pauperization."

forts to escape a similar fate, the old ethnic dregs take the skidder's fall as additional evidence of the meanness of social life, and the whimsy of destiny.

The Infirm

The infirm are the final element in the milieu of disreputable poverty. Before age, injury or illness made them infirm, these people belonged to other strata—especially the reputable sections of the working class. Their downward shift may take the form of physically moving from a reputable to a disreputable neighborhood but more frequently, perhaps, the infirm stay put and the neighborhood moves out from under them. Frequently, they belong to old ethnic groups, but since they have achieved or maintained reputable status they are not dregs. They slip because of some misfortune, aging being the most common. Their contribution is, in part, similar to the skidders', but without the blatant elements of neuroticism and degradation. Like the skidders, they testify to the flimsy foundations of respectability, the worthlessness of sustained effort, and the whimsical nature of fate or destiny. Like the skidders— even more so because they have done less to provoke their fate—they symbolize the beat (and not in the sense of beatific) aspects of life among the disreputable poor.

But the infirm have a distinctive contribution of their own to make. In a completely ineffective way, they oppose the tradition of disreputable poverty. Their cantankerous complaints, and what is surely perceived as their nosy interference, frequently precipitate a flagrant and vengeful show of license and sin; the infirm become a captive and powerless audience before whom the flaunting and mischievous youth can perform. Intruders in this world because they are of different stock, because they claim reputability, or both, they are simultaneously powerless and rejected. Those who claim reputability in a disreputable milieu inevitably appear to take on airs, and are thus vulnerable to ridicule and sarcasm—the typical sanctions for that minor vice. Furthermore, their opposition is weakened because the police cannot, after all, bother with their complaints if they are to attend to the serious violations that abound in these areas. The infirm are the one indigenous source of opposition, but their marginal status makes them powerless to effect change. Thus, their distinctive contribution is to demonstrate the pettiness of character and the incredible impotence of those who oppose disreputable poverty.

In the situation of disreputable poverty, the various elements that coincidentally inhabit its regions conspire to perpetuate immobilization.

Thus, part of the explanation for its anachronistic persistence lies in the relations among its components. But at best this is a partial explanation only; at worst it begs the more basic questions. To understand how disreputable poverty is produced and maintained, we must turn to the process of pauperization.

THE PROCESS OF PAUPERIZATION

Although disreputable poverty has always existed, we do not yet know how the ranks of the disreputable poor are periodically replenished on something approximating a mass basis, or how fractions of newcomers are selected to join them. These two related questions make up the topic of pauperization. My answers are intended only to illustrate certain facets of the process, not to present a general theory of pauperization.

Pauperization is the process that results in disreputable poverty. That aspect of it by which the population is periodically replenished may be termed *massive generation;* that by which newcomers pass into the ranks of disreputable poverty may be termed *fractional selection.*

Massive Generation

Let us begin cautiously by guarding against two antithetical beliefs, both common—one connected with that hardy variety of humanitarian conservatism we now call "liberalism," the other associated with that harsh variety of economic liberalism we now call "conservatism." The first view all but denies the possibility of pauperization, claiming that the very category of disreputable poverty is a prejudice with no substantive foundation, and that pauperization is merely an unwarranted imputation. The second view makes rather different assumptions, claiming that pauperization occurs whenever the compulsion to work is relieved. According to this latter view, the poor are readily susceptible to the immobilization and demoralization implicit in disreputable poverty and will succumb whenever they are given the slightest opportunity. My own view is intermediate: Pauperization, in the form of massive generation, is always a possibility, and occasionally occurs, but it requires extreme and special conditions. Pauperizing a significant part of a population is possible, but relatively difficult to accomplish. It must be worked at conscientiously, even if unwittingly.

The circumstances attending the early phases of industrialization in England offer a classic illustration of massive pauperization. As far as can be told, mass pauperization is not, and never has been, a necessary or even a normal feature or by-product of industrialization or, more specifically, of primitive accumulation. Instead, it was probably an un-anticipated consequence of purposive social action regarding the poor during the early phases of English industrialization. Mass pauperization was implicit in the sequence of Poor Laws by which the harsh reform of 1834 was built on the indulgent and slovenly base provided by Speenhamland. Neither the reform of '34 nor Speenhamland alone, I suggest, was sufficient to accomplish a massive generation of disreputable poverty. But together they achieved a major replenishing.

The principal consequence of Speenhamland was *potentially* to en-large the ranks of the disreputable poor. This was accomplished through the moral confusion associated with a policy that in essence violated normal expectations regarding the relation between conscientious effort and economic reward.[43] Under Elizabethan Law, which prevailed before Speenhamland, "the poor were forced to work at whatever wages they could get and only those who could obtain no work were entitled to relief." [44] In the 1790's, England experienced a series of bad harvests. This, combined with a rise in prices connected with the war with France, in the wider context of enclosures, caused distress and led to a number of disturbances, "an alarming combination in view of the horror with which the revolutionary aims of the French were regarded." [45] The reaction to this potential crisis was Speenhamland. Maurice Bruce de-scribes the conditions attending the adoption of this plan:

> Numerous were the remedies proposed, though any increase of wages was keenly deprecated lest it should prove impossible to lower them when prices fell again. . . . The influential and operative remedy, the spontaneous reaction to England's first wartime inflation, was the decision of the Berkshire Justices at Speenhamland in 1795 to supplement wages from the [poor] rates on a sliding scale in accordance with the price of bread and the size of families con-cerned. This historic "Speenhamland system" was given legislative sanction in the following year.[46]

Thus, one major aspect of Speenhamland was a peculiar system of outdoor relief in which "aid-in-wages" was regularly endorsed in such a way as to make indistinguishable independent laborers and paupers. The wage of the former was depressed,[47] while the lot of the latter was obviously improved. "The poor-rate had become public spoil. . . . To

[43] This interpretation is based on, but departs somewhat from that suggested in Polanyi, *op. cit.*

[44] *Ibid.*, p. 79.

[45] Maurice Bruce, *The Coming of the Welfare State* (London: Batsford, 1961), pp. 41-42.

[46] *Ibid.*

[47] Polanyi, *op. cit.*, p. 280.

obtain their share the brutal bullied the administrators, the profligate exhibited their bastards which must be fed, the idle folded their arms and waited till they got it; ignorant boys and girls married upon it; poachers, thieves and prostitutes extorted it by intimidation; country justices lavished it for popularity and Guardians for convenience. This was the way the fund went." [48]

Consequently, Speenhamland potentially enlarged the ranks of disreputable poverty by obscuring the time-honored distinction between independent laborer and the pauper. As Harriet Martineau observed, "Except for the distinction between sovereign and subject there is no social difference in England so wide as that between independent laborer and the pauper; and it is equally ignorant, immoral and impolitic to confound the two." [49] Describing some of the ways in which this occurred, Karl Polanyi has suggested the effect of such confounding on the productivity of the labor force so indiscriminately subsidized:

Under Speenhamland . . . a man was relieved even if he was in employment, as long as his wages amounted to less than the family income granted him by the scale. Hence, no laborer had any material interest in satisfying his employer, his income being the same whatever wages he earned. . . . The employer could obtain labor at almost any wages; however little he paid, the subsidy from the rates brought the worker's income up to scale. Within a few years the productivity of labor began to sink to that of pauper labor, thus providing an added reason for employers not to raise wages above the scale. For once the intensity of labor, the care and efficiency with which it was performed, dropped below a definite level, it became indistinguishable from "boondoggling," or the semblance of work maintained for the sake of appearance. [50]

Though boondoggling and other forms of demotivation were implicit in Speenhamland's peculiarly indiscriminate system of outdoor relief, that in itself was probably not sufficient for the massive generation of paupers. Pauperization implies more than demotivation of effort; it also implies a more general demoralization, the emergence of a view in which work is taken as punishment or penalty. These features of pauperization both appeared in substantial, though obviously limited, sections of the amorphous mass in which laborers and paupers were confounded, and both may perhaps be traced to an institution that was already apparent under Speenhamland but came to full fruition in the subsequent policies enacted in the Poor Law reforms of 1834. Pauperization awaited an institution in which persistent poverty was *penalized,* and in which the

[48] *Ibid.,* p. 99.
[49] Cited in *ibid.,* p. 100.
[50] *Ibid.,* p. 79; also see Marcus Lee Hansen, *The Atlantic Migration, 1607-1860* (Cambridge: Harvard University Press, 1940), p. 128.

form taken by penalization was *coerced labor* administered on an *indoor* basis.

Under Speenhamland, the penalizing of poverty in the workhouse was a minor appendage to its major feature, indiscriminate outdoor relief. Under the reform of 1834 poverty was penalized on an indoor basis as the major governmental method of regulating the poor. Since this policy of penalization was pursued, first side by side with and subsequently in the wake of a policy that confounded laborers with paupers, it was well suited to realize the enormous potential for massive pauperization implicit in that confounding. Penalizing poverty through the workhouse reinforced and established, inadvertently but effectively, whatever mere propensities resulted from the indiscriminate use of outdoor relief under Speenhamland. The indolence and boondoggling occasioned by Speenhamland created the propensity for mass pauperization, but to be transformed into true paupers, those exhibiting indolence had to be stigmatized or defamed, work had to be reconstituted as penal sanction, and demoralization centralized under the roof of a facilitating institution. All of this was accomplished by the workhouse system.

Under Spenhamland, a man and his family would be put in the poorhouse if they had been on the rates for an extended period of time.[51] Once there, suggests Polanyi, "the decencies and self-respect of centuries of settled life wore off quickly in the promiscuity of the poorhouse where a man had to be cautious not to be thought better off than his neighbor, lest he be forced to start out on the hunt for work, instead of boondoggling in the familiar fold." [52] In the poorhouse the ancient culture of paupers could now be disseminated to those who had been thrown together with them, and the potential for massive generation of disreputable poverty could be realized. Moreover, the confusion regarding the moral value of work could be compounded and finally resolved by the unmistakable lesson of the workhouse—work is a penalty, to be avoided and viewed with resentment.[53]

Collecting the indolent in an indoor setting was important for another reason. Persons receiving poor relief during Speenhamland were not yet overwhelmingly concentrated in the urban slums we have come to associate with a tradition of disreputable poverty. Most were still distributed over chiefly agricultural areas.[54] Thus, the concentration that

[51] Polanyi, *op. cit.*, p. 99.
[52] *Ibid.*
[53] The moral confusion regarding the status of work occasioned by this dual aspect of Speenhamland is discussed by Reinhard Bendix in *Work and Authority in Industry* (New York: Harper Torchbooks, 1963), pp. 40-42.
[54] Neil J. Smelser, *Social Change in the Industrial Revolution* (Chicago: University of Chicago Press, 1959), p. 350.

facilitates the formation of a subculture was aided by the poorhouse system. The poorhouses and workhouses served the same function for the disreputable poor that Marx assigned the factories in the development of an industrial proletariat and the same function assigned by criminologists to prisons in disseminating the standards and techniques of criminality. Each is a center for the collection of traits which can then be conveniently disseminated.

The defamation of character implicit in commitment to a workhouse is clearest after the Poor Law Reform of 1834. This reform was a direct reaction to Speenhamland. It was calculated to avoid the indulgence of indolence apparent in the previous system. The Webbs summarize the reformers' motives:

The decisive element [in the Poor Law Reform amendments of 1834] was undoubtedly a recognition of the bad behavior induced alike among employers and employed by the various devices for maintaining the able-bodied, wholly or partially, out of the Poor Rate. When, under the allowance system, the farmers and manufacturers became aware that they could reduce wages indefinitely, and the manual workers felt secure of subsistence without the need for exerting themselves to retain any particular employment, the standard of skill and conduct of all concerned rapidly declined. To single out the full-whitted employer and the lazy workman for special grants out of public funds, to the detriment of the keen organizer and the zealous worker, was obviously bad psychology as well as bad economics. When adding to the number of children automatically increased the family income, young persons hastened to get married, as it was, indeed, intended they should do by the Justices of the Peace who adopted the Speenhamland Scale. . . . The Elizabethan Poor Law had become, by the beginning of the nineteenth century, a systematic provision, not so much for the unfortunate as for the less competent and the less provident, whom the humanity or carelessness of the Justices and the Overseers had combined specially to endow out of public funds.[55]

The reform of 1834 was an extreme reaction to Speenhamland, but instead of undoing the effects of Speenhamland, it compounded them, for penalizing poverty completed the historic process of pauperization begun by the moral confusion occasioned by Speenhamland. The abolition of Speenhamland, in some respects, was as Polanyi suggests, "the true birthday of the modern working-classes" because it forced them to mobilize on their own behalf. But just as surely, the same abolition and the same enactment of the Reform was the "true birthday of the modern disreputable poor," for it signalled the last phase of the pauperization process. If "Speenhamland was an automation for demolishing the standards on which any kind of society could be based," then the

[55] Sidney and Beatrice Webb, *English Poor Law History*, Vol. 8 of *English Local Government* (London: Longmans, Green, 1929), pp. 14-15.

reform was an instrument for institutionalizing the standards which replaced those "on which any kind of society could be based."

The reform of 1834 was designed in the hope that the poor would
be severely discouraged from going on the rates by the stigma now
attached to the workhouse and the conditions characterizing it.

> The new law provided that in the future no outdoor relief should be given. . . .
> Aid-in wages was . . . discontinued. . . . It was now left to the applicant
> to decide whether he was so utterly destitute of all means that he would
> voluntarily repair to a shelter which was deliberately made a place of
> horror. The workhouse was invested with a stigma; and staying in it was
> made a psychological and moral torture. . . . the very burial of a pauper was
> made an act by which his fellow men renounced solidarity with him even in
> death.[56]

Surely, this was to reinstate the distinction between independent laborer
and pauper, but only after 40 years of confounding precisely that issue.
Together the two policies comprise the classic way to generate a mass
population of paupers.

Doubtless, pauperization is easier to accomplish when the population
in question is a subjugated national or ethnic group rather than an indigenous group of subjects or citizens. Subjugated people are regarded
as moral inferiors to begin with, capable of a variety of vices which
typically include indolence and immorality. Pauperizing an indigenous
population is more difficult in the measure that national affinities limit,
though without necessarily precluding the possibilities of imputing sub-
human stature. The English case is classic precisely because pauperizing
some part of an indigenous population is difficult; but in that case too,
the extent of indigenous pauperization is easily exaggerated, for many
who were caught in the curious combination of Speenhamland indulgence and Reform penalization were in fact not English but Irish. Some
of the Irish in England were pauperized by the same circumstances
that affected indigenous Englishmen, but many more were pauperized
by a separate process, one that illustrates the pattern of extreme subjugation by which the poor among captive or conquered peoples are
commonly pauperized. This second pattern of massive pauperization
is of paramount importance in the U.S. because it produced two of the
major ethnic contributors to the tradition of disreputable poverty—the
Irish and the Negro.[57]

The great Irish famine was only the culmination of a long period of

[56] Polanyi, *op. cit.*, pp. 101-102.

[57] For a general sense in which Irish and Negroes were at least somewhat dif-
ferent from other immigrant groups in America, see Nathan Glazer and Daniel P.
Moynihan, *Beyond the Melting Pot* (Cambridge: The M.I.T. Press and Harvard
University Press, 1963).

subjugated poverty that drove the Irish eastward across the channel to England and westward to America. Both before and during the famine it is very likely that England rather than America received the most profoundly pauperized sections of the Irish poor,[58] if only because migration to nearby England was economically more feasible.[59] Ireland was an impoverished colony, before, during, and after its great famine, and perhaps, as travellers during the period suggested, impoverished to an extent unrivalled in the rest of Europe.[60] Impoverishment, however, is not the same as pauperization. In the Irish experience, extreme economic impoverishment was combined with profound political subjugation. Just as penalization pauperizes an indigenous population, political subjugation of a captive or colonized people may transform the merely poor into paupers through the agency of oppression and degradation. The political subjugation experienced by the Irish was tantamount to the penalization of the entire island.

Beginning in 1695, the Irish were subjected to the infamous Penal Laws which Edmund Burke aptly described as "a machine of wise and elaborate contrivance, and as well fitted for the oppression, impoverishment and degradation of a people and the debasement in them of human nature itself, as ever proceeded from the perverted ingenuity of man." The Penal Laws were long, elaborate and developed over a number of generations.[61] Their character is perhaps conveyed by the fact that on two occasions it is stated that the law "does not suppose any such person to exist as a Roman Catholic." [62] Some provisions were potentially subversive of family life: "If the eldest son of a landholder apostatized and renounced the Catholic religion, he became sole owner of the property and immediately his father was inhibited from placing impediments on it. . . . The son could disinherit the father," [63] and in the process dispossess all of his younger brothers, who were otherwise entitled to an equal share.

---

[58] John A. Jackson, *The Irish in Britain* (London: Routledge and Kegan Paul, 1963), p. 9; also see Cecil Woodham-Smith, *The Great Hunger* (London: Hamish Hamilton, 1962), p. 270.

[59] One cannot help observing that there was a certain poetic justice in this preference for nearby England. The paupers came home to roost, sponging, as it were, on the very regime that had so ingeniously pauperized them. There is no evidence that the Irish paupers were prompted by so frivolous a motive, however; only the gypsies among the disreputable poor are regularly guided by such considerations. For a discussion of the peculiar gypsy version of disreputable poverty see my *Deviant Phenomena*, Prentice-Hall, forthcoming.

[60] Woodham-Smith, *op. cit.*, pp. 19-20.

[61] For a brief summary of the Penal Laws, see George Potter, *To the Golden Door* (Boston: Little, Brown and Company, 1960), pp. 26-28.

[62] *Ibid.*

[63] *Ibid.*

The effects of the Penal Laws are suggested by Woodham-Smith. She says:

The material damage suffered through the penal laws was great; ruin was widespread, old families disappeared and old estates were broken up; but the most disastrous effects were moral. The Penal Laws brought lawlessness, dissimulation and revenge in their train, and the Irish character, above all the character of the peasantry did become, in Burke's words degraded and debased. The upper classes were able to leave the country and many middle-class merchants contrived with guile, to survive, but the poor Catholic peasant bore the full hardship. His religion made him an outlaw; in the Irish House of Commons he was described as "the common enemy," and whatever was inflicted on him, he must bear, for where could he look for redress? To his landlord? Almost invariably an alien conqueror. To the law? Not when every person connected with the law, from the jailer to the judge, was a Protestant who regarded him as "the common enemy." [64]

The lingering effects of the Penal laws were instrumental in creating the two traditions for which the Irish later became noted, terrorist rebellion and disreputable poverty.

The pauperization of the Irish peasantry was not simply a consequence of the Penal laws. It was also facilitated by the Irish system of land tenure headed by absentee landlords and managed largely by local agents. Under the policy of surrender and regrant of land, most Irish farmers had become rent-paying tenants.[65] Moreover, the land system, and especially the institution of "cant," seemed almost calculated to punish conscientious effort and reward slovenliness.

The most calloused abuse by the landlord of his ownership was the practice of putting up farms for "cant" [or public auction] when leases expired. No matter how faithfully a tenant paid his rent, how dutifully he had observed regulations, or how well he had improved the property by his own labors, he was in constant danger of being outbid for his farm by the "grabber" upon the expiration of the lease. . . . Moreover, in the Catholic parts of Ireland . . . the tenant was not entitled to compensation for improvements brought by himself. . . . Hard experience had taught the tenant the penalties of improving the property he leased or hired and the self-interest of slovenliness. If he improved the property, his rent was raised! . . . Progress and improvement, instead of being encouraged by the landlord for his own interests, were penalized. This upside-down system withered the character, destroyed the initiative, and squelched the ambition of the Irish tenant.[66]

A key factor in pauperization, as in the English Poor Law policy, was the negative association of work with sanction. In one instance, conscientious effort was punished, whereas in the other it was used as a

[64] Woodham-Smith, *op. cit.*, 27-28.
[65] Ernst, *op. cit.*, p. 5.
[66] Potter, *op. cit.*, p. 44.

punishment. In either form, the association of work with a negative sanction facilitates pauperization. Mere indolence is converted to an active antagonism to work. By the time the Irish began to emigrate to America, the policy of political subjugation along with the economic impoverishment of the island had had its effect. A substantial proportion of the population had been pauperized though, almost certainly, it was nothing approaching a majority. So difficult is the process of pauperization that no more than a substantial minority are likely to succumb to it. Counteracting the forces for degradation and demoralization are always the stabilizing and moralizing forces of family, religion, and primary group solidarity; these are weakened but never obliterated. Beaumont, a French observer, put the partial effects of pauperization nicely: "All the faculties of his soul that despotism has touched are blighted; the wounds there are large and deep. All this part of him is vice, whether it be cowardice, indolence, knavery or cruelty; half of the Irishman is a slave."

In the years just before the famine and great emigration, the Irish poor were subjected to the workhouse system, which was instituted in the English parliament as part of the Irish Poor Law Act of 1838. Thus, in Ireland the penalizing of poverty in a workhouse system came in the wake of the political subjugation epitomized by the penal laws, whereas in the English case, the penalizing of poverty followed the indulgence of Speenhamland.

By the 1820's the poor rates in England had reached unprecedented heights. Whereas the total rate in 1696 was 400,000 pounds, in 1776 it was about one and a half million, in 1796 it passed two million, in 1802 it had risen to four and a quarter million, by 1818 close to eight million and still in 1832 seven million. [67] This represented only a small part of the national income, "probably no more than two per cent," but "it amounted to one-fifth of the national expenditure and to people who had no means of assessing the national income it loomed appallingly large and seemed to threaten the economic foundations of society." [68] The rate seemed especially high since a large number of able-bodied workers were being supported by it. Not surprisingly, many of the English rate-payers "blamed the Irish paupers in England and demanded a Poor Law for Ireland." [69] Irish emigration to England and Scotland was heavy throughout the 18th and early 19th centuries, first as seasonal agricultural labor and increasingly as more or less settled industrial workers. "By 1841, shortly before the great famine, fully 419,256 Irish-

[67] These figures are from Bruce, *op. cit.*, pp. 76-77, and Polyani, *op. cit.*, p. 110.
[68] Bruce, *op. cit.*, pp. 76-77.
[69] Ernst, *op. cit.*, p. 5.

born persons were living permanently in England and Scotland." [70]
Given the English knowledge of the pauperized state of the Irish, it was
to be expected that the Irish would be blamed for what were conceived
as staggeringly high poor rates. The enactment by the English of an
Irish Poor Law in 1838 was prompted by the desire to make Irish property responsible for its own poverty, and thus to slow the emigration
of the Irish poor to England. But Irish landlords were simply not up to
the task, and the major effect of the Act was to spur "Assisted Emigration" from Ireland, mostly to America via Quebec. Under the Irish Poor
Law of 1838, the workhouse became an intermediate step—a halfway
house between eviction from the land and emigration to America. The
Law taxed Irish landlords so highly that they showed "a sudden zeal to
promote emigration. The new law integrated emigration with evictions
by setting up workhouses for the dispossessed, and since the same act
provided for assisted emigration, the workhouse became the intermediate step between eviction and departure from Ireland." [71] This
sequence of eviction, sentence to the poorhouse and assisted emigration achieved special importance with the onset of the Irish famine
in 1845.

The penalization of poverty was the last phase in a long history of
English pauperization of the Irish poor. By coincidence, it occurred
shortly before the great emigration to America. Thus, a substantial proportion of emigrants to America had experienced *both* the punishing
of conscientious effort as a result of the cant system, and the use of
conscientious effort as punishment in the workhouse, along with political subjugation under the English. The disreputable poverty of the Irish
immigrant in America is best understood in the context of this dubious
legacy, and the subsequent tradition of disreputable poverty in urban
America is best understood by stressing that our first massive immigration of the very poor was that of already pauperized Irish fleeing in
"assisted" fashion from the great famine.[72]

In America, the Irish were almost immediately considered worthless
paupers. This stigma was applied not only to those who were already
truly pauperized but also to those who had somehow remained simply
poor. Since worthy poor too were frequently out of work, they were
lumped together with their more disreputable brethren. Potter summarizes their predicament:

[70] *Ibid.*
[71] *Ibid.*
[72] The other important stream feeding this tradition in America, and massively
replenishing the population of the disreputable poor, will be discussed in a later
publication. It consists, of course, of Negroes, many of whom were pauperized as a
result of enslavement and continued political subjugation after formal emancipation.

The "indolent Irish" had been a characterization fixed on the race by the English in Ireland that America inherited. Superficial observation gave it currency in America for two major reasons. One was the frequent spells of unemployment the Irishman suffered from the nature of his manual work—inclement weather, cyclical depressions, and job competition. On this score the description was unjust because of the elements beyond the individual Irishman's control. The other [reason] was the shiftlessness of a ragtag and bobtail minority, noisy, dissolute, troublesome, gravitating to public relief, which unfairly settled a distorted reputation on the race in the minds of people often initially prejudiced.[73]

Given the disreputability of the Irish, they probably encountered greater discrimination than other minorities in America. "Potential employers disliked and even feared their religion, shuddered at 'Irish impulsiveness' and turbulence, and were disgusted and morally shocked at the Irish propensity for strong drink." In all likelihood, "no other immigrant nationality was proscribed as the Catholic Irish were." [74]

Fractional Selection

Fractional selection is the process whereby some fraction of newcomers pass into the ranks of disreputable poverty. It is the more normal, less dramatic, process of pauperization, depending on existing traditions of disreputable poverty, which are only occasionally replenished on a massive scale by newly generated cohorts. Given the relative absence of massive generation, the process of fractional selection is the major hindrance to the gradual attrition of disreputable poverty. The conversion of newcomers to dregs provides for the partial replacement of the pauperized individuals who somehow transcend their circumstance, and pass into the reputable sections of society. Consequently, the survival of disreputable poverty has partly depended on barring newcomers from the normal routes of social mobility. Thus, the general conditions underlying fractional selection into the ranks of disreputable poverty are for the most part simply the reverse of those favoring social mobility. These general conditions need no special restatement. Insead, I want to stress the temporal context of the circumstances favoring mobility.

Strong family organization, a cultural heritage stressing achievement, an expanding economy, an upgraded labor force, a facilitating demographic context and other conditions generally favoring mobility, have their effect within a temporal context. Once a period, the length of which will be suggested, is over, these general circumstances favoring advancement are hampered by demoralization, first in the form of severe discouragement or immobilization, and subsequently in the form of relaxed moral standards. Demoralization signals the culmination of

[73] Potter, *op. cit.*, pp. 84-85.
[74] Ernst, *op. cit.*, pp. 66-67.

the process by which some proportion of newcomers are selected for disreputable poverty.

The period during which newcomers enjoy relatively high morale is the temporal context within which the general factors favoring social mobility flourish. Its length varies, but the limits may be suggested. Demoralization may be avoided until newcomers are reduced to dregs, and the reduction of newcomers to dregs occurs when the steady desertion of mobile ethnic brethren is dramatically climaxed by an ecological invasion of new bands of ethnic or regional newcomers. When newcomers to the milieu of disreputable poverty predominate as neighbors and workmates, the remnants of earlier cohorts resentfully begin to notice what they have finally come to. They must now live and work with "them," and suddenly the previously obscured relation between their lot and that of their more fortunate or succesful brethren from the original cohort is clear. They have become dregs, reduced to actually living and working with "Niggers," or some other newcomers in the milieu of disreputable poverty. Pauperization through fractional selection occurs, then, when newcomers take over the neighborhood and workplace. This kind of pauperization becomes more pronounced when the newcomers who have overtaken the dregs are themselves replaced by yet another cohort of newcomers. Thus, the milieu of disreputable poverty is temporally stratified: the older the vintage, the more thorough the pauperization.

The spiteful and condescending clucking of the now reputable segments of the original ethnic cohort is the main agency in demoralizing those who still live in a disreputable milieu. The attitudes of the reputable are illustrated by the comments of upper-lower class Irish, reported by Warner and Srole: [75]

"Maybe we haven't made a million dollars, but our house is paid for and out of honest wages, too," said Tim.

"Still, Tim, we haven't done so bad. The Flanagans came here when we did and what's happened to them? None of them is any good. Not one of them has moved out of the clam flats."

"You're right, Annie, we are a lot better than some. Old Pat Flanagan, what is he? He is worse than the clam diggers themselves. He has got ten or twelve kids—some of them born in wedlock, and with the blessings of the church, but some of them are from those women in the clam flats. He has no shame."

"His children," said Annie, "are growing into heathens. Two of them are in the reform school, and that oldest girl of his has had two or three babies without nobody admitting he was the father."

[75] W. Lloyd Warner and Leo Srole, *The Social Systems of American Ethnic Groups* (New Haven: Yale University Press, 1945), pp. 12-13.

When they are forced to live and work with newcomers, the remnants need no longer overhear the disparaging comments of the reputable members of their ethnic cohort. They disparage themselves. They know what they have come to, for they share the wider social view that the newcomers are profoundly inferior and detestable. The irony here is that the demoralization of old ethics and their subsequent transformation to dregs results from the provincialism that simultaneously maintains ethnic identity long after it has been partially obscured in other parts of society, and manifests itself in pervasive prejudices perhaps unmatched elsewhere.[76] The measure in which the old cohorts are reduced to dregs depends partly on the extent to which they themselves denigrate newcomers. For now they become in the eyes of significant others, and in that measure to themselves, "just like them." [77]

I suggest, then, that the general conditions facilitating social mobility, and, thus, the departure of newcomers from the milieu of disreputable poverty are rendered ineffective by the demoralizing encounter with a new contingent of ethnic or regional poor. Thereafter, though the conditions normally favoring social mobility persist, they are dampened by the pauperization of the remnant ethnic stock.

CONCLUSION

The disreputable poor are an immobilized segment of society located at a point in the social structure where poverty intersects with illicit pursuits. They are, in the evocative words of Charles Brace, "the dangerous classes" who live in "regions of squalid want and wicked woe." [78] This stratum is replenished only rarely through massive generation, and there is little evidence that anything in the current American political economy fosters this sort of pauperization. Still, the tradition of disreputable poverty persists, partly because the legacy of the pauperized Irish immigrants has been continued in some measure by the fractional selection of subsequent immigrants, and partly because the internal situation of disreputable poverty conspires toward that end. Additionally, however, it persists for a reason that I have hardly touched in this essay: it persists because the other main carrier of the tradition of disreputable

[76] See Seymour M. Lipset, "Working-Class Authoritarianism," in *Political Man* (Garden City, N.Y.: Doubleday & Company, 1960), Ch. 4.

[77] The viciousness and bigotry with which the previous ethnic cohort treats newcomers is not just a consequence of their higher levels of provincialism and prejudice; what we regard as residential and occupational desegregation is to ethnic remnants a visible social indication of pauperization.

[78] Bremner, *op. cit.*, p. 6.

poverty in America has only now begun to mobilize, and, thus, to undo the effects of its enduring pauperization. When the Negro mobilization has run its course, and if no other massive pauperization occurs, the tradition of disreputable poverty will have used up its main capital and be reduced to squandering the interest drawn from fractional selection and its own internal situation—a fitting fate for so improvident a tradition.

12

POLITICAL MOBILITY
AND ECONOMIC DEVELOPMENT

LESTER G. SELIGMAN, *University of Oregon*

THE MOST DRAMATIC and far reaching expression of political mobility in recent years is the rise of new nations. The products of a latter-day political messianism, most of these new nations are in a troubled way, beset with the practical translation of nationalistic ardor and vision into conditions for viable political independence and economic development.

The morning after independence has brought a "shock of recognition" of fragile underpinnings. Building a new nation is a rough, unchartered journey with many unanticipated problems. A recent description of Indonesia illustrates the problems of many developing nations in the last decade:

It [Indonesia] suffers from an acute shortage of qualified or experienced personnel, a predilection for political intrigue rather than administration, and an intense resentment of any outside counsels of moderation. Fragmented into many geographic and cultural entities, hampered by bad communications and regional animosities, Indonesia's task of unification seems almost impossibly difficult. The country has been beset with official incompetence, opportunism and corruption, public ignorance and excitability, and economic dislocation intensified by bureaucratic muddle and malice. It has dissipated upon an anti-colonial, anti-capitalist campaign at home and abroad the energies and resources which might far better have been expended upon critical domestic problems which remain not merely unresolved but unanalyzed.[1]

In the new states, allocation of economic resources is primarily a governmental decision. Comprehensive economic planning, whether called Arab Socialism or "guided democracy," is the path chosen to economic growth and development, which means that the character and capacities of the political elites are of critical importance.

Everywhere in the new states are signs of the vagaries of uninstitu-

[1] Willard Hanna, "Nationalist Revolution: Indonesia," in Kalman H. Silvert, (ed.), *Expectant Peoples* (New York: Random House, 1963), p. 135.

tionalized elite recruitment and mobility: autocratic cults of personality, self-contradictory policies of economic development; venal and incompetent public officials, political instability and violence, and a critical shortage of competent technical personnel in government services. These problems of political leadership can be traced to political recruitment and mobility processes. Patterns of political ascent and descent, recruitment and selection, are of great consequence for the direction and tempo of economic development. The organizations, associations and political parties that produce leaders are therefore also of importance.

Every political system structures political opportunity so that the rise of some to positions of political influence is facilitated while others are retarded and excluded. This opportunity structure stands between social and economic changes and changes in political elites [2] so that normally a sluggish reaction occurs between social and political spheres. Only crises stimulate a response. The normal gap between political actuality and social change itself impels much of the demand for political mobility.

The analysis of political mobility imposes certain difficulties: First, the concept of political mobility, as yet in its infancy, is very imprecise. Some of this imprecision derives from general problems of measurement in political science. Economists may use monetary units whose fluctuations are regularly reported and which they can chart with accuracy. Per capita or aggregate sums may be accurately used to measure growth and decline. Sociologists may use occupational positions and groupings (however imperfectly) for quantitative measures of social mobility. Lacking such units, political science has special problems. No one has as yet been able to quantify per capita influence or aggregate power. Political power and influence elude direct measurement, and political mobility, a process definable in terms of the distribution of influence, can therefore be no more exact. Our analyses of power have, so far, refined our notions of what power is *not*, rather than yielding generic indicators for comparative analyses.

Although political mobility is not directly measureable, its consequences are nevertheless observable and describable. One cogent theory, the circulation of elites, is based on such an assessment. The circulation theory attempts to explain gross or historical change in political direction. Turnover and change in the composition of political elites are principal mechanisms that alter political structure and values. The greater the change in the character of elites, the greater the change in the direction and methods of the regime.

[2] Lester G. Seligman, "Recruitment in Politics," *PROD*, (March, 1956).

As an explanation of historical change this theory has much to support it, but it is less useful for short run periods. Short-run political change entails complex role transformations and re-allocation of resources, often without personnel change, and for these, the circulation theory is too gross. A refined analysis of political mobility requires functional specification of all political positions and roles, and in systems undergoing rapid change, the scope of the political is as broad as the system itself and the boundary of the political roles is difficult to specify. Moreover, in such systems, new political roles are being created and others are being discarded or are changing content, and in any case political roles are rather indeterminate.[3] As a result, inter-generational and intra-generational measurements, comparable to those made of occupational structures are difficult. Cross-national comparisons face similar complications.

Political mobility does *not* correspond to conventional ideas about upward and downward social mobility, for upward mobility in politics must be judged against what is happening to the structure of political stratification. Political mobility is associated with a flattening of the pyramid of political stratification. The greater the degree of political equalitarianism, the greater the degree of political development, for greater political equalitarianism provides more opportunity for political mobility and also stimulates aspiration to politically influential positions.

With these limitations in mind, I shall use political offices and officeholders and political organizations as starting-point units for assessment, and I shall use the term *political mobility* to refer to changes in political *status*, assuming that the hierarchy of political positions approximately reflects both prestige and influence. This is not necessarily true, of course, for political systems sometimes depart from ascriptive bases, and political statuses are in part an outcome of competitive struggles. Formal political status and situational political influence are not always equivalent. *Neither* an assumption that formal office holders are *always* most influential, nor that they are always powerless "front men" is warranted by the evidence.

A term I shall use frequently is *political development*,[4] referring to the increasing political complexity of the system, commensurate with industrial development and its concomitants. This increasing complexity

---

[3] The concept of determinateness in occupational roles is elaborated in Raymond Mack, "Occupational Determinateness: Problem and Hypothesis in Role Theory," *Social Forces*, 35, (October, 1956) pp. 20-25.

[4] Various meanings of this term are evaluated in Leonard Binder, "National Integration and Political Development," *American Political Science Review*, 68 (September, 1964), pp. 622-24.

is not necessarily associated with a politically democratic system, as the example of many new nations amply attests.

Throughout this paper I shall draw on studies of many of the new nations in the world. Lumping together in one category these disparate systems absurdly strains the elasticity of the category; nevertheless, it has greater heuristic value for comparative analysis than an exclusive focus on one particular system.

Within the framework of political mobility and economic development this paper has the following scope: First, the significance of political elite recruitment among the New States; second, some of the observed changes in specific political roles—legislators, administrators and interest groups; third, political organizational and associational tendencies that express the reciprocal influence of economic changes and political mobility and finally some dilemmas and tensions in political elite recruitment and economic development.

POLITICAL ELITE RECRUITMENT AND
POLITICAL DEVELOPMENT

In any political system, political roles must be defined, filled and vacated. Elite recruitment refers to the process whereby such "staffing" takes place.

The political recruitment function takes up where the general political socialization function leaves off. It recruits members of the particular subcultures—religious communities, statuses, classes, ethnic communities and the like, and inducts them into the specialized roles of the political system.[5]

Thus the very notion of political positions and roles is inseparable from the processes of exit and entry into them; only by virtue of such movement can these positions and roles be considered structural categories. For the actors themselves, recruitment embraces two processes: (1) the transformation from non-political roles to eligibility for influential political roles, and (2) the assignment and selection of people for specific political roles. Recruitment includes both *eligibility* for elite status and further *selection* or *assignment* to specific elite positions.[6]

[5] Gabriel Almond and James S. Coleman, *The Politics of the Developing Areas* (Princeton: Princeton University Press, 1960), p. 31; Harold D. Lasswell, Daniel Lerner and E. Rothwell, *The Comparative Study of Elites* (Stanford: Stanford University Press, 1952); David Apter, "Nationalism, Government and Economic Growth," *Economic Development and Cultural Change*, 7 (January, 1959), pp. 117-36.

[6] Lester G. Seligman, "Political Recruitment and Party Structure," *American Political Science Review*, 55 (March, 1961), p. 77.

Recruitment is, therefore, a central function of any political system, and the process of recruitment is an indicator of the values and distribution of influence within the system itself.

As a dependent variable, elite recruitment expresses the consistencies and contradictions in the value system, the types of representation, and the articulation of social stratification with the political status system. As a factor that effects change, the pattern of elite recruitment defines avenues for political activity and status. These paths to political positions influence the distribution of status and prestige, as well as economic and political policies.

Whether a new state can maintain both stability and economic growth hinges to a large extent on the integration among the political elites. The elites stand in the strategic center of development possibilities. Development involves the assimilation of new values, the acquisition of new frames of reference, and new ways of believing and behaving. Planned development calls for organizing and rationalizing resource allocation in a way consistent with goals of growth, productivity and higher income levels. Development, therefore, disrupts older values of status, prestige, and income, and it can be self-defeating if in the process the fabric of the social and political order is threatened.

Economic development distributes its gains unevenly. Vested interests—occupational, religious, linguistic—may be dislocated and deprived, while other groups gain new opportunities. Political parvenus are created while other people are impoverished. Some parts of the nation advance; others remain in a static condition. Older status and prestige is disrupted to make way for new occupational and political roles. Political acceptance of the new balance of advantages and deprivations is critical to the stability of elites. [This will depend upon whether those who gain and those who lose are, or regard themselves, as adequately represented. Such representation is usually achieved by the participation of various interests and groups in the decision-making process. Thus tensions depend on the degree to which there is agreement on decision-making methods. This in turn will depend on the acceptance of the elites and upon their *integration*.]

The Legitimations of Elite Recruitment

THE CENTRAL VALUES

In general, political elites are legitimated by embodying or evoking core values of the system. In a new state, the goal of economic development is interwoven with the goals of nationalism. The political oligarchy that led the movement for independence heads the new state.

Thus, nationalism, modernization and industrialization are primary in the legitimation of the governing elites. Other, complementary goals are higher educational and technical levels, international prestige and cultural renaissance.

When political independence is gained the formal rules of political democracy are among the first changes introduced, including a parliament, a judicial system, universal suffrage, an electoral system, and a progressive written constitution. These formal innovations are, perhaps, among the easiest made. But gaps in the social structure, the loose articulation of various parts of the society make effective democracy a remote and elusive goal. The absence of both a democratic tradition and the necessary social and economic conditions to sustain democracy often means that the new constitution has only a superficial effect.[7]

This formal democracy symbolically fulfills the goal of popular consent. But the nation-state is more than a symbol, it is the primary instrument for solving a more egregious problem—the weakening of traditional pluralism and the creation of new common identification with the new state and its values. In the new states, the governing elite is *the* instrument of transition from the older pluralism to one more characteristic of industrialized societies.

DUALISTIC LEGITIMATIONS

Initially, the nationalist ideology does no more than cover the traditional cleavages with a patina of surface solidarity. Citizenship in the new state is superimposed on loyalties to tribe, region, ethnic background or language. The result is that legitimations remain dualistic. The groups and institutions of the traditional pluralism are deeply rooted and resist efforts to displace them. Such traditional ties cannot be quickly or totally rejected or suppressed without threatening national solidarity. Moreover, the new nationalism itself *stimulates* and reinforces the older parochial loyalties. In many instances traditional groups become more apprehensive and militant about preserving their *identity* and status.[8]

This dualism is reflected and nurtured by the new elite cadres. Though they are selected for their nationalist achievements, elite members are offshoots of traditional backgrounds, incorporating the old virtues of family background and respected status with the newer ones of

[7] See Chief H. O. Davis, "The New African Profile," *Foreign Affairs*, 40 (January, 1962), pp. 293-302.
[8] Rupert Emerson, *From Empire to Nation* (Cambridge: Harvard University Press, 1960), p. 329; Lucy Mair, *New Nations* (Chicago: University of Chicago Press, 1962), pp. 116, 117; and Clifford Geertz, "The Integrative Revolution," in Clifford Geertz (ed.), *Old Societies and New States* (New York: Free Press of Glencoe 1963), pp. 122 ff.

education, skill and heroic achievement in behalf of national liberation. The ruling elites are emancipated children of the traditional social structure.[9] While rejecting the old, they cannot help but embody it.

In older democratic systems elites are also legitimated by traditional and new values; traditional norms invest political roles, but expectations of political effectiveness may contradict them. Alongside legitimations based on public consent, vestigial traditional expectations about political leadership persist, derived from the mixed western heritage of monarchy and aristocracy.

CHARISMATIC LEADERSHIP AS LEGITIMATION

In the new states charismatic leadership, or "cults of personality," are quite typical. Nehru, Nasser, Nkrumah and Sukarno seem to fulfill many roles. In a symbolic way they stand "above" the cleavages in the society. As venerated leaders of a heroic past, they are symbols of the nation unified, to all segments of the population. As "heroes of renunciation," who gave much for the sake of the cause and thereby earned their right to power, they epitomize sacrifice and struggle against colonial rule, and by inviting popular identification with themselves, they help create a broader identification with the nation. They are also architects and spokesmen of the drive for economic development,[10] and their international prestige nourishes the pride of their citizenry. As politicians, they tactically adjust the balance among contending interests in the nation. In these several ways, charismatic leaders satisfy many conflicting needs in emerging nations.[11]

Charismatic leaders not only have a mass following; they also have an elite recruitment function. They draw around them a corps of younger "new intellectuals" who serve as acolytes to the master, in bureaucratic and party organization posts.[12] These technical and managerial cadres become catalysts and shock troops in the march toward modernization; they also elaborate and impart the ideology and leadership myths.

[9] On the "marginality" theory of new elites see Everett Hagen, "A Framework for Analyzing Economic and Political Change," in *Development of the Emerging Countries* (Washington: The Brookings Institution, 1962), pp. 23-24; and Bert Hoselitz, *Sociological Aspects of Economic Growth* (New York: Free Press of Glencoe, 1960), esp. Ch. 3.

[10] Dankwart Rustow, *Politics and Westernization; in the Middle East* (Princeton: Princeton University Press, 1956), p. 36; R. Schachter, "Single Party Systems in West Africa," *American Political Science Review*, 55 (June, 1961), p. 296; Douglas Ashford, *Political Change in Morocco* (Princeton: Princeton University Press, 1961), p. 412.

[11] See Anne Wilner, "Charismatic Leadership," *Annals*, v. 358 (March, 1965).

[12] Harry J. Benda, "Non-Western Intelligentsias as Political Elites," in John H. Kautsky (ed.), *Political Change in Underdeveloped Countries* (New York: John Wiley & Sons, 1962), p. 238.

The Bases of Eligibility and Selection

ELIGIBILITY AND THE DOMINANT VALUES

The recruitment process itself adheres to the dominant values in the system. In highly traditional systems like Yemen and Saudi Arabia, ascriptive kinship determines eligibility to rule, and family succession is the method of role selection. In sharp contrast are more modern democratic systems where popular election is associated with wide eligibility for elite role selection. In general, the broader the eligibility for political status and roles, the more democratic the system; those restricting elite eligibility and relying on ascriptive criteria are often, though not always, more traditional and authoritarian.

Political prestige and the exclusiveness of recruitment appear to be highly correlated. Political prestige is higher in the newer states,[13] for in general, where political power is concentrated, a political career enjoys high prestige, has instrumental influence, and is much sought after. Political offices are prized for their high status, emoluments and power.[14] Political values more exclusively embody and express the central values of the society.

REPRESENTATION

One of the important criteria for political eligibility and selection is representativeness. Representativeness is the expectation that elites will be responsive to group demands. It does not necessarily imply broad recruitment of the political elites. Broad recruitment may be of functional value, but in itself does not ensure representativeness.

Representation is legitimized by selection by a political party. In two or more party sequences, the procedure of nominating candidates is designed to make those chosen representative of the character of the party. In single-party regimes, representativeness is accomplished by equivalent procedures.

With economic development new bases of social differentiations emerge—occupational groups, working-class organizations, professionals, managers, etc. Society becomes cross-hatched along lines of the division of labor in industrial societies. These new interests protect and promote themselves through political representation. They are attracted to the dominant party, first, because the policies of this party are in the vanguard of modernization and, second, because this party *is* the government, capable of granting and withholding the resources necessary for development, and it controls all the coercive instrumentalities.

[13] Robert Marsh, *The Mandarins* (New York: The Free Press, 1961), Ch. 1, 3; Edward Shils, "The Concentration of Charisma," *World Politics*, 11 (1958), p. 2.
[14] Morroe Berger, *Bureaucracy and Society in Modern Egypt* (Princeton: Princeton University Press, 1953).

A significant shift in legitimation gradually takes place with economic development. Increasingly, elected and appointed officials become spokesmen for various groups. Leaders are chosen because they speak for occupational groups or specific geographic areas. This is a shift in the focus of representation,[15] or a transfer of those whom officials avowedly represent.

The groups represented may be sectarian, single-interest groups. Where the basis of group formation and cohesion is not a specific interest, but a broad outlook or *Weltanschauung,* then a sectarian group may become a political party. Groups may also be classified functionally in the manner suggested by Almond as institutional, non-associational, anomic, and associational.[16]

POLITICAL SKILL

Skill and talent are another basis of eligibility and selection. In the new states, oratorical ability is a valued and necessary talent for a political leader. The ability to arouse the public directly is essential for political success. Rhetorical skill in evoking the sacred symbols of past and present is highly valued; next come organizational capacity and education. More commonly, politicians are generalists and amateurs who approach political problems ideologically, rather than in a problem-solving manner.[17]

Economic development creates a new demand for men of professional skills, which accounts for the rapid rise of a new intelligentsia with professional abilities. Technicians and experts are tardily recognized as necessary in the political elites. While the usefulness of economists, public administrators and managers, and sociologists is disputed, not only because their skills are "new," but because they threaten to de-ideologize politics, men with older and more prestigeful scientific skills, e.g., engineers, chemists, physicists are more readily accepted. The recognition of those with newer technical skills in the recruitment of elites is one of the cutting edges of change.[18]

In Western states, political roles are more differentiated.[19] Political elites include specialists in entrepreneurship, bargaining, organization,

---

[15] Heinz Eulau, John Wahlke, W. Buchanan, L. Ferguson, "The Role of the Representative: Some Empirical Observations on the Theory of Edmund Burke," *American Political Science Review,* 53 (September, 1959), pp. 744-55.

[16] Almond and Coleman, *op. cit.,* pp. 33-38.

[17] Lucian Pye has emphasized this point in *Politics, Personality and Nation Building* (New Haven: Yale University Press, 1962), pp. 28-29 passim.

[18] Martin C. Needler, "The Political Development of Mexico," *American Political Science Review,* 55 (June, 1961), p. 309.

[19] Lucian Pye, "The Non-Western Political Process," *Journal of Politics,* 20 (August, 1958), pp. 468-86.

propaganda, and other skills. Political roles are so specialized that they resemble those in all occupations, and they also tend toward professionalization in the sense that the techniques predominate over the goals. The mastery of these techniques creates a "community of skills"— negotiating, bargaining and administrative skills—among politicians which transcends partisanship. Politicians tend to be pragmatic rather than ideological. Associated with economic and political development is a public demand for moral probity, political neutrality, and efficiency among both politicians and administrators.

SELECTION

Selection, the special process whereby those eligible for political roles are assigned their particular roles, takes several forms. Selection may be made by the ruling oligarchy of a party, or by component units of the party. The former method favors deserving veterans chosen for their party loyalty and length of service. A kind of bureaucratic succession to political office occurs. Members anticipate nomination to the highest political positions only at the end of their political careers.

The larger and more heterogeneous a party (pluralistic party), the more selection devolves to the component groups. Groups, accordingly, will focus their efforts on the nomination and selection of candidates. A primary objective then becomes a party slate that represents the constituent groups.

CAREER PATHS AND MOBILITY

Definable paths to political power exist in every society. The number and specificity of the routes distinguish one political system from another. In traditional societies the route to power is through kinship succession. The politically "eligible" are the aristocrats, and then kinship or family preferments determine the assignment of elite roles. Age and seniority weigh heavily in determining level and status.

In modern Western societies, the parliamentary bodies have provided the principal routes of political ascent.[20] Parliaments have been the principal training ground for political elite status, although here the "pure" politician, who uses the political escalator exclusively, and politicians who enter politics via other occupational routes, should be distinguished.

The "pure" politician is often the party official, who earns his livelihood from political activity and who moved into elective office. The other, or mixed type, usually enters politics from another occupation; for him politics is a part-time activity. To the extent to which political

[20] See John C. Wahlke and Heinz Eulau (eds.), *Legislative Behavior* (New York: Free Press of Glencoe, 1959), pp. 243-272.

career paths are various, prestige and influence are diffused. Increase in the diverse paths to power is a mark of the pluralism of the system.

The rate of mobility is a significant factor. "It can be shown that many events and developments of history were shaped, in part at least, by whether the actors involved were improving, declining, or remaining stationary in their social and political positions." [21] In general, in normal periods, political ascent tends to be a *bureaucratic step-by-step escalation*. Circulation follows a more or less regular pattern where political attention vetoes some, and new elements enter. Regular rates of political mobility, however, are not incompatible with more rapid *entrepreneurial ascent*. This is characteristic of periods of crises and rapid change when new skills and personalities are in great demand. The innovators are those who have experienced high upward mobility, as a direct result of an expanding economy.[22] Descending mobility and political mortality are equally significant in elite behavior. From the casualties among the ambitious come the politically dissident: the ranks of the defeated are fertile recruiting grounds for the disaffected. All systems are beset by the problem of finding an appropriate status and rationale for those displaced.

POLITICAL ROLES

The Legislators

Parliamentary bodies chosen by the electorate are everywhere instituted in the new states. At the outset the new parliaments enjoy high prestige, and membership in them is a sought-after honor, for they symbolize the new representative democracy. The rituals and procedures of the English Parliament or the French National Assembly are usually adapted, even though the legislator's role differs from that of his Western counterpart.

Election campaigns for parliament, however, are unrestrained by rules of the game. Corruption and bribery are widely practiced, and the traditional methods of rivalry for power come into play in the guise of a democratic election.[23]

The new legislators are often the veteran party leaders and activists of the nationalist movement. Parliament is an honorific assembly of nationalist notables who were yesterday's conspirators, propagandists,

[21] Marsh, *op. cit.*, p. 11.
[22] On this point see W. L. Guttsman, *The British Political Elite* (London: McGildron and Lee), p. 172.
[23] This is elaborated in Chief Davis, *op. cit.*, pp. 303 ff.

prestigeful spokesmen, and old intellectuals. For many, politics has been their sole or primary occupation.

Many of the new legislators would have been eligible for elite status in the traditional social structure. One of the few studies of candidates for parliamentary election reports:

When new political institutions replace old ones, political influence tends to flow into the hands of people not exclusively identified with either the old or the new. Perhaps there are few genuinely new men of power and new elites. One sector of the old elite dons the robes of the new.[24]

The pre-independence career patterns of the parliamentary majority conditions their behavior in confronting tasks of national reconstruction. The old party politicians are often ill-suited to the demands of the legislative process; the complex issues of national economic planning are beyond their grasp and training. The new legislators are more inclined to use the parliamentary forum to voice the shibboleths of the movement and party, rather than as a problem-solving body. These limitations become more apparent as the executive furnishes the initiative for decision-making, while the legislators rubberstamp its proposals.

Members of the opposition are not equipped to play the constructive role of minority in parliamentary tradition. What Shils has called "the oppositional mentality"—narrow, extravagant, uninformed opposition—characterizes parliamentary conflict. The resulting inadequacies of both majority and opposition lead to parliamentary breakdowns, stalemate, and ultimately, a coerced opposition.[25]

After a time parliaments have been suspended altogether. Legislatures have ceased to function in Egypt, Indonesia, Burma, and even where the legislature is operative, as in India, Israel and the Philippines, its prestige diminishes as the state embarks on programs of economic development. The bureacracy grows in importance, and the legislature remains an assembly of past revolutionary notables. Only a few roles—chairmen of powerful committees, party leaders—retain significant influence.

Where parliaments remain viable, economic development problems, among others, and the complexity of government tasks modify the legislative role. "Amateur generalism" becomes dysfunctional. Some legislators become educated and adjust to representing interests in an indus-

[24] Robert O. Byrd, "Characteristics of Candidates for Election in a Country Approaching Independence: The Case of Uganda," *Midwest Journal of Political Science*, 7:21 (February, 1963).

[25] Edward Shils, *Political Development in the New States* (The Hague: Mouton, 1962), p. 34.

trializing society.[26] Occupational groups, geographic areas and other newer lines of social differentiation demand and receive representation. Some of the generalist-ideologist legislators become transformed into group representatives. Legislators educated by the bureacracy cease to be "orators," and become more expert in particular policy areas.

Turnover in the membership of parliament is slow, and the sluggish circulation of bureaucratized parties keeps younger people low on the parliamentary list. To satisfy the clamor of youthful elements some young people are coopted, often to provide symbolic representation more than change in direction. The legislature, because it tends to become an assembly of the old guard, is less sensitive to mobility demands. Eschewing the role of legislator to take important bureaucratic posts, the younger elements serve the desuetude of parliament; as an institution of "government by talk," it becomes an obstructive anachronism.

The Administrators

The bureaucracy occupies a commanding position in the economic development of new states. Empowered by the broad authority of the executive, the bureaucracy initiates and directs economic policies, unchallenged by the weak parliament, interest groups and public opinion. Fallers has observed that with regard to economic development, the bureaucracy is, or has become, the functional equivalent of the entrepreneur in Western historical economic development.[27]

The burgeoning public service of new states attracts many to join its ranks because the prestige and power of public service are high. Other occupations, such as teaching and law, have considerably lower status and prestige and draw the less talented.[28]

In countries with relatively little private industrial enterprise a government job has been the goal of a large proportion of the educated youth. With fewer outlets for their talents than are found in areas that are more advanced technologically, young people have looked to the government to provide both the income and the prestige or status they expect as the reward for their educational achievement.[29]

A rationalized bureaucracy along Western lines was established in

[26] Lester G. Seligman, *Leadership in a New Nation* (New York: Atherton Press, 1964).
[27] Lloyd Fallers, "Equality, Modernity and Democracy in the New States," in Geertz (ed.), *Old Societies and New States, op. cit.,* p. 185.
[28] Edward A. Tiryakian, "Occupational Satisfaction and Aspiration in an Underdeveloped Country: The Philippines," *Economic Development and Cultural Change,* 7, (July, 1959), p. 437.
[29] Berger, *op., cit.,* p. 68.

French and British colonies. Staffs were recruited by merit, rather than ascriptive criteria. Selection on this basis is resisted by established patterns of patronage to political party, geographic area, ethnic groups, etc., however, and the new bureaucracies are made up of mixed patronage and merit appointments.[30]

The civil service is the career line for the sons of the middle and upper classes, Western-educated and eager for power. The status system and the narrow base of education precludes any lower-class recruitment. Because of these restrictions, the social differences between public and public officials are very great. If all public officials are better educated and receive more income than the ordinary people (but are not especially competent), then the result can only be mutual estrangement, fear and resentment.[31]

The recruitment methods for public employment are not appropriate to the skills that are needed: "The training of new public servants . . . is often more related to their participation in nationalistic political parties than it is to bureaucratic skills."[32] In the training of public servants and would-be public servants literary-historical and narrowly legal training is emphasized. The notion that an official is not a "generalist," but a specialist in a particular field, lags behind in underdeveloped countries.[33]

The obligations and loyalties incurred in the process of gaining positions contradict the professed administrative goals. Appointive jobs are regarded as political opportunities to reward friends and punish enemies. Public service positions are used to bargain for monetary and power advantages.[34] The socialization of bureaucrats to fit the Western model remains partial at best, as long as recruitment and its obligations ties them to an ascriptive base. Riggs, Presthus, and others have explored some of the economic consequences of narrow, ascriptive administrative recruitment. National planning is frustrated by administrators who excessively favor special groups and subvert national goals.[35]

[30] R. S. Milne, "Comparisons and Models in Public Administration," *Political Studies,* 10 (February, 1962), p. 11.

[31] Berger, *op. cit.,* p. 15.

[32] S. N. Eisenstadt, "Bureaucracy and Political Development," in Joseph La Palombara (ed.), *Bureaucracy and Political Development* (Princeton: Princeton University Press, 1963), p. 107.

[33] Bert Hoselitz, "The Recruitment of White-Collar Workers in Underdeveloped Countries," in Lyle W. Shannon (ed.), *Underdeveloped Areas* (New York and Chicago: Harper & Row, 1957), p. 188.

[34] Leonard Binder, *Iran: Political Development in Changing Society* (Berkeley: University of California Press, 1963).

[35] Fred W. Riggs, "Economic Development and Local Administration: A Study in Circular Causation," *Philippine Journal of Public Administration,* 3 (January, 1959), pp. 56-147; Robert Presthus, "The Social Bases of Bureaucratic Organization," *Social Forces,* 38 (December, 1959), pp. 103-109.

While these generalizations are valid overall, national bureaucracies vary in their ascriptiveness, and variations also occur within the administrative establishments of particular countries. Some agencies are relatively rationalized and economizing; others are pockets of patronage and corruption.

The new patterns thrive best at the center and in the higher levels of society; the older patterns persist most vigorously at the periphery, in the rural hinterlands and at the lower levels of society.[36]

The ascriptive recruitment of the new administrators makes bureaucratic form a mere façade, a bureaucracy manqué. The forms of rational bureaucracy have been adopted; the job classifications, the organizational hierarchy are present, but efficiency and economizing behavior are lacking.

POLITICAL GROUPS

New Associational Interest Groups

Mobility efforts by associational interest groups (in Almond's usage) are important indicators of economic and political development. Interest articulation requires more than an economic base. It requires a fellowship of skill among members of an occupation, organizational skills, and a leadership effective in representing group claims. Because these qualities are scarce in developing systems, interest groups are rare.

Because interest groups express new loyalties, some governing elites view them as potential sources of dissidence. For this reason autonomous interest groups are found only in nations such as India and Israel, which are growing economically and have some stability as democracies. Most interest associations in developing systems are agents of the dominant political party, i.e., the governmental regime.[37] Others are created as instruments of governmental bureaucracies, to enhance administrative control.[38] A recent survey of trade unions in developing countries reports that many unions are mere "labor fronts" of the state.[39]

Despite their lack of independence, these interest groups have far-reaching consequences for political mobility. A developing economy

[36] Fred W. Riggs, "Bureaucrats and Political Development: A Paradoxical View," in Palombara (ed.), *op. cit.*, p. 123.

[37] Ashford, *op. cit.*, pp. 373-87.

[38] Riggs, "Bureaucrats and Political Development," *op. cit.*, p. 140.

[39] Walter Galenson (ed.), *Labor in Developing Economies* (Berkeley: University of California Press, 1962), p. 5.

requires a national market and a nation-wide use of its human resources. Since occupational interest groups are nation-wide, they serve as "nationalizing" agencies that tend to dissolve local attachments.

Economic growth and democratization give rise to expectations that economic interest groups will use political avenues to achieve higher status and income. Trade unions, professional associations, chambers of commerce begin to appear.[40] Associations and collectivities formed to protect and fulfill the status expectations of skill register their demands politically. Such rapidly expanding professions as teaching, engineering, and law—everywhere closely articulated with politics—insistently demand political recognition and higher status.[41] Teachers, engineers, and lawyers are Westernized early and inspired to emulate established professional organizations in the West. Because the state controls economic resources, these groups orient themselves toward political influence.

Though group claims may be limited in scope, one is reminded that the most revolutionary demands are not the utopian claims, but the insistent clamor for "more." Myron Weiner, in his perceptive analysis of India, has stated this well:

The popular notion of the "revolution of rising expectations" is in reality an explosion of social competition. Rising expectations are not aimed at American, Russian, or British living standards, but are demands by one group for improvement in its economic and social position vis-à-vis another group within India. . . . Clearly, for most Indians, the great competition is not between India and the West, or even India and China, but between social groups within India.[42]

The higher level of wants that interest groups articulate creates acute policy dilemmas for developing economies. On one hand, the newer occupational interest groups support the industrialization of the economy. They identify with the governing elite's goals of efficiency and higher production. On the other hand, they expect standards of income, status, and consumption that strain the capacities of the economy. Consumption demands must be restrained to permit saving and consequent reinvestment in the economy.

The new interest groups do serve several political mobility functions. They recruit and train new political leaders and foster a political outlook based more on interest than on ideology; they create new channels

[40] William H. Friedland, "The Institutionalization of Labor Protest in Tanganyika," *Sociologus*, 11 (1961), pp. 133-48.

[41] Binder cites a political party of engineers in Iran, *op. cit.*, p. 210.

[42] *Op. cit.*, p. 66. Hirschman regards such group demands as helpful to effective decision-making in economic development. Albert O. Hirschman, *The Strategy of Economic Development* (New Haven: Yale University Press, 1958).

for political influence and new avenues for social status. These political
innovations are conducive to economic change.

Traditional Groups

In contrast to new groups, the accommodations of older, traditional
associations to political democratization and the new mobility expectations exhibit another pattern. Nationalism and democratization intensify
particularistic loyalties. Old loyalties, threatened by the new nationalism, rally to protect their identities. Social castes in India are a case in
point:

> The caste association is no longer a natural association in the sense in which
> caste was and is. It is beginning to take on features of the voluntary associa-
> tion. Membership in caste associations is not purely ascriptive; birth in the
> caste is a necessary but not sufficient condition for membership.[43]

Castes adapt to new political opportunity for registering social demands by becoming quasi-interest groups. This collective change in role
weakens the traditional basis of cohesion, but substitutes a new basis,
i.e., a common stake in political gains that enhance collective social
status.[44]

Leadership in caste associations has changed in response to new
political demands. Seniority as a basis for selection to leadership positions is replaced by literacy in the ways of the new democratic politics.
The new leaders come from educational and occupational backgrounds
that train them to articulate group demands. Thus, traditional groups
like castes are transformed as they acquire new political roles. New
goals are grafted on to the traditional cohesion, and new methods for
attaining them are employed.

Similar associational transformations have been observed in West
African nations. Some tribal and traditional ethnic groups identify with
the governing nationalist-pluralist parties, and this politicization links
them to the larger society. The boundaries of identification are stretched
beyond family, village, and tribe.

Apprehensiveness about ethnic survival in a changing society activates
group claims. Common status and concern for social mobility lead to
group action to equalize opportunity. As a political participant in the
development process, an ethnic group avoids a caste-like status: this is

[43] Lloyd I. Randolph and Suzanne H. Randolph, "The Role of India's Caste
Associations," *Pacific Affairs*, 33 (1960), p. 8.
[44] Randolph and Randolph, *op. cit.*, and Selig Harrison, "Caste and Andhara
Communists," *American Political Science Review*, 50 (June, 1959).

one of the functional values of ethnic group political mobility.[45] Traditional identifications become "bridges," over which the new politicization and the new logic of economic rationalization can take hold in traditional groups. The new leadership is not a product of revolutionary turnover, but a gradual transition to acceptance of new political skills.[46]

THE POLITICS OF ECONOMIC DEVELOPMENT

These elite recruitment tendencies and mobility patterns are related to the dynamics of political orientations in developing systems. In most of the new nations, tendencies we can call Populist, Pluralist, and Sectarian operate in the context of a single governing party. Less often, these tendencies are expressed through separate political parties. In either case, the three categories suggest a synthesis of recruitment pattern and political mobility, as well as the basis for their relation to economic growth.

From the policies of the dominant nationalist-pluralist party flows the influence of economic growth. Decisions about priorities in allocating economic resources, made by the leaders of this party, have far-reaching political consequences, for they benefit some and deprive others. To maintain its cohesion, this party must adopt a flexible recruitment policy. This policy influences the competing parties in the following manner.

Decisions made in pursuit of economic growth divide the dominant Pluralist Party, producing a cleavage between Sectarians and Populists. These latter two groups are thus nurtured by *both the successes and the defeats of the governing Nationalist-Pluralists*. The Sectarians draw the Old Guard who regress to traditional idealism—ethnic separatists, religious groups, pre-independence idealists. The Populists attract the more anomic victims of social change—the ambitious but unsuccessful.

The Nationalist-Pluralist Party compensates for its losses by aggressive recruitment and co-optation of new groups; its leaders make strenuous efforts to attract new associations and new leaders to the regime. These include the professionals and technicians, new immigrants, youth groups and so forth. In addition to co-opting new elements, the Pluralists

[45] Not all new interest groups respond so effectively, nor do all traditional groups adapt so harmoniously. Separatism and violence are not uncommon, because the gains and benefits of economic change may be distributed unequitably, and political leadership is not always sufficiently adept or responsive to all group demands.

[46] Immanuel Wallerstein, "Ethnicity and National Integration in West Africa," *Sociologie Politique de l'Afrique Noire* (1960), pp. 136-137; David Apter, *The Gold Coast in Transition* (Princeton: Princeton University Press, 1955), p. 127. W. B. Birmingham and G. Jahoda, "A Pre-Election Survey in a Semi-Literate Society," *Public Opinion Quarterly*, 19 (Summer, 1955), p. 152.

thrive on the special generational cleavages characteristic of the Sectarians and the Populists. Some of the younger Sectarians come to regard traditional dogmas as anachronistic and dysfunctional and are attracted to the more progressive Pluralists, and some of the younger Populists discover that affiliation with the Nationalist-Pluralists yields more opportunities for social advancement.

Recruitment policies are themselves a dynamic agent of change. Economic development increasingly demands that economic and political roles be assigned according to achievement rather than ascription. The governing Nationalist-Pluralist Party, despite its bias toward ascriptive recruitment, is impelled by economic considerations toward achievement criteria, recognizing (however gradually) the need for administrative and technical experts in industrial and agricultural enterprises. The Pluralists also foster education that will produce skilled people. This policy threatens ascriptive patronage and embitters the older elements.

The Sectarians oppose the newer achievement criteria because such criteria "de-ideologize" politics. The displacement of the amatuer generalist by the new technician-intellectuals undermines Sectarian values. Moreover, achievement criteria revolutionize the basis of social stratification. The prestige of older pursuits, e.g., agriculture, traditional scholarship, diminishes drastically as the demand for the new professional men increases. Accordingly, the traditional Sectarians rally those of diminished prestige, the disaffected and disillusioned older idealists who are indignant at the change in values.

The Populists, in contrast, favor industrialization but deplore its political consequences. They see in the new achievement values support for the continued growth of a powerful, more centralized bureaucracy, and they regard the elevation of skill as an elitism that strengthens the power of the regime. Economic development, as the Populists see it, is a fine thing, but it is corrupted by a cumulative increase in venality and corruption, disguised by the honorific term "expertness," among officials.

The Nationalist-Pluralists govern because only they can coalesce a majority; only they can govern. If development proceeds within a reasonable consensus, the Sectarians and Populists steadily lose their political effectiveness. If development is too rapid, so that new groups (because of rapid mobility) and old groups (because of sharply declining mobility) begin to express extreme demands, then strong counter-reactions may emerge in behalf of either Sectarians or Populists. *There are thus two processes involved. The Pluralists grow by winning support from new groups and defectors from the Sectarians and Populists. At the same time, the Populists and Sectarians divide the "spoilage" in the manner indicated. If the Pluralists decline, then the Populists and Sectarians grow more rapidly.*

The Pluralists thrive symbiotically on their differences with the Populists and Sectarians. They *need* the opposition on either side to justify their governing policies. Each tendency uses the others as counter-images, to sharpen its own identity and cohesion. The Pluralists can stress their responsible realism, while charging the Sectarians with romanticism, and the Populists with irresponsible demagoguery. The Pluralists may thus create an ever-broadening center that drives the opposition to the fringes. In the same symbiotic fashion the Populists and Sectarians grow by setting themselves apart from the Pluralists. Each party or tendency thus *supports* each of the others in particular ways. Their competitiveness is more apparent than real, related to the political consequences of development more than to competition for office.

Only the Pluralists can govern. The Sectarians and Populists are *not* contenders for power, but pressure groups whose intent is to influence party policies, and except in periods of crisis they cannot mobilize the requisite mass support. Since they do not calculate on power, they would be embarrassed to achieve it. Their leadership is opposition-oriented. Balancing internal cohesion, mass support, and control of the opposition with effective government imposes severe strains on the Pluralists, but they control the majority party and have the state's ample sanctions at hand. The Pluralist leaders hold the opposition in contempt anyway, and they are strongly tempted to resort to coercive and dictatorial measures. Suppressing the opposition would make the Pluralists' position more secure; coercive methods could contain the ambitiously mobile who want *more*, and the disaffected anomic who want *less*, development.

Relations among these three political *tendencies*, then, embody some of the dilemmas of recruitment and economic development.

RECRUITMENT AND ECONOMIC DEVELOPMENT

Elite Representativeness and Its Dislocations

In general, the stability of an elite rests on the degree of its representativeness. An elite must be both *symbolically* and *functionally* representative. Various segments of the society must have formal decision-making opportunity and also appear to share the prestige of elite political status. The maintenance of representation is difficult and critical. If the elite becomes too exclusive it jeopardizes the broad public participation and support it needs to further development goals. But if it becomes too diffuse in its desire to be representative it may lose some of its effectiveness.

New elements in the population that seek political recognition are both products and catalysts of change. A persistent problem for any political elite is to decide how much of the new element it should incorporate. How many newcomers can an elite accept without jeopardizing its prestige and influence? By the same token, how can "obsolete" elite members be retired without risking revolt and dissension? This is part of an ongoing problem in any political system, i.e., the relation between internal mobility and stability.[47] We can better understand this by examining some of the dislocations produced by unbalanced representation.

A good index of dysfunction is the political weight of those excluded from and denied opportunities for access to elite positions. In developing nations, a common pattern is that opposition elements are denied legitimate participation in decision-making. Ruling oligarchies refuse to consult them or give them recognition. Under extreme conditions, which nevertheless appear to be characteristic of developing systems, opposition is *openly* suppressed. The most recent to succumb to this practice are Nigeria and Algeria. Successful suppression of opposition depends on severe restriction of opportunities for revolt. In certain Latin American and Middle Eastern countries, where armies are closely linked to political cliques, suppression feeds the overthrow of the regime.

Alienated Aspirants

Societies undergoing rapid change unleash influences that break up traditional patterns before new associations with socially constructive functions are prepared to stand in their place. This creates a category of displaced persons, the "transitionals," whom Daniel Lerner has so poignantly described.[48] These are individuals thrust out of former positions of authority. Related to this is excessive selection by particularistic criteria. That is, people from the "right" families and backgrounds are overrepresented. The skilled elements, who wish their merit recognized, are restricted and their qualifications insufficiently recognized. Another possibility is new groups, e.g., "unemployed intellectuals," with high aspirations and no place to go (as in India).

---

[47] Seymour M. Lipset and Reinhard Bendix, *Social Mobility in Industrial Society* (Berkeley: University of California Press, 1959), p. 3.

[48] Daniel Lerner, *The Passing of Traditional Society* (New York: Free Press of Glencoe, 1958), pp. 43-52.

When such groups and individuals find the normal routes to political influence blocked (as commonly occurs in overbureaucratized parties), they may resort to violence or provocative acts to gain political recognition.[49] New political cliques, cabals, or political parties may be formed, and under condtions of severe political repression they may become a revolutionary underground.

Acute Generational Cleavages

The post-independence generation, the men of technical skill and high status aspirations, are denied opportunities for appointive or elective public office. In many of the new nations, young intellectuals are among the most politically volatile elements—witness student demonstrations in the Middle East, the suppression of youth organization in Africa. Coleman points out that

. . . the generation of younger university-educated radicals . . . [tends] to be impatient or disenchanted with the older group, either because of their alleged use of public office for personal aggrandizement, or because of their failure to fulfill nationalistic objectives and complete the "revolution." [50]

Another factor responsible for generational conflict is that the channels of elite recruitment may have disappeared, and the younger generation cannot follow in the footsteps of the older. Pye notes that:

When this happens, as it has happened in all former colonial countries in which the national leadership was mobilized during a conspiratorial or agitational phase of limited duration, the new generation may feel that it is being denied legitimate opportunities. Such is the case in Burma.[51]

Still another reason for such conflict is that the skills demanded in nation building are different from those useful in the independence movement. The older politicians are likely to be expert organizers, conspirators, and agitators. The "new men" are administrators who admire technical expertness. The younger men are contemptuous of the obsolete, amateur talents of the older men. Where older elites can no longer be emulated, generational tensions are very high.

When generational cleavage is coupled with irregular rates of change, the mixture is politically combustible. If the rate of change is too rapid, then religious and linguistic groups rebel and demand a

[49] Apter, *op. cit.*, p. 117.

[50] James Coleman, "The Character and Viability of African Political Systems," in Walter Goldschmidt (ed.), *The United States and Africa* (New York: Frederick A. Praeger, 1958), p. 43.

[51] *Politics, Personality, and Nation Building, op. cit.*, p. 245.

return to fundamentalism.[52] If the rate of economic change is too slow, less mass unrest occurs, but expectations generated by the independence movement cannot be fulfilled. On such unfulfilled expectations are fed the new leaders, espousing rapid modernization through drastic methods.

The tensions between these two pulls—modernization and tradition—may become intellectualized and result in a new movement, a new ideology. The new ideology may come from the new bureaucracy—those with greatest experience in dealing with the new problems. Or it may come from the army. These people are also most sensitive to the tensions of inducing change. In Israel sluggish mobility is in part responsible for a new and vague outlook that might be called the "New Nationalism." These are younger people who are impatient with the old ways. Two values seem to be cardinal in this newer outlook. First, effectiveness, getting things done expediently without too much regard for form and custom, is worshipped. Second, a new identification, different from the traditional, and yet uniquely "national," is sought. In some ways it parallels the poetic extolling of "Negritude" in French West Africa, in linguistic revivals, in the new interest in archaeology, and in the intellectual quests for authenticity in Turkey, India and in other new nations.

This groping for ideological definition reflects the low status of old romantic scholarship, and the heightened status of scientific and technological skills. An intellectual rationale is necessary to legitimize violent rejections in the face of sharp change and a hazy future. In societies undergoing rapid mobility, the process of mobility and change can *itself* become the core of intellectual definition.

New social differentiations—chiefly occupational groups—accompany economic development. These groups seek political representation as an expression of their social status.[53] Where change is too rapid, the mobility of these groups fosters high expectations, which may impel them toward becoming autonomous centers of power. On the other hand, if change is too slow, then traditional elements may be intransigent in their resistance to the new differentiations.[54]

Another dilemma revolves around the exclusiveness of the political elite. An expansion of elite membership may diminish control and

[52] Bert Hoselitz, "Tradition and Economic Growth," in Ralph Braibanti and Joseph Spengler (eds.), *Tradition, Values and Socio-Economic Development* (Durham, N.C.: Duke University Commonwealth Studies Center, 1961), pp. 90-113.

[53] S. N. Eisenstadt, "Sociological Aspects of Political Development in Underdeveloped Countries," reprinted in S. M. Lipset and N. J. Smelser (eds.), *Sociology: The Progress of a Decade* (Englewood Cliffs, N.J.: Prentice-Hall, 1961), p. 19.

[54] Max Millikan and Donald Blackmer, *The Emerging Nations* (Boston and Toronto: Little, Brown and Company, 1961), p. 19.

extend the range of conflict, but an elite too restricted is insufficiently representative. Elites must channel or co-opt newly differentiated groups and allow them representation. If individuals from new strata are not permitted entry into elite positions, then collective mobility efforts may result. On the other hand, if extremely anti-traditional groups are too rapidly absorbed into power positions, then active dissension may result.

CONCLUSION

I have attempted to show that political recruitment and mobility are central to nation-building and economic development. Current evidence suggests some salient patterns. New nationalism reactivates the traditional pluralism—the ties to area, tribe, religion and language. Threatened by the modernizing nationalism of the political elites, these deep-rooted ties are expressed in new political movements. New political demands are also generated by the dislocations and imbalances caused by economic development.

The core problem is to modify the traditional pluralism to form a *new pluralism* based on acceptance of methods and goals compatible with the new national identification. Political recruitment and mobility mediate this transformation. Political mobility bestows or withholds the representation, status, and influence that accommodates the tensions of change. When recruitment and mobility policies are faulty, then they exacerbate cleavages that make political mobility itself a basis for ideological reconstruction.

13

SOCIAL AND POLITICAL

CONSEQUENCES OF MOBILITY

GINO GERMANI, *Institute of Sociology, University of Buenos Aires**

ONLY ONE CONCLUSION about the social consequences of mobility is likely to encounter general agreement: an enormous variety of social and individual consequences can be imputed to social mobility. Not only will different kinds of mobility produce different consequences under different circumstances, but the number and variety of processes that can be distinguished under the general concept of mobility (even limiting this to *vertical* mobility), and above all the complexity and diversity of historical circumstances that may affect mobility and of course its consequences, make it extremely difficult to formulate even a few valid empirical generalizations.

An adequate analysis of the consequences of mobility—either social or individual—requires both a theory, that is, a series of clearly specified, logically interrelated hypotheses, and relevant data. Unfortunately neither theory nor empirical evidence is adequate at present. Most of the empirical material consists of impressionistic studies, vague historical generalizations, indirect inferences and sheer guesses, and though many interesting theoretical suggestions have been made, few specific hypotheses and certainly no systematic theory has been formulated.

Among the many possible consequences of mobility [1] the present paper will be concerned only with its impact on the attitudes of accepting or rejecting the existing social and political order, with special reference to the effects of mass mobility in the lower strata.

* Visiting Professor of the Institute of Latin American Studies, Columbia University.
[1] For a general review see Pitirim A. Sorokin, *Social Mobility* (New York: Harper & Row, 1927), Ch. 21.

THE GENERAL SOCIAL CONTEXT OF MOBILITY

"Individual" and "social" consequences of mobility stem from the same basic social processes. The former affect individuals *qua* individuals, whereas the latter affect the social structure, or some of its aspects through the individuals and groups involved. Thus, some of the "individual" effects of mobility play a role as intervening variables in the causation of social consequences. The impact on *individuals,* however, is not to be considered a purely psychological phenomenon; in fact, the "individual effects" are themselves the outcome of socially and culturally patterned processes.

In Tables 1 and 2 I have summarized the main categories of variables which in my opinion should be taken into account in analyzing the consequences of mobility. Their relevance depends, of course, on the kind of impact being studied. The list is by no means exhaustive; it should be considered only an illustration of the kind of factors that determine the social effects of mobility.

"Objective mobility" as an independent variable. The notion of "objective" mobility is based on the procedures commonly used to

TABLE 1

RELEVANT FACTORS IN THE ANALYSIS OF THE SOCIAL CONSEQUENCES OF MOBILITY

1. INDEPENDENT VARIABLE:	"OBJECTIVE" MOBILITY
1.1 *Nature of the movement*	Direction (up or down). Distance. Starting point. Dimensions (occupation, power, wealth, prestige, consumption, social participation, etc.). Time (number of years or generations required to complete movement).
1.2 *Characteristics of the individuals* (or other units) *involved* both (mobile and non-mobile)	Criteria for selection (intelligence, personality traits, ethnicity, rural/urban origin, etc.).
1.3 *Quantitative importance of the movement*	Proportion of mobile and non-mobile individuals (or other units), by specific kind of mobility as defined by factors mentioned in 1.1 and with regard to (a) sending stratum; (b) receiving stratum.

2.	INTERVENING PSYCHOSOCIAL VARIABLES:	"SUBJECTIVE" MOBILITY AND IMPACT ON INDIVIDUALS
2.1	*Gratification/frustration of individuals* (mobile and non-mobile) involved in the process	Balance between level of aspiration and actual mobility.
2.2	*Acculturation*	Acquisition of cultural traits of the receiving stratum; varying from over-conformity to retention of the traits of the sending stratum.
2.3	*Identification*	Degree of identification with receiving stratum (or retention of identification with sending stratum).
2.4	*Personal adjustment*	Capacity to bear psychological stresses (if any) caused by movement into a different sociocultural and interpersonal setting.
3.	INTERVENING CONTEXTUAL VARIABLES:	SOCIAL STRUCTURE AND RATE OF CHANGE
3.1	*Structure of the stratification system and degree and rate of modernization of the society*	
3.2	*Degree and rate of economic growth*	
3.3	*Configuration of mobile and non-mobile sectors*	Various possible combinations originated by the simultaneous occurrence of different types of mobility and its coexistence with non-mobile sectors.

measure positional changes in the manifest status of individuals (or other units, such as families or groups) along one or more stratification dimensions. A large number of types of "objective" mobility can be constructed on the basis of the traits indicated in Table 1; some of them may not be empirically relevant or even theoretically important, but it is obvious that the social impact of mobility should be *specifically* related to *specific* types of objective mobility.[2]

"Subjective" mobility and "individual" effects as intervening variables. "Objective" mobility requires an interpretation in terms of social action. How mobility is perceived by both mobile and non-mobile individuals concerned, and how they react, is determined not only by

[2] This degree of specificity is not usually achieved in empirical studies of the effects of mobility.

the specific type of "objective mobility," but also by a number of psychosocial processes.

The relevance of reference group theory for the analysis of mobility is well known: [3] whether an individual experiences gratification or frustration depends on his reference groups, his aspirations, and the discrepancy between such aspirations and the actual opportunity for mobility perceived. Not the kind or amount of objective mobility, but the *balance* between aspirations and mobility is the dynamic factor (among others) in determining individual and social consequences. And, as others have observed, more objective mobility may increase the level of aspiration, or create aspirations that previously did not exist in both mobile and non-mobile persons. Thus, the notion of *relative deprivation* (and *relative gratification*) is highly relevant in this context.

Although level of aspiration and choice of reference groups may be in part the result of idiosyncratic factors, they are to a much greater extent the result of the socially and culturally patterned experiences in early socialization and in later stages of individuals' lives. Intervening contextual variables in such patterning include the structure of the stratification system and the impact of particular events during the life of coexisting generations.[4]

Displacement from one stratum to another may involve acculturation, change of class identification and adjustment to a different social environment. Most research on the consequences of mobility and on its "cost" is concerned with precisely such processes. Here the available empirical evidence reveals different "effects." For instance, "normative" mobility,[5] that is, mobility involving a change in class subculture, may result sometimes in "overconformity," sometimes in "assimilation" or average conformity, and in other cases in "retention" of the older norms characterizing the original or sending stratum.[6] Fairly similar alternatives have been observed with regard to class self-identification.[7] And, finally, for

[3] Robert K. Merton, *Social Theory and Social Structure* (New York: Free Press of Glencoe, 1957), pp. 262-280.

[4] Harold L. Wilensky, "Orderly Careers and Social Participation," *American Sociological Review*, 26 (August, 1961), pp. 521-539.

[5] Arnold S. Feldman, "The Interpenetration of Firm and Society," in International Social Science Council (ed.), *Les implications sociales du progrès technique* (Paris, 1962), p. 192.

[6] See Peter M. Blau, "Social Mobility and Interpersonal Relations," in *American Sociological Review*, 21 (June, 1956), pp. 290-295.

[7] The tendency seems to be "retention" of father's status; this effect was quite clear in the author's Buenos Aires study: Gino Germani, "Class Social subjectiva e indicadores objetivos de estratificación" (Buenos Aires: Instituto de Sociologia, 1963). Effects of mobility on self-affiliation were also observed by Bertram A. Hutchinson, "Class Self-Assessment in a Río de Janeiro Population," *América Latina* 6 (1963), pp. 53-64, and by F. M. Martin, "Some Subjective Aspects of Social Stratification," in David V. Glass (ed.), *Social Mobility in Britain* (London: Routledge and Kegan Paul, 1954), Ch. 3.

individuals and groups displaced from one socio-cultural and inter-personal environment to another different one, the conflict between internalized norms and the requirements of the new situation results in personal or collective disorganization, or anomie.[8] Other important effects have been imputed to the conflict between culturally favored aspirations and socially permissible means.[9] These processes—acculturation, identification and personal adjustment—may play an important role in shaping the impact of mobility on social structure and social processes.

Intervening contextual variables. My concern here is with the general social context not as a *cause* of mobility but only as it conditions its social consequences. The general framework in which mobility occurs is the *system of stratification,* which conditions the impact of mobility not only through specific mobility norms and values, and the actual distribution of real life-chances, but also through the other characteristics listed in Table 2.[10] A few remarks will illustrate their relevance in this respect.

The *profile* of stratification is very important in determining the quantitative impact of mobility: given the same proportion of mobile or non-mobile individuals, the impact depends on the relative sizes of the sending and receiving strata. When the middle and higher strata are relatively small, even complete permeability (i.e., an empirical mobility approaching the "perfect" mobility formalized in certain indexes) means very little in terms of actual chances for individuals in the lower strata. The opposite effect may occur when the middle strata are larger and include at least a proportion of the population not much smaller than the proportion located in the lower strata.

Given the direction, distance, starting point, etc., of "objective" mobility, and the level of aspirations and anticipatory socialization, accul-

[8] Emile Durkheim, *Le Suicide* (Paris: Alcan, 1897), Ch. 5; Maurice Halbwachs, *Les causes de suicide* (Paris: Alcan, 1930), Ch. 15 (an interesting early reformulation of the classic Durkheimian hypothesis by a prominent member of the school); Merton, *op. cit.,* p. 188. On the disorganizing effects of social mobility, see the summary and bibliography in Seymour M. Lipset and Reinhard Bendix, *Social Mobility in Industrial Society* (Berkeley: University of California Press, 1959), pp. 64 ff., 252, and *passim.* See also Morris Janowitz, "Some Consequences of Social Mobility in the United States," in *Transactions of the Third World Congress of Sociology* (London: International Sociological Association, 1956), pp. 191-201. More recent contributions to this topic are Robert J. Kleiner and Seymour Parker, "Social Striving, Social Status, and Mental Disorder: A Research Review," *American Sociological Review,* 28 (April, 1963), pp. 189-203 and Warren Breed, "Occupational Mobility and Suicide Among White Males," *American Sociological Review,* 28 (April, 1963), pp. 174-188. For a review of earlier literature, see Sorokin, *op. cit.* Ch. 21.

[9] Merton, *op. cit.,* pp. 135 ff.

[10] See also Melvin Tumin, "Competing Status Systems" in Wilbert E. Moore and Arnold S. Feldman (eds.), *Labor Commitment and Social Change in Developing Areas* (New York: Social Science Research Council, 1960), pp. 279-280.

turation, identification, and personal adjustment will be more traumatic and more conducive to anomic reactions when a high *degree of discontinuity* exists between strata. *Hierarchization of interpersonal relations* may be considered a particular kind of discontinuity, and in this sense it may have similar effects. At the same time, however, its impact on mobility may be indirect, with different social consequences. Under conditions of a high degree of hierarchization, individuals in the lower strata feel segregated: the cleavage between strata is highly visible. Although the actual chances of mobility may be the same, upward mobility is likely to be less *visible* under these conditions. Downward mobility, or relative deprivation for the non-mobile, may be expected to have more severe effects where discontinuity and hierarchization are high.[11] In addition, these characteristics are usually accompanied by a *highly institutionalized image of stratification*, which may be quite important in determining the nature and the impact of status congruence. With a clear image of congruence, the psychosocial effects of incongruence should be much stronger than they are in a society where class lines are blurred and a clear notion of the "equivalents" in each stratification dimension is absent.

The probability of incongruence is related, of course, to the degree of homogeneity of *mobility norms* and to *actual chances* in the various dimensions. Where the mobility norms and empirical chances are the same in all dimensions, mobility is not likely to produce status incongruence, but if inheritance is the dominant norm in some dimensions, while other channels are open according to achievement criteria, incongruence will be a frequent outcome of mobility. This situation is particularly important for the social effects of mobility: partially blocked mobility is usually considered one of the more powerful sources of resentment and social tension. *Mobility values, attitudes and beliefs* condition the level of aspiration, and together with mobility norms and the real chances open to individuals, determine the degree of satisfaction or frustration induced in both mobile and non-mobile persons. Also, as suggested above, beliefs and attitudes may alter the visibility of actual mobility.

With the characteristics listed in Table 2 a typology of stratification systems could be constructed. The most widely used—either explicitly or implicitly—is the dichotomous classification (or, better, the continuum) in which the polar types are the "traditional" and "modern" patterns. The first is frequently described as a two-class system, with the great majority of the population in the lower stratum. It is characterized by high degrees of discontinuity and hierarchization and a highly

[11] Lipset and Bendix, *op. cit.*, esp. Ch. 3.

institutionalized image of stratification, in which inheritance norms, values and attitudes are dominant and real chances for mobility are slight. The second, the "modern" pattern of stratification, is defined by the opposite traits: multiple strata, or even a "stratification continuum," low degrees of discontinuity and hierarchization, an unclear image of the system, frequent status incongruence, predominant achievement norms, values and attitudes and high chances for effective mobility. As is well known, this typology does not describe concrete systems: on the contrary, various mixtures of "modern" and "archaic" traits exist not only in transitional societies—because of their transitional character—but in more stable societies as well. In fact, "modern" traits have been observed in many pre-industrial societies, and vice versa; the degree of compatibility between "traditional" traits—including aspects of stratification—and urban, industrial, modern structures seems to be quite large. On the other hand, many traits enumerated in the table are not completely independent of one another. They *tend* to cluster, and the combinations in which "modern" traits prevail are more frequently observed in industrial urban societies, while more "traditional" configurations seem fairly common in pre-industrial ones. At the same time, however, many important social consequences of mobility can be understood only in the context of a "mixed" stratification system.

Other aspects of modernization also affect the results of mobility: urbanization, literacy, diffusion of communication media, mobilization, political participation, secularization of the family, the church and other institutions, and so on. Many of these traits are somewhat related to the stratification system and exercise their influence mostly through it; some aspects of modernization, however, such as attitudes toward change, ability to adjust to new situations and especially to social and ecological displacement, and various others intervene more directly in determining the social consequences of mobility.

The *level and rate of economic growth* (as distinguished from degree and rate of modernization) are also likely to modify the impact of mobility. I am suggesting here that at a given level of modernization, the same type of "objective" mobility may produce one set of social consequences under conditions of economic growth and another during an economic depression, and that the stage of economic development reached by the society comprises analogous modifying conditions.

Finally, different types of mobility may occur at the same time, and the particular configurations resulting from simultaneous processes may introduce new conditions relevant to the effects of mobility.

TABLE 2

CHARACTERISTICS OF THE STRUCTURE OF THE STRATIFICATION
SYSTEM RELEVANT TO THE ANALYSIS OF THE CONSEQUENCES OF
MOBILITY

---

1. *Profile of stratification:* proportion of the population located in each stratum.

2. *Degree of discontinuity between strata:* ranges from maximum discontinuity, with clear cleavages between strata coupled with gross differences and inequalities in all dimensions, to minimum discontinuities in all the dimensions and a "stratification continuum."

3. *Degree of hierarchization of interpersonal relations:* ranges from maximum to minimum emphasis (overt or covert) on status inequalities in most or all social situations.

4. *Degree of institutionalization of the "image" of the stratification system:* ranges from maximum to minimum degree of institutionalization involving also maximum to minimum clarity of the "image" of each stratum, and of "ideal" congruence.

5. *Mobility norms:* predominance of inheritance or of achievement among the stratification dimensions, with various intermediate possibilities.

6. *Mobility values, beliefs and attitudes:* ranges from a maximum emphasis on stability and inheritance to a maximum emphasis on mobility and achievement (combined with varying degrees of consensus in the different strata).

7. *Real possibilities of mobility:* ranges from very few, unequally distributed among the strata, to many, equally distributed among the strata.

MOBILITY AS A FACTOR IN RADICAL OPPOSITION

Mobility has its most disruptive effects on the social order when it is *non-institutionalized mobility* and when there is an *imbalance between aspirations and actual chances of mobility,* that is, a lack of mobility when it is expected and institutionalized. In this sense mobility is disruptive in a "traditional" society with an "ascriptive" system of stratification, while in an "industrial" society that approaches the opposite ideal type, it is a normal recurrent process favorable to (or even required for) the maintenance of system equilibrium.

Non-institutionalized mobility by definition introduces status incongruencies: it involves opening some dimensions while the dominant norms and values (or at least the norms and values of the dominant groups) remain geared to the requirements of the previous structure.

This situation is a powerful potential source of social tension because the groups involved tend to re-equilibrate their status.[12] I shall consider two types of situation: *upward partial mobility*, and *downward partial mobility*.

Upward partial mobility: the case of developing countries. Typically, in this situation, the groups affected try to remove the obstacles blocking their social ascent and in doing so become innovating or revolutionary groups. The well known theory of the strategic role of the "partially deprived group" in the earlier stages of development is based precisely on an hypothesis of this kind.[13] According to this theory, if complete mobility had been possible (that is, if the possibility of status equilibration had existed), no innovating or revolutionary attitudes would have developed. Analogous consequences have been attributed to the partial mobility created by the diffusion of education. The rising expectations of newly educated groups remain unsatisfied because other groups— foreign or domestic—virtually monopolize the higher positions available in the society, or because the new supply of educated persons exceeds the demand or fails to correspond to the specific technical or intellectual skills required. Thus the formation of a "rootless intellectual proletariat" has been counted as one factor in the development of communism in Asia.[14] "Distinct ideological polarization" between "old" and "new" (educated) elites, giving rise to similar innovating movements, has been

[12] Lipset and Bendix, *op. cit.*, consider status incongruency one of the major intervening factors in conditioning the social consequences of mobility. Some effects of low crystallization on political or ideological orientation were found by Lenski, who also formulated a statistical definition of incongruency; see Gerhard E. Lenski, "Status Crystallization: A Non-Vertical Dimension of Social Status," *American Sociological Review*, 19 (June, 1954), pp. 405-413. Analogous results were found by Erving W. Goffman, "Status Consistency and Preference for Change in Power Distribution," *American Sociological Review*, 22 (February, 1957), pp. 275-281. Lenski also studied effects on social participation: "Social Participation, Status Crystallization and Class Consciousness," *American Sociological Review*, 21 (June, 1956), pp. 458-464. Degree of status congruence also seems to affect self-affilation to class: see Werner S. Landecker, "Class Crystallization and Class Consciousness," *American Sociological Review*, 28 (April, 1963), pp. 219-229. Similar results were obtained in Buenos Aires by Germani, *op. cit.*

[13] Marion Levy, "Contrasting Factor in the Modernization of China and Japan," in Simon Kuznets, Wilbert E. Moore and Joseph J. Spengler (eds.), *Economic Growth: Brazil, India, Japan* (Durham, N.C.: Duke University Press, 1955); Everett E. Hagen, *On the Theory of Social Change* (Homewood, Ill.: The Dorsey Press, 1962).

[14] Morris Watnick, "The Appeal of Communism to the Peoples of Underdeveloped Areas," in Seymour M. Lipset and Reinhard Bendix (eds.), *Class, Status and Power* (New York: Free Press of Glencoe, 1953); Myron Weiner, "The Politics of South Asia," in Gabriel A. Almond and James S. Coleman (eds.), *The Politics of the Developing Areas* (Princeton: Princeton University Press, 1960); Jerome M. v.d. Kroef, "Social Conflict and Minority Aspirations in Indonesia," *American Journal of Sociology*, 55 (1950), pp. 450-463.

observed in Africa and elsewhere. Their sense of superiority, born of acquaintance with modern ideas and methods, supports their ambition to achieve power through revolution or reform.[15]

In Latin America, extremist or at least radical movements have been promoted by groups whose ascent was partially blocked by the persisting rigidities of the stratification system. The rising middle strata created by the first steps toward economic development and social modernization, were led by their newly acquired class identification and their desire to gain political power and prestigeful positions to oppose the poltical and social order that gave the traditional elites a virtual monopoly on power and prestige. Supported by recently mobilized sectors of the lower strata, which usually lacked political experience, intellectuals, professionals, industrial entrepreneurs and similar groups organized the "national-popular" movements that have appeared in most of the Latin American countries in the last few decades. These include, among others, the APRA in Peru, the National Liberation party in Costa Rica, the Venezuelan Acción Democrática, the MNR in Bolivia, the radical parties in Chile and Argentina, at least at an earlier stage of their political evolution, and the PRI in Mexico. Peronism and Varguism (which I will examine later) must also be classified in this broad category, so far as they included middle-class sectors, partially blocked in their political and social ascent, as an important dynamic element.[16]

These political movements did vary a great deal, and for the purposes of a more specific analysis more refined distinctions should be introduced, but all of them were multiclass parties with an ideology favoring basic social changes, and all of them were equally and emphatically nationalistic, anti-imperialist and anti-oligarchic. From country

---

[15] Richard F. Behrendt, "The Emergence of New Elites and New Political Integration Forms and their Influence on Economic Development," in *Transactions of the Fifth World Congress of Sociology* (Louvain: International Sociological Association, 1962). An interesting example of the contrasting effects of modern education in a traditional setting when accompanied or not accompanied by status discrepancies is mentioned in a study on the political evolution of Uganda: David E. Apter, *The Political Kingdom of Uganda* (Princeton: University Press, 1961), pp. 199 ff. and 313 ff.

[16] On the populist alliance of the rising middle class and the lower strata, see Victor Alba, *Historia del Movimiento Obrero en América Latina* (Mexico: Liberos Mexicanos Unidos, 1964), Ch. 7; Armando Villanueva-del-Campo, "Partidos Democráticos Revolucionarios en Indoamérica," *Combate* (September 1961 and February 1962); Mario Monteforte-Toledo, *Partidos Políticos de Iberoamérica* (México: Instituto de Investigaciones Sociales de la Universidad Nacional Autónoma, 1961). Torcuato Di Tella has analyzed the role of partially blocked mobility in the anti-statusquo attitudes of Latin American intellectuals and middle-class groups: "Los Procesos Políticos y Sociales de la Industrialización," *Desarrollo Económico*, 2 (1962), pp. 19-48 and *El Sistema Político Argentino y la Clase Obrera* (Buenos Aires: Eudeba, 1964), Ch. 9.

to country, and from time to time within the same country, the extent of their real opposition to the *status quo* also varied, however, according to the success of the leading middle-class components in their efforts to equilibrate their status. The typical evolution of these movements has been from revolutionary and radical opposition to the political and social order to a more moderate orientation. Such change seems to correspond to the level of integration of the middle-class groups. The Radical Party in Argentina, for example, maintained its revolutionary impetus until the beginning of the century. But an unusually high rate of mobility and very rapid modernization produced an independent urban working class, and the party became a typical centrist party more homogeneously based on the middle classes. In Chile a similar evolution occurred.

The Peruvian APRA started with a more extremist orientation characteristic of the rigid stratification system, but later increased its political participation, and—probably—the increased legitimacy of its leaders moderated the APRA position.[17] The national revolution in Bolivia was a more extreme consequence which may be attributed largely to the severe deprivation of the leading middle-class sectors, combined with the more complete mobilization of the lower strata, which made available for the MNR far more popular support than the Peruvian party achieved.

Downward partial mobility: a European example. One of the most impressive symptoms of major social tension created by downward partial mobility was the middle-class support of rightist totalitarian movements in the interwar period, in Europe. Downward mobility resulted from the accumulation of various factors: inflation reduced drastically the savings and real income of the majority of the middle strata, their relative position was deeply affected by the substantial gains the workers were obtaining at that time, both in income and in political power, and finally unemployment among professional people contributed to their "proletarianization." Under the impact of this process, the intellectuals provided the leadership for both radical extremes of the political spectrum, but mostly for the rightist totalitarians.[18]

[17] The typical evolution of the APRA and other similar Latin American movements is examined from a leftist standpoint by Álvaro Mendoza-Diez in *La Revolución de los Profesionales e Intelectuales en Latinoamérica* (México: Instituto de Investigaciones Sociales, Universidad Nacional Autónoma, 1962).

[18] Social status and degree of modernization of the region of origin have been important in determining political orientation. In Germany, intellectuals of higher status and from more traditional and peripheral regions most frequently adopted the Nazi ideology, while the opposite was true for the "cosmopolitans" and those of lower social origins. In Argentina, extreme right-wing nationalism, during the thirties, was supported by a downwardly mobile traditional élite drawn disproportionately from the backward rural regions.

This European example suggests that when downward mobility affects a high proportion of the individuals in the middle or higher strata, the anomic effects of the displacement are likely to be transformed from an individual to a mass phenomenon. Mannheim and others have suggested that individual insecurity caused by inflation, status panic, or mass unemployment may stimulate collective insecurity, thus creating the conditions for the acceptance of totalitarian solutions.[19] In a similar general climate of depression, analogous consequences have been observed in lower-class groups at the individual level.[20] In the European example, another essential factor in this process was the high discontinuity and high hierarchization of the stratification system of the time, which increased the anomic consequences of the displacement and rendered intolerable the threat of the rising working class, especially for the lower middle groups. A similar process of decreasing differentials, occurring in the same countries after the Second World War, did not have mass effects. As I shall suggest in the next section, recent changes in the stratification system are one important source of this difference.

The preceding illustrations have shown that the direction of mobility may be correlated with specific ideological orientation: blocked *upward* mobility creates a propensity for "progressive" ideology, while a reactionary orientation expresses the experience of downward mobility. The relationship is much more complex, of course, because many other factors intervene. For instance, the specific configuration of mobile and non-mobile groups, and their availability for political action comprised another condition that promoted the "national-popular" parties in Latin America, and the rightist totalitarian movement in Europe. In Latin America the incongruent sectors of the middle-class were small, but the support of recently mobilized lower groups was available to them, and this required a "populist," "social justice" ideology. Even the downwardly mobile elements in the traditional élite (which had failed in their previous attempts to produce Fascist-like movements) joined the mass national-popular Peronist and Varguist parties in Argentina and Brazil. In Europe the working class had been politically organized for

[19] Karl Mannheim, in *Man and Society in an Age of Social Reconstruction* (New York: Harcourt, Brace & World, 1940), aptly describes the difference between the effects of *individual* unemployement and *mass* unemployment: "If in normal times an individual loses his job, he may indeed despair, but his reactions are more or less prescribed and he follows a general pattern in his distress. The panic reaches its height when the individual comes to realize that his insecurity is not simply a personal one, but is common to masses of his fellows, and when it becomes clear to him that there is no longer any social authority to set unquestioned standards and determine his behaviour," p. 130.

[20] See Harold L. Wilensky and Hugh Edwards, "The Skidder," *American Sociological Review*, 24 (April, 1959), pp. 215-231, on the different consequences of downward mobility in a climate of depression as compared with a period of prosperity.

a long time and was historically associated with a progressive ideology: the only "available" masses were the displaced middle-class groups, which included enough people for a mass movement, though less than a majority of the population.[21] Available élites, available masses and available ideologies are the important conditions shaping the specific ideological orientations of the movements originating in partial downward or upward mobility.

MOBILITY AS A FACTOR IN POLITICAL AND SOCIAL INTEGRATION

Implicit in the foregoing discussion are the general conditions under which mobility is likely to be an integrative force in the society. Such conditions may be summarized as follows: Mobility aspirations are of some importance for individuals and are widely diffused in the population; aspirations and actual mobility are balanced [22] in all strata and for the great majority of individuals (failures being perceived as "deviant") with respect to the institutionalized mobility norms; mobility is equally possible along all the relevant dimensions (that is, serious incongruencies are rare); hierarchization and cultural and interpersonal discontinuities (or at least their *visibility* for the majority of the individuals) are minimal; and finally, individual and social mechanisms of adjustment to mobility are effective. Under these conditions the individual "costs" of mobility are likely to be negligible, while the balance between aspirations and actual chances tends to increase (or at least to maintain) a strong feeling of participation in the society and to promote, as a consequence, a high degree of involvement in and acceptance of its social and political order.

The historical experience of the presently advanced countries, as well as certain developing nations, indicates that under the *cumulative* impact of some of the processes typical of economic development and social modernization, the contextual factors that made mobility disruptive or neutralized its integrative consequences in an earlier stage tend to be replaced by the opposite conditions. These processes include changes in the profile of stratification—broadening of the middle strata and a resulting "structural" mobility; additional mobility created by demo-

[21] For a comparison between Italian Fascism and Argentine Peronism, see Gino Germani: "La Integración Política de las Masas," *Cursos y Conferencias*, 42 (June, 1956).
[22] That is, *specific* aspirations are related to *specific* kinds of actual mobility; relative deprivation is minimized and optimum relative gratification ensured.

graphic differentials; greater "fluidity" [23] stemming from the "exchange" mobility produced by a wider application of achievement criteria; continuous transference of status symbols from top to bottom through increased participation in the "higher" consumption patterns and styles of living, or mobility by increasing participation.

This entire process is powerfully reinforced by mobility itself, once it reaches a relatively high quantitative level and has achieved a certain duration. First, as a reinforcing factor in structural change mobility helps to modify the psychological meaning of incongruence and to diminish its effects. During the initial stages of the transition the "incongruence" continues to be perceived because the traditional stratification pattern provides an "ideal image" of congruence. This situation may last for a long time, and it may co-exist with more modernized aspects. But once a persisting high mobility rate increases the proportion of incongruent individuals beyond a certain level the "ideal image" is likely to lose much of its validity as a criterion of evaluation. Except in certain special cases where castelike elements exist, the higher the proportion of the incongruent individuals in a population, the weaker the previously institutionalized image. At a given point, as has occurred in advanced areas, congruence becomes either a matter of opinion (one polls the population to discover what the image is in that society), or a statistical fact, based on the frequency distribution of stratification indicators.[24] A high frequency changes incongruence into a property of the stratification system, and its psychological meaning, its individual and social effects, and the very possibility of being aware of it, tend to decrease. A second consequence of an enlarged proportion of incongruents, when the rates of downward and upward mobility are high, is that the internal homogeneity of classes is decreased and, consequently, the gap between them is diminished, thus tending to blur discontinuities. This observation is far from original,[25] but the phenomenon does not seem to have stimulated studies of the extent to which this process may alter the structure of the stratification system.[26] It is unnecessary to

[23] The term fluidity is used by S. M. Miller: "Comparative Social Mobility," *Current Sociology*, 9 (1960).

[24] See, for example, the procedure used by Lenski, *op. cit.*

[25] Sorokin, *op. cit.*, Ch. 22.

[26] In the Buenos Aires metropolitan area a sample survey showed that the occupational origins of the present generation were quite mixed. In the two lower (manual) strata, taken together, only 34.7 per cent had remained stable (within either stratum); within the two manual categories 21.7 per cent had moved up, and 6.6 per cent down; finally, 37.0 per cent had fathers who were non-manual. In the three middle categories only 23.8 per cent had remained in the same middle category as their fathers; another 20 per cent had moved up or down within the middle strata; 17.4 per cent were born in the two upper most strata; and finally 38.7 per

insist on the *immediate* effects its tendency to weaken class solidarity [27] has on political orientations; what I want to emphasize here is the *structural* impact of fluidity, once it reaches a high, fairly constant level.

Finally, the experience of mobility shared by a wide and increasing proportion of the population through many generations contributes to the diffusion of more equalitarian values and beliefs, and to less hierarchical attitudes, manners, interpersonal relations.

This self-reinforcing process may be associated with the process of economic growth. "Self-sustained" mobility is possible only after a number of strategic aspects of the social structure have been modified, and the time this transition takes depends on the structural characteristics of the society at the "starting point." When the positive feedback of the self-sustaining stage is achieved, mobility becomes a normal, permanent process. The changes required by industrial development begin to broaden the stratification profile and bring about other modifications of the occupational structure, causing an initial mass mobility. At the same time the changing requirements for allocating personnel—especially educational requirements [28]—tend to increase "exchange" mobility, while the growth of the national product and its more equalitarian distribution increases consumption. On the other hand, the mobility so originated eventually reacts on the new structural conditions, reinforcing the previous changes. Technological innovation as a normal process

---

cent were of lower-class origin. In two higher strata, 29 per cent were stable, 8.5 per cent had been mobile within the two strata, and the majority—62.5 per cent— had lower origins (42.0 per cent were born in the middle strata and 20.5 per cent in the manual strata). While this situation seems rather common in urban areas, it is still important here to clarify the pyschological and cultural meaning of the occupational classification. (In this example it was based, as usual, on occupational prestige.) Gino Germani, *La Mobilidad Social en la Argentina* (Buenos Aires, Instituto de Sociología, P. Interna 60, 1963), p. 21.

[27] Sorokin, *op. cit.*, Chs. 21-22; Lipset and Bendix, *op. cit.*, pp. 66 ff; Wilensky and Edwards, *op. cit.* Ralf Dahrendorf expresses the same opinion but he notes that "mobility within classes is entirely irrelevant" in the context of *class* conflict: *Class and Class Conflict in an Industrial Society* (London: Routledge and Kegan Paul, 1959), pp. 220-221. But then one may ask where class boundaries are, in metropolitan urban society.

[28] The rate of downward mobility is likely to increase with the growth of occupations to which access is based on aducational requirements rather than inheritance of wealth, because there is the risk that an individual will fail to achieve the education level required to maintain his family position while virtually no such risk is involved in inheriting property. In the stratification and mobility survey in Buenos Aires (already quoted), and in a similar survey in Sao Paulo (Brazil), a considerable proportion of downward mobility was associated with failure to achieve the educational level "required" at any given occupational level (the "requirement" being defined statistically). See Gino Germani, *La Mobilidad, op. cit.*, and Bertrand Hutchinson: "A Educacao e a Mobilidade Social" in Bertrand Hutchinson (ed.), *Mobilidade e Trabalho* (Rio de Janeiro, Centro Brasileiro de Pesquisas Educacionais, 1960).

seems to be a basic mechanism in maintaining the rate of mobility needed to produce the integrative effects. ("Exchange" mobility alone is insufficient, because the maximum degree of fluidity possible in any society has a definite limit.) Technological innovation increases mobility in two ways: it produces a continuous occupational upgrading by transferring "lower" tasks to machines, and at the same time creates new needs and new products to satisfy them. Thus, a constant flow of new status symbols is circulated from top to bottom.

Massive mobility in advanced countries in recent years. The changes that have taken place in Europe seem to have made the European countries more similar to the kind of industrial society typified by the United States. In spite of remarkable differences among such countries, all of them have been approaching the various conditions under which mobility has an integrative impact: decreasing interclass tensions, greater acceptance of the social order by the lower strata and a substantial re-orientation of their political parties. The two basic aspects of the process are mass "individual" (exchange and structural) mobility and mobility by increasing participation.

On the mass character of individual occupational mobility, a number of points are relevant. Using a manual/non-manual dichotomy Miller showed that in the nine most industrialized countries, upward intergenerational mobility out of the manual strata was 20 to 30 per cent.[29] Now, whether these figures are "high" depends on one's expectations concerning this process in the type of society in question. In any case, however, rates of this size must leave unsatisfied a majority of the people belonging to the manual strata, assuming that all of them really aspired to the non-manual level. On the other hand, it has been observed that the manual/non-manual categorization, though very useful for international comparisons, may grossly underestimate the extent of *psychologically meaningful* mobility. The rate of mobility certainly depends on the number and kind of categories employed. For instance, when one discriminates within the manual stratum, separating the skilled from the unskilled workers, the rate of movement out of the unskilled includes, in many industrialized countries, a majority of the people.[30] Moreover, there are indications that upward (or downward) short-distance mobility may be perceived and experienced as deeply

[29] Miller, *op. cit.*

[30] Published data show that mobility from the unskilled or lowest level may be very high in some countries: 79.6 per cent in the Netherlands; 80.0 per cent in the U.S., 72.6 per cent in Great Britain, 54.6 per cent in Denmark, and lower in Japan (36.2 per cent) and Italy (34.0 per cent). In the former countries, however, upward mobility from the semi-skilled level includes the majority of those born in the stratum (53.7 per cent); high mobility is also observed when one takes into account only movement from the lowest *urban* stratum: Puerto Rico, 86.0 per cent; U.S., 63.0 per cent but in West Germany only 38.5 per cent. Cf. Miller, *op. cit.*

important by the mobile subjects,[31] especially in the case of intragenerational mobility. One's ability to discriminate on the basis of prestige is higher when comparing occupations in the proximity of one's own than it is when the occupations are more distant. More important, individual aspiration levels may usually be restricted to a very small range of the social hierarchy.

Thus, many mobility studies based on a set of broad occupational categories probably underestimate the extent of psychologically and socially relevant mobility. More precise knowledge of modal and deviant levels of aspiration and reference groups characteristic of each stratum, and the factors determining these characteristics, is needed. Data now available show that even in the United States, which could be taken as an extreme example of a culture emphasizing occupational and economic success, workers' levels of aspiration are much lower than those of the middle and upper classes. Social values that emphasize individual success tend to be seen in realistic terms, according to the possibilities actually available.[32]

Other general tendencies also transform the work situation, shaping mobility aspirations in terms of an ordered sequence of steps: this is the so-called professionalization of work. This process itself results from a series of other technological and economic factors, but in turn one of its general consequences is to introduce "career" mobility. Even when it is limited to the range of "working-class" positions, individuals nevertheless experiences it as an orderly process of advancement conforming to a series of expectations.[33]

True, orderly careers during the larger part of the individual's life are probably still a small proportion of all careers, according to recent studies by Wilensky.[34] But, as he points out, the psychological effects of

[31] The possibility of an inverse relation between distance and the effects of downward mobility has been mentioned by Seymour M. Lipset and Joan Gordon, "Mobility and Trade Union Membership," in Lipset and Bendix (eds.), *Class Status and Power, op. cit.*

[32] Leonard Reissman, "Level of Aspiration and Social Class" in *American Sociological Review*, 18 (April, 1953), pp. 233-242 and the bibliography in his *Class in American Society* (New York: Free Press of Glencoe, 1959), Ch. 6. In his research on automobile workers Chinoy found that a stable job was experienced as mobility or "getting ahead." Ely Chinoy, *Automobile Workers and the American Dream* (Garden City, N.Y.: Doubleday & Company, 1955), p. 125. According to Zweig, the worker "wants to better himself not so much by promotion, but by higher wages," and he wants security more than anything else. Ferdynand Zweig, *The Worker in an Affluent Society* (London: Heinemann, 1961), pp. 205-206.

[33] Nelson N. Foote, "The Professionalization of Labor in Detroit," *American Journal of Sociology*, 58 (1953), pp. 371-380. For the same trend in France, see Serge Mallet, *La Nouvelle Classe Ouvrière* (Paris: Editions du Seuil, 1963), pp. 56 ff.

[34] Wilensky, *op. cit.*

the "career" depend on other circumstances, including among others, the generational experience, which affects the aspiration levels of individuals of different ages according to the different historical circumstances through which they have lived.

One of the most important aspects of mass mobility hardly needs mentioning: the great rural-urban migrations and the successive displacement from primary to secondary and tertiary activities. Although the interpretation of these movements in terms of mobility is far from simple,[35] the indisputable long-run result—whatever the difficulty of adaptation and whatever the internal contradictions—is the massive upgrading of great strata of the population.[36] In the past century through part of the present one, in the United States and several other countries, rural-urban migration was combined with great international migrations. Most European countries, and especially the less advanced ones, have experienced great changes in this respect.[37]

Downward mobility seems to have been quite considerable in Europe in recent decades.[38] Although not much attention has been devoted to this phenomenon, it is known that mobile individuals tend to maintain for a time their original attitudes and even their original class identification. But this is in advanced industrial societies in a period of economic growth. Mobile individuals' retention of cultural traits related to their class origins may increase heterogeneity within each stratum, but the "cost" of mobility may at the same time be reduced by the decreasing

[35] Arnold S. Feldman, "Economic Development and Social Mobility," *Economic Development and Cultural Change*, 8 (1960), pp. 311-320; see his remarks on the interaction between status and situs mobility.

[33] International data on mobility connected with rural-urban migration have been summarized and analyzed by Lipset and Bendix, *Social Mobility. . . , op. cit.*, pp. 216 ff. While the circumstances of migration, the selection of the migrants, the distribution of occupational opportunities, and so on, condition the consequences of migration, in a time of industrial growth and in the contemporary work situation, rural-urban displacements are likely to be experienced as upward mobility. In a recent research on French workers of rural origin, Touraine says: "Their presence in the factory is the proof—for them—of mobility, if not of an achieved mobility at least of a first step, of a first victory: their entrance into urban economy and into urban life." Alain Touraine and Onetta Ragazzi: *Ouvriers d'origine Agricole* (Paris: Editions du Seuil, 1961), p. 117.

[37] Italy is probably one of the most extreme among Western European countries: in 1951 40 per cent of the labor force was concentrated in agriculture; in 1961, this proportion had been reduced by half, i.e., to 20 per cent. This process will probably continue in many European countries: the European Parliament has estimated at many millions the labor force to be transferred from the primary sector to the others. See Gaston Beijer, *Rural Migrants in an Urban Setting* (The Hague: Martinus Nijhoff, 1963), p. 23.

[38] Miller, *op. cit.;* the published figures show a minimum of approximately 20 per cent to a maximum of 43 per cent moving out of the non-manual into the manual strata.

class differentials. Also, for contemporary generations, socialization in a period of rapid change and widespread ecological and vertical mobility may encompass mechanisms for adjustment to what seems to be a *normal* occurrence.[39] The frustrating effects of downward mobility may be partially neutralized by a widespread sense of increasing opportunities, as already noted. In any case, this climate may have prevented individual cases of downward mobility from creating a *mass* phenomenon.

To what extent is the progressive participation of growing sectors of the population in the consumption patterns, the style of life and the education levels that were once symbols of upper-class status, experienced as personal mobility? In other words: when do such elements lose their psychosocial value as status symbols? For example, new items of consumption tend to be included in the family budget very soon, on a permanent basis, as normal expectations.[40]

Nevertheless, at least at present, many of the new consumption patterns are still viewed as symbols of personal success.[41] In any case, we do not need to belabor the fact that this process has narrowed considerably the distance between the working-class style of life and that of the middle classes, giving rise in the working population to a certain degree of "embourgeoisement." The progressive elevation of education, so that each new generation has access to levels that were out of the reach of the preceding one, not only promotes opportunities for individual betterment, but also permits fathers to transfer to their children their mobility aspirations. Thus, what is in fact a generalized improvement for the whole population may be felt by the subjects themselves as an individual attainment.

Two very important elements of this type of collective mobility are its continuity and its relative rapidity, so that most members of the present generation have experienced a progressive expansion of the possibilities of the individual. *The expansion of aspirations has been*

---

[39] Mobility seems not to be disruptive for those who are trained for it; this provisional conclusion refers to *ecological mobility*, but may have some application to vertical mobility as well. See Phillip Fellin and Eugene Litwak, "Neighborhood Cohesion Under Conditions of Mobility," *American Sociological Review*, 28 (June, 1963), pp. 364-376.

[40] This process of progressive change in the normal expectations of consumption was observed and described more than 30 years ago by Maurice Halbwachs, *L'Evolution Des Besoins Dans Les Classes Ouvrières* (Paris: Alcan, 1933), pp. 148 ff.

[41] Conspicuous consumption is becoming common among workers. "He [the worker] wants to show something for his labor, something tangible which can be seen by everybody and speaks clearly the language of success. He wants to show that he has not wasted his life, but achieved something which does not fall behind the standard of others. In this way a large section of the working-class population becomes a property-owning class" (Zweig, *op. cit.*, p. 206). Durable goods, cars and home ownership retain their value as status symbols, even if increasingly common ("My neighbours would call me middle class because I have my own house." *Ibid.*, p. 138).

simultaneous with the expansion of the possibilities of their satisfaction.

In a well known hypothesis, Lipset and others have suggested that "high" rates of individual mobility are equally characteristic of all industrial societies and that some consequences attributed to this process with respect to the United States, particularly the greater integration of the lower classes and the absence of typical class movements, are due not so much to mobility but rather to other aspects of social structure: equalitarian values and associated attitudes, especially the "equalitarianism of manners" which undoubtedly has helped to conceal or diminish class differences in power and prestige. In many European countries these differences are (or were) much more visible and exerted a much greater influence in accentuating the isolation of the working class. Other factors linked to the persistence of archaic traits in the stratification system, and some of the main conditions blocking mobility and facilitating the radicalization of the subordinated or isolated groups, were typical of the Western European situation. But as European countries approached the conditions required to facilitate the integrative effects of mobility, the integration of the working class increased considerably, as Lipset and others have observed. This change was clearly expressed in the substantial modification of working-class political and ideological attitudes, even though the old labels and party organization remained unchanged.[42]

The hypothesis that mobility occurs at an equally high rate in all industrial societies is limited, in any case, to "individual" mobility and mainly to the manual/non-manual distinction. But this kind of mobility is only one of several forms that may create the mass mobility conditions needed to break the isolation of the lower strata and ameliorate their feelings of inferiority and rejection. Values, attitudes and ideologies are indeed determining factors in the consequences of mobility, but we must recognize that under conditions of mass mobility these same values, attitudes and ideologies are likely to be substantially modified. This is, in fact, the process that occurred in Europe in the post-war decades.[43] The contrast between the American and the European experiences in-

[42] Seymour M. Lipset, "The Changing Class Structure and Contemporary European Politics," *Daedalus* (Winter, 1964), pp. 271-303; see also the articles by Ralf Dahrendorf, Alessandro Pizzorno and Alain Touraine in the same issue.

[43] It is interesting to compare the necessary conditions for a distinct working class consciousness as summarized by de Man some 30 years ago on the basis of a survey among workers, and Zweig's obervations on the contemporary English working class. According to de Man, the conditions are: (i) membership in a class deprived of any property; (ii) insecurity; (iii) low status, lack of consideration; (iv) lack of mobility. Henri de Man, *La Gioia nel Lavoro* (Bari: Laterza, 1931), p. 393. According to Zweig, (i) "the working-class population becomes a property-owning class;" (ii) has "security mindedness;" (iii) "has a recognized niche and social position;" (iv) even apart from those who are mobile within the working class, "a quarter of the boys coming from factory workers' families are reaching middle-class levels," Zweig, *op. cit.*, pp. 146-147; 205-206.

dicates that a rather long period of isolation under a highly hierarchical and discontinuous stratification system is a necessary condition for establishing political organizations of a predominantly or exclusively working-class composition. Such organizations evidently are stable enough to persist after the conditions of isolation have disappeared or greatly diminished, although the ideological orientation of their political action will be deeply modified as the lower strata they still represent become integrated with the national society. In the United States the integration occurred much earlier, and the greater and more diffused acceptance of the existing social order evidently inhibited the formation of specifically working-class parties of any importance.

MASS MIGRATIONS, MASS MOBILITY AND SOCIAL CONSENSUS IN ARGENTINA AND BRAZIL

Argentina in two stages of its socioeconomic development, and Brazil more recently, in its rapidly industrializing regions, have approached the conditions most conducive to the integrative effects of mobility.

The Argentinian experience during six decades of mass international migration (1870-1930) involves an almost complete transformation of the stratification system, and remarkable changes in values and attitudes, under the impact of mass mobility. At the beginning of the period the social structure and predominant values of this society were fairly similar to those of other Latin American countries, with the traditional Spanish emphasis on ascriptive norms and values, family origin and stability. At the national level the socio-occupational structure exhibited the typical two-class pattern,[44] with the bulk of the population in the lower stratum and the usual high discontinuity and high hierarchization prevailing between classes. In the decade 1860-1870 an accelerated process of economic growth and modernization was initiated, which in little more than 40 years completely transformed the social structure and the economy of the country, at least in its "central" region where two-thirds of the population live. The innovating agent was the liberal elite, composed

[44] Di Tella has observed, in Chile, Argentina and elsewhere, an "intermediate" stratum of a traditional nature (artisans, small shopkeepers and the like) which includes a considerable proportion of the *urban* population even if in the national average it is very small. Downgraded by the "first impact" of economic development it could have some political role. This hypothesis, however, does not alter the basic assumption of a two-class system at the national level. See Torcuato Di Tella, "Economía y Estructura Ocupacional en Un País Subdesarrollado," *Desarrollo Económico*, 1 (1961), pp. 123-153.

mostly of big landowners, who undertook the task of organizing Argentina as a modern nation, within the limits of the economic conceptions of the time and in accordance with their own political and economic interests. Their program involved mass foreign immigration, massive imports of foreign capital, building railways, roads and means of communications, establishing and diffusing modern education at all levels, creating modern bureaucratic organization and a stable representative democracy, occupying all the available land, incorporating all the national territory in the market economy, and finally integrating the national with the world economy by modernizing agriculture and cattle breeding, changes that turned Argentina from an importer nation into one of the main exporters of cereals, meat and other food products. The amazing growth of the society in the first three or four decades of the process is illustrated in Tables 3 and 4.

The conditions of mass mobility were created chiefly by the rapid expansion of the middle-class, whose proportion more than doubled in the 25 years before the turn of the century and has continued to grow at a very high rate ever since. This increase involved mass recruitment from the lower strata: during the period from 1890 to the end of mass immigration in 1930, more than two-thirds of the middle-class were of lower-class origin and in many cases the mobility was intragenerational.[47] In fact, most of the recruitment took place among the foreign immigrants who long formed the majority of the adult male population in the "central" regions of the country.[48] Until 1900, more than 95 per cent of the foreigners who arrived in Argentina were lower-class, mostly rural laborers, and in the following decades the proportion of middle-class immigrants increased a little but never exceeded 10 per cent during the period under consideration.[49]

As one of the consequences of this process, "open society" attitudes came to prevail in Argentina, including equalitarian values, manners and interpersonal relations, with diffused beliefs in the possibilities of individual success conceived in material terms, and less formalism and less tendency to make hierarchical distinctions than in the other Latin American countries.[50]

This change (with respect to the original situation) was much less marked or even absent in the "peripherical" areas not affected by the

[47] Germani, La Mobilidad Social, op. cit., p. 10.
[48] More than 70 per cent in the Buenos Aires area and more than 50 per cent in the Litoral. Gino Germani, "La Asimilación de los Inmigrantes en la Argentina," Revista Interamericana de Ciencias Sociales (Washington), 1 (1961), no. 1.
[49] Germani, La Mobilidad Social, op. cit., p. 7.
[50] Except for Uruguay, where development took a form closely similar to Argentina's.

TABLE 3

SOME INDICATORS OF GROWTH AND SOCIAL MODERNIZATION IN
ARGENTINA: 1869-1960 [45]

	1869	1895	1914	1947	1960
Population (000's)	1,700	4,000	7,900	15,900	20,000
Crude Birth Rate (0/000)	°	°	38	25	23
Crude Death Rate (0/000)	°	°	19	10	10
Mean No. Persons per Household	6.05	5.48	5.24	4.32	†
Per Cent of Population in Cities of 2,000 or More	27	37	53	62	†
Per Cent of Population in Cities of 20,000 or More	14	24	36	48	58 ‡
Percentage Foreign-Born	12	26	30	15	12
Percentage of Active Population in:					
Primary Activities	41 ‡	39 ‡	28 ‡	25	23
Secondary Activities	31 ‡	25 ‡	34 ‡	32	33
Tertiary Activities	28 ‡	36 ‡	38 ‡	43	44
Percentage of National Product: §					
Agricultural	°	37	25	18	°
Industrial	°	13	16	24	°
Percentage of Active Population in Middle Occupational Level ‡	11	25	30	40	45
Percentage Literate	22	47	65	84	92
University Students Per Thousand Inhabitants	°	°	1	3	7

° Data not available or not published.
† 1960 Census: data not yet available.
‡ Estimates based on census and other information.
§ Information refers to an approximate date, not precisely the year of the census.

TABLE 4

PERCENTAGES OF THE ACTIVE POPULATION IN DIFFERENT
SOCIO-OCCUPATIONAL STRATA: ARGENTINA, 1869-1960 [46]

Year	Middle and Higher Occupational Levels		Lower Occupational Levels		
	Secondary and Tertiary Activities	Primary Activities	Secondary and Tertiary Activities	Primary Activities	Total
1869	5.1	5.5	53.5	35.9	100
1895	14.6	10.6	46.2	28.6	100
1914	22.2	8.2	50.0	19.6	100
1947	31.0	9.2	43.8	16.0	100
1960	37.3	7.9	39.7	15.1	100

[45] Sources for the data are the National Censuses and other official statistics; estimates and analysis in Gino Germani, *Estructura Social de la Argentina* (Buenos Aires: Raigal, 1955), and Ruth Sautu, "The Socio-occupational Structure of Argentina, 1869-1914" (Buenos Aires, Instituto de Sociología, 1961) (unpublished paper).
[46] Same sources as Table 3.

developmental process, which was concentrated mainly in the *litoral* region.

With regard to the acceptance of the social and political order, the impact of mobility during this period (1870-1930), seems to be analogous to the European experience. The innovating elite—the so-called "oligarchy"—conceived its political regime as a liberal democracy, with limited popular participation. The radical changes the elite itself had promoted, in fact, initiated the social and political forces that would in time challenge its monopoly of power and prestige. As indicated earlier, the outcome of this situation of "partial mobility" was a "populist" reform movement led by the middle-class, but its relatively easy political success—enlarged political participation and access to power, coupled with a persisting high rate of mobility—evidently dissipated a great deal of its reformist zeal. In the lower strata the newly formed urban proletariat originated, in the first decade of the century, extreme radical protest movements, prone to violence but of relatively short duration as they were rapidly absorbed in the unions and in the very moderate socialist party that emerged in the twenties and thirties as a left-of-center alternative to the middle-class parties. Communism in its different varieties has remained an extremely limited group in Argentina, both before 1930 and afterwards.[51]

The relatively rapid integration of the urban proletariat in the "central" region can be explained partly as a consequence of individual mobility from the manual strata. This mobility rate was high,[52] but even if it had been low, similar effects would have been produced by complementary mechanisms. Certainly the country did not reach the stage of mass consumption at that time, but the process of uninterrupted economic growth may have contributed to satisfy the modest aspirations of the majority. However the most effective "multiplier" of the effects of individual mobility was the continuous renewal of a high proportion of the lower strata, by the constant flow of new immigrants into the lowest level, replacing those who were upwardly mobile. When this well known mechanism of replacement from the bottom occurs fairly quickly, as it did in Argentina, there is not enough time to form a real "proletarian tradition," which requires, as in the European experience, a long period of isolation and class homogeneity.

[51] In the twenties Argentine Communists numbered fewer than 3,500. See Rollie Poppino, *International Communism in Latin America* (New York: Free Press of Glencoe, 1964), p. 64. The maximum vote obtained by Communists, in a coalition with democratic non-communist groups, was less than 5 per cent in 1946, in the Buenos Aires area. In the rest of the country they were nonexistent.

[52] The national average may be estimated at some 20-25 per cent as a minimum. But since the process was concentrated in the central areas the actual upward mobility rates in this region must have been much higher, especially in Buenos Aires and other large urban centers.

The 70-year period under consideration was quite stable, with a succession of civilian governments and no military intervention, and with popular participation in elections and normal political activity increasing. The large foreign population did not vote,[53] however, and in the "outer" underdeveloped regions the political influence of the lower strata remained fairly low.

A second stage in the modernization and economic development of Argentina, and similar changes in Brazil, illustrate the integrative effects of mobility in presently developing countries. In both countries mass mobility approaching the required conditions seems to have attenuated the tensions generated by the very rapid process of "social mobilization" through which large elements of the population are incorporated in the national life. The process is similar to what occurred in many European countries during the past century, but the much faster uprooting from traditional or rural milieux, coupled with the higher aspirations created by the "demonstration effect" in an age of mass consumption, introduced important differences.

In Argentina the recently mobilized masses came chiefly from the "peripheral" regions, still largely underdeveloped and more traditional, but they also came from the "central" modernized areas where large sectors had been economically and socially uprooted as a result of the drastic reduction of exports during the world crisis and the long depression of the early thirties. The interruption of world trade set in motion a new cycle of industrialization, much more intensive and faster than the first one,[54] and the mobilized and displaced sectors of the population provided the necessary labor. Mass internal migrations replaced foreign immigration, which had completely stopped in 1930; the Buenos Aires Metropolitan area received an average of nearly 100,000 migrants annually, from the middle thirties to the fifties. The growth of internal migration also affected the other large cities, and by 1947 nearly one-fourth of the population were living in a state different from the one in which they were born.[55] A large mass of rural and small-town laborers, small farmers (mostly tenants), petty artisans, peddlers, small shopkeepers and the endemic unemployed from the underdeveloped provinces, became industrial workers in the large cities and in the Buenos

[53] Only 2 per cent of the foreigners had Argentine citizenship; the procedure was open to all, and relatively simple, but nobody really cared since the legal situation of foreigners was quite favorable in every respect.

[54] During this period the share of the national product contributed by industry became larger than the proportion generated by agriculture and cattle breeding; see Table 3.

[55] Gino Germani, "El Proceso de Urbanización en la Argentina," *Revista Interamericana de Ciencias Sociales* (Washington), 3 (1963), no. 3.

Aires area,[56] with the usual impact on housing and general social conditions. Labor turnover was higher and productivity was probably lower than for urban workers previously; [57] personal and family relations were disorganized, and workers were more isolated, more alienated and less likely to participate in voluntary associations, less rational in economic behavior and so forth.[58] But reorganization according to the urban pattern also occurred very quickly,[59] and the social tensions caused by the large influx of migrants and the new industrial situation, though serious, never reached the high intensity of the similar situation that occurred at the beginning of the century.[60]

More recent tensions were reduced by mass mobility in its various forms, better living conditions, general upgrading through increased exposure to education, material and immaterial culture, and by individual mobility. In the Buenos Aires area upward mobility out of the manual strata was even more intense than at the turn of the century, and it was based on the same mechanism of upgrading the successive generations who immigrated to the city.[61] Even when individual chances deteriorated the newcomers did not feel frustrated in their hopes; [62] after ten years of economic stagnation and a decreasing level of living, most of the urban proletariat still believed in success through hard work

[56] The industrial demand for labor far exceeded the total annual increase in the labor force. The internal migrants, who comprised only 11 per cent of the population of the Buenos Aires metropolitan area in 1914 and still did not exceed this percentage in 1936, had increased to 26 per cent in 1947. At the same time the foreign population was rapidly decreasing. The same process took place in the majority of the urban centers.

[57] Knox found much higher labor turnover and absenteeism among the internal migrants than among the foreign born workers or those born in the city. John B. Knox, "Absenteeism and Turnover in an Argentine Factory," *American Sociological Review*, 26 (June, 1961), pp. 424-428.

[58] Gino Germani, "An Inquiry into the Social Effects of Industrialization and Urbanization in Buenos Aires," in Phillip Hauser (ed.); *Urbanization in Latin America* (Paris: UNESCO, 1962).

[59] Living in a shanty town was an effective barrier to the acculturation of the migrants to urban life, though only some 2 per cent of the total population lived in such conditions. Even a slum was a more favorable situation for the rapid adjustment of the migrant.

[60] Germani, "El Proceso de Urbanización," *op. cit.*

[61] In 1960, in Buenos Aires among sons of unskilled fathers, more than 80 per cent of those born in the area, and some 75 per cent of the internal migrants, had achieved some upward mobility. Mobility into the non-manual categories was also high, and it revealed larger differentials among the city-born, the migrants and the foreigners. Germani, *La Mobilidad Social, op. cit.*

[62] Only 3 per cent of the migrants with longer residence in the city said that their hopes had been frustrated. For those with shorter residence the proportion was higher (20 per cent) but they had arrived in a period of economic decline. (See Germani, "An Inquiry into the Social Effects," *op. cit.*)

and personal initiative.[63] On the whole, the workers seemed quite willing to accept the existing economic and social order, even if they wanted moderate reforms.

In any case the political instability of the last three decades cannot be imputed to overwhelming social pressure from a revolutionary lower class; these political troubles resulted from other historical circumstances, although they also reflected the impact of the sudden political incorporation of recently mobilized groups and the beginning of democracy based on total participation. That incorporation occurred through an authoritarian "national-popular" movement was mostly the result of the severe limitations under which the political system had functioned since 1930. To accommodate the recently mobilized groups and adapt to the changing composition of the urban lower strata, either the existing political parties had to be altered or a new one created, within the framework of representative democracy. But, on the one hand, the attempt to re-establish a "limited" democracy on behalf of the old "oligarchy" added new rigidities precisely at the moment when maximum flexibility was deeply needed.[64] On the other hand, the political élite was unable to understand the economic and social changes that were occurring so rapidly and the Socialist Party especially, as well as the unions, did not effectively take advantage of the political potential offered by the new industrial workers.[65] The Communists and other leftist groups were active, but failed to win their support, which was given instead to Perón.

The success of Perón can only partially be explained as an expression of the need for charismatic leadership, except with regard to the most traditional sectors of the lower class. For most workers Peronism presented the only realistic opportunity for moderate reform under the existing social order, which they basically accepted. In supporting Peronism they chose a moderate alternative: beneath the anti-imperialist, anti-oligarchic proclamations usually emphasized in Latin American populism, Peronism was much more conservative than most movements of this type. It never contested the basis of the existing economic order—private property and private enterprise—it only insisted on "social justice," social legislation, industrialization, agrarian reform, planning and other changes compatible with the interests of some sectors of the

[63] Germani, *La Mobilidad Social, op. cit.* The rapid increase of per capita income (more than 6 per cent per year) had ceased in 1950-52.

[64] This attempt took place in 1930, when a military coup put an end to 70 years of political stability. Widespread electoral fraud limited the functioning of the representative system. From 1943 to 1945 another military coup attempted to establish a fascist dictatorship of the European type. In 1946 the Constitution was re-established and Peronism won some 55 per cent of the vote in regular elections.

[65] The periodicals of the Labor Confederation and the Unions gave no attention to the mass of new industrial workers, and they remained largely unorganized until mass unionization occurred under the Peronist Unions.

middle classes.[66] Its leaders' undemocratic and authoritarian orientation had a very different meaning for the followers or the union members.[67]

Political events of the post-Peronist years have shown that the majority of workers, while maintaining their organizations and their readiness to defend their economic and social interests through the normal pattern of industrial conflict, were not available for extreme solutions. In the various recent elections most of the previously Peronist votes were given to democratic parties, and the Peronist movement itself, profoundly divided, seemed ready for an analogous re-orientation.[68]

The process that occurred in Brazil since 1930 is similar in many ways to the one just described. A cycle of intense urbanization and industrialization has deeply modified the social structure in some regions, creating a more modern pattern of social stratification with a new urban proletariat and a new middle class. This change has not affected large areas of the country: Brazil is still mostly rural, with marked contrasts between the highly industrialized and urbanized areas and the large underdeveloped regions, highly traditional, and economically marginal.[69] But internal migration and the absorption of an increasing

[66] Especially the new industrial middle class, which probably had experienced partially blocked mobility; Peronism was not fully accepted by the older middle class.

[67] For a specific analysis of the meaning of freedom and authoritarianism for the lower class under Peronism, see Germani, "La Integración Política," *op. cit.*

[68] From the high mark reached by the Peronist vote under the regime (some 65 per cent of the vote), the "blank" (Peronist) vote was reduced to some 18 per cent in the 1963 election, in spite of Perón's "order." Survey data on the political attitudes of the population of the Buenos Aires area (in 1960) seem also to indicate wide support for political pluralism as against the one-party system:

Socioeconomic Status	Per cent Preferring One-Party System
1 (low)	
2	20.1
3	17.1
4	13.4
5	13.7
6 (high)	6.3
	3.2

(The two lower groups contain 41 per cent of the total population.) See Gino Germani, "Authoritarianism and Prejudice in Buenos Aires" (unpublished). Many indications suggest that these authoritarians are of the "traditional" type. Another survey (1962) showed that the rest of the hard-core Peronists came disproportionately from the migrant sector of the population, and that their orientation was mostly determined by their "loyalty" to the charismatic leader: José L. de Imaz, *Motivación Electoral* (Buenos Aires: Instituto de Desarrollo Económico Social, 1962).

[69] See Charles Wagley, "The Brazilian Revolution: Social Changes since 1930," in Richard N. Adams and others, *Social Change in Latin America Today* (New York: Harper & Row, 1960); Fernando H. Cardoso, "Le Proletariat Brésilien," *Sociologie du Travail*, 4 (1961), pp. 50-65; Bertrand Hutchinson, "The Migrant Population of Urban Brazil," *América Latina*, 6 (1963), pp. 41-71. According to this survey, conducted in six of the most important Brazilian cities, some 65 per cent of the population were internal migrants.

proportion of the population into the new urban and industrial environment have occurred under conditions of rapid economic growth and mass mobility. Compared with Western Europe and the United States, the emergent groups are more traditionalist, the stratification system is less modern, even in the more advanced regions, and the society is characterized by marked internal discontinuities in modernization, but other factors have compensated for these differences and the impact of mass mobility has produced similar integrative mechanisms in the rapidly changing areas.

A number of studies describe the role of mobility in the assimilation of rural migrants. In this transition two main phases have been distinguished. The first one consists of the simple transposition of traditional patterns to the new situation; the second one involves a new definition of the situation, with new attitudes and new modes of action.

In the first stage the specific tasks associated with the job are identified with traditional "obligations" to the "Patrão," which were "reciprocated" with a "fair" salary. The enterprise is expected to give the same particularistic "protection" as the landowner. Although a diffuse feeling of solidarity is not absent, it expresses the traditional distinction between the "poor people" and "the rich" rather than the solidarity of the workers' group as such.[70] As a result, the new workers either lack a basis for organized collective action, or depend exclusively on the primary relations of kinship and friendship. A union may initiate and organize collective action, but even when it succeeds in imposing the discipline required for a strike, it is still perceived as an external factor, lacking the active and psychological participation of the migrant workers. They view the union as a provider of services; often they make no distinctions between the State and the union. Aspirations are predominately oriented toward escape from the industrial situation itself.[71] Nevertheless, adaptation to the new urban industrial culture does take place: at least some of the migrants develop new modes of interaction and a clearer consciousness of being an industrial worker facing a new set of social relations. But even if these changes do involve a higher level of political awareness, and more conscious and mature union participation, they do not involve more readiness to accept ideological

---

[70] The change of class-identification from "poor" to "worker" decreases with education and seems also to be inversely correlated with political awareness; Glaucio A. Dillon Soares, "Classes Sociais, Strata Sociais e As Eleçoes Presidenciadis de 1960," Sociologia (1961), pp. 217-238.

[71] Brandao Lopes, op. cit. and "Relations Industrielles dans deux Communautés Brésiliennes," Sociologie du Travail (1961), pp. 18-32. Fernando H. Cardoso, "Atitudes e Expectativas Desfavoráveis a Mudanca Social," Boletín (Río de Janeiro: Centro Latino Americano de Pesquizas em Ciencias Sociais, 1960), No. 3, pp. 15-22.

radicalism. Cardoso believes that the behavior of workers who have reached this second stage is determined

more by their demands of *better* conditions *within* the capitalist system than by a political action addressed to transform the total social system. Such an evaluation of the future is based on the fact of the existence of career possibilities within the industry, on the fact of economic growth and of the reasonable level of skilled workers' salaries.

At present, the Brazilian urban proletariat has little revolutionary potential. On the contrary, Cardoso thinks that workers' action will probably be increasingly oriented toward movements demanding better working and living conditions more than anything else.[72]

Individual mobility assumes a central role in this transition. Touraine has applied to it a typology based precisely on different levels of aspiration and different mobility experiences. At the lowest level there are no aspirations and no mobility, and we find a simple denial of the industrial situation, leading to a kind of apathetic *adaptation*—perhaps the condition most favorable to *populismo;* on the other hand, when aspirations are higher the experience of some measure of upward mobility within the industrial situation will produce a higher level of integration and increase political and union participation. Under conditions of economic growth, and if this individual mobility is part of a general process of *national* development, the workers' political orientation is likely to be more moderate than revolutionary.[73]

The political evolution of Brazil reflects the reformist and moderate orientation of the new urban proletariat. In this sense, Varguism is similar to Peronism with respect to its moderate character and the composition of its leadership, as well as its authoritarianism.[74] Given the more traditional element in the mobilized sectors, the paternalistic and charismatic factor must have been stronger,[75] but Varguism also represented a moderate choice when other more extreme possibilities were available.[76] President Goulart's failure to win the support of the industrial workers at a crucial moment may be considered another expression of the absence of revolutionary potential in the urban lower class.

While moderation may in part reflect the passivity of a still tradi-

[72] Cardoso, "Le Proletariat . . ." *op. cit.,* p. 377.

[73] Alain Touraine, "Industrialisation et Conscience Ouvriere a São Paulo," *Sociologie du Travail* (1961), pp. 389-407.

[74] Wagley, *op. cit.;* John Johnson, *Political Change in Latin America* (Stanford: Stanford University Press, 1958), p. 171.

[75] Andrew Pearse, "Algunas Características de la Urbanización en Rio de Janeiro," Hauser (ed.), *op. cit.,* pp. 194-207.

[76] The Communist party won 8 per cent of the vote; it was well organized with a prestigeful leader.

tional (and submissive) population, it is also the result of an evolution of working-class consciousness which is remarkably different from the European experience. In Europe the awakening of class consciousness in the traditional groups involved an intermediate stage of predominant alienation and extreme radicalization (which could last many decades), and only later did a third stage take place in which workers were progressively integrated and increasingly apt to accept the existing social order. In Brazil and in Argentina only two stages have occurred: the lower strata move from traditionalism directly to integration and moderate reformism. Mass mobility and other conditions eliminate or considerably reduce the period of working-class isolation and segregation of the working class: at the same time they eliminate the possibility of an intermediate radical stage.

Given the other necessary intervening conditions I have described, these are the specific consequences of mass mobility in developing countries.

INDEX